INTERPRETATIONS OF

INTERPRETATIONS OF
Beowulf
A CRITICAL ANTHOLOGY

EDITED BY
R. D. FULK

INDIANA UNIVERSITY PRESS
Bloomington & Indianapolis

© 1991 by Indiana University Press
All rights reserved

The paper used in this publication meets the minimum requirements of
American National Standard for Information Sciences--Permanence
of paper for Printed Library Materials, ANSI Z39.48-1984.

Manufactured in the United States of America

Library of Congress Cataloging-in-Publication Data

Interpretations of Beowulf : a critical anthology / edited by R.D.
Fulk.
    p. cm.
  Includes index.
  ISBN 0-253-32437-8. -- ISBN 0-253-20639-1 (pbk.)
  1. Beowulf. 2. Epic poetry, English (Old)--History and criticism.
I. Fulk, R. D. (Robert Dennis)
PR1585.I58   1991
829'.3--dc20   90-47555

1 2 3 4 5 95 94 93 92 91

for Heidi and Rick

CONTENTS

PREFACE

This anthology grew out of a need perceived in my 1989 graduate *Beowulf* seminar at Indiana University for an inexpensive collection of representative critical approaches to the poem, to function as a complement to Klaeber's edition. Although each of the currently available anthologies has its own merits, none seems entirely appropriate to this purpose. The most useful of these is undoubtedly Lewis E. Nicholson's *Anthology of 'Beowulf' Criticism*, and Anglo-Saxonists owe a debt of gratitude to the University of Notre Dame Press for keeping this collection in print for more than a quarter of a century, and at a remarkably reasonable price. But its very longevity is a fault, since there is no essay in it more recent than 1962. Its age is also evident in the nature of the critical selection it offers, since its focus on religious controversy, perhaps better warranted in 1963, is hard to justify to students in 1990, when the religious nature of the poem is no longer such a burning issue. Likewise, Joseph F. Tuso's edition of Talbot Donaldson's translation of the poem (New York: Norton, 1975), with more than a hundred pages of background studies and criticism, has served *Beowulf* students well, introducing them to an admirable variety of approaches. Yet this variety also limits the book's usefulness, since it is achieved only by presenting short excerpts from books and articles, a problem aggravated by the severe length limitations that the translation-and-criticism format imposes. The other currently available anthology, Harold Bloom's *Beowulf*, in the immense Modern Critical Interpretations series (New York: Chelsea House, 1987), while drawing attention to some worthy recent publications, is too limited in scope for use as a secondary classroom text, containing just six essays, none but J. R. R. Tolkien's "*Beowulf*: The Monsters and the Critics" older than 1978, and one previously unpublished. It is also available only in a hardcover edition.

What should an anthology such as this contain? One possible goal is convenience, assembling perhaps the most frequently cited scholarship in the field, thereby furnishing easy reference. But then there is also the more immediate question of pedagogical aims: if it should be a goal in the classroom to expose students to a wide variety of approaches and methodologies, the selection of criticism cannot easily coincide with that other aim of using the most frequently cited scholarship. Given that literary studies are rapidly coming to be dominated by theory, it is also desirable pedagogically to present *Beowulf* scholarship in the context of its historical development, and thus to represent a variety of discrete critical movements, from nineteenth-century philology to post-structuralist hermeneutics. More important, it is essential to make students aware of the variety of issues involved in *Beowulf* scholarship, and so the ideal anthology would not concentrate just on the staples of literary interpretation (theme, style, meaning, structure, etc.), but would also include the bases of literary interpretation, such as textual criticism, cultural studies, folklore and analogue scholarship, historical backgrounds, linguistic, metrical and dating studies, and so forth. Ideally, of course, the selection would also represent that Arnoldian aim of "the best that had been thought and spoken."

Satisfying any one of these aims would be difficult. And this is especially true because of one remaining aim, which is to insure that the dimensions of this book are reasonable, and that it will therefore remain inexpensive enough to be used as a course text to supplement an edition of the poem. To that end it has been imperative to keep it under three hundred pages in length, in a paperback edition, printed from the editor's camera-ready copy. This length requirement the book does meet; and in compromising among those other goals it does aspire to provide such a selection of *Beowulf* scholarship as to promote worthwhile classroom discussion of a wide range of issues.

One editorial guideline has been to avoid overly technical issues, particularly dating and manuscript studies. However important such philological problems may be for the interpretation of the poem, the complexity of the issues involved is such that an anthology such as this could not do justice to them: problems of interpretation need not be covered exhaustively to be worth including, while to cover philological issues such as dating with anything less than absolute thoroughness is to render all conclusions valueless, and to deceive students with the impression that the issues can be so simplified. And at least for the problem of dating there already exists a separate collection, Colin Chase's *Dating of 'Beowulf'* (Univ. of Toronto Press, 1981), which is much better able to do justice to the variety of problems involved in dating the poem. Of particular merit for students requiring an introduction to the issues involved in dating the poem is Eric Stanley's contribution to the collection ("The Date of *Beowulf*: Some Doubts and No Conclusions," pp. 197-211). Although I must admit to believing Stanley too readily discards valuable evidence—particularly linguistic evidence—this essay is nonetheless an admirably broad survey of the issues. The linguistic issues in dating, which are paramount, are treated in most detail by Ashley Crandell Amos in her *Linguistic Means of Determining the Dates of Old English Literary Texts* (Cambridge, MA: Medieval Academy of America, 1980), and in my forthcoming book on Old English metrics.

My determination to include a wide range of critical approaches, coupled with the desire to include only complete articles, without excerpting, has also dictated that some pieces have had to be excluded simply on the basis of their length. Particularly noteworthy in this regard is Patrick Wormald's much-discussed "Bede, *Beowulf* and the Conversion of the Anglo-Saxon Aristocracy," in *Bede and Anglo-Saxon England*, ed. Robert T. Farrell, British Archaeological Reports 46 (Oxford: B.A.R., 1978), 32-95. Rather than excluding the fine second chapter of Thomas Shippey's *Old English Verse* altogether, only the section titled "The Ironic Background" is reproduced here—the one exception to my practice of not excerpting. And as the pages of this anthology filled up it became necessary to exclude a number of familiar and frequently cited essays, perhaps the most obvious omission being Robert Kaske's "*Sapientia et Fortitudo* as the Controlling Theme of *Beowulf*," *Studies in Philology* 55 (1958),

423-57. And just as Christian interpretations of *Beowulf* are no longer the preoccupation they once were, so with oral-formulaic approaches to the poem, and as a result it has been necessary to exclude such course staples as Francis P. Magoun, Jr., "The Theme of the Beasts of Battle in Anglo-Saxon Poetry," *NM* 56 (1955), 81-90; Robert P. Creed, "The Making of an Anglo-Saxon Poem," *ELH* 26 (1959), 445-54; Robert D. Stevick, "The Oral-Formulaic Analyses of Old English Verse," *Speculum* 37 (1962), 382-89; Larry D. Benson, "The Literary Character of Anglo-Saxon Formulaic Poetry," *PMLA* 81 (1966), 334-41; Stanley B. Greenfield, "The Canons of Old English Criticism," *ELH* 34 (1967), 141-55 (in revised form worked into his *Interpretation of Old English Poems* [London: Routledge, 1972], pp. 30ff.); and Franz H. Bäuml, "Medieval Texts and the Two Formalist Theories of Oral-Formulaic Composition: A Proposal for a Third Theory," *NLH* 16 (1984), 31-49.

The criticism that has been included is arranged in chronological order. In part because Klaeber's notes, introduction and bibliographical apparatus cover nineteenth- and early twentieth-century scholarship so well, it has been un- necessary to include examples here—especially since the historical and philo- logical bent of this scholarship rarely leads to serious literary interpretation, as J. R. R. Tolkien argues in a clever allegory in his lecture on the monsters and the critics. But it must not be supposed that no one ever realized *Beowulf* is a poem until Tolkien pointed it out. It was precisely the penchant of scholars like Klaeber and Raymond Chambers for viewing *Beowulf* not as an oral but a literary production—with all the forethought as to literary qualitites such as structure and theme that that assumption implies—that made Henry Chadwick, perhaps the leading English representative of the old Germanist school, so critical of their work (see Haarder, n. 1 below). This short-lived marriage of philology and literary interpretation in the years before Tolkien's lecture is admirably represented by Dame Bertha Phillpotts' "Wyrd and Providence in Anglo-Saxon Thought" (1928). Here the evidence of early Germanic heroic literature as a whole is brought to bear on such literary concerns as the character of the hero and the moral outlook of the poet and the world he represents—questions that were to become major preoccupations of the anti- philological scholarship of the 1950s and '60s.

Any editor worth his salt, and with an adequate understanding of the changing critical winds in the profession, would no doubt remark at this point that Tolkien's lecture on the monsters and the critics has become the object of mindless veneration, is over-anthologized, hopelessly retrograde, and much too long, and so can safely be set aside now to make way for more important matters. But since my wit is short (as you may well understand), against all reason Tolkien is included here. No one denies the historical importance of this lecture as the first sustained effort at viewing the poem on its own terms, according to aesthetic guidelines discoverable in the work itself, thus opening the way to the formalist principles that played such a vital role in the subsequent development of *Beowulf* scholarship. But Tolkien's study is not just a pilgrims' stop on the road to holier shrines: his explanation of the poem's larger structure, though frequently disputed, has never been bettered, and the methodology inherent in his practice of basing claims about the macro- structural level on patterns everyone discerns in the microstructure remains a model for emulation. His view of the poet as an artist of an antiquarian bent remains enormously influential (and a major obstacle to dating the poem); and although the issue of the appropriateness of the monsters is not as pressing as it was in 1936, it is not superfluous in the context of some subsequent criticism, in which themes of even nobler conception than the Romantic vision of the Heroic Age are attributed to the poet, and he is credited with such ingenuity of design as a James Joyce or T. S. Eliot never dreamed of.

Between Tolkien and the New Critics stands the oral-formulaic theory—not just chronologically, but also conceptually, since the theory seemed, to most, to present an insurmountable obstacle to the formalist view that the poem is carefully designed, and thus worthy of detailed reading and close interpretation. How could this be if the poem is simply the transcript of a single performance, related loosely to other improvised and different performances, and not the studied product of monastic endeavors? Accordingly, the question of "the possibility of criticizing Old English poetry" (to borrow the title of one familiar essay) is a recurrent theme, as demonstrated by some of the articles on oral-formulaic theory mentioned three paragraphs above. In this sense, then, the oral-formulaic theory is a return to the primitivism of the nineteenth century, harnessing little of its vast Germanist learning, but much of its rigorousness. It is difficult to improve on the original essay of F. P. Magoun, Jr. (1953), to exemplify the oral-formulaic theory, since not only does he set out the hypothesis in its most radical form, insisting that all formulism implies orality; he also demonstrates in close detail the formulaic nature of specific passages in *Beowulf* and *Christ and Satan*, as his students were to do later for other passages and poems. One opposing view in the oral-formulaic controversy is represented here by Geoffrey Russom's 1978 article on three Old English poets' avoidance of handy formulas. From this avoidance Russom concludes that the economical use of formulas is not nearly as important a compositional aim in Anglo-Saxon verse as in Homeric epic, and therefore a feature essential to formulaic composition, at least according to Parry and Lord's formulation of the hypothesis, is missing from Old English. This essay is especially useful because in the process of making his point Russom surveys many of the major issues in the controversy over oral-formulaic composition, up to 1978, since which time the theory, though it continues to inspire significant research, has provoked little controversy over its basic premises.[1]

As the title of the anthology implies, the main emphasis in the selection of criticism has been on interpretation of the poem, and the result is that New Critical approaches are well represented. This seems particularly appropriate for students approaching the poem for the first time, and for graduate students translating it from Old English: for these students, examples of the insights to be gained from close reading are particularly important. The father of detailed

---

[1]For a recent issue-oriented survey of the field see Alexandra Hennessey Olsen, "Oral-Formulaic Research in Old English Studies," *Oral Tradition* 1.3 (1986), 548-606, and 3.1-2 (1988), 138-90; and John Miles Foley has written no fewer than three survey-oriented summaries: see "Introduction: The Oral Theory in Context," in *Oral Traditional Literature: A Festschrift for Albert Bates Lord*, ed. John Miles Foley (Columbus: Slavica, 1980, rpt. 1983), pp. 27-122, at 51-95; pp. 41-7 of his *Oral Formulaic Theory and Research: An Introduction and Annotated Bibliography* (New York: Garland, 1985); and pp. 65-74 of his *Theory of Oral Composition: History and Methodology* (Indiana Univ. Press, 1988). Good but now dated is Andreas Haarder, *Beowulf: The Appeal of a Poem* (Copenhagen: Akademisk Forlag, 1975), pp. 171-204.

formalist analysis of *Beowulf* of course is Arthur G. Brodeur, whose 1959 book remains unsurpassed for sensitivity to interpretive detail, and chiefly at a distance of about an inch from the text. One of the foremost of Brodeur's many accomplishments is exemplified in the second chapter of that book, reproduced here, in which he teaches us to discern purpose in the poet's selection of expressions in variation—a method still emulated even in criticism of the 1980s, most prominently in Fred C. Robinson's *'Beowulf' and the Appositive Style* (Knoxville: Univ. of Tennessee Press, 1985). A different sort of New Criticism is practiced by Stanley B. Greenfield in "Geatish History: Poetic Art and Epic Quality in *Beowulf*" (1963). Here he examines the references to the Frisian campaign and the Swedish-Geatish wars in the second half of the poem in order to demonstrate how they are linked thematically to the epic purposes of the poem. The original aspect of his approach is his method of identifying the most important thematic resonances of a passage on a *linguistic* basis, e.g. by discerning an envelope pattern of formulaic expressions that refer to survival bracketing one passage. Here we see the first glimmerings of a Jakobsonian style of poetics that was to become a major preoccupation for Greenfield in some later essays. The significance of this article resides not just in its conclusions about the poem, but also in that it is one of the first applications of structuralism to a text in any literary field. And it amounts to a particularly clear demonstration of how closely New Criticism is linked to Saussurean linguistics, beginning as it does from the assumption of inextricably interrelated properties at various levels of analysis within a closed and consistent system.

Richard N. Ringler's explication of Grendel's last visit to Heorot (1966) is a specific instance of the general principle urged in Tolkien's lecture, of not locating the elements of discourse in the ready-made aesthetics of literary tradition, but of reconstructing the aesthetic principles of the poem from the poem itself. His demonstration of the subordination of suspense to the poet's ironic aims is masterful. Edward B. Irving, Jr.'s *A Reading of 'Beowulf'* (1968) is in the tradition of Brodeur's close reading of the text. The first chapter is reproduced here as an exemplary demonstration of the myriad manifestations of the one structural principle of contrast that underlies a wide variety of rhetorical constructions. Like Brodeur, Irving teaches us to read carefully and discern purpose in even the most formulaic of rhetorical patterns. The second chapter of Thomas Shippey's *Old English Verse* (1972) is self-admittedly indebted to Irving's book on several counts. Shippey's study represents perhaps both an extension and an attenuation of the formalist tradition, employing the methods of close reading not to arrive at an aesthetic appreciation, but at an understanding of both the heroic philosophy underlying the moral system of the poem and, more important, a set of interpretive assumptions that must have been shared by the poem's audience. This pushing at the limits of New Criticism, onward into literary structuralism itself, is evident in some of Shippey's other work, and nowhere more clearly than in his application to *Beowulf* of Vladimir Propp's study of the plot structure of folktales.[2]

---

[2]See "The Fairy-Tale Structure of *Beowulf*," *N&Q*, n.s. 16 (1969), 2-11. Other articles dealing with Proppian approaches to morphology include Daniel R. Barnes's "Folktale Morphology and the Structure of *Beowulf*," *Speculum* 45 (1970), 416-34; Bruce A. Rosenberg's "Folktale Morphology and the Structure of *Beowulf*: A Counter-Proposal," *Journal of the Folklore Institute* 11 (1975), 199-209; and Kent Gould's "*Beowulf* and Folktale Morphology:

Old English scholarship was fated to diverge from trends in more recent fields, where the direction of critical thought was conditioned by the inevitable reaction to formalism. The reason for this divergence is that the seeds of anti-formalism were sown in the field of Anglo-Saxon scholarship at about the same time as New Criticism first made its appearance there, so that the two schools of thought grew at least at the same rate if not together. It was inevitable that New Criticism should never entirely dominate medieval scholarship the way it did more recent fields, since it has never been possible to comprehend medieval literature in accord with the New Critical dictum excluding historical and cultural contexts. And while the textual basis of, say, American literature is relatively stable, the study of *Beowulf* has always demanded close attention to the textual and philological context so carefully excluded by formalism. The opponents of New Criticism may be broadly characterized as espousing inter-textuality, if "text" may be interpreted metaphorically to include such cultural artifacts as manuscript illuminations and archaeological finds. Of course the chief form of intertextual *Beowulf* criticism since the late 1950s has been the religious one. It perhaps has its start with Klaeber's studies of "the Christian elements" (appearing in *Anglia* in 1911 and 1912), which annoyed Chadwick so; such elements were at any rate before this largely regarded as inter-polations in an otherwise pristine Germanic production. Half a century later, even Klaeber's views looked conservative: where he had felt "inclined to recognize features of the Christian savior in the destroyer of hellish fiends," a parallel nonetheless "delicately kept in the background," and had insisted that it would be "going too far to say that the author set out with the deliberate purpose of writing an allegorical poem with Christ himself as the true hero" (edition, pp. li, cxx), by 1960 that was no longer going too far. Christian interpretation of *Beowulf* tends to fall into two categories, the allegorical and the exegetical. The former category is best represented by Maurice B. McNamee's "*Beowulf*—An Allegory of Salvation?" (1960), an article of lasting influence. Father McNamee's methods are actually somewhat reminiscent of Freudian and Jungian interpretation, and his view of the hero, who stands in for Christ, is naturally an admiring one. This is in stark contrast to the scholarship of the second and much larger category, of studies placing *Beowulf* in one or another patristic context. Here the hero's actions, especially in his final exploit, are weighed against the prescriptions of the patrology, with the result that he is almost invariably deemed a failure. This, for instance, is the judgment of such influential critics as Larry D. Benson, Whitney F. Bolton, James E. Cross, Eric Stanley, and many others. The section of the poem commonly referred to as "Hrothgar's sermon" (1700-84) acquires enormous significance in many such studies, placed as it is at the physical center of the poem, and constituting the most elaborate instance of moralization in *Beowulf*. Moreover, it contains some elements reminiscent of Christian didactic liter-ature (the *sāwele hyrde* of 1742 and the *bona . . . sē þe of flānbogan fyrenum scēoteð* at 1743-44), and is concerned with the proper behavior of a king, a

God as Magical Donor," *Folklore* 96 (1985), 98-103. On the other hand, mythic/archetypal approaches are too numerous to list in a short footnote: a particularly notable example is the Jungian approach of John Miles Foley in "*Beowulf* and the Psychohistory of Anglo-Saxon Culture," *American Imago* 34 (1977), 133-53.

subject of particular relevance to the remainder of the poem. Though it is not the fullest statement of her views, Margaret Goldsmith's "The Christian Perspective in *Beowulf*" (1962) remains perhaps the most nearly perfect succinct example of the exegetical category, as it begins with a defense against the charge of improbable reasoning, moves to an account of the hero's overweening pride, explains the basis of this judgment in Hrothgar's sermon, and finally illustrates the conventional wisdom on pride in the writings of the Church Fathers that might have been available to an Anglo-Saxon scholar at the time *Beowulf* was composed.[3]

John Leyerle in "The Interlace Structure of *Beowulf*" (1967) shares Goldsmith's critical attitude toward the hero,[4] though the basis of his intertextual approach is very different. He presents an analogy between the interlace patterns of the Anglo-Saxon visual arts and interweaving at various levels in *Beowulf*: in the poet's own description of his craft as *wordum wrixlan*; at the level of the sentence, in which ideas are interlaced through the elaborate syntax and the use of variation; at the level of the episodes and digressions, particularly the fragmented allusions to the wars of the Geats in the latter part of the poem; and at the level of the theme.

As already noted, *Beowulf* criticism has been little affected so far by deconstruction and other recent developments in American literary theory that derive their force from the reaction to formalism. Aside from some unpublished conference papers, the only self-characterized example of what Paul Ricoeur calls the "hermeneutics of suspicion" that comes to mind is Linda Georgianna's "King Hrethel's Sorrow and the Limits of Heroic Action in *Beowulf*," *Speculum* 62 (1987), 829-50, an essay that I think illustrates why this is so: the thesis, that the poet is critical of Beowulf's heroic values by the time of the dragon fight, was anticipated in the Old English anti-New-Critical schools of the 1960s by Goldsmith, Leyerle, and others, as mentioned above, the difference generally being that in one instance the ploy is ascribed to the poet's moral and religious outlook, in the other to his rhetorical strategy.[5] An article that is not distinctly deconstructionist in design, and yet does borrow a few of the more useful aspects of deconstruction's terminology and premises is Laurence N. de Looze's "Frame Narratives and Fictionalization: Beowulf as Narrator" (1984), an article that approaches the same critical task as Georgianna's—to account for the internal and contextual structure of Beowulf's long speech before his fight with the dragon. De Looze's argument is that the speech represents the hero's attempt to work through his insoluble dilemma,

---

[3]Two very useful articles on the school of Christian interpretation of the poem appeared together in *ASE* 2 (1973), the one surveying patristic approaches and the other (actually the record of an MLA forum, rather than an article) weighing the plausibility of allegorical interpretation, and whether in fact Goldsmith's approach can be called allegorical: they are, respectively, Philip B. Rollinson's "The Influence of Christian Doctrine and Exegesis on Old English Poetry: An Estimate of the Current State of Scholarship" (pp. 271-84), and "Allegorical, Typological, or Neither? Three Short Papers on the Allegorical Approach to *Beowulf* and a Discussion" (pp. 285-302).

[4]His views on this point are more fully developed in "Beowulf the Hero and the King," *Medium Ævum* 34 (1965), 89-102.

[5]Pre-publication publicity for Gillian R. Overing's *Language, Sign, and Gender in 'Beowulf'*, to appear in 1990 from Southern Illinois University Press, suggests its methodology will be deconstructionist, though it also suggests feminist and reader-centered methods.

and its elements epitomize his alternatives. The most strikingly original facet of this approach is that it relocates what has heretofore been a major element of critical discourse to a position within the poem itself. Just as Derrida argues that the distinction between the discourses of literature and criticism is artificial and delusive, and ought to be violated at the critic's every opportunity, so a major preoccupation of *Beowulf* criticism of the 1960s and '70s, the insoluble question of the rightness of the king's fighting the dragon, becomes Beowulf's own preoccupation in this speech.

Nor have reception theory/affective criticism and the new historicism made any headway at all in *Beowulf* scholarship, as far as I can discern (though Joseph Harris's essay in this anthology represents another type of renewed historicism, and shares some of the same generic concerns as Hans Robert Jauss's version of reception theory). In regard to the former this is surprising, since reader-centered criticism represents what ought to be a tool as powerful for the analysis of Old English texts as it is for more recent ones. Interestingly enough, some of the essays in this volume use methods reminiscent of reader-response criticism—e.g., John Leyerle's idea that monster-fighting "pre-empts the reader's attention just as it pre-empts Beowulf's," with the result that "the reader gets caught up in the heroic ethos like the hero and easily misses the warnings" (pp. 153-4 below), and Thomas Shippey's analysis of the effect on the reader of the sudden reversals in the story of the battle at Ravenswood (pp. 200-201 below), are highly reminiscent of Stanley Fish's readings of purposeful indeterminacy in Milton, though of course both of these essays antedate Fish's work. As for the new historicism, given its origins in Renaissance studies and its growing importance in later medieval studies, it is not a sufficient explanation for Anglo-Saxonists' disinterest that New Criticism never managed to separate *Beowulf* studies from the old historicism. Rather, the Marxist basis of "cultural poetics" seems more culpable, for while Marxism acknowledges heroic society as a stage in the development of human institutions, it actually has little to say about it, or any stage of human society before the rise of the bourgeoisie. As a result, at least at this point in time the idea of a Marxist interpretation of *Beowulf* still seems odd. In a sense, the Christian interpretations of the 1960s were the new historicism of *Beowulf* studies, the (particularly colonialist) texts of social commentary that are such a preoccupation for cultural materialists having no equivalent in the Anglo-Saxon period but religious texts.[6] Thus the view of Old English studies as a backwater to which drops from the well of critical theory trickle down[7] is wrong-headed, and the innovations in Anglo-Saxon scholarship ought to have a broader effect on other fields than they do. The one post-structuralist critical movement that has

---

[6]Recognition of such an equivalence is implicit in frequently encountered references to the work of D. W. Robertson, Jr., and his school as "historical criticism"—e.g. by Stanley Greenfield, "The Authenticating Voice in *Beowulf*," *ASE* 5 (1976), 51-62, at 52 (see also his *Interpretation of Old English Poems*, p. 10); and Derek Pearsall, "Chaucer's Poetry and Its Modern Commentators: The Necessity of History," in *Medieval Literary Criticism: Ideology and History*, ed. David Aers (Brighton: Harvester Press, 1986), pp. 123-47, at p. 138.

[7]Lee Patterson rehearses some stereotypical views of this sort about medieval studies, and attempts to explain their causes and devise a solution to the problem, in "On the Margin: Postmodernism, Ironic History, and Medieval Studies," pp. 87-108 in the issue of *Speculum* mentioned in n. 9 below.

actually scored some successes in this field is gender studies—another anti-formalist school to the extent that it is disdainful of New Criticism's isolation of the text from social and political contexts, though it borrows freely from some of New Criticism's methods. Jane Chance's chapter on *Beowulf* from her *Woman as Hero in Old English Literature* (1986) is typical of the eclecticism of feminist studies, drawing on structural analysis to locate Grendel's mother at both the physical and conceptual center of the poem, and (perhaps reflecting the influence of current French feminist theory on American criticism) on Freudian methods to interpret the sexual nature of the encounter between the hero and his female adversary.[8]

A more vital trend in recent Anglo-Saxon scholarship than American post-structuralism has been a renewed interest in philology of all sorts—both Germanic philology of the traditional sort and what has (perhaps prematurely) been called the "New Philology," which one recent collection of essays identifies as a fairly loose congeries of critical concerns, particularly the study of manuscript culture, the application of linguistic pragmatics and discourse analysis to texts, and post-structuralist hermeneutics in general.[9] The linguistic aspects of this renewed interest in philology are well exemplified by such studies as Ashley Crandell Amos' 1980 book mentioned above, a project of a wider scope than any dating study undertaken by Eduard Sievers' contemporaries; Geoffrey Russom's *Old English Meter and Linguistic Theory* (Cambridge Univ. Press, 1987); Bruce Mitchell's *Old English Syntax* (Oxford: Clarendon, 1985); and by several collaborative projects, the foremost of which is the *Dictionary of Old English* now appearing from the University of Toronto. And though of course it has not always been the best of research, the resurgence of philological interest is perhaps most familiar in the preoccupation of the 1980s with the *Beowulf* manuscript and non-linguistic methods of dating the poem. As applied to *Beowulf*, on its linguistic side the philology of the 1980s, like the old philology, was largely concerned with comparative Germanic and Indo-European language studies, but now with improved tools (both research tools and theoretical frameworks) and, more important, with literary rather than linguistic aims. An example is John C. Pope's "*Beowulf* 505, 'gehedde,' and the Pretensions of Unferth" (1986). This contains all the elements of a classic lexicographical study, but to a much larger purpose, since Pope's aim is to illuminate the much-disputed character and function of a major participant in the action of the poem.[10] Moreover, the essay seems especially characteristic of the "New Philology" inasmuch as the study of the semantics of *gehedde* is not limited to the traditional, comparative realm, but extends into the realm of linguistic pragmatics, employing the principle of

---

[8]For another study that places Grendel's mother at the center of the poem see Jacqueline Vaught, "*Beowulf*: The Fight at the Center," *Allegorica* 5 (1980), 125-37, not listed in Chance's bibliography, which is otherwise a good source of information on gender studies of Old English literature. Helen Damico and Alexandra Hennessey Olsen provide a survey of Old English literary criticism on women in the Introduction to their just-published *New Readings on Women in Old English Literature* (Bloomington: Indiana Univ. Press, 1990), pp. 1-26.

[9]*The New Philology*, ed. Stephen G. Nichols (= *Speculum* 65, No. 1 [January, 1990]).

[10]Recent studies employing linguistic analysis with literary aims are too numerous to list, but Mary Blockley, Roberta Frank, Bruce Mitchell, Paul Beekman Taylor, and myself may be mentioned as frequent practitioners.

presupposition to determine the relative likelihood of competing interpretations. On the literary side, recent philological work on *Beowulf* tends to
return to the Germanic roots of the poem: a familiar example is the set of
studies placing Beowulf's exchange of words with Unferth in the context of the
Old Icelandic *senna* or flyting.[11] As these studies illustrate, this sort of critical
approach again has frankly literary aims and methods, and so at least in that
respect it is not a return to a pre-Tolkien critical agenda. It is of course free
of the romanticizing impulse, chronicled by E. G. Stanley, that characterized
earlier philology, and idolized *die echt germanischen Elemente* to the extent of
branding as interpolations all apparently Christian allusions in the poem.
Rather, current philology does for the poem roughly what its Christian
interpreters did, though now using the eddas and the *Hildebrandslied* rather
than Augustine and Origen, and etymology rather than exegesis. Like most
post-structuralism it is intertextual, though it tends to assimilate rather than
reject both formalist and anti-formalist methodologies, and to that extent, like
gender studies, it is eclectic.[12] Theodore M. Andersson's "Tradition and Design
in *Beowulf*" (1980) is a good example. Andersson starts with an analytical
structural model, proposed by P. G. Buchloh, reminiscent of type-scene and
Proppian folktale analysis, that prescribes a narrative pattern of incidents for
early Germanic lays. In true eclectic fashion, when he finds the framework
more useful in general conception than in detail, he retains only its identification of scene types, and armed with these he proceeds in the manner of
Brodeur to identify a pattern of dramatic reversals in *Beowulf*. Overall these
contribute to the development of a theme of mutability that is highly credible
because it is characteristic of other Old English verse, is explicitly argued in
Beowulf, and extends Tolkien's structure of contrast to another level of
analysis. Joseph Harris, in *"Beowulf* in Literary History" (1982), identifies a
wide variety of early Germanic genres represented within the framework of
Beowulf, lending the poem the character of an anthology that, like the
Canterbury Tales, summarizes and synthesizes the entire range of its literary
antecedents. Then selecting just two of those constituent types, genealogical
verse and the praise poem, he surveys the surviving parallels in skaldic verse,
in order to reconstruct paradigmatic generic outlines from which the *Beowulf*
poet diverges more or less.[13]

In addition to representing an historical range of critical movements, this
selection of essays has the advantage of touching from a variety of critical
positions on most of the major interpretive issues with which *Beowulf* criticism
has concerned itself, including structure (Tolkien, Leyerle, Andersson, Chance),
style (Magoun, Brodeur, etc.), genre (Tolkien, Greenfield, McNamee, Harris),

---

[11]See, among others, Joseph Harris, "The *senna*: From Description to Literary Theory,"
Michigan Germanic Studies 5 (1979), 65-74; Carol J. Clover, "The Germanic Context of the
Unferth Episode," *Speculum* 55 (1980), 444-68; and Earl R. Anderson, "Formulaic Typescene
Survival: Finn, Ingeld, and the *Nibelungenlied*," *English Studies* 61 (1980), 293-301.

[12]It is natural that feminist approaches to the poem should intersect with philological
ones, since the problem of establishing the social and cultural context for women's roles must
inevitably draw on other Germanic records. This is particularly clear in Helen Damico's
Wealhtheow and the Valkyrie Tradition (Madison: Univ. of Wisconsin Press, 1984).

[13]This reprint afforded an opportunity to remedy the typographic limitations imposed on
the original publication. I am grateful to the author for providing typographical improvements.

and theme (Phillpotts, Goldsmith, Andersson, etc.). In addition, many are frankly explicative of important passages, and as such are particularly useful to students. And so it is to be hoped that this collection will serve the purposes for which it is designed, of introducing students to a broad range of ideas, of presenting *Beowulf* scholarship in historical perspective, and of stimulating worthwhile classroom discussion.

Grateful acknowledgement is due to the publishers of the journals and books in which these essays originally appeared, and in some instances to the authors themselves, for permission to reprint them here. For granting their permission gratis I am particularly grateful to Maurice B. McNamee, Margaret Goldsmith, and Laurence de Looze; to the publishers of *Essays and Studies*, *Speculum*, *Comparative Literature*, *Neophilologus*, *Studies in Philology*, and *Pacific Coast Philology*; and to Boydell & Brewer Ltd and Syracuse University Press. So also those institutions holding rights to the objects illustrated in the plates are to be thanked for their permission to use these illustrations. I should especially like to thank Father McNamee for locating and providing an offprint of an article that is now thirty years old, and for kindly consenting to the substitution mentioned in a note on page 95. Edward B. Irving, Jr., read a draft of the preface and offered some invaluable suggestions, among them the addition of an index. Thanks are also due to Deans Morton Lowengrub and Roger Farr of Indiana University for authorizing funding for the purchase of the computer software necessary for the preparation of camera-ready copy, and especially to Associate Dean Albert Wertheim and Professor Mary Burgan, who were instrumental in securing this funding. Joan Catapano and Harriet Curry of Indiana University Press were unstinting of their advice and assistance in the preparation of this volume. The assistance of Jeff Hale and Fang Tsui of Bloomington Academic Computing Services in the optical scanning of the articles, and of Linda Gray and the late Jeffrey Vickman in editing the scanned files and proofreading the copy, was indispensable. Lastly I should like to thank the participants in the seminar mentioned at the beginning of this preface for their frank and generous advice in selecting the articles for this anthology.

R. D. F.
BLOOMINGTON, 1990

Wyrd and Providence in Anglo-Saxon Thought

By Bertha S. Phillpotts

I

However much scholars may differ in the dates they assign to *Beowulf* and to *Widsith*, and however much—or little—Christianity they may ascribe to the authors of the poems, they would doubtless agree on one point, that those authors are still influenced to some extent by the pagan attitude to life. But what is this pagan attitude to life? Some kind of coherent philosophy forms the background of even the most primitive faith, and there must be something more in Anglo-Saxon paganism than the worship of Woden and Thunor, more than the sanctions of loyalty to a chief, more than the recognition of Wyrd as an impersonal and unapproachable force.

If we can descry the shadowy outline of this earlier, unformulated philosophy, it must be through the medium of the stories and memories of the Heroic Age. The Anglo-Saxons shared in that common stock as freely as any other of the Nordic[1] peoples, and it seems safe to assume that the ideas which lie behind it were also common property. At any rate it is worth seeing what these stories will yield, because there can be no doubt that a better under-standing of the pagan philosophy would throw light on some dark places in early Anglo-Saxon literature.

Our first task, then, is to analyse the stories known to have been celebrated in verse by the Anglo-Saxons. And here we will leave the main themes of *Beowulf* on one side for the present, for amid the multiplicity of theories about that poem there is unanimity on one point, and that is that the subject-matter of the poem is an anomaly. We certainly know of no other heroic poem which turns wholly on the slaying of monsters.

But though *Beowulf*'s main theme is anomalous, the poem contains several allusions to other heroic poems, and we can begin by considering these.

1. First there is the story of Finn, sung by Hrothgar's *scop* or minstrel, at the banquet celebrating the killing of Grendel. The details of the story are obscure, and not much light is thrown on them by the actual extant fragment of the *Finnsburh Lay*. It is, however, clear that the interest of the story centres in the conflict in the mind of Hengest, who having defended his own lord, Hnæf, with the greatest devotion, is forced by circumstances to make peace and to swear fealty to Hnæf's slayer and brother-in-law, Finn. The song in *Beowulf* describes the tragic conflict in his mind between the duty of vengeance for his late lord on the one hand, and the tremendous sanctions of loyalty to a chief on the other.

[1]In the use of the term Nordic in this connexion I follow Professor Trevelyan in his *History of England*, cp. p. 29.

Reprinted, with permission, from *Essays and Studies* 13 (1928), 7-27.

2. The other heroic poem referred to in *Beowulf*, and recited by a king's thegn, is that of Sigemund. The *Beowulf* poet seems to have attempted to bowdlerize this story, or at any rate to stress its more presentable features. The dragon-slaying, an exploit attributed in later versions to his son Sigurd or Siegfried, is here ascribed to Sigemund, and he is expressly said to be the maternal uncle of Fitela, as if the poet did not wish to dwell on the closer relationship in which Sigemund stood to Fitela in all Germanic stories—father as well as uncle. But the reference to '*fæhðe ond fyrene*'—feuds and fearful crimes—suggests that the poet and his audience were acquainted with some such story as is preserved to us in the North, and was evidently known in Germany. Signý, Sigemund's sister, is faced with a choice of evils. The only alternatives before her are to commit horrible crimes or to leave unavenged her father and brothers, treacherously slain by her husband. The story tells of the alternative she chose, and how she carried it through to the bitter end, not flinching at incest nor at the murder of her sons.

3. *Beowulf* contains another allusion to what must have been an heroic poem, for Alcuin alludes disapprovingly to its recitation at Lindisfarne. It is the story of the choice placed before Ingeld, king of the Heathobards. To end a feud with the Danes, due to his father's death in battle at their hands, he has accepted in marriage the Danish king's daughter Freawaru. Is he to hold sacred his marriage and the oaths of peace, or is it not, in spite of all, his duty to wipe out the disgrace of letting Danish nobles wear in his court weapons and heirlooms stripped from his father in the field of battle?

These three epic lays mentioned in *Beowulf* all turn, then, on a forced choice between two evil courses, each of which presents itself as a duty.

4. In *Waldere* the conflicting duties are of a slightly different order. As we know the story from other sources, Hagena has to choose between the oath of brotherhood sworn by him to Waldere, and his duty to his king Guthhere, who demands that he shall attack Waldere.

Now let us look at the references in *Widsith* to heroes whom we know to have been celebrated in heroic song.[2] We can of course only tell the plots of the stories from later sources, Scandinavian and German, but since they agree in essentials there is no reason to suppose that the Anglo-Saxon forms of the stories were fundamentally different.

5. The Hild story. As the Danish Saxo recounts this story a slanderer tells Högni (Hagena, l. 21) that Heðinn (Heoden), his sworn brother, who is plighted to his daughter Hild, has already betrayed her. Is Högni to avenge this dire insult on his sworn brother, or shall he let it pass unavenged?

In Snorri's account, apparently founded on a lost poem, Heðinn abducts Hild—a terrible insult, as we know from Egilssaga. Högni has to choose between killing his son-in-law and letting this insult remain unavenged.[3]

6. Hagbard is secretly betrothed to Signe, daughter of Sigarr (Sigehere, l. 28). Her brothers kill his brothers owing to a slander, in spite of oaths of

[2]The Anglo-Saxon forms of the names mentioned in *Widsith* are given in brackets, with the line of the poem in which they occur.

[3]I do not give the story of Wade (Wada l. 22) because we do not know it. In *Widsith* he is a king ruling over his people, in the German *Kudrun* a champion of Hetele: in late medieval story his adventures seem to have been of a mythical order, in a boat with a Norman name.

sworn brotherhood. Is Hagbard to kill them or spare Signe? He kills them: Signe has to choose between him and the memory of her brothers.

7. The story of Alboin (Ælfwine, 1. 70) is only told by Paul the Deacon, but it is generally recognized that his account is based on a poem. Alboin, who has slain Thurisind's son, comes to his court and claims hospitality. Thurisind has to choose between the duty of hospitality and the duty of vengeance.

8. The story of Hlithe and Incgentheow (1. 116), as known to us in the verses in Hervarar Saga, concerns a battle between two half-brothers, there called Hlöðr and Angantýr. Hlöðr, grandson of the king of the Huns, having been taunted with being base-born, refuses Angantýr's offer of magnificent gifts from their father's property, as his honour demands that he shall share the inheritance equally with his half-brother. This leads to the great battle between the Goths and the Huns, in which Hlöðr falls. The poem ends with Angantýr's lament over his half-brother: 'A curse has been laid upon us, my brother: I have brought about thy death. . . . Evil is the decree of the norns.'[4]

9. Witega, Viðga (Wudga, 1. 130) having been a retainer of Theodoric, enters the service of Ermanaric with Theodoric's consent. When Ermanaric and Theodoric quarrel, what is he to do? He chooses loyalty to his present master, even though it involves killing Theodoric's brother in battle.

This then is the type of story celebrated in heroic poems by the Anglo-Saxons in the seventh century and earlier.

But if we are to understand the true force of those in which vengeance plays a part, we must utterly rid ourselves of the haunting idea, natural to members of a policed society, that the pursuit of vengeance was a yielding to a passion, to a temptation. On the contrary; it was very often a deliberate sacrifice of wealth, happiness, even of personal honour, in order to fulfil an obligation which might be the holiest of all. The claim became thus paramount, as Professor Chambers so admirably explains,[5] when the original slaying had been accomplished by treachery or any kind of baseness. Such deeds struck at the very foundations of human society, and since society had no means of punishing the evil-doer, it is not to be wondered at that the individual most affected should be held to fail utterly in his duty if he did not manage somehow to compass retribution.

In each story there is thus a situation entailing a choice between conflicting alternatives, both of which are felt to be evil.

If we look at the stock of early German and Scandinavian poems not mentioned in Anglo-Saxon sources we find that they are of the same type. In Germany we have the early *Hildebrandslied*. Father and son have challenged each other to single combat in front of the hostile armies. Hildebrand discovers that his antagonist is his son, but the latter will not believe him and suspects treachery. What is Hildebrand to do?

In the North the Nibelungen story[6] turns on similar situations. Gunnarr's

[4]Tr. Kershaw, *Anglo-Saxon and Norse Poems.*

[5]Introduction to *Beowulf*, pp. 276 ff.

[6]I do not mention this story among those alluded to in *Widsith*, as, though Gunnarr is

choice is put before him by Brynhild, who herself has to choose between the duty of avenging her brothers and her duty to her husband. The other heroic poems in the Elder Edda are similar in plot. The lay of Helgi Hundingsbane presents the same problems as the story of Hagbard and Signe.[7] The Lay of Helgi Hjörvarðsson tells how Heðinn has sworn an oath of awful sanctity that he will wed his brother's bride. What is he to do?

In the flotsam and jetsam of heroic poems preserved in various Norwegian sources and in Saxo there are the outlines of many more stories of this type,—e.g. the story of Hamlet—all turning on a choice between dire alternatives. And all the best of the Icelandic prose Sagas are inspired by the same theme.

It is not too much to say that it is the characteristic Nordic type of heroic story.

II

Before we consider the relation of these stories to the pagan philosophy of these peoples, it will be well to consider what else we can learn of their attitudes to life from the memories of heroic figures and events which they have preserved.

It is usual to marvel at what the Nordic peoples, including the Anglo-Saxons, remembered from the Heroic Age. But far more remarkable, and far more significant, is what they forgot. Few peoples can have had as spectacular successes as those who took part in the national migrations. They swept across Europe: they founded kingdoms from the Black Sea to Spain, from Africa to England. Yet what their poets remember is always connected with failure, defeat, disaster.[8] They have utterly forgotten Alaric and the sack of Rome, but Gundahari, who was defeated by the Huns not much later, is remembered for eight centuries or more, and sung of from Austria to Greenland. So too with Ermanaric, under whom the Gothic people were subdued by the Huns. The Anglo-Saxons have left no word in poetry of the victories they gained over the Britons, but they still remember the defeat and death of Hygelac in Friesland.

Strangest of all, perhaps, the Nordic peoples chose to forget how Theodoric the Ostrogoth ruled gloriously in Italy for thirty years, and in their poems one of the most successful figures in history, as Professor Chambers says, came to be the type of endurance under consistent and undeserved misfortune.[9]

There is something more in this interest in defeat than the mere poetic value of a lost battle against overwhelming odds, for very often no hint of odds has come down to us. Perhaps we shall get nearest to the secret of this interest if we see how the Scandinavians, at any rate, apply the ideas of failure

---

mentioned in that poem (Guthhere ll. 65-7), scholars do not consider that the Anglo-Saxons knew the combination of his story with the story of Sigurd.

[7]So also the Gram-Gro poem in Saxo.

[8]Even the songs recited by Hrothgar at the festivity after Grendel's slaying are 'soð ond sarlic'—true and *sad*, notwithstanding the joyful occasion. *Beow.* 2108 f.

[9]It is instructive to contrast the epic memories of another people—the Greeks. There is tragedy in the Iliad, but the Greeks did capture Troy, and the Odyssey ends with the hero's successful defeat of the suitors.

and defeat to their gods. It may be that the myth of Ragnarök, the Doom of the Gods, is a late product of the Viking Age, but it seems to me to be the logical outcome of the Northern philosophy of life, and therefore to throw light on our problem. The gods are mortal and subject to defeat not, surely, because the Northerners could not imagine immortality or permanent success, but because disaster is the final acid test of character. The valour of Odin and his peers, like the valour of human heroes, can only be proved by their fighting a losing battle, with defeat foreordained and foreknown. They must fight against tremendous and terrifying adversaries, with the universe crashing about them, the sun darkened, the stars falling from their places, flames playing against the sky itself, the earth sinking into the sea. They must bear it out even to the crack of doom: they must strive against the shape of disaster and destruction to the end, however much they know, and all the world knows, that the fight will be vain. It is the only way that they can be justified, and that the loyalty of their followers can be justified.

And so with human heroes. The quality of a man is not known until he is sore beset, either by defeat in battle or by being placed in a situation in which he must do violence to his sense of right. Fate can put men and women into positions whence it seems impossible for them to emerge with honour. They are judged by their choice, still more, perhaps, by the steadfastness with which they carry out their chosen aim, never looking back. Signý, in the Volsung story, is everything that the Northern peoples most contemn: a treacherous wife, a murderous mother. Yet she is a heroine, worthy of men's admiration, because having chosen her path she never looks back until her purpose is accomplished. When that is done, the Völsunga Saga, which is founded on ancient poems, makes her refuse to come out of the burning house, her husband's hall, which she has helped to set on fire for his destruction. To compass his undoing she has done things which make her, as she says, not fit to live, and now that right is done, treachery avenged, she can behave like a true wife and die with him.

Signý perhaps vindicates herself by her end: but many of the heroes and heroines have no chance of doing this: for them there is simply the awful choice between two evils.[10] But the point is that there is a choice.[11] It may be no more than a choice between yielding and resisting to the uttermost what is bound to happen: it may be only a choice between two courses each of which is hateful. But the intense interest of poets in this type of story does seem to show that the aristocracies of the Nordic peoples felt that man's will was free and, therefore, in some way superior to the Fate that crushes him. If this is not the ultimate significance of the stories, we should be forced to think that the Northern poets put their heroes and heroines into unendurable positions merely in order to see what they would do—as a child pulls the wings off a fly. But they justify themselves and redress the balance by their

[10]One of the alternatives may be suicide: Helga, in *Hervarar Saga*, ch. vii, chooses this way out instead of avenging her father and mother on her husband. See also the interesting story of the old comrades of Ingimund the Old, whose slayer is too low-born for satisfactory vengeance, *Vatnsdœla Saga*, ch. xxiii.

[11]Quite distinct from these are the misfortunes befalling men as a result of their own folly or credulity or cruelty: e.g. to Nithhad in the Weland story: to Ermanaric, to Thiadric (the Frank), and to Atli in the Northern versions.

conception of Fame. Fame is for the man who has the courage to choose: whether he chooses resistance to the uttermost against hopeless physical odds, knowing that his death is ordained, or whether he chooses one course rather than another of two that are hateful to him, and makes something magnificent of it by a single-minded pursuit of it. About the references to Fame in Anglo-Saxon and Scandinavian poetry there is a warmth and a passion which ought to warn us against regarding it as the meed of mere physical prowess. It is an assertion that there is something greater than Fate: the strength of will and the courage of human beings, and the memory which could preserve their deeds. Fame and human character: these were the two things against which Fate could not prevail. 'Wealth perishes, kinsfolk perish, one's very self perishes', says the Northern *Hávamál*, 'but fame dies never for him who gets it worthily.'[12]

For the Northern peoples there was no reward in a future life, since the doctrine of Valhöll never seems to have made much headway against the far older beliefs that the dead man lived on in his grave-mound or led a shadowy existence in Hell. So, as the Anglo-Saxon gnomic verse says: Dom bið selast—'Fame is the best of all.'[13]

This attitude to life deserves, I think, the name of a philosophy,[14] and it is none the less a coherent philosophy for being unformulated. It depends equally on the conception of Fate and on the conception of Fame. Neither can be taken away without shattering the web of thought.

To understand the influence of medieval Christianity on Anglo-Saxon thought we must imagine some such ideas as these in the minds of those who listened to Augustine or to Paulinus. But we must first consider two questions. The first question is, what parts of medieval Christian doctine would be most readily apprehended by men with this background of thought? The second is, how far could the new ideas be assimilated to the old philosophy?

III

It is abundantly clear, and has been well pointed out by Ehrismann,[15] and Haase,[16] that the ideas of heaven and hell dominated the early converts. This comes out very clearly in Bede's account of the conversion. Augustine's first message to Æthelbert of Kent is that he brings him 'a joyful message which most undoubtedly assured to him that hearkened to it everlasting joys in heaven'.[17] In Northumbria it is the first thing the heathen priest Coifi seizes upon: 'The truth of this doctrine can confer on us the gifts of life, of salvation,

---

[12]Beowulf utters much the same thought, ll. 1386 ff.

[13]There is a tacit appeal to this sentiment in the song sung by an Icelandic court poet to the Norwegian army before the battle of Stiklastaðir, in 1030, in which St. Olaf fell. The poet chants of no victory, but of the attack on Hrólfr Kraki (*Widsith*'s Hrothulf) and his retainers in their hall, and of how they perished every one.

[14]Cp. W. P. Ker, *Dark Ages*, p. 57.

[15]Paul and Braune's *Beiträge*, xxxv (1909), pp. 209 ff.

[16]Haase, *Kirchengeschichte*, ii. 47, quoted by Ehrismann.

[17]*H. E.* i. 25 (Sellar's tr.).

of eternal happiness.'[18] The famous simile of the sparrow[19] shows that the conception of a future life among the heathen Anglo-Saxons was vague and unsatisfying. It is, therefore, natural that this should be the point they would seize on first, and which would influence them most. But we need not suppose that the interest of the better converts in Heaven and Hell was merely selfish. Though the Northern peoples had a high appreciation of the ethical value of law and justice in society they had never, so far as we can tell, conceived of a reign of law and justice in the world order. Yet it is easy to see that it is a conception which would have an immediate appeal to them even in the crude form in which medieval Christianity presented it to them.

These ideas of Heaven, Hell, and the justice of God, are the three ideas connected with the new faith which we find clearly indicated in *Beowulf*, and they were no doubt specially characteristic of the first few generations after the conversion. How did they blend with the old heathen philosophy of life?

Clearly mere misfortune, mere defeat, was easier to understand in the light of the new knowledge. The victim could be compensated in the next life for his sufferings in this one, though that resistance to the uttermost, that defiance of Fate, so much admired in the heathen times, was now very liable to become mere impiety. As for all the rest of the heathen philosophy, it could have needed no special acumen to see that it was wholly incompatible with the new Christian doctrines.

In a universe governed by justice and not by a capricious Fate, in a universe where men go to Heaven or Hell according to their deeds, the old Nordic type of story leads to grave difficulties. If the world is governed by justice, how can men and women be forced into following one of two evil courses? What place in a future world could be assigned to Signý, of the Volsung story, to Hagena, who breaks the oaths of sworn brotherhood, to Ingeld who breaks the oaths of peace, and kills his wife's nearest kinsfolk? They cannot be thought of in Heaven, yet all the ancient traditions must have risen up in protest against consigning them to Hell, as Alcuin does Ingeld. It is surely not merely because Ingeld was a heathen that he is a *rex perditus*.[20] It is because he must be judged by the sins he committed, which were very great, and not, as the heathens would have considered, by the heroism which broke a way out of a network of evils.

At this stage it is useful to see what happened to these old stories in Germany. Just this feature which must have been repugnant to medieval Christianity, is smoothed away in a very interesting fashion. Even poets in a monastery may treat of Waltharius, Waldere, if they like. The conflict of motives is still there: Hagen is still faced with the alternatives of breaking his oath of brotherhood to Waltharius, or failing in loyalty to his king, and it is only when his nephew is slain by Waltharius that he enters the fight. Here are all the ingredients for one of the old heathen tragedies. But they are not allowed to clash beyond a certain point. The heroes each lose a limb in the battle, but they are mended, and go home happily after a reconciliation. It is

---

[18]Ibid., ii. 13.

[19]Loc. cit.

[20]Cp. Chadwick, *Heroic Age*, p. 465 f.

an ending that is generally recognized to be grotesque, but it is evidently the price the story-tellers had to pay for the survival of the story in a Christian atmosphere. So with the story of Hildebrand and Hadubrand. The ancient poem undoubtedly ended in the tragic slaying of the son by the father.[21] But in the *Jüngere Hildebrandslied*, though the stage is set in the same way, the ending is cheerful. So, too, with the originally tragic poem of Heðinn and Högni. The Middle High German *Kudrun* lets Hetel and Hagen wound each other sorely, but then it reconciles them, heals their wounds, and gives a happy ending to the story.

Such violence as this cannot be done to the greatest of all the tales, the Nibelungen story. But all the balance of the story has been altered in the *Nibelungenlied*. Tragedy remains, and much of the heathen spirit, but here it is the conflict of motives in the minds of the heroines which has been smoothed away. The Scandinavian Brynhild cuts the knot of her love for Sigurd by inducing her brothers to kill him. The conflict in the mind of a woman in such a situation continued to interest the Icelanders at the very time the *Nibelungenlied* was committed to writing, for it is studied afresh in the Laxdale Saga. But in the *Nibelungenlied* it is Hagen who decides to take vengeance on Siegfried for Brunhild's humiliation, though later she is said to have been in the plot.[22] She disappears from the story before Siegfried's death, and it is not suggested that she loved him. Kriemhild, Siegfried's widow, in revenge for his slaying, compasses the death of her brothers, but the sympathy of the poet is not with her, and the end of the poem shows her simply as a very wicked woman, who meets a righteous death at the hands of Hildebrand. Indeed, she is represented as more concerned with getting hold of the Nibelungen treasure possessed by her brothers than with her vengeance on them. The old conflict of duties in the minds of Brunhild and Kriemhild has disappeared.[23] 'The *Nibelungenlied* is glorious, but its glory, like its metre, is not that of the ancient lays.'[24]

IV

In early Anglo-Saxon poetry the interaction between the heathen attitude to life and the new doctrines seems to have been more creative and more interesting than in Germany. Let us first consider *Beowulf*.

Two things are certain about this poem. The first is that its author had thoroughly assimilated, not Christianity,[25] but the three ideas of medieval Christianity which dominated the minds of the early converts: Heaven, Hell, and the reign of justice in the universe.[26] The second is that its plot is an anomaly. W. P. Ker observed that the construction of the poem is in a sense preposterous: the irrelevances, the monster-slayings, are in the centre, and the

---

[21]Ehrismann, *Gesch. der d. Lit.* (Munich, 1918), p. 123.

[22]*Nibelungenlied*, ed. Bartsch, Leipzig, 1875, xiv. Av. str. 864; ibid., xvi. Av. str. 917.

[23]On the other hand the *Nibelungenlied* has preserved, or developed, an interesting conflict of motives in the mind of the Markgraf Rüdiger.

[24]Chambers, *Widsith*, p. 3.

[25]Chadwick, *Heroic Age*, p. 47 f.

[26]Ll. 588 f., 977 ff., 2741 ff., 2819 f.

serious things—the references to heroic story—are on the outer edges.[27] In *Widsith*, which shows us, as Professor Chambers says, the stock in trade of the old Anglian bard, the hall Heorot is not thought of as the place where Beowulf overcomes monsters, but as the scene of strife within the kindred, and of the Ingeld story. 'In that conflict between plighted troth and the duty of revenge', Professor Chambers adds, 'we have a situation which the old heroic poets loved, and would not have sold for a wilderness of dragons.'[28]

The choice of the story seems to become more mysterious still as the suspicion of scholars about its hero deepens. Beowulf's long reign of fifty years over the Geatas does not fit the chronology, and his name does not fit with the names of the Geatic dynasty, nor with those of his father's house.

These two anomalies—that the great epic deals with monster-slayings instead of with heroic story, and that the hero does not quite belong to his environment—have led Professor Klaeber[29] to suggest that the author imported the figure of Beowulf into heroic story with a definitely Christian aim. He took him as his hero because a prince who delivered his people from a dragon would remind his audience of the Redeemer of their new faith. The story, in fact, lent itself to being made into a symbol or allegory of the central fact of the Christian faith.

While fully admitting that there must have been some special reason for the choice of the theme of *Beowulf*, there seems to me to be unsurmountable difficulties in Professor Klaeber's theory. If the poet had the Christian Redeemer in his mind, the absence of any allusion to Him, or to anything in the New Testament except the Day of Judgment, becomes stranger than it already is. And would it not be too strange an irony, if the author had such a prototype in his mind, to make the dying hero exult in the dragon's gold, and insist on seeing it as he lies dying—gold which is buried with him, 'as unprofitable to men as it had been before'? And why, with such a hero, describe with such gusto a markedly heathen funeral? But there is a more serious objection than these—namely, that the poet has not troubled to omit from the story a feature which makes Beowulf actually more primitive than the ordinary epic hero. Beowulf may be forgiven for fighting Grendel without a sword, whether from chivalrous motives (ll. 679 ff.), or because weapons will not bite the monster (ll. 433 ff.). But when he goes out of his way to boast of having hugged to death a human antagonist, the warrior Dæghrefn (ll. 2506 ff.), he seems to show bear or troll-like attributes,[30] which would surely have been omitted by an author who had selected him for the reasons suggested by Klaeber.

Let us now suppose that the poet of *Beowulf* was a *scop* devoid of the slightest missionary aim—on the contrary, delighting (as he evidently does) in pagan antiquity. Yet he is anxious to compose a poem which could fitly be

[27]Ker, *Dark Ages*, p. 253. Cp. also Chadwick, *Heroic Age*, p. 116; Ehrismann, *Anglia*, xxxvi (1912), p. 195.

[28]No one would suggest that heroes did not kill dragons: Sigurd did, and Sigemund too, and Theodoric the Ostrogoth seems to have been particularly active in this sphere. But dragon-slaying is only an incidental glory to these heroes: their interest for heroic poets lies elsewhere.

[29]*Die christlichen Elemente im Beowulf*, iv, *Anglia*, xxxvi (1912), pp. 169 ff.

[30]Cp. Chadwick, *Heroic Age*, p. 121.

sung in the hall of such a king as Oswald, Oswin, or Oswy.[31] He and his audience are still so near to pagan times that no one will expect him to celebrate the past with no references to paganism, but on the other hand, he must have a respectable hero and plot. He must not take one of the old traditional plots which turn on an evil choice being offered to man or woman; because in a world governed by justice, and leading to Heaven or Hell, it is obviously impossible that a human being should be forced to do one wrong in order to avoid another. Yet our poet wants to keep the heroic atmosphere, and to use all the knowledge of the kings and peoples of the pagan past, which is his stock in trade. In this dilemma he chooses a dragon-slayer as his hero: but a dragon-slayer who can be placed in the environment of which he has always sung—the dynasties of Southern Sweden and Denmark. He loses the close-knit structure of a story of the old type, and the Wyrd of the old religion becomes a mere body-snatcher.[32] But at least he can have fighting, and ceremonial,[33] and loyal and disloyal retainers, and he can put fine speeches into the mouths of his characters, and he can allude constantly to the web of ancient stories which is still present in the minds of his audience.

He sacrifices, in fact, as little as he possibly can, and the result is that his poem is liked both by the Christian and the more conservative elements of the aristocracy, and comes ultimately to be written down in a fine MS., together with the Christian poem *Judith*. *Beowulf* may thus be considered the first English compromise.

Perhaps, however, he was not the first *scop* to discover that allusions to the old pagan stories were inoffensive to Cristians, and nearly as satisfactory as the stories themselves to the less ardent converts. It may be significant that out of the five poems referring to the pagan period surviving in England, three, *Beowulf*, *Widsith*, and *Deor*, use this allusive method of recalling ancient stories. They are the only three of the poems to be preserved entire.[34]

V

I have said above that the poet of *Beowulf* sacrifices as little of the old poetic traditions as he possibly can. But one thing he has lost without being aware of it, and the loss is typical of early Anglo-Saxon poetry as a whole. It is the loss of a certain spirit, a sort of grim satisfaction in recounting the actions of men driven into a corner by adverse circumstances. The modern reader feels this spirit even in Saxo's prolix Latin version of the old Lay of Hrólfr Kraki, and still more, of course, in the references to Ragnarök, the Doom of the Gods, in the Eddic poems. So far as the shortness of the

---

[31]I follow Chadwick in regarding the poem as very early: cp. *Heroic Age*, p. 46 f.

[32]Except in l. 572 f.

[33]It is difficult to follow Klaeber in regarding courtly behavior as necessarily Christian. The courtesies of Beowulf are after all outdone by the supreme courtesy of King Hringr in wholly heathen times, when he gives his fallen enemy a chariot and saddle in the grave-mound, so that he made ride or drive to Valhöll as he wishes (*Sögubrot af Fornkonungum*, ch. ix).

[34]I subscribe to everything said by Professor Chambers in his *Lost Literature of Medieval England* as to the element of chance in what has been kept and what lost of Anglo-Saxon poems. But still it is clear that poems which could be included in mainly religious MSS. were far more likely to survive than others.

fragment allows, I think it can be felt in the *Finnsburh Lay*. But in *Beowulf* it is replaced by a wholly alien spirit, one of melancholy resignation. As Professor Legouis says: 'This poem, which is a glorification of bold enterprise, leaves a bitter taste, or at least an impression of universal melancholy.'

Owing to the markedly elegiac note of such poems as the *Wanderer*, and the *Ruin*, scholars usually assume that melancholy was an inborn trait of the Anglo-Saxons. Yet it seems strange that these peoples, delighting in the same stories as the rest of the Northern world, should have differed so greatly in temperament from their close kinsfolk. The one difference we can trace is a difference in the nature of their conversion to Christianity. The Anglo-Saxons were converted by persuasion and not by compulsion, at a time of great religious fervour, and under the direct influence of Roman, Greek, and Celtic culture. It is, therefore, not strange that Christian ideas should have a much more rapid influence on the thought of aristocratic circles in England,[35] than in countries converted later, mainly by compulsion, like North Germany and Norway, by missionaries who could not compare in ability and enlightenment with those who converted England.

It therefore seems more natural to explain the melancholy in Anglo-Saxon poems as a result of the clash between the pagan philosophy of life and the new doctrine, so readily accepted. On the one hand we have what W. P. Ker saw in the myth of Ragnarök, 'the assertion of the individual freedom against all the terrors and temptations of the world, . . . absolute resistance, perfect because without hope,'[36] sometimes reaching an intensity of defiance which does not fear to arraign the gods.[37] On the other hand, there is the new knowledge that the world is ordered by a just Providence, so that resistance to what must be becomes no longer glorious but simply impious and foolish. It is surely natural that the revulsion from the old attitude should lead to an undue stressing of resignation.

Other causes, similar in origin, contribute to the tendency to melancholy. The old idea of resistance was stimulated by the thought of Fame, the one certain and enduring reward of the morally and physically valiant. But what is Fame, when all that matters is the whereabouts of the soul in the next world? And what of physical prowess, of the glory of weapons and of gold, since Fame is a shadow, and life not what it seems?

The old idea of resistance is still of course respectable in battles against mortal enemies, and in this connexion, in the words uttered by Byrhtwold in the *Battle of Maldon*, we find it more finely expressed in Anglo-Saxon than in any other Northern literature:

> Soul shall be the more stalwart, heart the higher,
> Courage the greater, the more our might 'minisheth.

[35]Cp. Brandl, *Paul's Grundriss*, ii. 1, p. 963: all Anglo-Saxon secular poetry is 'im innersten Kern Adelspoesie'.

[36]*Dark Ages*, p. 57. See whole passage.

[37]Cp. Biarki in the *Lay of Hrólfr Kraki*, boasting that if he could meet with Odin he would kill him in vengeance for the disaster that is overtaking his king (Saxo, *Holder*, p. 66); Egill, in the *Sonatorrek*, wishing that he could fight the sea-god Ægir, who has bereft him of his sons; Hervör, in the poem in *Hervarar Saga*, defying the decrees of Fate.

There is still one connexion in which resistance to the decree of God can be freely described without offence to Christian doctrine—in telling the story of Satan. Here many strings of the old heathen harp can be touched—disaster and defeat, as well as resistance and defiance, all in surroundings that surely owe something to Niflheim. The finest flower of religious narrative deals with the Fall of the Angels: and this is surely no accident. Though the poem is translated from Old Saxon, the very fact of the translation suggests that the subject made a powerful appeal to the Anglo-Saxons.

It is interesting that the nearest approach, in the religious narratives, to the old heathen stories of choice between two evils occurs in the poem written in the same manuscript as *Beowulf*, and by the same hand as the latter part of the poem. Of course it is a duty for Judith to kill Holofernes, and it is the proper alternative for her to choose. Nevertheless, the poem has something of the old interest and the old gusto in depicting the choice of a man or woman, driven to desperate straits by Fate, and it is significant that just these two poems—the *Fall of the Angels* (*Genesis B.*), and *Judith*, should appear to W. P. Ker to be the best of the religious narrative poems.[38] Both poems, of course, owe much to the circumstance that their plots enable their poets to use the ancient heroic vocabulary. The self-will of women was a subject quite as dear to the pagan poets as that of men,[39] so that in describing Judith the poet had an immense traditional vocabulary to draw upon.[40]

But the pagan ideas are responsible for much more than the excellence of these two poems. It seems too paradoxical to see their influence in the Anglo-Saxon version of the *De Consolatione* of Boethius, yet it might never have been translated by Alfred but for paganism. A glance at the book will show how profoundly it must have interested a people torn like the Anglo-Saxons between rather crudely apprehended Christian doctrine on the one hand, and, on the other, the philosophy incorporated in their old stories, with its Fate, its Fame, and its defiant consciousness of free will. W. P. Ker said that Boethius saved the thought of the medieval world. But he could only save it because the ideas which he treated were fermenting in the minds of the converted barbarians. 'What the onefold Providence of God is, and what Fate is, what happens by chance, and what are divine intelligence, divine predestination, and human free will'[41]—were not these questions which every thoughtful Anglo-Saxon must have pondered, so long as he was acquainted with the old tales of his people,

---

[38] *Dark Ages*, p. 256.

[39] The very strong-willed, ruthless women of heroic tradition seem to have been more repugnant to Christian sentiment than the men. The St. Gall poet turns Hildegund into a weak and gentle character, most unlike the impression given by the Anglo-Saxon fragment, if the speech to Waldere is rightly attributed to her. It is noticeable that the women in *Beowulf* play very minor parts and are models of propriety, though Beowulf refers to another, Thryth, who seems to have been in the old Valkyrie tradition.

[40] Is it not possible that the choice of subject in the religious narrative poems may have been considerably influenced by the existence of an old poetic vocabulary and convention? *Elene* and *Juliana* offer some of the same advantages to poets as *Judith*: the story of *Andreas* may have been chosen for the adventures at sea, for which an immense traditional vocabulary was at hand. Probably poems about the beginning of the world also had pagan prototypes which could be followed to a certain extent.

[41] *Consolation of Philosophy*, Book VI, Alfred's version, tr. Sedgefield. The discussion of Free will is much expanded by Alfred or by some previous commentator.

as Alfred himself was? And Book II, on the nothingness of Fame, must also have had a deep, if melancholy, interest for the Anglo-Saxon. We may well owe the preservation of this work, and with it the best thought of the Middle Ages, to the fact that it made a bridge between the ancient philosophy of the Nordic peoples and their new religion.

VI

If the old pagan attitude to life has been rightly interpreted, one or two problems confronting Anglo-Saxon scholars become less difficult of solution. Stories born of the heathen philosophy could not but be unacceptable in the courts of newly converted kings, and it is, at least, a possible explanation of *Beowulf*'s main theme that it is a gallant attempt to keep the traditions of heroic poetry while sacrificing the hero torn between two conflicting duties. So also the transition in Anglo-Saxon thought from pagan defiance to Christian resignation, from the glory of undying Fame to the nothingness of this world, might well produce the melancholy in Anglo-Saxon poetry, which strikes such an alien note in the chorus of heroic song.

But there is a greater mystery in Anglo-Saxon literature than these. Why did it die of no notifiable disease, as W. P. Ker said somewhere, and in a manner puzzling to literary historians, long before the Norman Conquest? If the theory advanced above has any truth in it, this decay of poetic literature is perfectly explicable. Whereas in Norway and Iceland, so long as the old ideas still have creative force, the native literature is like a plant perpetually putting forth new shoots, in England the principle of life in the old stories was dead, though the old poems, no doubt, continued to be sung. (It was not, I suppose, till the Tudor period that the English people again occupied themselves with the problem of men and women faced by evil alternatives.) And except for historical events, there were no new stories to be got save by borrowing. The impulse to treat in verse stories from the Bible and from lives of Saints died out, perhaps, because they necessarily lacked the close-knit dramatic structure of the heroic poems, perhaps owing to the decay of religious fervour. Then comes a long silence, and when next we meet stories treated in verse they no longer treat of the clash of character with Destiny. They are stories of adventure, and they are borrowed. Some the new Norman aristocracy brings, most come from the conquered Britons, a few from the conquering Danelaw. None appear to be the original property of the Anglo-Saxon element in the population.

The other Northern peoples whose literature has survived seem to have had the same intellectual history, except that no silence supervenes on the abandonment of the old themes. By the time that they were conscious of the incongruity of their stories and their beliefs, there was plenty of new material to borrow. In some ways the transition in Iceland from the stories of character to the stories of adventure and chivalry is even more striking than the course of literary history in England. But that is another story. What we can say here is that the Anglo-Saxons were the quickest of all the Nordic peoples to observe the discrepancy between their heroic stories and the new doctrines, and the most original in their efforts to create a new poetry on the lines of the old, yet in accord with the teaching of medieval Christianity.

Beowulf: The Monsters and the Critics

BY J. R. R. TOLKIEN

In 1864 the Reverend Oswald Cockayne wrote of the Reverend Doctor Joseph Bosworth, Rawlinsonian Professor of Anglo-Saxon: 'I have tried to lend to others the conviction I have long entertained that Dr. Bosworth is not a man so diligent in his special walk as duly to read the books . . . which have been printed in our old English, or so-called Anglosaxon tongue. He may do very well for a professor.'[1] These words were inspired by dissatisfaction with Bosworth's dictionary, and were doubtless unfair. If Bosworth were still alive, a modern Cockayne would probably accuse him of not reading the 'literature' of his subject, the books written about the books in the so-called Anglo-Saxon tongue. The original books are nearly buried.

Of none is this so true as of *The Beowulf*, as it used to be called. I have, of course, read *The Beowulf*, as have most (but not all) of those who have criticized it. But I fear that, unworthy successor and beneficiary of Joseph Bosworth, I have not been a man so diligent in my special walk as duly to read all that has been printed on, or touching on, this poem. But I have read enough, I think, to venture the opinion that *Beowulfiana* is, while rich in many departments, specially poor in one. It is poor in criticism, criticism that is directed to the understanding of a poem as a poem. It has been said of *Beowulf* itself that its weakness lies in placing the unimportant things at the centre and the important on the outer edges. This is one of the opinions that I wish specially to consider. I think it profoundly untrue of the poem, but strikingly true of the literature about it. Beowulf has been used as a quarry of fact and fancy far more assiduously than it has been studied as a work of art.

It is of *Beowulf*, then, as a poem that I wish to speak; and though it may seem presumption that I should try with *swich a lewed mannes wit to pace the wisdom of an heep of lerned men*, in this department there is at least more chance for the *lewed man*. But there is so much that might still be said even under these limitations that I shall confine myself mainly to the *monsters—* Grendel and the Dragon, as they appear in what seems to me the best and most authoritative general criticism in English—and to certain considerations of the structure and conduct of the poem that arise from this theme.

There is an historical explanation of the state of *Beowulfiana* that I have referred to. And that explanation is important, if one would venture to criticize the critics. A sketch of the history of the subject is required. But I will here

[1] *The Shrine*, p. 4.

This paper was delivered as the Sir Israel Gollancz Memorial Lecture of 1936 to the British Academy. It is reprinted here, by permission of the Academy, from *Proceedings of the British Academy* 22 (1936), 245-95.

14

only attempt, for brevity's sake, to present my view of it allegorically. As it set out upon its adventures among the modern scholars, *Beowulf* was christened by Wanley Poesis—*Poeseos Anglo-Saxonicæ egregium exemplum*. But the fairy godmother later invited to superintend its fortunes was Historia. And she brought with her Philologia, Mythologia, Archaeologia, and Laographia.[2] Excellent ladies. But where was the child's name-sake? Poesis was usually forgotten; occasionally admitted by a side-door; sometimes dismissed upon the door-step. 'The *Beowulf*', they said, 'is hardly an affair of yours, and not in any case a protégé that you could be proud of. It is an historical document. Only as such does it interest the superior culture of today.' And it is as an historical document that it has mainly been examined and dissected. Though ideas as to the nature and quality of the history and information embedded in it have changed much since Thorkelin called it *De Danorum Rebus Gestis*, this has remained steadily true. In still recent pronouncements this view is explicit. In 1925 Professor Archibald Strong translated Beowulf into verse;[3] but in 1921 he had declared: '*Beowulf* is the picture of a whole civilization, of the Germania which Tacitus describes. The main interest which the poem has for us is thus not a purely literary interest. *Beowulf* is an important historical document.'[4]

I make this preliminary point, because it seems to me that the air has been clouded not only for Strong, but for other more authoritative critics, by the dust of the quarrying researchers. It may well be asked: why should we approach this, or indeed any other poem, mainly as an historical document? Such an attitude is defensible: firstly, if one is not concerned with poetry at all, but seeking information wherever it may be found; secondly, if the so-called poem contains in fact no poetry. I am not concerned with the first case. The historian's search is, of course, perfectly legitimate, even if it does not assist criticism in general at all (for that is not its object), so long as it is not mistaken for criticism. To Professor Birger Nerman as an historian of Swedish origins *Beowulf* is doubtless an important document, but he is not writing a history of English poetry. Of the second case it may be said that to rate a poem, a thing at the least in metrical form, as mainly of historical interest should *in a literary survey* be equivalent to saying that it has no literary merits, and little more need in such a survey then be said about it. But such a judgement on *Beowulf* is false. So far from being a poem so poor that only its accidental historical interest can still recommend it, *Beowulf* is in fact so interesting as poetry, in places poetry so powerful, that this quite overshadows

[2]Thus in Professor Chambers's great bibliography (in his *Beowulf: An Introduction*) we find a section, § 8. Questions of Literary History, Date, and Authorship; Beowulf in the Light of History, Archaeology, Heroic Legend, Mythology, and Folklore. It is impressive, but there is no section that names Poetry. As certain of the items included show, such consideration as Poetry is accorded at all is buried unnamed in § 8.

[3]*Beowulf translated into modern English rhyming verse*, Constable, 1925.

[4]*A Short History of English Literature*, Oxford Univ. Press, 1921, pp. 2-3. I choose this example, because it is precisely to general literary histories that we must usually turn for literary judgements on *Beowulf*. The experts in *Beowulfiana* are seldom concerned with such judgements. And it is in the highly compressed histories, such as this, that we discover what the process of digestion makes of the special 'literature' of the experts. Here is the distilled product of Research. This compendium, moreover, is competent, and written by a man who had (unlike some other authors of similar things) read the poem itself with attention.

the historical content, and is largely independent even of the most important facts (such as the date and identity of Hygelac) that research has discovered. It is indeed a curious fact that it is one of the peculiar poetic virtues of *Beowulf* that has contributed to its own critical misfortunes. The illusion of historical truth and perspective, that has made *Beowulf* seem such an attractive quarry, is largely a product of art. The author has used an instinctive historical sense—a part indeed of the ancient English temper (and not unconnected with its reputed melancholy), of which *Beowulf* is a supreme expression; but he has used it with a poetical and not an historical object. The lovers of poetry can safely study the art, but the seekers after history must beware lest the glamour of Poesis overcome them.

Nearly all the censure, and most of the praise, that has been bestowed on *The Beowulf* has been due either to the belief that it was something that it was not—for example, primitive, pagan, Teutonic, an allegory (political or mythical), or most often, an epic; or to disappointment at the discovery that it was itself and not something that the scholar would have liked better—for example, a heathen heroic lay, a history of Sweden, a manual of Germanic antiquities, or a Nordic *Summa Theologica*.

I would express the whole industry in yet another allegory. A man inherited a field in which was an accumulation of old stone, part of an older hall. Of the old stone some had already been used in building the house in which he actually lived, not far from the old house of his fathers. Of the rest he took some and built a tower. But his friends coming perceived at once (without troubling to climb the steps) that these stones had formerly belonged to a more ancient building. So they pushed the tower over, with no little labour, in order to look for hidden carvings and inscriptions, or to discover whence the man's distant forefathers had obtained their building material. Some suspecting a deposit of coal under the soil began to dig for it, and forgot even the stones, They all said: 'This tower is most interesting.' But they also said (after pushing it over): 'What a muddle it is in!' And even the man's own descendants, who might have been expected to consider what he had been about, were heard to murmur: 'He is such an odd fellow! Imagine his using these old stones just to build a nonsensical tower! Why did not he restore the old house? He had no sense of proportion.' But from the top of that tower the man had been able to look out upon the sea.

I hope I shall show that that allegory is just—even when we consider the more recent and more perceptive critics (whose concern is in intention with literature). To reach these we must pass in rapid flight over the heads of many decades of critics. As we do so a conflicting babel mounts up to us, which I can report as something after this fashion.[5] '*Beowulf* is a half-baked native epic the development of which was killed by Latin learning; it was inspired by emulation of Virgil, and is a product of the education that came in with Christianity; it is feeble and incompetent as a narrative; the rules of narrative are cleverly observed in the manner of the learned epic; it is the confused product of a committee of muddle-headed and probably beer-bemused Anglo-Saxons (this is a Gallic voice); it is a string of pagan lays edited by monks; it

---

[5]I include nothing that has not somewhere been said by some one, if not in my exact words; but I do not, of course, attempt to represent all the *dicta*, wise or otherwise, that have been uttered.

is the work of a learned but inaccurate Christian antiquarian; it is a work of genius, rare and surprising in the period, though the genius seems to have been shown principally in doing something much better left undone (this is a very recent voice); it is a wild folk-tale (general chorus); it is a poem of an aristocratic and courtly tradition (same voices); it is a hotchpotch; it is a sociological, anthropological, archaeological document; it is a mythical allegory (very old voices these and generally shouted down, but not so far out as some of the newer cries); it is rude and rough; it is a masterpiece of metrical art; it has no shape at all; it is singularly weak in construction; it is a clever allegory of contemporary politics (old John Earle with some slight support from Mr. Girvan, only they look to different periods); its architecture is solid; it is thin and cheap (a solemn voice); it is undeniably weighty (the same voice); it is a national epic; it is a translation from the Danish; it was imported by Frisian traders; it is a burden to English syllabuses; and (final universal chorus of all voices) it is worth studying.'

It is not surprising that it should now be felt that a view, a decision, a conviction are imperatively needed. But it is plainly only in the consideration of *Beowulf* as a poem, with an inherent poetic significance, that any view or conviction can be reached or steadily held. For it is of their nature that the jabberwocks of historical and antiquarian research burble in the tulgy wood of conjecture, flitting from one tum-tum tree to another. Noble animals, whose burbling is on occasion good to hear; but though their eyes of flame may sometimes prove searchlights, their range is short.

None the less, paths of a sort have been opened in the wood. Slowly with the rolling years the obvious (so often the last revelation of analytic study) has been discovered: that we have to deal with a poem by an Englishman using afresh ancient and largely traditional material. At last then, after inquiring so long whence this material came, and what its original or aboriginal nature was (questions that cannot ever be decisively answered), we might also now again inquire what the poet did with it. If we ask that question, then there is still, perhaps, something lacking even in the major critics, the learned and revered masters from whom we humbly derive.

The chief points with which I feel dissatisfied I will now approach by way of W. P. Ker, whose name and memory I honour. He would deserve reverence, of course, even if he still lived and had not *ellor gehworfen on Frean wære* upon a high mountain in the heart of that Europe which he loved: a great scholar, as illuminating himself as a critic, as he was often biting as a critic of the critics. None the less I cannot help feeling that in approaching *Beowulf* he was hampered by the almost inevitable weakness of his greatness: stories and plots must sometimes have seemed triter to him, the much-read, than they did to the old poets and their audiences. The dwarf on the spot sometimes sees things missed by the travelling giant ranging many countries. In considering a period when literature was narrower in range and men possessed a less diversified stock of ideas and themes, one must seek to recapture and esteem the deep pondering and profound feeling that they gave to such as they possessed.

In any case Ker has been potent. For his criticism is masterly, expressed always in words both pungent and weighty, and not least so when it is (as I occasionally venture to think) itself open to criticism. His words and judgements are often quoted, or reappear in various modifications, digested, their source probably sometimes forgotten. It is impossible to avoid quotation of the well-known passage in his *Dark Ages*:

A reasonable view of the merit of *Beowulf* is not impossible, though rash enthusiasm may have made too much of it, while a correct and sober taste may have too contemptuously refused to attend to Grendel or the Fire-drake. The fault of *Beowulf* is that there is nothing much in the story. The hero is occupied in killing monsters, like Hercules or Theseus. But there are other things in the lives of Hercules and Theseus besides the killing of the Hydra or of Procrustes. Beowulf has nothing else to do, when he has killed Grendel and Grendel's mother in Denmark: he goes home to his own Gautland, until at last the rolling years bring the Fire-drake and his last adventure. It is too simple. Yet the three chief episodes are well wrought and well diversified; they are not repetitions, exactly; there is a change of temper between the wrestling with Grendel in the night at Heorot and the descent under water to encounter Grendel's mother; while the sentiment of the Dragon is different again. But the great beauty, the real value, of *Beowulf* is in its dignity of style. In construction it is curiously weak, in a sense preposterous; for while the main story is simplicity itself, the merest commonplace of heroic legend, all about it, in the historic allusions, there are revelations of a whole world of tragedy, plots different in import from that of *Beowulf*, more like the tragic themes of Iceland. Yet with this radical defect, a disproportion that puts the irrelevances in the centre and the serious things on the outer edges, the poem of *Beowulf* is undeniably weighty. The thing itself is cheap; the moral and the spirit of it can only be matched among the noblest authors.[6]

This passage was written more than thirty years ago, but has hardly been surpassed. It remains, in this country at any rate, a potent influence. Yet its primary effect is to state a paradox which one feels has always strained the belief, even of those who accepted it, and has given to *Beowulf* the character of an 'enigmatic poem'. The chief virtue of the passage (not the one for which it is usually esteemed) is that it does accord some attention to the monsters, despite correct and sober taste. But the contrast made between the radical defect of theme and structure, and at the same time the dignity, loftiness in converse, and well-wrought finish, has become a commonplace even of the best criticism, a paradox the strangeness of which has almost been forgotten in the process of swallowing it upon authority.[7] We may compare Professor Chambers in his *Widsith*, p. 79, where he is studying the story of Ingeld, son of Froda, and his feud with the great Scylding house of Denmark, a story introduced in *Beowulf* merely as an allusion.

---

[6]*The Dark Ages*, pp. 252-3.

[7]None the less Ker modified it in an important particular in *English Literature, Mediæval*, pp. 29-34. In general, though in different words, vaguer and less incisive, he repeats himself. We are still told that 'the story is commonplace and the plan is feeble', or that 'the story is thin and poor'. But we learn also at the end of his notice that: 'Those distracting allusions to things apart from the chief story make up for their want of proportion. They give the impression of reality and weight; the story is not in the air . . . it is part of the solid world.' By the admission of so grave an artistic reason for the procedure of the poem Ker himself began the undermining of his own criticism of its structure. But this line of thought does not seem to have been further pursued. Possibly it was this very thought, working in his mind, that made Ker's notice of *Beowulf* in the small later book, his 'shilling shocker', more vague and hesitant in tone, and so of less influence.

Nothing [Chambers says] could better show the disproportion of *Beowulf* which 'puts the irrelevances in the centre and the serious things on the outer edges', than this passing allusion to the story of Ingeld. For in this conflict between plighted troth and the duty of revenge we have a situation which the old heroic poets loved, and would not have sold for a wilderness of dragons.

I pass over the fact that the allusion has a dramatic purpose in *Beowulf* that is a sufficient defence both of its presence and of its manner. The author of *Beowulf* cannot be held responsible for the fact that we now have only his poem and not others dealing primarily with Ingeld. He was not selling one thing for another, but giving something new. But let us return to the dragon. 'A wilderness of dragons.' There is a sting in this Shylockian plural, the sharper for coming from a critic, who deserves the title of the poet's best friend. It is in the tradition of the Book of St. Albans, from which the poet might retort upon his critics: 'Yea, a desserte of lapwyngs, a shrewednes of apes, a raffull of knaues, and a gagle of gees.'

As for the poem, one dragon, however hot, does not make a summer, or a host; and a man might well exchange for one good dragon what he would not sell for a wilderness. And dragons, real dragons, essential both to the machinery and ideas of a poem or tale, are actually rare. In northern literature there are only *two* that are significant. If we omit from consideration the vast and vague Encircler of the World, Miðgarðsormr, the doom of the great gods and no matter for heroes, we have but the dragon of the Völsungs, Fáfnir, and Beowulf's bane. It is true that both of these are in *Beowulf*, one in the main story, and the other spoken of by a minstrel praising Beowulf himself. But this is not a wilderness of dragons. Indeed the allusion to the more renowned worm killed by the Wælsing is sufficient indication that the poet selected a dragon of well-founded purpose (or saw its significance in the plot as it had reached him), even as he was careful to compare his hero, Beowulf son of Ecgtheow, to the prince of the heroes of the North, the dragon-slaying Wælsing. He esteemed dragons, as rare as they are dire, as some do still. He liked them—as a poet, not as a sober zoologist; and he had good reason.

But we meet this kind of criticism again. In Chambers's *Beowulf and the Heroic Age*—the most significant single essay on the poem that I know—it is still present. The riddle is still unsolved. The folk-tale motive stands still like the spectre of old research, dead but unquiet in its grave. We are told again that the main story of *Beowulf* is a *wild folktale*. Quite true, of course. It is true of the main story of *King Lear*, unless in that case you would prefer to substitute *silly* for *wild*. But more: we are told that the same sort of stuff is found in Homer, yet there it is kept in its proper place. 'The folk-tale is a good servant', Chambers says, and does not perhaps realize the importance of the admission, made to save the face of Homer and Virgil; for he continues: 'but a bad master: it has been allowed in *Beowulf* to usurp the place of honour, and to drive into episodes and digressions the things which should be the main stuff of a well-conducted epic.'[8] It is not clear to me why good *conduct* must depend on the main *stuff*. But I will for the moment remark only that, if it is so, *Beowulf* is evidently not a well-conducted epic. It may turn out to be no epic at all. But the puzzle still continues. In the most recent discourse

[8]*Foreword* to Strong's translation, p. xxvi; see note 3.

upon this theme it still appears, toned down almost to a melancholy question-mark, as if this paradox had at last begun to afflict with weariness the thought that endeavours to support it. In the final peroration of his notable lecture on *Folk-tale and History in Beowulf* given last year, Mr. Girvan said:

Confessedly there is matter for wonder and scope for doubt, but we might be able to answer with complete satisfaction some of the questionings which rise in men's minds over the poet's presentment of his hero, if we could also answer with certainty the question why he chose just this subject, when to our modern judgment there were at hand so many greater, charged with the splendour and tragedy of humanity, and in all respects worthier of a genius as astonishing as it was rare in Anglo-Saxon England.

There is something irritatingly odd about all this. One even dares to wonder if something has not gone wrong with 'our modern judgement', supposing that it is justly represented. Higher praise than is found in the learned critics, whose scholarship enables them to appreciate these things, could hardly be given to the detail, the tone, the style, and indeed to the total effect of *Beowulf*. Yet this poetic talent, we are to understand, has all been squandered on an unprofitable theme: as if Milton had recounted the story of Jack and the Beanstalk in noble verse. Even if Milton had done this (and he might have done worse), we should perhaps pause to consider whether his poetic handling had not had some effect upon the trivial theme; what alchemy had been performed upon the base metal; whether indeed it remained base or trivial when he had finished with it. The high tone, the sense of dignity, alone is evidence in *Beowulf* of the presence of a mind lofty and thoughtful. It is, one would have said, improbable that such a man would write more than three thousand lines (wrought to a high finish) on matter that is really not worth serious attention; that remains thin and cheap when he has finished with it. Or that he should in the selection of his material, in the choice of what to put forward, what to keep subordinate 'upon the outer edges', have shown a puerile simplicity much below the level of the characters he himself draws in his own poem. Any theory that will at least allow us to believe that what he did was of design, and that for that design there is a defence that may still have force, would seem more probable.

It has been too little observed that all the machinery of 'dignity' is to be found elsewhere. Cynewulf, or the author of *Andreas*, or of *Guthlac* (most notably), have a command of dignified verse. In them there is well-wrought language, weighty words, lofty sentiment, precisely that which we are told is the real beauty of *Beowulf*. Yet it cannot, I think, be disputed, that *Beowulf* is more beautiful, that each line there is more significant (even when, as sometimes happens, it is the same line) than in the other long Old English poems. Where then resides the special virtue of *Beowulf*, if the common element (which belongs largely to the language itself, and to a literary tradition) is deducted? It resides, one might guess, in the theme, and the spirit this had infused into the whole. For, in fact, if there were a real discrepancy between theme and style, that style would not be felt as beautiful but as incongruous or false. And that incongruity is present in some measure in all the long Old English poems, save one—*Beowulf* has thus an inherent *literary* improbability.

Why then have the great critics thought otherwise? I must pass rather hastily over the answers to this question. The reasons are various, I think, and would take long to examine. I believe that one reason is that the shadow of research has lain upon criticism. The habit, for instance, of pondering a summarized plot of *Beowulf*, denuded of all that gives it particular force or individual life, has encouraged the notion that its main story is wild, or trivial, or typical, *even after treatment*. Yet all stories, great and small, are one or more of these three things in such nakedness. The comparison of skeleton 'plots' is simply not a critical literary process at all. It has been favoured by research in comparative folk-lore, the objects of which are primarily historical or scientific.[9] Another reason is, I think, that the allusions have attracted curiosity (antiquarian rather than critical) to their elucidation; and this needs so much study and research that attention has been diverted from the poem as a whole, and from the function of the allusions, as shaped and placed, in the poetic economy of *Beowulf* as it is. Yet actually the appreciation of this function is largely independent of such investigations.

But there is also, I suppose, a real question of taste involved: a judgement that the heroic or tragic story on a strictly human plane is by nature superior. Doom is held less literary than ἁμαρτία. The proposition seems to have been passed as self-evident. I dissent, even at the risk of being held incorrect or not sober. But I will not here enter into debate, nor attempt at length a defence of the mythical mode of imagination, and the disentanglement of the confusion between myth and folk-tale into which these judgements appear to have fallen. The myth has other forms than the (now discredited) mythical allegory of nature: the sun, the seasons, the sea, and such things. The term 'folk-tale' is misleading; its very tone of depreciation begs the question. Folk-tales in being, as told—for the 'typical folk-tale', of course, is merely an abstract conception of research nowhere existing—do often contain elements that are thin and cheap, with little even potential virtue; but they also contain much that is far more powerful, and that cannot be sharply separated from myth, being derived from it, or capable in poetic hands of turning into it: that is of becoming largely significant—as a whole, accepted unanalyzed. The significance of a myth is not easily to be pinned on paper by analytical reasoning. It is at its best when it is presented by a poet who feels rather than makes explicit what his theme portends; who presents it incarnate in the world of history and geography, as our poet has done. Its defender is thus at a disadvantage: unless he is careful, and speaks in parables, he will kill what he is studying by vivisection,

---

[9]It has also been favoured by the rise of 'English schools', in whose syllabuses *Beowulf* has inevitably some place, and the consequent production of compendious literary histories. For these cater (in fact, if not in intention) for those seeking knowledge about, and ready-made judgements upon, works which they have not the time, or (often enough) the desire, to know at first hand. The small literary value of such summaries is sometimes recognized in the act of giving them. Thus Strong (op. cit.) gives a fairly complete one, but remarks that 'the short summary does scant justice to the poem'. Ker, in *E. Lit. (Med.)* says: 'So told, in abstract, it is not a particularly interesting story.' He evidently perceived what might be the retort, for he attempts to justify the procedure in this case, adding: 'Told in this way the story of Theseus or Hercules would still have much more in it.' I dissent. But it does not matter, for the comparison of two plots 'told in this way' is no guide whatever to the merits of literary versions told in quite different ways. It is not necessarily the best poem that loses least in précis.

and he will be left with a formal or mechanical allegory, and, what is more, probably with one that will not work. For myth is alive at once and in all its parts, and dies before it can be dissected. It is possible, I think, to be moved by the power of myth and yet to misunderstand the sensation, to ascribe it wholly to something else that is also present: to metrical art, style, or verbal skill. Correct and sober taste may refuse to admit that there can be an interest for *us*—the proud *we* that includes all intelligent living people—in ogres and dragons; we then perceive its puzzlement in face of the odd fact that it has derived great pleasure from a poem that is actually about these unfashionable creatures. Even though it attributes 'genius', as does Mr. Girvan, to the author, it cannot admit that the monsters are anything but a sad mistake.

It does not seem plain that ancient taste supports the modern as much as it has been represented to do. I have the author of *Beowulf*, at any rate, on my side: a greater man than most of us. And I cannot myself perceive a period in the North when one kind alone was esteemed: there was room for myth and heroic legend, and for blends of these. As for the dragon: as far as we know anything about these old poets, we know this: the Prince of the heroes of the North, supremely memorable—*hans nafn mun uppi meðan veröldin stendr*—was a dragon-slayer. And his most renowned deed, from which in Norse he derived his title Fáfnisbani, was the slaying of the prince of legendary worms. Although there is plainly considerable difference between the later Norse and the ancient English form of the story alluded to in *Beowulf*, already there it had these two primary features: the dragon, and the slaying of him as the chief deed of the greatest of heroes—*he wæs wreccena wide mærost*. A dragon is no idle fancy. Whatever may be his origins, in fact or invention, the dragon in legend is a potent creation of men's imagination, richer in significance than his barrow is in gold. Even today (despite the critics) you may find men not ignorant of tragic legend and history, who have heard of heroes and indeed seen them, who yet have been caught by the fascination of the worm. More than one poem in recent years (since *Beowulf* escaped somewhat from the dominion of the students of origins to the students of poetry) has been inspired by the dragon of *Beowulf*, but none that I know of by Ingeld son of Froda. Indeed, I do not think Chambers very happy in his particular choice. He gives battle on dubious ground. In so far as we can now grasp its detail and atmosphere the story of Ingeld the thrice faithless and easily persuaded is chiefly interesting as an episode in a larger theme, as part of a tradition that had acquired legendary, and so dramatically personalized, form concerning moving events in history: the arising of Denmark, and wars in the islands of the North. In itself it is not a supremely potent story. But, of course, as with all tales of any sort, its literary power must have depended mainly upon how it was handled. A poet may have made a great thing of it. Upon this chance must be founded the popularity of Ingeld's legend in England, for which there is some evidence.[10] There is no inherent magical virtue about heroic-tragic stories as such, and apart from the merits of individual treatments. The same

---

[10]Namely the use of it in *Beowulf*, both dramatically in depicting the sagacity of Beowulf the hero, and as an essential part of the traditions concerning the Scylding court, which is the legendary background against which the rise of the hero is set—as a later age would have chosen the court of Arthur. Also the probable allusion in Alcuin's letter to Speratus: see Chambers's *Widsith*, p. 78.

heroic plot can yield good and bad poems, and good and bad sagas. The recipe for the central situations of such stories, studied in the abstract, is after all as 'simple' and as 'typical' as that of the folk-tales. There are in any case many heroes but very few good dragons.

Beowulf's dragon, if one wishes really to criticize, is not to be blamed for being a dragon, but rather for not being dragon enough, plain pure fairy-story dragon. There are in the poem some vivid touches of the right kind—as *þa se wyrm onwoc, wroht wæs geniwad; stonc æfter stane*, 2285—in which this dragon is real worm, with a bestial life and thought of his own, but the conception, none the less, approaches *draconitas* rather than *draco*: a personification of malice, greed, destruction (the evil side of heroic life), and of the undiscriminating cruelty of fortune that distinguishes not good or bad (the evil aspect of all life). But for *Beowulf*, the poem, that is as it should be. In this poem the balance is nice, but it is preserved. The large symbolism is near the surface, but it does not break through, nor become allegory. Something more significant than a standard hero, a man faced with a foe more evil than any human enemy of house or realm, is before us, and yet incarnate in time, walking in heroic history, and treading the named lands of the North. And this, we are told, is the radical defect of *Beowulf*, that its author, coming in a time rich in the legends of heroic men, has used them afresh in an original fashion, giving us not just one more, but something akin yet different: a measure and interpretation of them all.

We do not deny the worth of the hero by accepting Grendel and the dragon. Let us by all means esteem the old heroes: men caught in the chains of circumstance or of their own character, torn between duties equally sacred, dying with their backs to the wall. But *Beowulf*, I fancy, plays a larger part than is recognized in helping us to esteem them. Heroic lays may have dealt in their own way—we have little enough to judge by—a way more brief and vigorous, perhaps, though perhaps also more harsh and noisy (and less thoughtful), with the actions of heroes caught in circumstances that conformed more or less to the varied but fundamentally simple recipe for an heroic situation. In these (if we had them) we could see the exaltation of undefeated will, which receives doctrinal expression in the words of Byrhtwold at the battle of Maldon.[11] But though with sympathy and patience we might gather, from a line here or a tone there, the background of imagination which gives to this indomitability, this paradox of defeat inevitable yet unacknowledged, its full significance, it is in *Beowulf* that a poet has devoted a whole poem to the theme, and has drawn the struggle in different proportions, so that we may see man at war with the hostile world, and his inevitable overthrow in Time.[12] The particular is on the outer edge, the essential in the centre.

Of course, I do not assert that the poet, if questioned, would have replied

---

[11]This expression may well have been actually used by the *eald geneat*, but none the less (or perhaps rather precisely on that account), is probably to be regarded not as new-minted, but as an ancient and honoured *gnome* of long descent.

[12]For the words *hige sceal þe heardra, heorte þe cenre, mod sceal þe mare þe ure mægen lytlað* are not, of course, an exhortation to simple courage. They are not reminders that fortune favours the brave, or that victory may be snatched from defeat by the stubborn. (Such thoughts were familiar, but otherwise expressed: *wyrd oft nereð unfægne eorl, þonne his ellen deah.*) The words of Byrhtwold were made for a man's last and hopeless day.

in the Anglo-Saxon equivalents of these terms. Had the matter been so explicit to him, his poem would certainly have been the worse. None the less we may still, against his great scene, hung with tapestries woven of ancient tales of ruin, see the *hæleð* walk. When we have read his poem, as a poem, rather than as a collection of episodes, we perceive that he who wrote *hæleð under heofenum* may have meant in dictionary terms 'heroes under heaven', or 'mighty men upon earth', but he and his hearers were thinking of the *eormengrund*, the great earth, ringed with *garsecg*, the shoreless sea, beneath the sky's inaccessible roof; whereon, as in a little circle of light about their halls, men with courage as their stay went forward to that battle with the hostile world and the offspring of the dark which ends for all, even the kings and champions, in defeat. That even this 'geography', once held as a material fact, could now be classed as a mere folk-tale affects its value very little. It transcends astronomy. Not that astronomy has done anything to make the island seem more secure or the outer seas less formidable.

Beowulf is not, then, the hero of an heroic lay, precisely. He has no enmeshed loyalties, nor hapless love. He is a man, and that for him and many is sufficient tragedy. It is not an irritating accident that the tone of the poem is so high and its theme so low. It is the theme in its deadly seriousness that begets the dignity of tone: *lif is læne: eal scæceð leoht and lif somod*. So deadly and ineluctable is the underlying thought, that those who in the circle of light, within the besieged hall, are absorbed in work or talk and do not look to the battlements, either do not regard it or recoil. Death comes to the feast, and they say He gibbers: He has no sense of proportion.

I would suggest, then, that the monsters are not an inexplicable blunder of taste; they are essential, fundamentally allied to the underlying ideas of the poem, which give it its lofty tone and high seriousness. The key to the fusion-point of imagination that produced this poem lies, therefore, in those very references to Cain which have often been used as a stick to beat an ass—taken as an evident sign (were any needed) of the muddled heads of early Anglo-Saxons. They could not, it was said, keep Scandinavian bogies and the Scriptures separate in their puzzled brains. The New Testament was beyond their comprehension. I am not, as I have confessed, a man so diligent as duly to read all the books about *Beowulf*, but as far as I am aware the most suggestive approach to this point appears in the essay *Beowulf and the Heroic Age* to which I have already referred.[13] I will quote a small part of it.

In the epoch of *Beowulf* a Heroic Age more wild and primitive than that of Greece is brought into touch with Christendom, with the Sermon on the Mount, with Catholic theology and ideas of heaven and hell. We see the difference, if we compare the wilder things—the folk-tale element—in *Beowulf* with the wilder things of Homer. Take for example the tale of Odysseus and the Cyclops—the No-man trick. Odysseus is struggling with a monstrous and wicked foe, but he is not exactly thought of as struggling with the powers of darkness. Polyphemus, by devouring his guests, acts in a way which is hateful to Zeus and the other gods: yet the Cyclops is himself god-begotten and under divine protection, and the fact that Odysseus has maimed him is a wrong which Poseidon is slow to forgive. But the gigantic foes whom Beowulf has

---

[13]*Foreword* to Strong's translation, p. xxviii. See note 3.

to meet are identified with the foes of God. Grendel and the dragon are constantly referred to in language which is meant to recall the powers of darkness with which Christian men felt themselves to be encompassed. They[14] are the 'inmates of Hell', 'adversaries of God', 'offspring of Cain', 'enemies of mankind'. Consequently, the matter of the main story of *Beowulf*, monstrous as it is, is not so far removed from common mediaeval experience as it seems to us to be from our own . . . . Grendel hardly differs[15] from the fiends of the pit who were always in ambush to waylay a righteous man. And so Beowulf, for all that he moves in the world of the primitive Heroic Age of the Germans, nevertheless is almost a Christian knight.[16]

There are some hints here which are, I think, worth pursuing further. Most important is it to consider how and why the monsters become 'adversaries of God', and so begin to symbolize (and ultimately to become identified with) the powers of evil, even while they remain, as they do still remain in *Beowulf*, mortal denizens of the material world, in it and of it. I accept without argument throughout the attribution of *Beowulf* to the 'age of Bede'—one of the firmer conclusions of a department of research most clearly serviceable to criticism: inquiry into the probable date of the effective composition of the poem as we have it. So regarded *Beowulf* is, of course, an historical document of the first order for the study of the mood and thought of the period and one perhaps too little used for the purpose by professed historians.[17] But it is the mood of the author, the essential cast of his imaginative apprehension of the world, that is my concern, not history for its own sake; I am interested in that time of fusion only as it may help us to understand the poem. And in the poem I think we may observe not confusion, a half-hearted or a muddled business, but a fusion that has occurred *at a given point* of contact between old and new, a product of thought and deep emotion.

One of the most potent elements in that fusion is the Northern courage: the theory of courage, which is the great contribution of early Northern literature. This is not a military judgement. I am not asserting that, if the Trojans could have employed a Northern king and his companions, they would have driven Agamemnon and Achilles into the sea, more decisively than the Greek hexameter routs the alliterative line—though it is not improbable. I refer rather to the central position the creed of unyielding will holds in the North. With due reserve we may turn to the tradition of pagan imagination as it survived in Icelandic. Of English pre-Christian mythology we know practically nothing. But the fundamentally similar heroic temper of ancient England and Scandinavia cannot have been founded on (or perhaps rather, cannot have generated) mythologies divergent on this essential point. 'The Northern Gods' Ker said, 'have an exultant extravagance in their warfare which makes them more like Titans than Olympians; *only they are on the right side, though it is not*

---

[14]This is not strictly true. The dragon is not referred to in such terms, which are applied to Grendel and to the primeval giants.

[15]He differs in important points, referred to later.

[16]I should prefer to say that he moves in a northern heroic age imagined by a Christian, and therefore has a noble and gentle quality, though conceived to be a pagan.

[17]It is, for instance, dismissed cursorily, and somewhat contemptuously in the recent (somewhat contemptuous) essay of Dr. Watson, *The Age of Bede* in *Bede, His Life, Times, and Writings*, ed. A. Hamilton Thompson, 1935.

the side that wins. The winning side is Chaos and Unreason'—mythologically, the monsters—*'but the gods, who are defeated, think that defeat no refutation.'*[18] And in their war men are their chosen allies, able when heroic to share in this 'absolute resistance, perfect because without hope'. At least in this vision of the final defeat of the humane (and of the divine made in its image), and in the essential hostility of the gods and heroes on the one hand and the monsters on the other, we may suppose that pagan English and Norse imagination agreed.

But in England this imagination was brought into touch with Christendom, and with the Scriptures. The process of 'conversion' was a long one, but some of its effects were doubtless immediate: an alchemy of change (producing ultimately the mediaeval) was at once at work. One does not have to wait until all the native traditions of the older world have been replaced or forgotten; for the minds which still retain them are changed, and the memories viewed in a different perspective: *at once they become more ancient and remote, and in a sense darker.* It is through such a blending that there was available to a poet who set out to write a poem—and in the case of *Beowulf* we may probably use this very word—on a scale and plan unlike a minstrel's lay, both new faith and new learning (or education), and also a body of native tradition (itself requiring to be learned) for the changed mind to contemplate together.[19] The native 'learning' cannot be denied in the case of *Beowulf*. Its display has grievously perturbed the critics, for the author draws upon tradition at will for his own purposes, as a poet of later times might draw upon history or the classics and expect his allusions to be understood (within a certain class of hearers). He was in fact, like Virgil, learned enough in the vernacular department to have an historical perspective, even an antiquarian curiosity. He cast his time into the long-ago, because already the long-ago had a special poetical attraction. He knew much about old days, and though his knowledge —of such things as sea-burial and the funeral pyre, for instance—was rich and poetical rather than accurate with the accuracy of modern archaeology (such as that is), one thing he knew clearly: those days were heathen—heathen, noble, and hopeless.

But if the specifically Christian was suppressed,[20] so also were the old gods.

[18]*The Dark Ages*, p. 57.

[19]If we consider the period as a whole. It is not, of course, necessarily true of individuals. These doubtless from the beginning showed many degrees from deep instruction and understanding to disjointed superstition, or blank ignorance.

[20]Avoidance of obvious anachronisms (such as are found in *Judith*, for instance, where the heroine refers in her own speeches to Christ and the Trinity), and the absence of all definitely *Christian* names and terms, is natural and plainly intentional. It must be observed that there is a difference beween the comments of the author and the things said in reported speech by his characters. The two chief of these, Hrothgar and Beowulf, are again differentiated. Thus the only definitely Scriptural references, to Abel (108) and to Cain (108, 1261), occur where the poet is speaking as commentator. The theory of Grendel's origin is not known to the actors: Hrothgar denies all knowledge of the ancestry of Grendel (1355). The giants (1688 ff.) are, it is true, represented pictorially, and in Scriptural terms. But this suggests rather that the author identified native and Scriptural accounts, and gave his picture Scriptural colour, since of the two accounts Scripture was the truer. And if so it would be closer to that told in remote antiquity when the sword was made, more especially since the *wundorsmiþas* who wrought it were actually giants (1558, 1562, 1679): they would know the true tale. See note 25.

Partly because they had not really existed, and had been always, in the Christian view, only delusions or lies fabricated by the evil one, the *gastbona*, to whom the hopeless turned especially in times of need. Partly because their old names (certainly not forgotten) had been potent, and were connected in memory still, not only with mythology or such fairy-tale matter as we find, say, in *Gylfaginning*, but with active heathendom, religion and *wigweorþung*. Most of all because they were not actually essential to the theme.

The monsters had been the foes of the gods, the captains of men, and within Time the monsters would win. In the heroic siege and last defeat men and gods alike had been imagined in the same host. Now the heroic figures, the men of old, *hæleð under heofenum*, remained and still fought on until defeat. For the monsters do not depart, whether the gods go or come. A Christian was (and is) still like his forefathers a mortal hemmed in a hostile world. The monsters remained the enemies of mankind, the infantry of the old war, and became inevitably the enemies of the one God, *ece Dryhten*, the eternal Captain of the new. Even so the vision of the war changes. For it begins to dissolve, even as the contest on the fields of Time thus takes on its largest aspect. The tragedy of the great temporal defeat remains for a while poignant, but ceases to be finally important. It is no defeat, for the end of the world is part of the design of Metod, the Arbiter who is above the mortal world. Beyond there appears a possibility of eternal victory (or eternal defeat), and the real battle is between the soul and its adversaries. So the old monsters became images of the evil spirit or spirits, or rather the evil spirits entered into the monsters and took visible shape in the hideous bodies of *þyrsas* and *sigelhearwan* of heathen imagination.

But that shift is not complete in *Beowulf*—whatever may have been true of its period in general. Its author is still concerned primarily with *man on earth*, rehandling in a new perspective an ancient theme: that man, each man and all men, and all their works shall die. A theme no Christian need despise. Yet this theme plainly would not be so treated, but for the nearness of a pagan time. The shadow of its despair, if only as a mood, as an intense emotion of regret, is still there. The worth of defeated valour in this world is deeply felt. As the poet looks back into the past, surveying the history of kings and warriors in the old traditions, he sees that all glory (or as we might say 'culture' or 'civilization') ends in night. The solution of that tragedy is not treated—it does not arise out of the material. We get in fact a poem from a pregnant moment of poise, looking back into the pit, by a man learned in old tales who was struggling, as it were, to get a general view of them all, perceiving their common tragedy of inevitable ruin, and yet feeling this more *poetically* because he was himself removed from the direct pressure of its despair. He could view from without, but still feel immediately and from within, the old dogma: despair of the event, combined with faith in the value of doomed resistance. He was still dealing with the great temporal tragedy, and not yet writing an allegorical homily in verse. Grendel inhabits the visible world and eats the flesh and blood of men; he enters their houses by the doors. The dragon wields a physical fire, and covets gold not souls; he is slain with iron in his belly. Beowulf's *byrne* was made by Weland, and the iron shield he bore against the serpent by his own smiths: it was not yet the breastplate of righteousness, nor the shield of faith for the quenching of all the fiery darts of the wicked.

Almost we might say that this poem was (in one direction) inspired by the debate that had long been held and continued after, and that it was one of the chief contributions to the controversy: shall we or shall we not consign the heathen ancestors to perdition? What good will it do posterity to read the battles of Hector? *Quid Hinieldus cum Christo?* The author of *Beowulf* showed forth the permanent value of that *pietas* which treasures the memory of man's struggles in the dark past, man fallen and not yet saved, disgraced but not dethroned. It would seem to have been part of the English temper in its strong sense of tradition, dependent doubtless on dynasties, noble houses, and their code of honour, and strengthened, it may be, by the more inquisitive and less severe Celtic learning, that it should, at least in some quarters and despite grave and Gallic voices, preserve much from the northern past to blend with southern learning, and new faith.

It has been thought that the influence of Latin epic, especially of the *Aeneid*, is perceptible in *Beowulf*, and a necessary explanation, if only in the exciting of emulation, of the development of the long and studied poem in early England. There is, of course, a likeness in places between these greater and lesser things, the *Aeneid* and *Beowulf*, if they are read in conjunction. But the smaller points in which imitation or reminiscence might be perceived are inconclusive, while the real likeness is deeper and due to certain qualities in the authors independent of the question whether the Anglo-Saxon had read Virgil or not. It is this deeper likeness which makes things, that are either the inevitabilities of human poetry or the accidental congruences of all tales, ring alike. We have the great pagan on the threshold of the change of the world; and the great (if lesser) Christian just over the threshold of the great change in his time and place: the backward view: *multa putans sortemque animo miseratus iniquam.*[21]

But we will now return once more to the monsters, and consider especially the difference of their status in the northern and southern mythologies. Of Grendel it is said: *Godes yrre bær.* But the Cyclops is god-begotten and his maiming is an offence against his begetter, the god Poseidon. This radical difference in mythological status is only brought out more sharply by the very closeness of the similarity in conception (in all save mere size) that is seen, if we compare *Beowulf*, 740 ff., with the description of the Cyclops devouring men in *Odyssey*, ix—or still more in *Aeneid*, iii. 622 ff. In Virgil, whatever may be true of the fairy-tale world of the Odyssey, the Cyclops walks veritably in the historic world. He is seen by Aeneas in Sicily, *monstrum horrendum, informe, ingens*, as much a perilous fact as Grendel was in Denmark, *earmsceapen on weres wæstmum . . . næfne he wæs mara þonne ænig man oðer*; as real as Acestes or Hrothgar.[22]

At this point in particular we may regret that we do not know more about pre-Christian English mythology. Yet it is, as I have said, legitimate to suppose

---

[21] In fact the real resemblance of the *Aeneid* and *Beowulf* lies in the constant presence of a sense of many-storied antiquity, together with its natural accompaniment, stern and noble melancholy. In this they are really akin and together differ from Homer's flatter, if more glittering surface.

[22] I use this illustration following Chambers, because of the close resemblance between Grendel and the Cyclops in kind. But other examples could be adduced; Cacus, for instance, the offspring of Vulcan. One might ponder the contrast between the legends of the torture of Prometheus and of Loki: the one for assisting men, the other for assisting the powers of darkness.

that in the matter of the position of the monsters in regard to men and gods the view was fundamentally the same as in later Icelandic. Thus, though all such generalizations are naturally imperfect in detail (since they deal with matter of various origins, constantly reworked, and never even at most more than partially systematized), we may with some truth contrast the 'inhumanness' of the Greek gods, however anthropomorphic, with the 'humanness' of the Northern, however titanic. In the southern myths there is also rumour of wars with giants and great powers not Olympian, the *Titania pubes fulmine deiecti*, rolling like Satan and his satellites in the nethermost Abyss. But this war is differently conceived. It lies in a chaotic past. The ruling gods are not besieged, not in ever-present peril or under future doom.[23] Their offspring on earth may be heroes or fair women; it may also be the other creatures hostile to men. The gods are not the allies of men in their war against these or other monsters. The interest of the gods is in this or that man as part of their individual schemes, not as part of a great strategy that includes all good men, as the infantry of battle. In Norse, at any rate, the gods are within Time, doomed with their allies to death. Their battle is with the monsters and the outer darkness. They gather heroes for the last defence. Already before euhemerism saved them by embalming them, and they dwindled in antiquarian fancy to the mighty ancestors of northern kings (English and Scandinavian), they had become in their very being the enlarged shadows of great men and warriors upon the walls of the world. When Baldr is slain and goes to Hel he cannot escape thence any more than mortal man.

This may make the southern gods more godlike—more lofty, dread, and inscrutable. They are timeless and do not fear death. Such a mythology may hold the promise of a profounder thought. In any case it was a virtue of the southern mythology that it could not stop where it was. It must go forward to philosophy or relapse into anarchy. For in a sense it had shirked the problem precisely by not having the monsters in the centre—as they are in *Beowulf* to the astonishment of the critics. But such horrors cannot be left permanently unexplained, lurking on the outer edges and under suspicion of being connected with the Government. It is the strength of the northern mythological imagination that it faced this problem, put the monsters in the centre, gave them victory but no honour, and found a potent but terrible solution in naked will and courage. 'As a working theory absolutely impregnable.' So potent is it, that while the older southern imagination has faded for ever into literary

---

[23]There is actually no final principle in the legendary hostilities contained in classical mythology. For the present purpose that is all that matters; we are not here concerned with remoter mythological origins, in the North or South. The gods, Cronian or Olympian, the Titans, and other great natural powers, and various monsters, even minor local horrors, are not clearly distinguished in origin or ancestry. There could be no permanent policy of war, led by Olympus, to which human courage might be dedicated, among mythological races so promiscuous. Of course, nowhere can absolute rigidity of distinction be expected, because in a sense the foe is always both within and without; the fortress must fall through treachery as well as by assault. Thus Grendel has a perverted human shape, and the giants or *jötnar*, even when (like the Titans) they are of super-divine stature, are parodies of the human-divine form. Even in Norse, where the distinction is most rigid, Loki dwells in Asgarðr, though he is an evil and lying spirit, and fatal monsters come of him. For it is true of man, maker of myths, that Grendel and the Dragon, in their lust, greed, and malice, have a part in him. But mythically conceived the gods do not recognize any bond with *Fenris úlfr*, any more than men with Grendel or the serpent.

ornament, the northern has power, as it were, to revive its spirit even in our own times. It can work, even as it did work with the *goðlauss* viking, without gods: martial heroism as its own end. But we may remember that the poet of *Beowulf* saw clearly: the wages of heroism is death.

For these reasons I think that the passages in *Beowulf* concerning the giants and their war with God, together with the two mentions of Cain (as the ancestor of the giants in general and Grendel in particular) are specially important.

They are directly connected with Scripture, yet they can be dissociated from the creatures of northern myth, the ever-watchful foes of the gods (and men). The undoubtedly scriptural Cain is connected with *eotenas* and *ylfe*, which are the *jötnar* and *álfar* of Norse. But this is not due to mere confusion—it is rather an indication of the precise point at which an imagination, pondering old and new, was kindled. At this point new Scripture and old tradition touched and ignited. It is for this reason that these elements of Scripture alone appear in a poem dealing of design with the noble pagan of old days. For they are precisely the elements which bear upon this theme. Man alien in a hostile world, engaged in a struggle which he cannot win while the world lasts, is assured that his foes are the foes also of Dryhten, that his courage noble in itself is also the highest loyalty: so said thyle and clerk.

In *Beowulf* we have, then, an historical poem about the pagan past, or an attempt at one—literal historical fidelity founded on modern research was, of course, not attempted. It is a poem by a learned man writing of old times, who looking back on the heroism and sorrow feels in them something permanent and something symbolical. So far from being a confused semi-pagan—historically unlikely for a man of this sort in the period—he brought probably *first* to his task a knowledge of Christian poetry, especially that of the Cædmon school, and especially *Genesis*.[24] He makes his minstrel sing in Heorot of the Creation of the earth and the lights of Heaven. So excellent is this choice as the theme of the harp that maddened Grendel lurking joyless in the dark without that it matters little whether this is anachronistic or not.[25] *Secondly*, to his task the poet brought a considerable learning in native lays and traditions: only by learning and training could such things be acquired, they were no more born naturally into an Englishman of the seventh or eighth centuries, by simple virtue of being an 'Anglo-Saxon', than ready-made knowledge of poetry and history is inherited at birth by modern children. It would seem that, in his attempt to depict ancient pre-Christian days, intending

[24]The *Genesis* which is preserved for us is a late copy of a damaged original, but is still certainly in its older parts a poem whose composition must be referred to the early period. That *Genesis A* is actually older than *Beowulf* is generally recognized as the most probable reading of such evidence as there is.

[25]Actually the poet may have known, what we can guess, that such creation-themes were also ancient in the North. *Völuspá* describes Chaos and the making of the sun and moon, and very similar language occurs in the Old High German fragment known as the *Wessobrunner Gebet*. The song of the minstrel Iopas, who had his knowledge from Atlas, at the end of the first book of the *Aeneid* is also in part a song of origins; *hic canit errantem lunam solisque labores, unde hominum genus et pecudes, unde imber et ignes*. In any case the Anglo-Saxon poet's view throughout was plainly that true, or truer, knowledge was possessed in ancient days (when men were not deceived by the Devil); at least they knew of the one God and Creator, though not of heaven, for that was lost. See note 20.

to emphasize their nobility, and the desire of the good for truth, he turned naturally when delineating the great King of Heorot to the Old Testament. In the *folces hyrde* of the Danes we have much of the shepherd patriarchs and kings of Israel, servants of the one God, who attribute to His mercy all the good things that come to them in this life. We have in fact a Christian English conception of the noble chief before Christianity, who could lapse (as could Israel) in times of temptation into idolatry.[26] On the other hand, the traditional matter in English, not to mention the living survival of the heroic code and temper among the noble households of ancient England, enabled him to draw differently, and in some respects much closer to the actual heathen *hæleð*, the character of Beowulf, especially as a young knight, who used his great gift of *mægen* to earn *dom* and *lof* among men and posterity.

Beowulf is not an actual picture of historic Denmark or Geatland or Sweden about A.D. 500. But it is (if with certain minor defects) on a general view a self-consistent picture, a construction bearing clearly the marks of design and thought. The whole must have succeeded admirably in creating in the minds of the poet's contemporaries the illusion of surveying a past, pagan but noble and fraught with a deep significance—a past that itself had depth and reached backward into a dark antiquity of sorrow. This impression of depth is an effect and a justification of the use of episodes and allusions to old tales, mostly darker, more pagan, and desperate than the foreground.

To a similar antiquarian temper, and a similar use of vernacular learning, is probably due the similar effect of antiquity (and melancholy) in the *Aeneid* —especially felt as soon as Aeneas reaches Italy and the *Saturni gentem . . . sponte sua veterisque dei se more tenentem. Ic þa leode wat ge wið feond ge wið freond fæste worhte, æghwæs untæle ealde wisan.* Alas for the lost lore, the annals and old poets that Virgil knew, and only used in the making of a new thing! The criticism that the important matters are put on the outer edges misses this point of artistry, and indeed fails to see why the old things have in *Beowulf* such an appeal: it is the poet himself who made antiquity so appealing. His poem has more value in consequence, and is a greater contribution to early mediaeval thought than the harsh and intolerant view that consigned all the heroes to the devil. We may be thankful that the product of so noble a temper has been preserved by chance (if such it be) from the dragon of destruction.

The general structure of the poem, so viewed, is not really difficult to perceive, if we look to the main points, the strategy, and neglect the many points of minor tactics. We must dismiss, of course, from mind the notion that *Beowulf* is a 'narrative poem', that it tells a tale or intends to tell a tale sequentially. The poem 'lacks steady advance': so Klaeber heads a critical section in his edition.[27] But the poem was not meant to advance, steadily or

---

[26]It is of Old Testament lapses rather than of any events in England (of which he is not speaking) that the poet is thinking in lines 175 ff., and this colours his manner of allusion to knowledge which he may have derived from native traditions concerning the Danes and the special heathen religious significance of the site of Heorot (*Hleiðrar, æt hærgtrafum,* the tabernacles)—it was possibly a matter that embittered the feud of Danes and Heathobeards. If so, this is another point where old and new have blended. On the special importance and difficulty for criticism of the passage 175-88 see the Appendix.

[27]Though only explicitly referred to here and in disagreement, this edition is, of course, of great authority, and all who have used it have learned much from it.

unsteadily. It is essentially a balance, an opposition of ends and beginnings. In its simplest terms it is a contrasted description of two moments in a great life, rising and setting; an elaboration of the ancient and intensely moving contrast between youth and age, first achievement and final death. It is divided in consequence into two opposed portions, different in matter, manner, and length: A from 1 to 2199 (including an exordium of 52 lines); B from 2200 to 3182 (the end). There is no reason to cavil at this proportion; in any case, for the purpose and the production of the required effect, it proves in practice to be right.

This simple and *static* structure, solid and strong, is in each part much diversified, and capable of enduring this treatment. In the conduct of the presentation of Beowulf's rise to fame on the one hand, and of his kingship and death on the other, criticism can find things to question, especially if it is captious, but also much to praise, if it is attentive. But the only serious weakness, or apparent weakness, is the long recapitulation: the report of Beowulf to Hygelac. This recapitulation is well done. Without serious discrepancy[28] it retells rapidly the events in Heorot, and retouches the account; and it serves to illustrate, since he himself describes his own deeds, yet more vividly the character of a young man, singled out by destiny, as he steps suddenly forth in his full powers. Yet this is perhaps not quite sufficient to justify the repetition. The explanation, if not complete justification, is probably to be sought in different directions.

For one thing, the old tale was not first told or invented by this poet. So much is clear from investigation of the folk-tale analogues. Even the legendary association of the Scylding court with a marauding monster, and with the arrival from abroad of a champion and deliverer was probably already old. The plot was not the poet's; and though he has infused feeling and significance into its crude material, that plot was not a perfect vehicle of the theme or themes that came to hidden life in the poet's mind as he worked upon it. Not an unusual event in literature. For the contrast—youth and death—it would probably have been better, if we had no journeying. If the single nation of the *Geatas* had been the scene, we should have felt the stage not narrower, but symbolically wider. More plainly should we have perceived in one people and their hero all mankind and its heroes. This at any rate I have always myself felt in reading *Beowulf*; but I have also felt that this defect is rectified by the bringing of the tale of Grendel to Geatland. As Beowulf stands in Hygelac's hall and tells his story, he sets his feet firm again in the land of his own people, and is no longer in danger of appearing a mere *wrecca*, an errant adventurer and slayer of bogies that do not concern him.

There is in fact a double division in the poem: the fundamental one already

---

[28]I am not concerned with minor discrepancies at any point in the poem. They are no proof of composite authorship, nor even of incompetent authorship. It is very difficult, even in a newly invented tale of any length, to avoid such defects; more so still in rehandling old and oft-told tales. The points that are seized in the study, with a copy that can be indexed and turned to and fro (even if never read straight through as it was meant to be), are usually such as may easily escape an author and still more easily his natural audience. Virgil certainly does not escape such faults, even within the limits of a single book. Modern printed tales, that have presumably had the advantage of proof-correction, can even be observed to hesitate in the heroine's Christian name.

referred to, and a secondary but important division at line 1887. After that the essentials of the previous part are taken up and compacted, so that all the tragedy of Beowulf is contained between 1888 and the end.[29] But, of course, without the first half we should miss much incidental illustration; we should miss also the dark background of the court of Heorot that loomed as large in glory and doom in ancient northern imagination as the court of Arthur: no vision of the past was complete without it. And (most important) we should lose the direct contrast of youth and age in the persons of Beowulf and Hrothgar which is one of the chief purposes of this section: it ends with the pregnant words *oþ þæt hine yldo benam mægenes wynnum, se þe oft manegum scod.*

In any case we must not view this poem as in intention an exciting narrative or a romantic tale. The very nature of Old English metre is often misjudged. In it there is no single rhythmic pattern progressing from the beginning of a line to the end, and repeated with variation in other lines. The lines do not go according to a tune. They are founded on a balance; an opposition between two halves of roughly equivalent[30] phonetic weight, and significant content, which are more often rhythmically contrasted than similar. They are more like masonry than music. In this fundamental fact of poetic expression I think there is a parallel to the total structure of *Beowulf*. *Beowulf* is indeed the most successful Old English poem because in it the elements, language, metre, theme, structure, are all most nearly in harmony. Judgement of the verse has often gone astray through listening for an accentual rhythm and pattern: and it seems to halt and stumble. Judgement of the theme goes astray through considering it as the narrative handling of a plot: and it seems to halt and stumble. Language and verse, of course, differ from stone or wood or paint, and can be only heard or read in a time-sequence; so that in any poem that deals at all with characters and events some narrative element must be present. We have none the less in *Beowulf* a method and structure that within the limits of the verse-kind approaches rather to sculpture or painting. It is a composition not a tune.

This is clear in the second half. In the struggle with Grendel one can as a reader dismiss the certainty of literary experience that the hero will not in fact perish, and allow oneself to share the hopes and fears of the Geats upon the shore. In the second part the author has no desire whatever that the issue should remain open, even according to literary convention. There is no need to hasten like the messenger, who rode to bear the lamentable news to the waiting people (2892 ff.). They may have hoped, but we are not supposed to. By now we are supposed to have grasped the plan. Disaster is foreboded. Defeat is the theme. Triumph over the foes of man's precarious fortress is over, and we approach slowly and reluctantly the inevitable victory of death.[31]

[29]The least satisfactory arrangement possible is thus to read only lines 1-1887 and not the remainder. This procedure has none the less been, from time to time, directed or encouraged by more than one 'English syllabus'.

[30]Equivalent but not necessarily equal, certainly not as such things may be measured by machines.

[31]That the particular bearer of enmity, the Dragon, also dies is important chiefly to Beowulf himself. He was a great man. Not many even in dying can achieve the death of a single worm, or the temporary salvation of their kindred. Within the limits of human life

'In structure', it was said of *Beowulf*, 'it is curiously weak, in a sense preposterous,' though great merits of detail were allowed. In structure actually it is curiously strong, in a sense inevitable, though there are defects of detail. The general design of the poet is not only defensible, it is, I think, admirable. There may have previously existed stirring verse dealing in straightforward manner and even in natural sequence with the Beowulf's deeds, or with the fall of Hygelac; or again with the fluctuations of the feud between the houses of Hrethel the Geat and Ongentheow the Swede; or with the tragedy of the Heathobards, and the treason that destroyed the Scylding dynasty. Indeed this must be admitted to be practically certain: it was the existence of such connected legends—connected in the mind, not necessarily dealt with in chronicle fashion or in long semi-historical poems—that permitted the peculiar use of them in *Beowulf*. This poem cannot be criticized or comprehended, if its original audience is imagined in like case to ourselves, possessing only *Beowulf* in splendid isolation. For *Beowulf* was not designed to tell the tale of Hygelac's fall, or for that matter to give the whole biography of Beowulf, still less to write the history of the Geatish kingdom and its downfall. But it used knowledge of these things for its own purpose—to give that sense of perspective, of antiquity with a greater and yet darker antiquity behind. These things are mainly on the outer edges or in the background because they belong there, if they are to function in this way. But in the centre we have an heroic figure of enlarged proportions.

Beowulf is not an 'epic', not even a magnified 'lay'. No terms borrowed from Greek or other literatures exactly fit: there is no reason why they should. Though if we must have a term, we should choose rather 'elegy'. It is an heroic-elegiac poem; and in a sense all its first 3,136 lines are the prelude to a dirge: *him þa gegiredan Geata leode ad ofer eorðan unwaclicne*: one of the most moving ever written. But for the universal significance which is given to the fortunes of its hero it is an enhancement and not a detraction, in fact it is necessary, that his final foe should be not some Swedish prince, or treacherous friend, but a dragon: a thing made by imagination for just such a purpose. Nowhere does a dragon come in so precisely where he should. But if the hero falls before a dragon, then certainly he should achieve his early glory by vanquishing a foe of similar order.

There is, I think, no criticism more beside the mark than that which some have made, complaining that it is monsters in both halves that is so disgusting; one they could have stomached more easily. That is nonsense. I can see the point of asking for no monsters. I can also see the point of the situation in Beowulf. But no point at all in mere reduction of numbers. It would really have been preposterous, if the poet had recounted Beowulf's rise to fame in a 'typical' or 'commonplace' war in Frisia, and then ended him with a dragon. Or if he had told of his cleansing of Heorot, and then brought him to defeat and death in a 'wild' or 'trivial' Swedish invasion! If the dragon is the right end for Beowulf, and I agree with the author that it is, then Grendel is an eminently suitable beginning. They are creatures, *feond mancynnes*, of a similar order and kindred significance. Triumph over the lesser and more nearly

Beowulf neither lived nor died in vain—brave men might say. But there is no hint, indeed there are many to the contrary, that it was a war to end war, or a dragon-fight to end dragons. It is the end of Beowulf, and of the hope of his people.

human is cancelled by defeat before the older and more elemental. And the conquest of the ogres comes at the right moment: not in earliest youth, though the nicors are referred to in Beowulf's *geogoðfeore* as a presage of the kind of hero we have to deal with; and not during the later period of recognized ability and prowess;[32] but in that first moment, which often comes in great lives, when men look up in surprise and see that a hero has unawares leaped forth. The placing of the dragon is inevitable: a man can but die upon his death-day.

I will conclude by drawing an imaginary contrast. Let us suppose that our poet had chosen a theme more consonant with 'our modern judgement'; the life and death of St. Oswald. He might then have made a poem, and told first of Heavenfield, when Oswald as a young prince against all hope won a great victory with a remnant of brave men; and then have passed at once to the lamentable defeat of Oswestry, which seemed to destroy the hope of Christian Northumbria; while all the rest of Oswald's life, and the traditions of the royal house and its feud with that of Deira might be introduced allusively or omitted. To any one but an historian in search of facts and chronology this would have been a fine thing, an heroic-elegiac poem greater than history. It would be much better than a plain narrative, in verse or prose, however steadily advancing. This mere arrangement would at once give it more significance than a straightforward account of one king's life: the contrast of rising and setting, achievement and death. But even so it would fall far short of *Beowulf*. Poetically it would be greatly enhanced if the poet had taken violent liberties with history and much enlarged the reign of Oswald, making him old and full of years of care and glory when he went forth heavy with foreboding to face the heathen Penda: the contrast of youth and age would add enormously to the original theme, and give it a more universal meaning. But even so it would still fall short of *Beowulf*. To match his theme with the rise and fall of poor 'folk-tale' Beowulf the poet would have been obliged to turn Cadwallon and Penda into giants and demons. It is just because the main foes in *Beowulf* are inhuman that the story is larger and more significant than this imaginary poem of a great king's fall. It glimpses the cosmic and moves with the thought of all men concerning the fate of human life and efforts; it stands amid but above the petty wars of princes, and surpasses the dates and limits of historical periods, however important. At the beginning, and during its process, and most of all at the end, we look down as if from a visionary height upon the house of man in the valley of the world. A light starts—*lixte se leoma ofer landa fela*—and there is a sound of music; but the outer darkness and its hostile offspring lie ever in wait for the torches to fail and the voices to cease. Grendel is maddened by the sound of harps.

And one last point, which those will feel who today preserve the ancient *pietas* towards the past: *Beowulf* is not a 'primitive' poem; it is a late one, using the materials (then still plentiful) preserved from a day already changing

---

[32]We do, however, learn incidentally much of this period; it is not strictly true, even of our poem as it is, to say that after the deeds in Heorot Beowulf 'has nothing else to do'. Great heroes, like great saints, should show themselves capable of dealing also with the ordinary things of life, even though they may do so with a strength more than ordinary. We may wish to be assured of this (and the poet has assured us), without demanding that he should put such things in the centre, when they are not the centre of his thought.

and passing, a time that has now forever vanished, swallowed in oblivion; using them for a new purpose, with a wider sweep of imagination, if with a less bitter and concentrated force. When new *Beowulf* was already antiquarian, in a good sense, and it now produces a singular effect. For it is now to us itself ancient; and yet its maker was telling of things already old and weighted with regret, and he expended his art in making keen that touch upon the heart which sorrows have that are both poignant and remote. If the funeral of Beowulf moved once like the echo of an ancient dirge, far-off and hopeless, it is to us as a memory brought over the hills, an echo of an echo. There is not much poetry in the world like this; and though *Beowulf* may not be among the very greatest poems of our western world and its tradition, it has its own individual character, and peculiar solemnity; it would still have power had it been written in some time or place unknown and without posterity, if it contained no name that could now be recognized or identified by research. Yet it is in fact written in a language that after many centuries has still essential kinship with our own, it was made in this land, and moves in our northern world beneath our northern sky, and for those who are native to that tongue and land, it must ever call with a profound appeal—until the dragon comes.

APPENDIX

(a) Grendel's Titles

The changes which produced (before A.D. 1066) the mediaeval devil are not complete in *Beowulf*, but in Grendel change and blending are, of course, already apparent. Such things do not admit of clear classifications and distinctions. Doubtless ancient pre-Christian imagination vaguely recognized differences of 'materiality' between the solidly physical monsters, conceived as made of the earth and rock (to which the light of the sun might return them), and elves, and ghosts or bogies. Monsters of more or less human shape were naturally liable to development on contact with Christian ideas of sin and spirits of evil. Their parody of human form (*earmsceapen on weres wæstmum*) becomes symbolical, explicitly, of sin, or rather this mythical element, already present implicit and unresolved, is emphasized: this we see already in *Beowulf*, strengthened by the theory of descent from Cain (and so from Adam), and of the curse of God. So Grendel is not only under this inherited curse, but also himself sinful: *manscaða, synscaða, synnum beswenced*; he is *fyrena hyrde*. The same notion (combined with others) appears also when he is called (by the author, not by the characters in the poem) *hæðen*, 852, 986, and *helle hæfton, feond on helle*. As an image of man estranged from God he is called not only by all names applicable to ordinary men, as *wer, rinc, guma, maga*, but he is conceived as having a spirit, other than his body, that will be punished. Thus *alegde hæðene sawle: þær him hel onfeng*, 852; while Beowulf himself says *ðær abidan sceal miclan domes, hu him scir Metod scrifan wille*, 978.

But this view is blended or confused with another. Because of his ceaseless hostility to men, and hatred of their joy, his superhuman size and strength, and his love of the dark, he approaches to a devil, though he is not yet a true devil in purpose. Real devilish qualities (deception and destruction of the soul), other than those which are undeveloped symbols, such as his hideousness and habitation in dark forsaken places, are hardly present. But he and his mother are actually called *deofla*, 1680; and Grendel is said when fleeing to hiding to make for *deofla gedræg*. It should be noted that *feond* cannot be used in this question: it still means 'enemy' in *Beowulf*, and is for instance applicable to Beowulf and Wiglaf in relation to the dragon. Even *feond on helle*, 101, is not so clear as it seems (see below); though we may add *wergan gastes*, 133, an expression for 'devil' later extremely common, and actually applied in line 1747 to the Devil and tempter himself. Apart, however, from this expression little can be made of the use of *gast, gæst*. For one thing it is under grave suspicion in many places (both applied to Grendel and otherwise) of being a corruption of *gæst, gest* 'stranger'; compare Grendel's title *cwealmcuma*, 792 = *wælgæst*, 1331, 1995. In any case it cannot be translated either by the modern *ghost* or *spirit*. *Creature* is probably the nearest we can now get. Where it is genuine it applies to Grendel probably in virtue of his relationship or similarity to bogies (*scinnum ond scuccum*), physical enough in form and power, but vaguely felt as belonging to a different order of being, one allied to the malevolent 'ghosts' of the dead. Fire is conceived as a *gæst* (1123).

This approximation of Grendel to a devil does not mean that there is any confusion as to his habitation. Grendel was a fleshly denizen of this world (until physically slain). *On helle* and *helle* (as in *helle gast* 1274) mean 'hellish', and are actually equivalent to the first elements in the compounds *deapscua, sceadugengea, helruna*. (Thus the original genitive *helle* developed into the Middle English adjective *helle, hellene* 'hellish', applicable to ordinary men, such as usurers; and even *feond on helle* could be so used. Wyclif applies *fend on helle* to the friar walking in England as Grendel in Denmark.) But the symbolism of darkness is so fundamental that it is vain to look for any distinction between the *þystru* outside Hrothgar's hall in which Grendel lurked, and the shadow of Death, or of hell after (or in) Death.

Thus in spite of shifting, actually in process (intricate, and as difficult as it is interesting and important to follow), Grendel remains primarily an ogre, a physical monster, whose main function is hostility to humanity (and its frail efforts at order and art upon earth). He is of the *fifelcyn*, a *þyrs* or *eoten*; in fact the *eoten*, for this ancient word is actually preserved in Old English only as applied to him. He is most frequently called simply a foe: *feond, lað, sceaða, feorhgeniðla, laðgeteona*, all words applicable to enemies of any kind. And though he, as ogre, has kinship with devils, and is doomed when slain to be numbered among the evil spirits, he is not when wrestling with Beowulf a materialized apparition of soul-destroying evil. It is thus true to say that Grendel is not yet a real mediaeval devil—except in so far as mediaeval bogies themselves had failed (as was often the case) to become real devils. But the distinction between a devilish ogre, and a devil revealing himself in ogre-form— between a monster, devouring the body and bringing temporal death, that is inhabited by an accursed spirit, and a spirit of evil aiming ultimately at the soul and bringing eternal death (even though he takes a form of visible horror, that may bring and suffer physical pain)—is a real and important one, even if both kinds are to be found before and after 1066. In *Beowulf* the weight is on the physical side: Grendel does not vanish into the pit when grappled. He must be slain by plain prowess, and thus is a real counterpart to the dragon in Beowulf's history.

(Grendel's mother is naturally described, when separately treated, in precisely similar terms: she is *wif, ides, aglæc wif*; and rising to the inhuman: *merewif, brimwylf, grundwyrgen*. Grendel's title *Godes andsaca* has been studied in the text. Some titles have been omitted: for instance those referring to his *outlawry*, which are applicable in themselves to him by nature, but are of course also fitting either to a descendant of Cain, or to a devil: thus *heorowearh, dædhata, mearcstapa, angengea*.)

(b) 'Lof' and 'Dom'; 'Hell' and 'Heofon'

Of pagan 'belief' we have little or nothing left in English. But the spirit survived. Thus the author of *Beowulf* grasped fully the idea of *lof* or *dom*, the noble pagan's desire for the *merited praise* of the noble. For if this limited 'immortality' of renown naturally exists as a strong motive together with actual heathen practice and belief, it can also long outlive them. It is the natural residuum when the gods are destroyed, whether unbelief comes from within or from without. The prominence of the motive of *lof* in *Beowulf*—long ago pointed out by Earle—may be interpreted, then, as a sign that a pagan time was not far away from the poet, and perhaps also that the end of English paganism (at least among the noble classes for whom and by whom such traditions were preserved) was marked by a twilight period, similar to that observable later in Scandinavia. The gods faded or receded, and man was left to carry on his war unaided. His trust was in his own power and will, and his reward was the praise of his peers during his life and after his death.

At the beginning of the poem, at the end of the first section of the exordium, the note is struck: *lofdædum sceal in mægþa gehwære man geþeon.* The last word of the poem is *lofgeornost*, the summit of the praise of the dead hero: that was indeed *lastworda betst*. For Beowulf had lived according to his own philosophy, which he explicitly avowed: *ure æghwylc sceal ende gebidan worolde lifes; wyrce se ðe mote domes ær deaþe: þæt bið dryhtguman æfter selest*, 1386 ff. The poet as commentator recurs again to this: *swa sceal man don, þonne he æt guðe gegan þenceð longsumne lof: na ymb his lif cearað*, 1534 ff.

Lof is ultimately and etymologically *value, valuation*, and so *praise*, as we say (itself derived from *pretium*). *Dom* is *judgement, assessment*, and in one branch *just esteem, merited renown*. The difference between these two is not in most passages important. Thus at the end of *Widsith*, which refers to the minstrel's part in achieving for the noble and their deeds the prolonged life of fame, both are combined: it is said of the generous patron, *lof se gewyrceð, hafað under heofonum heahfæstne dom*. But the difference has an importance. For the words were not actually synonymous, nor entirely commensurable. In the Christian period the one, *lof*, flowed rather into the ideas of heaven and the heavenly choirs; the other, *dom*, into the ideas of the judgement of God, the particular and general judgements of the dead.

The change that occurs can be plainly observed in *The Seafarer*, especially if lines 66-80 of that poem are compared with Hrothgar's *giedd* or sermon in *Beowulf* from 1755 onwards. There is a close resemblance between *Seafarer* 66-71 and Hrothgar's words, 1761-8, a part of his discourse that may certainly be ascribed to the original author of *Beowulf*, whatever revision or expansion the speech may otherwise have suffered. The Seafarer says:

> ic gelyfe no
> þæt him eorðwelan ece stondað.
> Simle þreora sum þinga gehwylce
> ær his tid[d]ege to tweon weorþeð:
> adl oþþe yldo oþþe ecghete
> fægum fromweardum feorh oðþringeð.

Hrothgar says:

> eft sona bið
> þæt þec adl oððe ecg eafoþes getwæfeð,
> oððe fyres feng, oððe flodes wylm,
> oððe gripe meces, oððe gares fliht,
> oððe atol yldo; oððe eagena bearhtm
> forsiteð ond forsworceð. Semninga bið
> þæt þec, dryhtguma, deað oferswyðeð.

Hrothgar expands *þreora sum* on lines found elsewhere, either in great elaboration as in the *Fates of Men*, or in brief allusion to this well-known theme as in *The Wanderer* 80 ff. But the Seafarer, after thus proclaiming that all men shall die, goes on: 'Therefore it is for all noble men *lastworda betst* (the best memorial), and praise (*lof*) of the living who commemorate him after death, that ere he must go hence, he should merit and achieve on earth by heroic deeds against the malice of enemies (*feonda*), opposing the devil, that the children of men may praise him afterwards, and his *lof* may live with the angels for ever and ever, the glory of eternal life, rejoicing among the hosts.'

This is a passage which from its syntax alone may with unusual certainty be held to have suffered revision and expansion. It could easily be simplified. But in any case it shows a modification of heathen *lof* in two directions: first in making the deeds which win *lof* resistance to spiritual foes—the sense of the ambiguous *feonda* is, in the poem as preserved, so defined by *deofle togeanes*; secondly, in enlarging *lof* to include the angels and the bliss of heaven. *lofsong, loftsong* are in Middle English especially used of the heavenly choirs.

But we do not find anything like this definite alteration in *Beowulf*. There *lof* remains pagan *lof*, the praise of one's peers, at best vaguely prolonged among their descendants *awa to ealdre*. (On *soðfæstra dom*, 2820, see below). In *Beowulf* there is *hell*: justly the poet said of the people he depicted *helle gemundon on modsefan*. But there is practically no clear reference to *heaven* as its opposite, to heaven, that is, as a place or state of reward, of eternal bliss in the presence of God. Of course *heofon*, singular and plural, and its synonyms, such as *rodor*, are frequent; but they refer usually either to the particular landscape or to the sky under which all men dwell. Even when these words are used with the words for God, who is Lord of the heavens, such expressions are primarily parallels to others describing His general governance of nature (e.g. 1609 ff.), and His realm which includes land and sea and sky.

Of course it is not here maintained—very much the contrary—that the *poet* was ignorant of theological heaven, or of the Christian use of *heofon* as the equivalent of *caelum* in Scripture: only that this use was of intention (if not in practice quite rigidly) excluded from a poem dealing with the pagan past. There is one clear exception in lines 186 ff: *wel bið þæm þe mot æfter deaðdæge Drihten secean, ond to Fæder fæþmum freoðo wunian*. If this, and the passage in which it occurs, is genuine—descends, that is, without addition or alteration from the poet who wrote *Beowulf* as a whole—and is not, as I believe, a later expansion, then the point is not destroyed. For the passage remains still definitely an aside, an exclamation of the Christian author, who knew about heaven, and expressly denied such knowledge to the Danes. The characters within the poem do not understand heaven, or have hope of it. They refer to *hell*—an originally pagan word.[33] Beowulf predicts it as the destiny of Unferth and Grendel. Even the noble monotheist Hrothgar—so he is drawn, quite apart from the question of the genuineness of the bulk of his sermon from 1724-60—refers to no heavenly bliss. The reward of virtue which he foretells for Beowulf is that his *dom* shall live *awa to ealdre*, a fortune also bestowed upon Sigurd in Norse (that his name *æ mun uppi*). This idea of lasting *dom* is, as we have seen, capable of being christianized; but in *Beowulf* it is not christianized, probably deliberately, when the characters are speaking in their proper persons, or their actual thoughts are reported.

The author, it is true, says of Beowulf that *him of hreðre gewat sawol secean soðfæstra dom*. What precise theological view he held concerning the souls of the just heathen we need not here inquire. He does not tell us, saying simply that Beowulf's

---

[33]Free as far as we know from definite physical location. Details of the original northern conception, equated and blended with the Scriptural, are possibly sometimes to be seen colouring the references to Christian hell. A celebrated example is the reference in *Judith* to the death of Holofernes, which recalls remarkably certain features in *Völuspá*. Cf. *Judith* 115: *wyrmum bewunden*, and 119: of *ðam wyrmsele* with *Völ.* 36 *sá's undinn salr orma hryggjum*; which translated into O.E. would be *se is wunden sele wyrma hrycgum*.

spirit departed to whatever judgement awaits such just men, though we may take it that this comment implies that it was not destined to the fiery hell of punishment, being reckoned among the good. There is in any case here no doubt of the transmutation of words originally pagan. *soðfæstra dom* could by itself have meant simply the 'esteem of the true-judging', that *dom* which Beowulf as a young man had declared to be the prime motive of noble conduct; but when combined with *gewat secean* it must mean either the glory that belongs (in eternity) to the just, or the judgement of God upon the just. Yet Beowulf himself, expressing his own opinion, though troubled by dark doubts, and later declaring his conscience clear, thinks at the end only of his barrow and memorial among men, of his childlessness, and of Wiglaf the sole survivor of his kindred, to whom he bequeathes his arms. His funeral is not Christian, and his reward is the recognized virtue of his kingship and the hopeless sorrow of his people.

The relation of the Christian and heathen thought and diction in *Beowulf* has often been misconceived. So far from being a man so simple or so confused that he muddled Christianity with Germanic paganism, the author probably drew or attempted to draw distinctions, and to represent moods and attitudes of characters conceived dramatically as living in a noble but heathen past. Though there are one or two special problems concerning the tradition of the poem and the possibility that it has here and there suffered later unauthentic retouching,[34] we cannot speak in general either of confusion (in one poet's mind or in the mind of a whole period), or of patch-work revision producing confusion. More sense can be made of the poem, if we start rather with the hypothesis, not in itself unlikely, that the poet tried to do something definite and difficult, which had some reason and thought behind it, though his execution may not have been entirely successful.

The strongest argument that the actual language of the poem is not in general the product either of stupidity or accident is to be found in the fact that we can observe *differentiation*. We can, that is, in this matter of philosophy and religious sentiment distinguish, for instance: (a) the poet as narrator and commentator; (b) Beowulf; and (c) Hrothgar. Such differentiation would not be achieved by a man himself confused in mind, and still less by later random editing. The kind of thing that accident contrives is illustrated by *drihten wereda*, 'lord of hosts', a familiar Christian expression, which appears in line 2186, plainly as an alteration of *drihten Wedera* 'lord of the Geats'. This alteration is obviously due to some man, the actual scribe of the line or some predecessor, more familiar with *Dominus Deus Sabaoth* than with Hrethel and the Weder-Geatish house. But no one, I think, has ventured to ascribe this confusion to the author.

That such differentiation does occur, I do not attempt here to prove by analysis of all the relevant lines of the poem. I leave the matter to those who care to go through the text, only insisting that it is essential to pay closer attention than has usually been paid to the *circumstances* in which the references to religion, Fate, or mythological matters each appear, and to distinguish in particular those things which are said in *oratio recta* by one of the characters, or are reported as being said or thought by them. It will then be seen that the narrating and commenting poet obviously stands apart. But the two characters who do most of the speaking, Beowulf and Hrothgar, are also quite distinct. Hrothgar is consistently portrayed as a wise and noble monotheist, modelled largely it has been suggested in the text on the Old Testament patriarchs and kings; he refers all things to the favour of God, and never omits explicit thanks for mercies. Beowulf refers sparingly to God, except as the arbiter of critical

---

[34]Such as 168-9, probably a clumsily intruded couplet, of which the only certain thing that can be said is that it interrupts (even if its sense were plain) the natural connexion between 165-7 and 170; the question of the expansion (in this case at any rate skilful and not inapt) of Hrothgar's *giedd*, 1724-60; and most notably lines 175-88.

events, and then principally as *Metod*, in which the idea of God approaches nearest to the old Fate. We have in Beowulf's language little differentiation of God and Fate. For instance, he says *gæð a wyrd swa hio scel* and immediately continues that *dryhten* holds the balance in his combat (441); or again he definitely equates *wyrd* and *metod* (2526 f.).[35] It is Beowulf who says *wyrd oft nereð unfægne eorl, þonne his ellen deah* (immediately after calling the sun *beacen Godes*), which contrasts with the poet's own comment on the man who escaped the dragon (2291): *swa mæg unfæge eaðe gedigean wean ond wræcsið, se ðe Wealdendes hyldo gehealdeþ.* Beowulf only twice explicitly thanks God or acknowledges His help: in lines 1658-61, where he acknowledges God's protection and the favour of *ylda Waldend* in his combat under the water; in his last speech, where he thanks *Frean Wuldurcyninge . . . ecum Dryhtne* for all the treasure, and for helping him to win it for his people. Usually he makes no such references. He ascribes his conquest of the nicors to luck—*hwæþre me gesælde*, 570 ff. (compare the similar words used of Sigemund, 890). In his account to Hygelac his only explanation of his preservation in the water-den is *næs ic fæge þa gyt* (2141). He does not allude to God at all in this report.

Beowulf knows, of course, of hell and judgement: he speaks of it, to Unferth; he declares that Grendel shall abide *miclan domes* and the judgement of *scir metod*; and finally in his last examination of conscience he says that *Waldend fira* cannot accuse him of *morðorbealo maga*. But the crimes which he claims to have avoided are closely paralleled in the heathen *Völuspá*, where the grim hall, *Náströndu á*, contains especially *menn meinsvara ok morðvarga* (perjurers and murderers).

Other references he makes are casual and formal, such as *beorht beacen Godes*, of the sun (571). An exceptional case is *Godes leoht geceas* 2469, describing the death of Hrethel, Beowulf's grandfather. This would appear to refer to heaven. Both these expressions have, as it were, inadvertently escaped from Christian poetry. The first, *beacen Godes*, is perhaps passable even for a heathen in this particular poem, in which the theory throughout is that good pagans, when not tempted or deluded by the devil, knew of the one God. But the second, especially since Beowulf himself is formally the speaker, is an item of unsuitable diction—which cannot be dismissed as a later alteration. A didactic reviser would hardly have added this detail to the description of the heathen king's death: he would rather have removed the heathen, or else sent him to hell. The whole story alluded to is pagan and hopeless, and turns on blood-feud and the motive that when a son kills his brother the father's sorrow is intensified because no vengeance can be exacted. The explanation of such occasional faults is not to be sought in Christian revision, but in the fact that before *Beowulf* was written Christian poetry was already established, and was known to the author. The language of *Beowulf* is in fact partly 're-paganized' by the author with a special purpose, rather than christianized (by him or later) without consistent purpose. Throughout the poem

---

[35]Of course the use of words more or less equivalent to 'fate' continued throughout the ages. The most Christian poets refer to *wyrd*, usually of unfortunate events; but sometimes of good, as in *Elene* 1047, where the conversion of Judas is ascribed to *wyrd*. There remains always the main mass of the workings of Providence (*Metod*) which are inscrutable, and for practical purposes dealt with as 'fate' or 'luck'. *Metod* is in Old English the word that is most nearly allied to 'fate', although employed as a synonym of *god*. That it could be so employed is due probably to its having anciently in English an agental significance (as well as an abstract sense), as in Old Norse where *mjötuðr* has the senses 'dispenser, ruler' and 'doom, fate, death'. But in Old English *metodsceaft* means 'doom' or 'death'. Cf. 2814 f. where *wyrd* is more active than *metodsceaft*. In Old Saxon *metod* is similarly used, leaning also to the side of the inscrutable (and even hostile) aspects of the world's working. Gabriel in the *Hêliand* says of John the Baptist that he will not touch wine: *so habed im* uurdgiscapu, metod *gimarcod endi maht godes* (128); it is said of Anna when her husband died: *that sie thiu mikila maht* metodes *todelda, uured* uurdigiscapu (511). In Old Saxon *metod(o)giscapu* and *metodigisceft*, equal Fate, as O.E. *metodsceaft*.

the language becomes more intelligible, if we assume that the diction of poetry was already christianized and familiar with Old and New Testament themes and motives. There is a gap, important and effective poetically whatever was its length in time, between Cædmon and the poet of *Beowulf*. We have thus in Old English not only the old heroic language often strained or misused in application to Christian legend (as in *Andreas* or *Elene*), but in *Beowulf* language of Christian tone occasionally (if actually seldom) put inadvertently in the mouth of a character conceived as heathen. All is not perfect to the last detail in *Beowulf*. But with regard to *Godes leoht geceas*, the chief defect of this kind, it may be observed that in the very long speech of Beowulf from 2425-2515 the poet has hardly attempted to keep up the pretence of *oratio recta* throughout. Just before the end he reminds us and himself that Beowulf is supposed to be speaking by a renewed *Beowulf maðelode* (2510). From 2444 to 2489 we have not really a monologue in character at all, and the words *Godes leoht geceas* go rather with *gewat secean soðfæstra dom* as evidence of the author's own view of the destiny of the just pagan.

When we have made allowance for imperfections of execution, and even for some intentional modification of character in old age (when Beowulf becomes not unnaturally much more like Hrothgar), it is plain that the characters and sentiments of the two chief actors in the poem are differently conceived and drawn. Where Beowulf's thoughts are revealed by the poet we can observe that his real trust was in his own might. That the possession of this might was a 'favour of God' is actually a comment of the poet's, similar to the comment of Scandinavian Christians upon their heathen heroes. Thus in line 665 we have *georne truwode modgan mægenes, metodes hyldo*. No *and* is possible metrically in the original; none should appear in translation: the favour of God was the possession of *mægen*. Compare 1272-3: *gemunde mægenes strenge, gimfæste gife ðe him God sealde.*[36] Whether they knew it or not, *cupon* (or *ne cupon*) *heofena Helm herian*, the supreme quality of the old heroes, their valour, was their special endowment by God, and as such could be admired and praised.

Concerning Beowulf the poet tells us finally that when the dragon's ruinous assault was reported, he was filled with doubt and dismay, and *wende se wisa þæt he Wealdende ofer ealde riht ecean Dryhtne bitre gebulge*. It has been said that *ofer ealde riht*, 'contrary to ancient law', is here given a Christian interpretation; but this hardly seems to be the case. This is a heathen and unchristian fear—of an inscrutable power, a *Metod* that can be offended inadvertently: indeed the sorrow of a man who, though he knew of God, and was eager for justice, was yet far estranged, and 'had hell in his heart'.

(c) Lines 175-88

These lines are important and present certain difficulties. We can with confidence accept as original and genuine these words as far as *helle gemundon on modsefan*—which is strikingly true, in a sense, of all the characters depicted or alluded to in the poem, even if it is here actually applied only to those deliberately turning from God to the Devil. The rest requires, and has often received, attention. If it is original, the poet must have intended a distinction between the wise Hrothgar, who certainly knew of and often thanked God, and a certain party of the pagan Danes—heathen priests, for instance, and those that had recourse to them under the

---

[36]Compare for instance, the intrusive commentary in *Fóstbrœðra saga* which observes in a description of a grim pagan character; *ekki var hjarta hans sem fóarn í fugli, ekki var þat blóð ult, svá at þat skylfi af hræðslu, heldr var þat hert af enum hæsta höfuðsmið í öllum hvatleik* (ch. 2); and again *Almáttigr er sá sem svá snart hjarta ok óhrætt lét í brjóst Þorgeiri: ok ekki var hans hugþryði af mönnum ger né honum í brjóst borin, heldr af enum hæsta höfuðsmið* (ib.). Here the notion is explicitly (if unseasonably and absurdly) expressed.

temptation of calamity—specially deluded by the *gastbona*, the destroyer of souls.[37] Of these, particularly those permanently in the service of idols (*swylce wæs þeaw hyra*), which in Christian theory and in fact did not include all the community, it is perhaps possible to say that they did not know (*ne cuþon*), nor even know of (*ne wiston*), the one God, nor know how to worship him. At any rate the hell (of fire) is only predicted for those showing malice (*sliðne nið*), and it is not plain that the *freoðo* of the Father is ultimately obtainable by none of these men of old. It is probable that the contrast between 92-8 and 175-88 is intentional: the song of the minstrel in the days of untroubled joy, before the assault of Grendel, telling of the Almighty and His fair creation, and the loss of knowledge and praise, and the fire awaiting such malice, in the time of temptation and despair.

But it is open to doubt whether lines 181-88 are original, or at any rate unaltered. Not of course because of the apparent discrepancy—though it is a matter vital to the whole poem: we cannot dismiss lines simply because they offer difficulty of such a kind. But because, unless my ear and judgement are wholly at fault, they have a ring and measure unlike their context, and indeed unlike that of the poem as a whole. The place is one that offers at once special temptation to enlargement or alteration and special facilities for doing either without grave dislocation.[38] I suspect that the second half of line 180 has been altered, while what follows has remodelled or replaced a probably shorter passage, making the comment (one would say, guided by the poem as a whole) that they *forsook* God under tribulation, and incurred the danger of hell-fire. This in itself would be a comment of the *Beowulf* poet, who was probably provided by his original material with a reference to *wigweorþung* in the sacred site of Heorot at this juncture in the story.

In any case the *unleugbare Inkonsequenz* (Hoops) of this passage is felt chiefly by those who assume that by references to the Almighty the legendary Danes and the Scylding court are depicted as 'Christian'. If that is so, the mention of heathen *þeaw* is, of course, odd; but it offers only one (if a marked) example of a confusion of thought fundamental to the poem, and does not then merit long consideration. Of all the attempts to deal with this *Inkonsequenz* perhaps the least satisfactory is the most recent: that of Hoops,[39] who supposes that the poet had to represent the Danish prayers as addressed to the Devil for the protection of the honour of the *Christengott*, since the prayers were not answered. But this attributes to the poet a confusion (and insincerity) of thought that an 'Anglo-Saxon' was hardly modern or advanced enough to achieve. It is difficult to believe that he could have been so singularly ill instructed in the nature of Christian prayer. And the pretense that *all* prayers to the *Christengott* are answered, and swiftly, would scarcely have deceived the stupidest member of his audience. Had he embarked on such bad theology, he would have had many other difficulties to face: the long time of woe before God relieved the distress of these Christian Danes by sending Scyld (13); and indeed His permission of the assaults of

---

[37]It is not strictly true to say, as is said, for instance, by Hoops that he is 'identified' with their heathen god. The Christian theory was that such gods did not exist, and were inventions of the Devil, and that the power of idols was due to the fact that he, or one of his emissaries, often actually inhabited them, and could be seen in their real hideousness if the veil of illusion was removed. Compare Aelfric's homilies on St. Bartholomew, and St. Matthew, where by the power of an angel or saint the devil residing in idols was revealed as a black *silhearwa*.

[38]Similarly it is the very marked character already by the poet given to Hrothgar which has induced and made possible without serious damage the probable revision and expansion of his sermon. Well done as the passage in itself is, the poem would be better with the excision of approximately lines 1740-60; and these lines are on quite independent grounds under the strongest suspicion of being due to later revision and addition. The actual joints have, nevertheless, if that is so, been made with a technical competence as good as that which I here assume for the earlier passage.

[39]*Kommentar zum Beowulf*, p. 39.

Grendel at all upon such a Christian people, who do not seem depicted as having perpetrated any crime punishable by calamity. But in fact God did provide a cure for Grendel—Beowulf, and this is recognized by the poet in the mouth of Hrothgar himself (381 ff.). We may acquit the maker of *Beowulf* of the suggested motive, whatever we may think of the *Inkonsequenz*. He could hardly have been less aware than we that in history (in England and in other lands), and in Scripture, people could depart from the one God to other service in time of trial—precisely because that God has never guaranteed to His servants immunity from temporal calamity, before or after prayer. It is to idols that men turned (and turn) for quick and literal answers.

The Oral-Formulaic Character of
Anglo-Saxon Narrative Poetry[1]

By Francis P. Magoun, Jr.

In the course of the last quarter-century much has been discovered about the techniques employed by unlettered singers in their composition of narrative verse. Whereas a lettered poet of any time or place, composing (as he does and must) with the aid of writing materials and with deliberation, creates his own language as he proceeds, the unlettered singer, ordinarily composing rapidly and extempore before a live audience, must and does call upon ready-made language, upon a vast reservoir of formulas filling just measures of verse. These formulas develop over a long period of time; they are the creation of countless generations of singers and can express all the ideas a singer will need in order to tell his story, itself usually traditional. This progress is primarily due to the work of two men, the late Milman Parry[2] and his former pupil and successor in this field, Professor Albert Bates Lord of Harvard University.[3] First in connection with Homeric language, later as a

---

[1]This paper is, with revisions, essentially the second ('The Formulaic Character of Anglo-Saxon Narrative Poetry') of three Special University Lectures (series-title 'Oral-Formulaic Tradition in Anglo-Saxon Poetry'), delivered at the invitation of the University of London in the Senate House on 10, 17, and 24 January 1952, and was written in March 1952. The first two pages or so present the sense of the first lecture ('The Art and Craft of Oral Poetry'), while the last few pages similarly digest the third ('Some Problems of the Future'). Charts I and II are revisions of mimeographed counterparts distributed at the second lecture.

[2]For a complete bibliography of the writings of Milman Parry, see A. B. Lord, 'Homer, Parry, and Huso,' *American Journal of Archaeology,* LII (1948), 43-44. Two of Parry's papers may be specially noted as representing the full development of his thought, 'Studies in the Epic Technique of Oral Verse-Making, I: Homer and Homeric Style,' *Harvard Studies in Classical Philology,* XLI (1930), 73-147, esp. pp. 118-121 for charts exposing the formulaic character of ll.1-25 of the *Iliad* and the *Odyssey* respectively; and 'II: The Homeric Language as the Language of Oral Poetry,' *ibid.,* XLIII (1932) 1-50, esp. pp. 12-17 ('The Art of Oral Poetry'). These papers are cited here as Parry I and II and by page.

[3]Parry in the summer of 1933, and Parry and Lord in the years 1934-35, studied the production of the oral epic style in Yugoslavia and collected some 12,500 texts, 'The Parry Collection of South-Slavic Texts,' now deposited in the Harvard College Library. Following Parry's lead and working with this opulent material Lord submitted in 1949 a Ph.D. thesis (Harvard, unpublished), 'The Singer of Tales: A Study in the Process of Yugoslav, Greek, and Germanic Oral Poetry.' Lord revisited Yugoslavia in 1950 and 1951; for his report on the collecting trip of 1950 see 'Yugoslav Epic Folk Poetry,' *Journal of the International Folk Music Council,* III (1951), 57-61. His thesis, revised and expanded, will be published by the Harvard

---

Reprinted, by permission, from *Speculum* 28 (1953), 446-67.

result of field-work in Yugoslavia, chiefly among unlettered Muslim singers, Parry, aided by Lord, demonstrated that the characteristic feature of all orally composed poetry is its totally formulaic character. From this a second point emerged, namely, that the recurrence in a given poem of an appreciable number of formulas or formulaic phrases brands the latter as oral, just as a lack of such repetitions marks a poem as composed in a lettered tradition. Oral poetry, it may be safely said, is composed entirely of formulas, large and small, while lettered poetry is never formulaic, though lettered poets occasionally consciously repeat themselves or quote verbatim from other poets in order to produce a specific rhetorical or literary effect. Finally, it is clear that an oral poem until written down has not and cannot have a fixed text, a concept difficult for lettered persons; its text, like the text of an orally circulating anecdote, will vary in greater or lesser degree with each telling.

The oral singer does not memorize either the songs of singers from whom he learns nor later does he memorize in our sense of the word songs of his own making. His apprenticeship involves the learning of thematic material, plots, proper names, and formulas with which he will gradually become able to compose in regular verse songs of his own. A good singer is one able to make better use of the common fund of formulas than the indifferent or poor singer, though all will be drawing upon essentially the same body of material. The length of a song or, better, the length of a given performance (since there is no fixed text) will largely depend upon the audience-factor, on how much time an audience has to give to the singer on any given occasion. A good singer can go on as long as an audience will listen to him, be it persons assembled in a Bosnian coffee-house, or in the presence of a tape-recorder or a stenographer. The analogies with musical improvisation will be evident.

The present paper is essentially an extension into the realm of Anglo-Saxon narrative poetry of the work of Parry and Lord, to whom it is indebted at every turn and in more ways than can easily be expressed. Indeed, without the stimulation of Parry's published works and the works and spoken words of Albert Lord, the present paper, or, indeed, anything like it would not have been written.

When one first reads of the existence of Anglo-Saxon poetry in the seventh century in Bede's account of Cædman (*H.E.*, IV, 22 [24]), there is every reason to believe that already behind this lay a long tradition, running back to the Continental homeland and into a distant common Germanic heritage, a tradition of at least seven centuries and probably more. Toward the end of the first century A.D. Cornelius Tacitus comments on the art of poetry among the Germanic peoples of his day, and from that time on there are allusions by authors from late antiquity to the singing of songs among various Germanic

University Press as *The Singer of Tales* in the series "Harvard Studies in Comparative Literature."

P.S. The work of Parry and Lord and the rich material preserved at Harvard were very familiar to Sir Cecil Maurice Bowra and utilized by him in his *Heroic Poetry* (London: Macmillan, 1952). This distinguished work appeared too late for me to use in preparing my London lectures or in preparing this paper, though I am happy to be able to add a specific reference or two in the footnotes below. For an excellent review of Sir Maurice's book see *The Times Literary Supplement*, Friday, 12 December 1952, p. 824.

tribes. Since these ancient Germanic singers were unlettered, their poetry must have been oral, and its diction, accordingly, must have been formulaic and traditional. The birth of this diction must have taken place in a very distant past and, like the birth of any diction, is beyond observation. As Parry observes of Homeric language:

A single man or even a whole group of men who set out in the most careful way could not make even a beginning at such an oral diction. It must be the work of many poets over many generations. When one singer . . . has hit upon a phrase which is pleasing and easily used, other singers will hear it, and then, when faced at the same (metrical) point in the line with the need of expressing the same idea, they will recall it and use it. If the phrase is so good poetically and so useful metrically that it becomes in time the one best way to express a certain idea in a given length of verse, and as such is passed on from one generation of poets to another, it has won a place for itself in the oral diction as a formula. But if it does not suit in every way, or if a better way of fitting the idea into the verse and sentence is found, it is straightway forgotten or lives only for a short time, since with each new poet and with each new generation of poets it must undergo the twofold test of being found pleasing and useful. In time the needed number of such phrases is made up: each idea to be expressed in the poetry has its formula for each metrical need, and the poet, who would not think of trying to express ideas outside the traditional field of thought of poetry, can make his verses easily by means of a diction which time has proved to be the best.[4]

At this late date speculation about origins is rather idle, but one may perhaps imagine that in its earliest beginnings isochronous utterances in Old Germanic, almost surely based on the rhythmic beat of some instrument, involved short sequences of verse at first almost accidentally arrived at and consisting, say, of a maxim of a few verses or a protective charm or encomiastic song of similarly modest dimensions. By the time of Tacitus it would seem that more ambitious compositions were possible and the order of the day. In his *Germania* (ch. 2) he says of the Germanic peoples:

In ancient songs (*carminibus antiquis*), which is the sole kind of record (*memoria*) or history (*annales*) among them, they celebrate the god Twisto, begotten of the earth, and his son Mannus, as the beginning and founder of their people. To Mannus they ascribe three sons from whose names those tribes nearest the Ocean are called Ingvaeones [North Sea Germans], the central Erminones [Elbe Germans?], and the rest Istvaeones [Western Rhine Germans?].

This suggests possibly rather elaborate narrative and there seems to be little reason to assume that the apparently more or less mythological or cult songs of the North Sea and Inland Germans were merely mnemonic verses on the order of the *þular* in *Widsith* or in the Old-Norse *Hervarar saga* (ch. 12, Stanza 69).[5] In the *Annales* (Book II, §88, *ad fin.*) Tacitus further reports that songs about Arminius, who had died nearly a century earlier, were still being sung by Germans of his day. These familiar statements are adduced only to emphasize the presumably high antiquity of Old-Germanic poetry and the

[4]Parry II, 7-8.
[5]E.g., Rudolf Much, *Die Germania des Tacitus* (Heidelberg, 1937), pp. 21-22.

length of tradition behind it. Furthermore, in order to suggest the antiquity not merely of the art of Germanic poetry in general but specifically the antiquity of the metrical-rhythmical forms of Anglo-Saxon poetry as we know it, one may point to the fact that Anglo-Saxon verse is cast in a form to all intents and purposes identical with all Old-Germanic poetry—Old-Norse, Old-Saxon, Old-High-German—in a word, identical with everything except the later skaldic *vísur* of Norway and Iceland. Since any theory of independent origins for the five basic metrical-rhythmical patterns, the 'Sievers Five Types,' is so exceedingly unlikely, one is forced to assume that something very close to the later preserved forms and patterns had been established and was in good running order before the Anglo-Saxons began to colonize Britain.

In the nature of the case we do not have and cannot have any record of Anglo-Saxon poetry before the introduction of the art of reading and writing by Christian missionaries from Rome and from Iona in the Hebrides; indeed, we have no poetical text which can in exactly the form preserved be thought of as having been put together very early at all. Consequently, it has been natural to think of the preserved poems as composed as we compose poetry, i.e., by lettered persons making use of writing materials, and until the time of Parry and Lord there was no available technique permitting one to decide on the basis of internal evidence alone to which tradition a given text might belong—to the oral or to the lettered. The recurrence of verses and verse-pairs in Anglo-Saxon poetry, the 'Parallelstellen' of German scholars, has been much noted and commented upon, and cross-references accumulated and often cited by editors of individual poems, with the main conclusion drawn from this phenomenon being that those parallels might constitute evidence of the direct influence of one poem upon another (see p. 59, below). But with the discovery of the dominant rôle of the formula in the composition of oral poetry and of the non-existence of metrical formulas in the poetry of lettered authors, we have suddenly acquired a touchstone with which it is now possible to determine to which of the two great categories of poetry a recorded text belongs—to the oral or to the lettered.

As a first test I have analyzed the first twenty-five lines or, better, the first fifty verses or twenty-five typographical lines of *Béowulf,* chosen because they deal with highly specialized thematic material not represented elsewhere in the poetry, for the presentation of which in verse one might suppose that a poet would need to create his own language if he would ever have to do so. The formulaic character of the verse is demonstrated by Chart I (pp. 62-63, below).[6] A word-group of any size or importance which appears elsewhere in *Béowulf* or other Anglo-Saxon poems unchanged or virtually unchanged is marked with solid underlining and is a formula according to Parry's definition that a formula is 'a group of words which is regularly employed under the same metrical conditions to express a given essential idea.'[7] A word-group

---

[6]Quotations and line-references from *Béowulf* are based on Fr. Klaeber's third edition with First and Second Supplements (Boston, 1950), those from *Judith* on the edition of Benno J. Timmer (London: Methuen, 1952); all others on *The Anglo-Saxon Poetic Records* (New York: Columbia University Press, 1931-42). Spellings are normalized on the basis of early W.S. as set forth in *Les Langues modernes,* XLV (1951), 63-69. Title-abbreviations, coded in three letters, are based on the titles used in *The Anglo-Saxon Poetic Records.*

[7]Parry I, 80.

marked with solid and broken underlining, or with broken underlining only, may be called a fomulaic phrase or system; such groups are of the same type and conform to the same verbal and grammatical pattern as the various other verses associated with them and cited in the supporting evidence. For verses which are unmarked I have found no supporting evidence. Following the marked text on the chart comes the supporting evidence assembled under numbers answering to the *a* and *b* parts of the respective typographical lines.

Looking at Chart I one notes first that of the fifty verses only some thirteen, or twenty-six per cent, are not matched wholly or in part elsewhere in Anglo-Saxon poetry. In a word, despite the relatively limited corpus of some 30,000 lines—a little more than the two Homeric poems—in which to find corresponding phrases, some seventy per cent of the text of this passage does occur elsewhere. Were the surviving corpus, say, twice as big and if, above all, we had other songs of any extent dealing with anything like the same thematic material, there well might be almost nothing in the language here used that could not be demonstrated as traditional.

Though usefulness rather than mere repetition is what makes a formula, it is instructive to look at the repeated formulas first, since it is easier to recognize a formula as such when it occurs a second or third time,[8] and from this regular use in various songs one readily sees how it helps this and that singer to compose his verses. Verses 1b, 3a, 3b, 4b, 5a, 5b, 8a, 10b, 11b, 13a, 14a, 15a, 16a, 17a, 23a, and 25a are of this sort. They occur exactly the same elsewhere or with only some insignificant change in inflection about which a singer would scarcely have to devote conscious thought in order to fit them into some different context or slightly different grammatical situation. The very fact of their recurrence in and/or outside of this poem bears witness to their usefulness not only to the singer of *Béowulf* but to singers of many other songs dealing with quite different themes.

A number of these formulas are something more than mere repeats and form part of larger formulaic systems used to express the same, or almost the same, idea or used to fit some larger rhythmical-grammatical pattern. As Parry observes of such formulas in Homer, 'any group of two or more such like formulas makes up a system, and the system may be defined in turn as a group of phrases which have the same metrical value and which are enough alike in thought and words to leave no doubt that the poet who used them knew them not only as a single formula, but also as formulas of a certain type.'[9] Here belong verses 1b, 6b, 11b, 16a, and 19a.

1b. *on géar-dagum* is one phase of a system *on* x-*dagum* used to express the idea 'long ago' and occurs twice elsewhere in *Béowulf* and in other poems as well. Either alone or with one or two preceding unstressed words it forms a complete C-verse. With the substitution for *géar,* with the sense 'of yore,' of *ǽr, eald,* or *fyrn,* the formula remains unchanged in meaning and meter, though the variant first elements of the compound are patently more than useful in meeting the exigencies of alliteration, a restrictive and technical problem with which neither Homeric nor Yugoslav verse, for instance, have to contend. The

---

[8]Parry I, 122.
[9]Parry I, 85 and ff.

degree of thrift that marks the use of formulas in Homeric verse[10] is scarcely conceivable in the construction of the much more restrictive alliterative Germanic verse.

6b. *siþþan ǽrest wearþ* shows us three words repeated as a formula in *Béowulf* where it serves to express the general idea 'after something or other has happened'; it must have often been used by singers to express this same idea in a complete D-verse. But *siþþan ǽrest* (or *furðum*) can be followed by any monosyllabic verb-form in the past tense and in the recorded instance with *wéox* expresses a closely related idea.

11b. *þæt wæs gód cyning!* is a formula that may well have come into being in connection with encomiastic verse, of which we hear so much and have so little. Stylistically this and related formulas stop the narrative for a moment and thus serve as a kind of emphatic punctuation. It is used twice in *Béowulf*, and elsewhere with unfavorable adjectives it serves as a parallel phrase of disapprobation. The system is *þæt wæs (is)* x *cyning*. There are other more distantly related formulas noted in the supporting evidence, all referring to persons.

16a. *lange hwíle* is part of a large system expressing the idea 'for a long time' and is closely related to a similar system with *þráge*, equally popular with the *Béowulf* singer. This formula or formulaic system occurs with *ealle*, *góde*, and *micele* substituting for *lange*, alternates which affect neither sense nor meter; here alliteration must dictate the singer's choice. Whether he uses *hwíle* or *þráge* is surely a matter of accident or indifference, since both words fill the same measure of verse and here will not enter into the alliteration.

19a. *Scieldes eafora* is not repeated elsewhere in the poetic corpus, for nowhere else does the need exist to use this particular patronymic. The value of this system, whereby an A-verse can be constructed with the genitive of any monosyllabic personal name, is obvious from the supporting evidence. For patronymics involving the numerous dithematic names it may be observed that *sunu* is the favorite keyword and automatically forms a D- or E-verse, as do the somewhat less common *maga* and *magu*.

The present passage includes three nominal compounds which I have underlined as formulas not merely because they are repeated elsewhere to make up whole verses but because their second elements constitute the core of many small systems of formulas. These are *þéod-cyninges* (2a), *ymbsittendra* (9b), and *willgesíðas* (23a).[11] If these words did not make up entire verses, one might perhaps be inclined to view them merely as repeated words, and just as formulas need not be mere repetitions, so mere repetitions need not constitute a formula.

þéod-cyninga (2a) is one of a large number of compounds with inflected forms of *cyning*, usually in the genitive singular, which express the idea 'king' within the limits of a D3-verse. In most cases the first element merely emphasizes in one way or another the importance of the king or kings in

---

[10]Parry I, 86.

[11]For further instances of words of similar structure, and thus with similar rhythmical patterns, in *Béowulf* see John Collins Pope, *The Rhythm of Béowulf* (New Haven, Conn., 1942), pp. 300, 358 (type D1, No. 1) and 248 (type A1, No. 2a). Examples from other poems and with other first elements can be found in Christian W. M. Grein—Ferd. Holthausen—J. J. Köhler, *Sprachschatz der angelsächsischen Dichter* (Heidelberg, 1912).

question, as here where the Danish *þéod-cyningas* are tacitly opposed, as it were, to *smákonungar* 'roitelets' of ancient Scandinavia. Occasionally the first element will be more functional and will define or locate a king. In the on-verse position *Béowulf* 2795 has *Wuldor-cyninge* and in the off-verse position *eorþ-, héah-, þéod-cyninges*, also *Frís-cyninge* and *sǽ-cyninga;* of the same general order is *weorold-cyninga.* Except for *Frís-*, used to place geographically Dæghræfn's overlord, the first elements add little to the thought and were presumably chosen for alliterative convenience.[12]

ymbsittendra (9b), a compound present participle forming a D1-verse, presents a quite similar situation; it handily expresses the idea of 'persons residing round about.' Very close is *ymbstandendra*. In a broader way *ymbsittendra* is to be associated with a large number of verses consisting of a compound present participle, of which there are many in *Béowulf*, which tend in turn to break down into various semantic systems such as the idea of 'sea-farer' expressed by *brim-* and *sǽ-liðende* in *Béowulf*, and in other songs with the substitution of *éa-, mere-*, and *wǽg-* as the first element but with no change in thought.

will-gestðas (23a) is but one of a largish formulaic system centering on *gestþ* to express in a complete A-verse the idea of 'follower(s)' 'retainer(s),' the large variety of available first elements being highly useful to the singers in connection with alliteration. Thus are found compounds with *dryht-, eald-, folc-, wéa-*, and *wynn-*.[13]

Within the first fifty verses of *Béowulf* occur three so-called kennings, two Christian: *Líf-fréa* (16b), varied by *wuldres Wealdend* (17a), and one non-Christian; *hran-ráde* (10a). Reserving the Christian formulas for later discussion in connection with the special diction of the Christian songs (pp. 55 ff. below), we may examine here the formulaic character of the C-verse *ofer hran-ráde* and some closely related expressions by the aid of which the singers were able to place people on the sea or to get them over it. Much has been written about Anglo-Saxon kennings by themselves and as part of Old-Germanic poetical technique, but there is one particular aspect of this problem which can probably support further thought and investigation, namely, the formulaic character of the kenning. Like the rest of the language of oral poetry, kennings must have developed over a long period of time and must be traditional and formulaic. An examination of the phrase *ofer hran-ráde* will tend to bear out this view. The feminine accusative singular *hran-ráde*, combined with the prepositions *geond, ofer*, and *on*, forms a complete C-verse, whose repeated use marks it as formulaic. Yet it is more than that, in that it is also one phrase of a formulaic system *on (ofer, geond) x-ráde*, where for *x* one can substitute any appropriate monosyllabic first element. With the substitution of *swan* one finds *ofer swan-ráde* in *Béowulf* and *Elene*, *on swan-ráde* in *Juliana*, while *on segl-ráde* appears in *Béowulf* with little or no real difference in meaning, and none in meter, from the other combinations. The singers are presumably concerned not primarily with some refinement of imagery produced by varying the first elements *hran, segl*, and *swan*—something for which an oral singer could scarcely have time—but with recalling a formula

---

[12]See further *ibid.*, p. 106, col. 1, under *cyning.*
[13]*Ibid.*, p. 608, under *gestþ.*

expressing the fundamental idea in question with availability for different alliterative situations. It is hard to believe that they had much concern with possible connotative effects produced by passing mention of sails, swans, or whales.

There is another aspect of this general problem that semantically at least is related to the *ofer hran-ráde* verse in *Béowulf*. Now this particular formula and related formulaic systems were obviously useful to Anglo-Saxon singers and provided them with a C-verse with the aid of which they could get their characters onto or across the sea. Nevertheless, this system imposed certain limitations, including the fact that a verse based on this formula cannot well contain a verb; yet the need for composing such verses was felt and was met in more than one way. A fair example centers on a parallel to *rád*, f., namely, *weg*, m. In the accusative singular of *weg* there will be no ending; hence any compound of *weg* in this grammatical case, where ending a verse, must be fitted into a metrical pattern other than C, one in which there will be place for a verb or some other important alliterating word at the beginning. The pertinent compounds of *weg* are *bæþ-*, *flód-*, *flot-*, and *hwæl-*, of which *bæþ-weg* is the most frequent combination. *Ofer bæþ-weg* occurs three times, always with some form of *brecan* in the sense 'pressing on across the sea': thus, *brecan ofer bæþ-weg* (*And* 223, *Ele* 244) and *brecaþ ofer bæþ-weg* (*And* 513), where the phrase *ofer bæþ-weg* combines with the alliterating verb to make a formula. The two *f*-compounds, *flód-* and *flot-weg*, serve their purpose in combination with *faran*. *Flód-weg* appears in an instrumental construction *fóron flód-wege* (*Exo* 106) '[the sailors] journeyed on or over the sea'; while in the accusative plural there is *Fór flód-wegas* (*Rid* 36, 9) '[it, probably a ship] traversed the seas.' With *on* the combination *flot-weg* appears in *faran on flot-weg* (*HbM* 42) '[was fated] to journey on the sea.' Finally comes *hwæl-weg*, in meaning identical with *hran-rád* of *Bwf* 10a and occurring in *hwetep on hwæl-weg* (*Sea* 63a) 'impels on [to?] the whale's route.' Beside offering various alliterative alternates this cluster of *weg*-formulas permits the inclusion of a verb in a single D-verse, an opportunity of which the singers were obviously glad to avail themselves.

I shall conclude this discussion of the formulaic character of the first 50 verses of *Béowulf* with a brief word on the first five verses (1a-3a) of the poem, where the singer appears to have adjusted, combined, and recombined a number of formulas. He begins with a formula much used to start songs or to introduce an important new section of a song, a formula built around the weakly exclamatory *hwæt* plus a personal pronoun. This is in effect a sort of filler-in, something to let the singer get going; the phrase, ordinarily metrically unstressed, opens the way to a B- or C-verse. The total system, embracing all personal pronouns in the nominative and a few in oblique cases, cannot be presented here, but looking at all instances of the subvariety *Hwæt, wé* (1a), collected on Chart I, one is struck by two points: (1) that in each case the singer includes his audience in assuming familiarity with the thematic material of his song,[14] and (2), more important, the fact that he is saying 'we have all

[14]See Dorothy Whitelock, *The Audience of Béowulf* (Oxford University Press, 1950), pp. 34-44 and ff. *passim* on audience-familiarity in gross and detail with the *Béowulf* stories and substories introduced for purposes of embellishment: the latter are not in any ordinary sense 'digressions.'

heard or learned about something or other,' at times adding that the events took place long ago. *Hīeran* is the verb favored in preserved song, with *frignan* of *Bēowulf* running (perhaps by chance), a poor second. It will be noticed that the singers ordinarily work in the important verbal idea 'hearing about,' 'learning about' in the course of the first two verses, but the *Bēowulf* singer introduced mention of the Spear-Danes (*Gār-Dena*) before proceeding farther. This apparently spoiled his chance of getting in a verb in what appears to be the favored or ordinary position in the first verse. Comparable to Cynewulf in *Ele* 397b, he might in some fashion have worked in a suitable verb in 1b, had there been such a one capable of *g*-alliteration, but at all events he next called upon one of the several available formulas expressing the idea 'long ago,' already discussed (p. 49, above) under *on gēar-dagum* (1b). Thus *gefrugnon* is put off to the fourth verse (2b), while the *hū* of the total phrase *wē gefrugnon hū* has to wait for the fifth (3a). The basic formula is all there and the singer has used every scrap of it, though not in what would appear to be the usual way. One might interpret this exceptional treatment as an example of a first-rate singer coping quickly and deftly with an almost awkward situation into which he had got himself, even though the resulting order of words is perhaps not quite natural. To suggest that this order of words is [in] any sense 'literary' is virtually to deny oral technique in the composition of the poem, a technique demonstrated in the preceding analysis of the first fifty verses of the poem. The traditional character of the recorded text is further borne out by the fact that at least fifteen per cent of the verses of the poem are to all intents and purposes repeated within the poem,[15] a phenomenon unthinkable in lettered tradition.

In the opening lines of *Bēowulf* are two formulas which must be called Christian: *Līf-frēa* (16b) and *wuldres Wealdend* (17a). Neither of these so-called kennings could well refer to anything but the Deity and hence could not have formed part of the traditional language of pre-Christian poetry. They must be relatively young and their presence in *Bēowulf* raises the general question of the relation of the language of Christian narrative poetry—by far the largest genre in the corpus—to the older traditional poetic language. There are no means of knowing when first a singer or singers started making songs based on such novel thematic material as that found in the Old Testament, Apocrypha, saints' lives, and homilies, but it cannot well have been before the arrival of Augustine in Kent in 597 and of Paulinus in York in 625, an influence fortified by the settlement of Aidan on Lindisfarne (Holy Island) off the Northumberland coast in 635. Yet somewhere in the neighborhood of 675 St. Aldhelm was quite possibly singing religious verse, interspersed among diverting secular songs, in public at Malmesbury in Wiltshire in order to get the local populace to stay on after mass for the sermon,[16] and sometime

---

[15]Communicated orally by Mr Robert P. Creed of Smith College, who is presently studying the oral style in *Bēowulf*.

[16]Reported by William of Malmesbury (d. 1125) in his *De Gestis Pontificum Anglorum* (ed. N. E. S. A. Hamilton, Rolls Ser. No. 52, London, 1870), Bk. V, Pt. 1 ('Life of Aldhelm'), p. 336, based on Alfred the Great's lost *Handbōc* (William's *Manuale, ed. cit.*, pp. 332-333):

'Litteris itaque ad plenum instructus nativae quoque linguae non negligebat carmina, adeo ut, teste libro Elfredi de quo superius dixi, nulla umquam aetate par ei fuerit quisquam. Poesim Anglicam posse facere, cantum componere, eadem apposite vel canere vel dicere.

between 658 and 680, the years during which Hild ruled as abbess of Whitby in the North Riding, the unlettered Cædman, farm-hand on the monastic estate, is said on first-rate authority[17] to have been successfully composing all sorts of songs based on Christian story. There is no way of learning more about Aldhelm's compositions but, as I hope to show elsewhere, Cædman was probably the father of nothing but his own songs and composed these against the background of a developed tradition.

In talking or thinking about the chronology, real or relative, of Anglo-Saxon poems one is notoriously treading on very swampy ground, but if one adopts the conservative view that a *Béowulf* song in form fairly close to the preserved performance had come into being not far from, say, 730 or even somewhat later, it is clear that by that time Christian poetry was a commonplace and that its recitation was a familiar form of entertainment not only in monasteries but in lay circles. Were this not the case, the recitation in Heorot of a song about the Creation (*Bwf* 90-98) would, as Dr Whitelock has recently pointed out, 'surely have been incongruous, or even ludicrous, if minstrels never sang on such themes to lay audiences.'[18] As it is, the Creation song seems to enjoy a status no different from that of songs sung about Sigemund and Fitela or the tragedy of Finn's stronghold in the same hall on another occasion. Indeed, apart from this, the entire fabric of *Béowulf* is shot through with the language and thought of Christianity and must be viewed as a Christian poem though of an unusual sort.[19]

Now, as Parry emphasizes, the traditional language of unlettered singers develops very, very slowly and over a long period of time and is created to

---

Denique commemorat Elfredus carmen triviale adhuc vulgo canitatur Aldelmum fecisse. . . . Populum eo tempore semibarbarum, parum divinis sermonibus intentum, statim cantatis missis domos cursitare solitum. Ideo sanctum virum super pontem qui rura et urbem continuat abeuntibus se opposuisse obicem quasi artem cantandi professum. Eo plus quam semel favorem et concursum emeritum. Hoc commento, sensim inter ludicra verbis Scripturarum insertis, cives ad sanitatem reduxisse.'

'And thus fully instructed in [Latin] literature he also did not neglect the songs of his native tongue, so that, according to Alfred's book of which I spoke above, at no time was anybody ever his equal. He was able to make English poetry, compose a melody, and properly sing or recite the same. Finally, Alfred remarks that Aldhelm composed a light song which was still [i.e., in Alfred's day] being commonly sung. . . . The people, at that time [about 675] semibarbarous and too little intent on divine discourses, were in the habit of hurrying to their homes after masses had been sung. Therefore, the holy man stationed himself on a bridge [over the Avon] which connects the town [of Malmesbury] and the countryside as an obstacle to those going away, as though professing the art of song. After he had done this several times [lit. 'more than once'] he gained the good-will and the attendance of the common people. By this device, gradually working in words of the Scriptures among entertaining words, he led the people back to right reason.'

It may be remarked that the Scriptural words introduced in the course of the recitation of secular poems need not have been in verse, though this is a reasonable inference. It should also be noted that nothing is said about writing despite the rendering 'write a poem' (*Poesim . . . facere*) of George F. Browne, *St. Aldhelm: His Life and Times* (London, 1903), p. 79.

[17] I refer not merely to Bede himself but to the tradition of the Whitby community on which Bede drew, surely completely reliable in this local matter, unless one assumes a monstrous conspiracy of falsification.

[18] Whitelock, *op. cit.*, p 9: on pp. 9-11 Whitelock is on the verge of suggesting what I suggest here.

[19] *Idem*, pp. 3-4: Klaeber, *ed. cit.*, p. xlix, *ad fin.*

deal only with traditional themes with which singers and audiences are in the main familiar. On his visits to Yugoslavia in 1950 and 1951 Professor Lord noted that the traditional singers were proving unable to cope with such radically new themes of a social-political nature as Marxism and related matters, for the simple reason that they lacked formulas necessary to express these new ideas in just measures of verse.

Except for rather obvious substitutions of key-words in an old formula (e.g. *engla Dryhten* for *eorla dryhten*), no one singer ever creates many new formulas and most of them never create any at all. Thus, standing on the threshold, so to speak, of the year 600, one might well have wondered whether and how Anglo-Saxon singers would be able to meet the challenge of adapting their traditional verses to the needs of singing about themes so different as Christian material would seem to be. In actual fact they did rise to this occasion and often magnificently.

A glance of Chart II (pp. 63-65) analyzing ll. 512-535 of *Christ and Satan*, a poem of appreciably later date than *Béowulf* and mainly telling a story of Christ's harrowing of hell, exhibits plainly the formulaic character of the language. If not as many verses are underlined as in Chart I, this can, in the case of the unmarked verses, only mean that the surviving corpus of Anglo-Saxon poetry does not happen to contain verses which furnish supporting evidence, that is, either exactly similar verses or, equally significant, verses constructed on closely similar formulaic patterns.

It will be unnecessary to take up the text of this chart in detail, for the supporting evidence will now be telling its own story. There are, however, two matters, quite different from one another, which the present passage brings to one's attention. The first concerns the 'Christianity' of the language of this and perhaps any other Christian poem, while the second concerns the possibility of occasionally making use of an understanding of the nature and function of the formula in textual criticism.

The prime point of interest in the sample of verse analyzed on Chart II lies in the fact that it is from a Christian poem. It is a passage treating a most central event in Christian belief, the Ascension of Jesus Christ, and in that sense at least could scarcely be more Christian as opposed to the opening verses of *Béowulf*. What, as far as the language is concerned, is Christian about it? Very largely references to God, specifically Jesus Christ. This passage of forty-six verses includes thirteen such references, more than one for every four verses: *wuldres Weard* (512a), *Meotod mann-cynnes* (513a), *Dryhten God* (514a), *engla Dryhten* (518b), *God* (522b), *Godes Sunu* (526b), *Sunu Meotodes* (527b), *se Éca* (530b), *Þéodne* (532a), *Scieppend engla* (533b), and *Dryhten* (535a). These are all in one way or another different from one another. In addition there are ten other 'Christian' words, that is, words which would normally only appear in a Christian context: Galilee is mentioned twice (522a, 529a), Simon called Peter twice (521b, 536b); there is one reference to the Holy Spirit (525b), two to the disciples (520b, 529b), and three to angels (518b, 520a, 533b), of which two occur as parts of kennings designating the Deity. In all these forty-six verses include twenty-three Christian words, or words used in a Christian way; thus there is one Christian word for every other verse or one for each typographical line. It might be hard to find a more 'Christian' passage, and for these words and formulas used in a Christian way only *giengran* lacks supporting evidence. This is no doubt due to the limits of the surviving corpus and, had the singer happened to have preferred formulas with the much more frequent equivalent of 'disciple,' namely *þegn*, it would probably be possible to collect no little supporting evidence.

In this so very Christian passage there may be a hint and more as to how Anglo-Saxon singers were able, apparently from early on, to sing in a slightly adjusted traditional language songs based on these novel and untraditional themes. In the first place and stated in most general terms, the Christian themes that the singers apparently liked best to sing about are in the main stories involving extraordinary and exciting adventures and events, such as the stories on which center Andreas, *Azarias, Daniel, Elene, Exodus, Judith,* and *Juliana.* To the ear of Anglo-Saxons not yet fully initiated in this new development most immediately striking and strange were no doubt the presence of non-Germanic proper nouns, names of persons such as Simon Peter and places such as Galilee. These could be and were, however, readily fitted into older formulas created to embody Germanic proper names, and since these strange new names were all but invariably accented on the first syllable, regardless of the stress in the original tongues, they offered few, if any, metrical problems to the singer. Some of them must have been awkwardly long and more than queer sounding, such as *Nabochodonossar*, used five times in *Daniel* (48, 411, 497, 618, 663) and once in *Azarias* (183) to form a complete A-type on-verse, yet the singers made do with them. Aside from the pre-Christian word *God* and elsewhere *Críst,* to be viewed as ordinary personal names, the singers had available from pre-Christian tradition, already evidently rich in words and kennings to express the idea of 'ruler,' a large number of expressions ready to take off the rack, available as substitutory epithets for the Deity. As a result of new formations on the analogy of the old, e.g., the weaving into compounds of such characteristically Christian word-elements as *heofon* and *wuldor,* the number of epithets for the Deity was increased to a point where this is by all odds the largest single group of kennings in the poetical corpus.[20] The frequency and hence importance of this group can scarcely be overestimated. The concept 'angel' is new as is the loan-word *engel,* an idea also capable of being expressed by the old word *gást.* The Latin titles *Sanctus* and *Beatus* were easily handled by the old words *hálig* (originally 'inviolate') and *éadig* ('favored by fortune,' 'prosperous'). Expression of general conceptions of theology, dogma, and Christian doctrine is notably rare in the Christian songs,[21] as it is in *Béowulf,* where action predominates, and even in that most beautiful song of meditation or devotion, *The Dream of the Rood.* This lack is surely due neither to mere accident nor to ignorance or indifference, but to a lack of formulas capable of adaptation to such ideas. The lyrically keyed poem on the Advent (*Christ I*) and the song on the Ascension (*Christ II*), based on the latter part of Pope Gregory the Great's Ascension homily, are both traditional in diction and adhere pretty strictly to narrative.[22]

---

[20]See Hendrik van der Merwe Scholtz, *The Kenning in Anglo-Saxon and Old-Norse Poetry* (Utrecht-Nijmegen, 1929), pp. 92-98, and Hertha Marquardt, *Die altenglischen Kenningar,* etc. (Schriften der Königsberger gelehrten Gesellschaft, XIV, 3, Halle, 1938), pp. 269-292, and cp. *ibid.,* pp. 266 ff. *passim* (§D 'Christliche Begriffe').

[21]Cp. Klaeber, *ed. cit.,* p. xlix, *ad init.*

[22]P.S. Mr Robert E. Diamond, presently engaged in the study of 'The Diction of the

It would be wrong to suggest that the adaptation of the traditional language of the ancient poetry to this new and different thematic material did not take doing on the part of the singers or to withhold from them full credit for the successful exercise of what at the outset particularly must have called for skill and ingenuity. It is, however, fair to point out, in view of the obviously traditional language of the Christian poems—a matter that in essence has long since been noticed and stressed—that the singers did not make things unnecessarily hard for themselves by attempting to sing about matters for the expression of which the old diction would have been inadequate. As it was singers and audience probably felt little difference between the general style and narrative technique of, say, *Béowulf* and *Christ and Satan*, to mention two poems of very different thematic backgrounds. This marked uniformness or unity of style is largely to be accounted for by the continuity of the traditional formulaic language of the Anglo-Saxon singers, a continuity that seems to live until the Norman Conquest.

Many factors, political and social as well as linguistic, probably contributed to the death of the traditional poetry after the Conquest, and one must also reckon with the difficulties, probably insuperable, which the relatively swift introduction of ideas and activities incidental to the advent of the feudal age brought in their train, ideas which could not easily be sidestepped by singers trying to sing in the old tradition and for which they had no formulas.

Quite by chance the present passage from *Christ and Satan* offers an opportunity to consider the general possibility of the use of an understanding of the role of the formula in occasional matters of textual criticism. Verse 513b, with the manuscript reading *ǽr on morgen* (A), 'early in the morning,' technically violates a basic principle of alliteration in that the first downbeat or ictus in the off-verse does not here alliterate with the preceding on-verse where the alliteration is *m*. Acting on a suggestion of Professor Holthausen, Professor M. D. Clubb emended this verse in his edition of 1925 to read *on morgen ǽr*, thus producing which he rightly described as a normal (B) verse. Nevertheless, in the light of the supporting evidence which demonstrates the existence of a formula *ǽr on morgen*, taken together with the phrase *on ǽr-morgen*, with which may also be compared *mid ǽr-dǽge* of similar meaning, one may wonder whether the singer did not himself violate the usual procedures of alliteration in order to make use of a formula that he needed, a formula or system in which *ǽr* preceded the word it modified. Consequently, one might do well, not only here but in other similar situations, to test such alliteratively defective verses for their formulaic character before embarking on a course of emendation, however much better emendation may make, or may seem to make, matters. If given time to think his verse over, in a word to compose at a more leisurely pace, a singer might well agree with what a

Signed Poems of Cynewulf (Harvard thesis in preparation) tells me (30 April 1953) that 20 per cent of the 5194 verses (i.e., 2598 numbered typographic lines of the editions) in the signed poems of Cynewulf are repeated in the signed poems themselves. A series of samples, amounting to 581 verses (including the entire *Fates of the Apostles*, the runic passages in the other three poems, and several 15-20 line samples chosen at random from the other three poems), checked against the entire Anglo-Saxon poetical corpus, shows 30.8 per cent of repeated verses, and 61.1 per cent of verses, of which parts, by virtue of recurrence elsewhere, demonstrate themselves to be formulaic.

modern editor was proposing to do; on the other hand, such an emendation might produce a sequence of words which would strike him as stranger than the technical defect in versification.

If this discussion of manuscript *ær on morgen* suggests that it should be left regardless of the technical imperfection that its use and retention produces, the case of manuscript *on þæm fæstenne* (519a) would seem to speak in favor of emendation to *of þæm fæstenne*, 'from, out of the tomb,' an emendation adopted by certain earlier editors, though not by Clubb or Krapp, last to edit the poem. The supporting evidence on Chart II exhibits two expressions, one with *fram* or *of*, meaning 'from or out of the prison, stronghold or tomb,' the other with *on*, always except here with the obvious meaning 'in the prison, stronghold or tomb.' Now it is true that Old-English uses expressions with *on* which are convenient to render by 'from,' generally in connection with removing something from a surface on which the object in question is lying or reposing (see B.T. *s.v.* 'on,' III, 2). From the Anglo-Saxon point of view *on* is in these cases entirely appropriate, though the approach to the act is different from ours. It is as if one said 'he took the pencil on the table,' that is, 'he took the pencil which was lying on the table,' in the sense that he took it from the table. When Grendel assails *Béowulf*, it is said that the troll *nam . . . rinc on ræste* (ll. 746-47), 'took the warrior from his resting place.' This is, however, far from saying that OE *on* means 'from'; it is simply to say that the image of the action is different. In the verse in *Christ and Satan* such an image would in the nature of things be highly unlikely if not out of the question altogether. The singer must be trying to say that Our Lord went out of the tomb and thus it is all but certain that the manuscript *on* does not go back to the words of the singer or to anybody who was giving attention to the thought but to a miscopying by a scribe somewhere along the line of written transmission. If this is so, then in the small verbal matter of the preposition, manuscript *on*, the supporting evidence involving *on*'s does not support the manuscript reading, but rejects it rather.

The future is full of many problems involving a reappraisal of certain aspects of Anglo-Saxon poetical style and compositional technique and what these are, or at present seem likely to be, can here be merely adumbrated. First of all let it be said that, if further study of the formulaic character of the poetry is to be conducted in a thoroughgoing way, the first and most crying need is the construction of a concordance of the entire poetical corpus; without this the collecting of supporting evidence to test the formulaic character of a given verse or group of verses will prove to be incredibly laborious and often uncertain.[23]

More sample analyses of narrative verse are certainly desirable, though it

---

[23]For any comparative study of Old-Germanic formulaic diction concordances are equally needed for the Old-Norse Edda-type verse (*Eddukvæði* of Mod. Icel. parlance) and for the Old-Saxon corpus (see n. 27, below).

Efficient techniques for concordance-making have been worked out by Professor Emeritus Lane Cooper of Cornell University and are set forth in considerable detail in 'The Making and the Use of a Verbal Concordance,' *Sewanee Review* XXVII (1919), 188-206, esp. pp. 191-195, reprinted in his *Evolution and Repentance* (Ithaca, N. Y., 1935), esp. pp. 24-33. See also his 'Instructions for Preparing the Slips,' three pages, inserted in *A Concordance to the Works of Horace* (Washington, D. C., 1916). No concordance should ever be attempted without consulting these writings.

seems doubtful that any narrative poem will be found to be non-traditional in language. Particularly interesting will be a study from this point of view of the diction of the rather small body of lyrical-elegaic poetry. One might suspect that lyrical composition would call for formulas not elsewhere used and that for many of the verses there would be little or no supporting evidence of their formulaic character, due to the limited size of the body of lyric-elegaic verse. The same may be said of the literary *Riddles* of the *Exeter Book,* a genre new to the Anglo-Saxons and a direct imitation of Latin enigmas, specifically those 685-705? of Aldhelm, of which two are translated into Old English. At least some of the language of the *Riddles* is traditional, since verses from these appear in the support-evidence in the charts above, but it may turn out that many riddles, often very short compositions, were composed word by word. And what of the verses that embody runes other than isolated logograms (e.g., *éðel* and *mann*), notably Cynewulf's signature passages?[24]

Mention of Cynewulf raises a question concerning the relation between lettered persons and orally composed poetry. Not all Anglo-Saxon Christian poetry needs to have been composed by lettered singers—witness the story of Cædman. Any good unlettered singer who had translated for, or expounded to, him the *Apocryphal Gospel of St. Matthew and St. Andrew* could easily have composed *Andreas.* But Cynewulf was surely a lettered person, else how could he have conceived a plan to assure mention of his name in prayers by means of runic signatures which depend on a knowledge of spelling and reading for their efficacy?[25] If, however, the narrative parts of his poems prove on testing to be formulaic, one must assume that those parts at least he composed in the traditional way. That he subsequently got them written down, whether dictating to himself, as it were, or to another person—possibly a more convenient procedure—is beside the point. In any event there would be no conflict with, or contradiction to, tradition.[26]

A different view will, I think, have to be taken of the significance or lack of significance of phrasal similarities between this and that poem and poems than has prevailed up to now.[27] Certain verbal similarities among poems may in a

[24]P.S. Mr. Diamond further informs me that the four verse paragraphs which include the runic signatures (72 typographic lines in all), checked against the entire Anglo-Saxon poetical corpus, show 25.6 per cent of repeated verses and 52.7 per cent of verses, of which parts, by virtue of recurrence elsewhere, show themselves to be formulaic.

[25]From *Juliana* 718b-22 it is clear that the poem was intended for recitation (*þe þis giedd wrece*) and that a prayer was hoped for from a singer rather than some indefinite reading public. Does this suggest that Anglo-Saxon poems got put on record primarily for memorization by a class of later, memorizing entertainers, answering somewhat to the Greek rhapsodes of post-oral times? One thinks here of Asser's familiar ch. 23 (ed. W. H. Stevenson, p. 20, notes on p. 221) where we are told that Alfred learned by heart native poems read aloud to him by his mother.

[26]On oral-formulaic verse making by lettered persons see Parry II, 29, and Bowra, *op. cit.,* esp. pp. 370-372.

[27]E.g., Klaeber, *ed. cit.,* pp. cx-cxiii. For a competent survey of thought on 'the testimony of the parallels' see Claes Schaar, *Critical Studies in the Cynewulf Group* (Lund Studies in English, XVII, Lund, 1949), pp. 235 ff. Over sixty years ago J. Kail, 'Über die Parallelstellen in der angelsächsischen Poesie,' *Anglia,* XII (1889-90), 21-40, was clearly nearer right than he lived to know. In the case of Old Saxon poetry a start was made by Eduard Sievers in his ed. of the *Hêliand* (Halle, 1878) through his very comprehensive though inconveniently arranged 'Formelverzeichnis,' pp. 391-463, a reference for which I am most grateful to Professor Ferdinand Mossé of the Collège de France.

sense represent borrowing from one poem to another, for traditional singers perforce learn from other singers. But one verbal similarity or even a number of verbal similarities in themselves prove nothing beyond suggesting that given singers have found the same formulas useful to express a certain idea in a similar measure of verse. To quote Parry, 'Plagiarism is not possible in traditional literature. One oral poet is better than another not because he has by himself found a more striking way of expressing his thought, but because he has been better able to make use of the tradition.'[28] When by the aid of a concordance we gradually get to know what the Anglo-Saxon formulas are and what, indeed, constitute their dimensions[29] and the like, it will perhaps be possible to begin to detect individual styles. Apart from general over-all organization of material, the broad architectonics of a given poem, a singer's individuality will, as in other traditional poetry, presumably emerge in rather small matters,[30] verbal and stylistic, and will not be revealed by the large and rather obvious components known to all or almost all singers.

Lack of truly early material will preclude our ever knowing much about the relative age of the formulas encountered in the preserved poems, but perhaps something can be done with verses containing words which in earlier times had suffered contraction, either from the simple contraction of two vowels (as *dón* < *dó-an*) or as a secondary result of the loss of intervocalic *h* (as *héan* < *héahan*).[31] The poetry abounds in such verses as *héan landes* (*Gen* 2854b) which, if pronounced as they almost surely were pronounced in later times, were metrically deficient though at the time created they formed metrically regular verses: *héahan landes* (A). The becoming unmetrical of such a verse would have been a gradual process and singers would naturally have hung on

[28]Parry II, 13.

[29]Parry I, 84-85, n. 3, would for Homeric verse regard as a formula or a possible formula nothing less than four words or five syllables, a restriction that could not be applied to Anglo-Saxon verse.

[30]I am thinking of such small points as the *þe* of the formula *þe hit riht ne wæs* (*Mal* 190) contrasted to the *swá*'s of the parallel formula in *Gen* 901, *Vainglory* 61, with *gerisne* (*Gen* 1564) *gedéfe* (*PPs* 105, 22; *Met* 26, 90), *gepíewe* (*Bwf* 2331), references for which I am grateful to Dr. Randolph Quirk of University College, London. Without the negative cp. *Bwf* 561, 1670 (with *gedéfe*).

[31]For a somewhat analogous phenomenon see Parry II, 10, 30-31, and *idem*, 'Traces of the Digamma in Ionic and Lesbian Greek,' *Language*, X (1934), 130-144, esp. 131 and n. 6, for reference to *Béowulf*. See also Whitelock, *op. cit.*, p. 27 and n. 1, for general observations on intervocalic *h* and for references. Since the formulas in which contracted forms occur are, like the rest of the diction, traditional, their occurrence can tell us little about the age of a text in which they appear.

P.S. In his splendid and welcome edition *Béowulf with the Finnesburg Fragment* (Boston; Heath, 1953; 2d ed., London: Harrap, 1958), Professor C. L. Wrenn has taken the revolutionary step of decontracting the various contracted forms over which previous editors have placed a circumflex (see pp. 31-32), e.g., *fré[ge]a* (16b) for manuscript *fréa*, *dó[a]n* (1116b) for manuscript *dón*. Were there any evidence that such words (discussed in Luick, §§242-249, pp. 218-226) were pronounced as if uncontracted at the time when the text was first committed to writing, one would welcome such a procedure, however daring, as restoring the meter of otherwise metrically deficient verses (for literature see Luick §242, nn. 2-3, p. 219). But the phenomenon of contraction had almost surely quite run its course by, say, 650. (See Luick, §249, pp. 225-226: after the working of *i*-umlaut; for a few exceptional survivals of sorts see Sievers-Brunner, 2d ed., §218, 3, p. 197; Northumbrian *dóan*'s and the like are late and are analogical restorations comparable to Mod. Icel. *smáum* for *smám* of the old language and do not help here.)

to it as long as possible, down, in fact, to the time when the contraction-process had long since been completed. This would suggest that later-day singers and their audiences became habituated to such metrical irregularities and accepted these 'deficient' verses as traditional.[32] This matter might profitably be further explored.

Just as the half-hexameter is the basis of most Homeric formulas, so is the single verse that of Old-Germanic poetry. But in the Homeric poems there are also whole-line formulas[33] answering in a sense apparently to such Anglo-Saxon verse-pair formulas as *on þǽm dæge þisses lífes* (*Bwf* 197, 790, 806), *þæs oferéode: þisses swá mæg* (*Déo* 7, 13, 17, 20, 42), and *siþþan of líc-haman lǽded wǽre* (Vercelli *SlB* 21) with which cp. *Bwf* 3177, where *of líc-haman lǽded weorðan* is almost surely the right reading (cp. *Jul* 670a).

Oral singers are often faced with situations where enjambement is required,[34] and the Anglo-Saxon singers appear to be no exception. *Béowulf* offers at least one interesting example where enjambement is accomplished with the aid of a two-verse formula: *ende gebíden / weorolde lífes* (*Bwf* 1386b-87a, 2342b-43a); Dr Whitelock has already pointed out how the formula *God éaðe mæg* (*Bwf* 478b, *And* 425b, *Chr* 173b) operates in this situation.[35]

There is perhaps much that will never be known about the origin and special function, if any, of the expanded or hypermetric verses, but a casual survey suggests that, whereas the second measure of each such verse seems to be formulaic and out of its context would form a complete verse, the organization of the first measure would appear to be somewhat different, perhaps somewhat less rigid in structure, thus perhaps allowing the singer certain freedoms not available in a normal verse. Here, too, a concordance will be necessary for further study of the character of these first measures.[36]

At the end of these rather miscellaneous remarks on possible problems of the future, problems which will require the thought of many persons to test and solve, I should like to comment on the possible relation of one aspect of the physical preservation of our Anglo-Saxon poems that may reflect their oral background, namely, the fact of their all being written out as prose. It is a not uncommon view that this method was employed as a measure of economy, that the vernacular poetry was perhaps felt not quite worth, or worthy of, as much parchment as writing the poetry out as we today print it would require. I find it hard to believe this to be the case and suspect it was written as prose merely because neither scribes nor singers understood in a formal sense the metrics of the verse, even when they may have had an understanding of Latin verse studied in monastic schools. That tenth-eleventh century scribes at times separate verses (not our typographical lines) by dots may merely reflect a

---

[32]See Parry II, 22-23, n. 1, for instances in Homeric verse where the retention of a formula leads to a violation of meter.

[33]Parry, 'Whole Formulaic Verses in Greek and Southslavic Heroic Song,' *Transactions of the American Philological Association*, LXIV (1933), 179-197.

[34]See Lord, 'Homer and Huso III: Enjambement in Greek and Southslavic Song,' *ibid.*, LXXXIX (1948), 113-124.

[35]*Op. cit.*, p. 10. This formula is a phase of the system *x éaðe mæg*; cp. *B* 2764 *sinc éaðe mæg*. There are other systems with forms of *magan* to express the idea of the possibility of something happening or being done.

[36]An impetus to a revaluation of the expanded verses has recently been given by Benno J. Timmer, 'Expanded Lines in Old-English Poetry,' *Neophilologus*, XXXV (1951), 226-230.

feeling for the basic rhythm, the onset of a down-beat, comparable to a musically unschooled person's tapping time with foot or finger though knowing nothing of the writing of music or of musical composition.

CHART I
(Béowulf, ll. 1-25)

Hwæt wé Gár-Dena   on géar-dagum
þéod-cyninga   þrymm gefrugnon,
hú þá æðelingas   ellen fremedon.
Oft Scield Scéafing   sceaðena þréatum,
5   manigum mægðum   medu-setla oftéah,
egesode Eorle,   siþþan ǽrest wearþ
féasceaft funden;   hé þæs frófre gebád,
wéox under wolcnum,   weorþ-myndum þáh,
oþ-þæt him ǽghwelć   ymbsittendra
10   ofer hran-ráde   híeran scolde,
gamban gieldan;   þæt wæs gód cyning!
Þǽm eafora wæs   æfter cenned
geong on geardum,   þone God sende
folce to frófre;   firen-þearfe ongeat
15   þe híe ǽr drugon   ealdorléase
lange hwíle;   him þæs Líf-fréa,
wuldres Wealdend   weorold-áre forgeaf
Béow wæs bréme   —blǽd wíde sprang—
Scieldes eafora   Sceden-landum on.
20   Swá sceal geong guma   góde gewyrćan
framum feoh-giftum   on fæder bearme
þæt hine on ielde   eft gewunien
will-gesíðas   þanne wíg cume,
léode gelǽsten;   lof-dǽdum sceal
25   on mǽgða gehwǽm   man geþéon.

SUPPORTING EVIDENCE

1a-2b Hwæt, wé feorr and néah / gefrigen habbaþ (*Exo* 1), Hwæt, wé gefrugnon / on fyrn dagum (*And* 1); Hwæt, wé þæt gehíerdon / þurh hálge béć (*FAp* 63, *Ele* 364, 852); Hwæt, wé éac gehíerdon / be Ióhanne (*FAp* 23); Hwæt, wé nú gehíerdon / hú þæt Hǽlu-bearn (*Chr* 586, *with whose* gehíerdon cp. *Bwf* 2b-3a gefrugnon hú); Hwæt, wé híerdon oft / þæt se hálige wer (*Glc* 108); Hwæt, wé þæt gehíerdon / hæleþ eahtian (*Jul* 1); Hwæt, wé Ebréisce ǽ leornodon / þá on fyrn-dagum fæderas cúðon (*Ele* 397-98), 1b *XSt* 367, *Wan* 44. Cp. *Chr* 251 þe on géar-dagum; *Bwf* 1354 þone on géar-dagum, 2233 swá híe on géar-dagum. *Note also instrum. use without* on: *And* 1519 giefum géar-dagum; *Ele* 290 þæt gé géar-dagum, 834 swá hie géar-dagum (*also Bwf* 2233). *Note closely related formulas:* on fyrn-dagum, on ǽr-dagum, *and* on eald-dagum (*Chr* 303, *SFt* 1). **2a** *Nom. pl. Gen* 1965 þéod-cyningas / þrymme mićele; *gen. sg. Bwf* 2694 þá ić æt þearfe gefrægn / þéod-cyninges; *FAp* 18 Ne þréodode hé fore þrymme / þéod-cyninges; *Edw* 34 þæs-þe þearf wæs / þæs þéod-cyninges. **2b** *See 1-2 above for combination of formulas to express the idea of 'having heard or learned long ago.'* **3a** *FAp* 3 hú þá æðelingas / ellen cýðon, 85 þus þá æðelingas; *Rid* 49, 7 þá æðelingas. *Cp. without def. art. but with a preceding word, usually of light stress Gen* 1059 þára-þe æðelingas, 1647 þá nú æðelingas, 1868 ellor æðelingas; *Dan* 689, *And*

805 þǽr æðelingas, 857 *Him þá æðelingas.* **3b** *And* 1208 Scealt þú, Andréas, / ellen fremman. **4b** *Jul* 672 sceaðena þréate; *cp. Glc* 902 féonda þréatum. **5a** *Bwf* 75 manigre mǽgðe, 1771 manigum mǽgða. **6b** *Bwf* 1947; cp. 1775 siþþan Grendel wearþ; *Ele* 913 siþþan furðum wéox. *Note the more general metrical scheme involving siþþan plus a two- or three-syllable word plus verb: And* 1223 siþþan ge-ypped wæs; *Ele* 18 siþþan wǽpen ahóf, 841 siþþan béacen geseah; *Bwf* 1077, 2124 siþþan morgen (mergen) cóm, 1233 siþþan / ǽfen cóm, 1689 siþþan flód ofslóg. **7a** *Cp. And* 181 onfindaþ féasceaftne. **8a** *Gen* 1702 wéox þá under wolcnum; cp. *Bwf* 714 Wód under wolcnum; *Phx* 27 wrídaþ under wolcnum; *Gen* 1438 wǽre under wolcnum; *Phx* 247 awierde under wolcnum. **8b** *Exo* 258 weorþ-myndum spræc. **9a** *Ele* 865 oþ-þæt him gecýðe, 885 oþ-þæt him uppan. **9b** *Bwf* 2734, *Ele* 33. *Cp. other inflections: dat. pl.* ymbsittendum *PPs* 78, 4; 88, 35; *fem. acc. pl. Met* 35, 14 ymbsittenda. *Cp. closely related Gen* 2490 ymbstandendra; *PPs* 140, 4 ymbstandende. **10a** *Gen* 205 geond hran-ráde; *And* 266, 821 on hran-ráde. *Cp. Bwf* 200, *Ele* 996 ofer swan-ráde; *Jul* 675 on swan-ráde; *Bwf* 1429 on segl-ráde. **10b** *Dan* 135; *Ele* 367; *Met* 9, 45; *Met* 1, 31 híeran scoldon. **11a** *Gen* 1977b-78a níede scoldon, / gamban gieldan. **11b** *Bwf* 863, 2390. *Cp. Bwf* 1885 þæt wæs án cyning; *Jul* 224 þæt is sóþ cyning; *Déo* 23 þæt wæs grimm cyning; *Wíd* 67 Næs þæt sǽne cyning, *and further Bwf* 1075 þæt wæs geómru ides, 1812 þæt wæs módig secg; *Met* 26, 35 (?) þæt wæs geó cyning, *etc.* **12a** *Gen* 1188 Se eafora wæs / Énoc háten. *Note and cp. Bwf* 12a-b eafora . . . cenned *with Gen* 1159 þá wearþ on éðle / eafora féded, 2394 of idese biþ / eafora wæcned. **12b** *Cp. Cæd* 8 æfter téode; *Rid* 40, 44 and ić giestran geong cenned. **13a** *Phx* 355, 647; *Chr* 201 geongre on geardum. *Cp. Jul* 35 geong on gáste; *Bwf* 2446 geong on gealgan. **13b** *Dan* 525 þe þider God sende; cp. *Gen* 1371 Dryhten sende. **14a** *Exo* 88; *And* 606; *Ele* 1142; *Men* 228 folcum to frófre; *Ele* 502 folca to frófre; *Rid* 39, 19 manigum to frófre; *Men* 57, *Ps 50* 148 mannum to frófre. **15a** *Bwf* 831, 1875; *Chr* 615 þe wé ǽr drugon; *Jud* 158 þe gé lange drugon. **15b** *Cp. Bwf* 2935; *And* 405 hláfordléase. *Ealdorléas is ordinarily used in the sense 'lifeless.'* **16a** *Bwf* 2159, 2780; *Dan* 660; *DrR* 24; *Jul* 674; *Rid* 28, 9; *Met* 4, 46. *For numerous formulas to express a 'long' or 'short time' cp. DrR* 70 góde hwíle, *also* mićele, lýtle, sume hwíle, *and with* þráge: ealle, lýtle, lange, sume, *also* ǽnige stunde. **16b** *Cp. Exo* 271 and éow Líf-fréa; *Chr* 27 hwanne ús Líf-fréa. **17a** *Bwf* 183, 1752; *Dan* 14; *And* 193, 539. **18a** *Sol* 182 Saloman wæs brémra; *Dan* 104 Þá wæs bréme; *Sol* 238 béć sind bréme. **18b** *FAp* 6 Lof wíde sprang; *cp. Bwf* 1588 hráw wíde sprang; *Jul* 585 Léad wíde sprang; *also Max I* 194 wíde gesprungen. **19a** *Bwf* 897 Wælses eafora; 1847 Hréðles eaforan; *Gen* 1133 Séthes eafora, 2054 Þáres eafora; *Met* 26, 36 Ióbes ('Jove's') eafora; *Men* 136 Zebedes eafora. *Cp. also Gen* 1578 eafora Nóes, 2834 eafora Þáres. **19b** *Bwf* 2357 Frís-landum on; *Gen* 1052 éast-landum on. *Cp. Jul* 83 wín-(wynn?) burgum on. **20a** *Bwf* 1172, 1534 Swá sceal man dôn; *cp.* 2066 Swá sceal mǽg dôn, 2590 swá sceal ǽghwelć mann. **21b** *Cp. Bwf* 35, *Exo* 375 on bearm scipes, 896 bær on bearm scipes, 214 on bearm nacan. *Note related formula with* fæðm: *Bwf* 188 and to Fæder fæðmum; *Max II* 661 on Fæder fæðm; *And* 616 on banan fæðme; *Ele* 765 on dracan fæðme. **22a-b** *Cp. FoM* 60 and on ielde eft / éadig weorðan. **22b** *See* 22a-b, *also Phx* 481 lang gewunien. **23a** *Gen* 2003. **25a** *Pre* 74 þá-þe hér on mǽgðe gehwǽm.

CHART II

(Christ and Satan, ll. 512-35)

Swá wuldres Weard   wordum sægde,

Meotod mann-cynnes,   ǽr on morgen,

þæs-þe Dryhten God   of déaðe árás.

515   Næs nán þæs stranglić   stán gefæstnod,

> þéah hé wǽre mid írne   eall ymbfangen
> þæt meahte þǽm miċelan   mægene wiþhabban,
> ac Hé út éode,   engla Dryhten
> on þǽm fæstenne.   And gefetian hét
> 520 englas eall-beorhte   endleofan giengran,
> and húru secgan hét   Símon Pétre
> þæt hé móste on Galiléam   God sċéawian,
> éċne and trumne,   swá hé ǽr dyde.
> Þá iċ gangan gefrægn   giengran ætsamme
> 525 ealle to Galiléam;   hæfdon Gástes blǽd,
> (ongéaton) háligne   Godes Sunu
> swá híe gesáwon,   hwǽr Sunu Meotodes
> þá on upp (a-?) stód,   éċe Dryhten
> God on Galiléam.   To þæs giengran þider
> 530 ealle urnon,   þǽr se Éċa wæs.
> Féollon on foldan,   to fótum hnigon;
> þancodon Þéodne   þæt hit þus gelamp
> þæt híe sċéawodon   Sċieppend engla.
> Þá sóna spræc   Símon Pétrus:
> "Eart þú þis, Dryhten,   dómes geweorðod?"

SUPPORTING EVIDENCE

512a *XSt* 659. *Cp. Gen* 941 Híe þá wuldres Weard; *And* 596 hú ús wuldres Weard; *Ele* 84 (beseoh) on wuldres Weard; *Chr* 527 þá wæs wuldres Weard. **512b** *Gen* 707, 2053, 2704, *Glc* 451. *Cp. Exo* 377, *Phx* 425 wordum secgaþ; *And* 624 wordum gesecgan; *Chr* 64 wordum sægdon; *Bwf* 2795 wordum secge. **513a** *Sat* 457, *Gen* 459, *And* 172, 357, 446. **513b** *Frag. Ps* 5, 3; *also cp. PPs* 107, 2, 118, 148 on ǽrmergen, *PPs* 62, 7 and on ǽrmergen; *Met* 28, 37; *PPs* 56, 10 and iċ on ǽrmergene. **514a** *XSt* 313 mid Dryhtne Gode; *And* 1281 Geseoh nú Dryhten God, 1462 Þá cóm Dryhten God; *Pan* 55 Swá is Dryhten God; *Bwf* 181 ne wisson híe Dryhten God; *Jud* 300 him féng Dryhten God; *LPr* 3 18 Críst, Dryhten God. *Cp.* God Dryhten *in And* 897 Nú iċ God Dryhten, *Ele* 759 Þæs þú, God Dryhten; *also* Dryhten Críst *in Glc* 592 gief éow Dryhten Críst; *Sol* 337 Dryhtne Críste. **514b** *Ele* 187; *FAp* 56 þæt hé of déaðe arás; *Chr* 467 fram déaðe arás. **515a** *Cp. Chr* 241 for-þon n'is ǽnig þæs horsc; *GfM* 8 Ne biþ ǽnig þæs / earfoþ-sǽlig; *Sea* 39 For-þon n'is þæs mód-wlanc. **515b** *Cp. Jul* 499 folde (*subj.*) gefæstnod. **516b** *XSt* 143b (*cp.* 145a selfe mid sange); *cp. Bwf* 2691 heals eallne ymbeféng. **518b** *Exo* 559; *XSt* 395; *Sol* 462. **519a** *Wha* 71; *And* 1034 fram þǽm fæstenne, 1177 of fæstenne; *cp. Gen* 2536, *And* 1068 to þǽm fæstenne; *Sol.* 320 on fæstenne; *Met* 1, 79 né on þǽm fæstenne. **519b** *Gen* 525 and meċ hér standan hét; *XSt* 521 and húru secgan hét; *And* 330 and ús féran hét, 587 and wendan hét; *Bwf* 3095 and éowiċ grétan hét. *Cp. with subordination: Gen* 1865 oþ-þæt hé lǽdan hét; *And* 823 Þá gelǽdan hét, 931 swá iċ þeċ féran hét; *Ele* 863 ǽr hé asettan hét, *also* 129 arǽran hét. *With finite verb first: Gen* 2667 hét him fetian tó; *Ele* 1160, *Jul* 60 hét þá gefetian; *Bwf* 2190a-b hét . . . inn fetian. **520a** *Chr* 880; *Aza* 52 engel ealle-beorhta; *Dan* 336 engel eall-beorht. *For this formula used to connect a verse-pair of consecutive off- and on-verses see Chr* 506 Gesáwon híe eall-beorhte / englas twégen, 548 þæt him eall-beorhte / englas togéanes. **521a** *see* 519b, *above.* **521b** *XSt* 534b Símon Pétrus. **522a-b** *Cp.* 529a. **522b** *For* sċéawian *with preceding object entering into the alliteration: see Gen* 979 (tíber), 1679 (weorc), 1780, 1920 (land), 2595 (wíċ), *Chr* 1136 (weorod), 1206 (dolg), *Rid* 59, 2 (menn); *Bwf* 840, 3032 (wundor), 1391 (gang), 1413 (wang), 2402 (dracan), 2744 (hord). **523a** *Cp. Chr* 1071 éċe and edgeong. **523b** *Gen* 1840; *XSt* 116, 278. *Cp. Chr* 1233 swá híe geworhton ǽr, 161 þá þú geworhtest ǽr. **524a** *Gen* 2060 þá iċ néðan gefrægn; *And* 1706 Þá iċ lǽdan gefrægn; *cp. Sol* 179 Hwæt, iċ flítan gefrægn. **525b** *Cp. Phx* 549 þurh gástes blǽd; *XSt* 644 gemunan Gástes blǽd; **526b** *Gen* 1163 Enoses sunu; *XSt* 118 Wealdendes Sunu. *Bwf* 1009 Healf-Denes sunu; 2602, 2862, 3076 Wéoh-stánes sunu: *Wal I,* 11 Ælf-heres sunu. *For the closely parallel and more common patronymic formula* sunu X's *see* 527b. **527b** *XSt* 142 þær Sunu Meotodes, 172 Sunu Meotodes; *And* 881 Swelċe wé gesáwon / for Sunu Meotodes; *Ele* 1318 and to Suna Meotodes, 461, 564 sóþ Sunu Meotodes, 474 hú híe Sunu Meotodes, 686 þurh Sunu Meotodes. *Cp. XSt* 394 Sunu Wealdendes. *With the substitution of various personal names cp.: Gen* 1064 (Enoses), 1081, 1086 (Lámeches), 1240 (Nóes), 2465 (Arones); *Bwf* 524 (Béan-stánes), 590 (Ecg-láfes), 645, 1040 (Healf-Denes), *etc. For a patronymic formula centering on* eafora *see Chart I,* 19b. **528a** *Cp. And* 443 Hwílum upp astód, *and note other combinations of* upp *and* astandan *in Grein-Holthausen-Köhler, suggesting the XSt* 530a *Ms.* stod *should, perhaps, be emended to* astód *vs.* gestód *of the editors.* **528b** *Frag. Ps.* 5, 1, 3; *PPs* 53, 4; 70, 18, 20; 71, 19; 73, 17; 78, 1, *etc.; Cæd* 4; *and in inflected cases as follows: gen. sg. Bru* 16, *Men* 12 éċes Dryhtnes; *Gen* 7, 1885; *Chr* 396, 711; *Phx* 600; *PPs* 67, 3, 9; 68, 29 éċan Dryhtnes; *dat. sg. Bwf* 2796 éċum Dryhtne, 1779, 2330 éċan Dryhtne; *acc. sg. PPs* 55, 9; 65, 1, 3, 7 éċne Dryhten; *Bwf* 1692 éċan Dryhten.

530a *Cp. PPs* 61, 4 wíde urnon. **531a** *XSt* 544 féolon to foldan, *And* 918 Féoll þá to foldan; *Bwf* 2975 féoll on foldan. *Cp. Phx* 74 Ne feallaþ þǽr on foldan; *Sol.* 298 afielleþ hine on foldan. **531b** *Cp. Gen* 2441 þá to fótum [féoll / on foldan] Loth; *Mal* 119 þæt him æt fótum féoll. **532a** *Glc* 778, *and cp. with object (usually God) first: Dan* 86, *And* 1011, *Ele* 1138, *Bwf* 1397 Gode þancode; *Bwf* 227, 1626 Gode þancode; *Note the combined formulas of Ele* 961-62, *Bwf* 625-26 Gode þancode . . . þæs(-þe) hire se willa gelamp (see* 532b, *below).* **532b** *XSt* 568 þá hít þus gelamp, *and cp. Ele* 961-62 *and Bwf* 625-26 *under* 532a, *above.* **533b** *And* 434; *And* 119, *XSt* 562 enġla Scieppend. **534a** *Cp. Gen* 862 þá sóna ongann, 1589 and þá sóna ongeat; *Chr* 233 And þá sóna gelamp; *Bwf* 1280 þá þǽr sóna warþ; *Fin* 46 þá hine sóna frægn. **534b** *XSt* 522 Símon Pétre. **535a** *Bwf* 506 Eart þú sé Béo-wulf.

Variation

By Arthur Gilchrist Brodeur

Variation, "by far the most important rhetorical figure, in fact the very soul of the Old English poetical style, . . . may be studied to perfection in the *Beowulf*."[1] Variation is indeed the chief characteristic of the poetic mode of expression; the poetic appellations, however striking in themselves, and however often they may serve as pure substitutions, find their most effective use as the materials of variations or of variation-like structures. Variation restrains the pace of Old English poetic narrative, gives to dialogue or monologue its leisurely or stately character, raises into high relief those concepts which the poet wishes to emphasize, and permits him to exhibit the object of his thought in all its aspects. But it could be a dangerous instrument in the hands of an inferior poet: it could impart on the one hand an effect of sheer redundancy, on the other an unpleasing jerkiness of pace; it could stiffen the flow of style, and clog the stream of thought.

Paetzel, in his very solid and careful study of variation, defines the figure in these terms: ". . . ein für das Verständnis genügend gekennzeichneter Begriff wird, entgegen dem Gebrauch der Prosa, noch einmal und zwar oft mit Unterbrechung des syntaktischen Zusammenhanges dem Hörer oder Leser vor die Seele gerückt. Diese Ausdrucksform nenne ich Variation. Ihre Hauptkennzeichen sind also 1) begriffliche, 2) syntaktische Entbehrlichkeit."[2] In his application of this definition he appears to me, on the one hand, to tend to excessive rigor, and on the other, to overlook the distinction between variation and parallelism. I have therefore undertaken to provide, in Appendix C, a correction of these shortcomings, with illustrations from the text of *Beowulf*.[3]

I should prefer to define variation as a double or multiple statement of the same concept or idea in different words, with a more or less perceptible shift in stress: one member of a variation may state the thought either more generally or more specifically than the other; or the second member, while restating essentially the same concept or idea, may do so in a manner which emphasizes a somewhat different aspect of it. When the members of a variation possess

---

[1] Klaeber's edition, p. lxv.

[2] Walther Paetzel, *Die Variationen in der altgermanischen Allitterationspoesie* (*Palaestra*, XLVIII; Berlin, 1913). The reference is to pp. 3, 4.

[3] Correction of so careful and systematic a work may seem presumptuous. Actually the limits of variation are not easy to define; but Paetzel's exclusions (see his p. 20) appear needlessly arbitrary.

This selection represents Chapter Two of the author's *The Art of 'Beowulf'* (Berkeley and Los Angeles: University of California Press, 1959), pp. 39-70. Reprinted by permission.

the same grammatical structure, they constitute a parallelism as well as a variation; but not all variations are parallelisms, nor are all parallelisms variations. I should insist that there are legitimate variations the members of which do not stand in the same grammatical construction: consider the opening lines of *Beowulf*:

> Hwæt, we Gar-Dena   in geardagum,
> þeodcyninga   þrym gefrunon,
> hu ða æþelingas   ellen fremedon!

Since *Gar-Dena* is intended to apply, not to the whole Danish nation, but to the members of the royal house, it and *þeodcyninga* constitute a substantival variation, the two members of which stand in parallel structure. The clause *hu ða æþelingas ellen fremedon* is, like *þeodcyninga þrym*, the object of *gefrunon*; these two objects say the same thing in different terms, and form a variation, the first member of which is a substantive with qualifying genitive, the second a clause. Variation of substantive by clause is not uncommon; there is a fine instance in lines 350-353:

> . . . .   'Ic þæs wine Deniga,
> frean Scyldinga   frinan wille,
> beaga bryttan   swa þu bena eart,
> þeoden mærne   ymb þinne sið . . .'

Here we have, first, a multiple substantive variation *wine Deniga—frean Scyldinga—beaga bryttan—þeoden mærne*, with King Hrothgar as referent; but that which is to be asked of Hrothgar is also phrased in a variation—this time without parallelism: the first element is a pronoun in the genitive, the second a clause, the third a prepositional phrase. There is no identity of structure between *þæs—swa þu bena eart—ymb þinne sið*; but the identity of meaning is absolute. Identity of sense is more essential to variation than identity of structure.

In my first chapter I mentioned the fondness of the poet of *Beowulf* for grouping together different poetic appellations for a single referent in variations, each appellation expressing one aspect of the referent, so that the sum of the members of the variation presents a total description or characterization. An excellent instance is the sequence of terms applied to Hrothgar in Wulfgar's second speech, which I have just quoted (lines 350-353): the first appellation (*wine Deniga*) stresses the warm and affectionate relation between Hrothgar and his retainers; the second refers to him in terms of his lordship over them; the third emphasizes his generosity; the fourth, his renown. This is true variation: each member has the same referent as the others; the several members express it in somewhat different, and cumulative, terms. Unless each member of the sequence has the same referent, we have not a variation but an enumeration—or, in certain cases, a progression. The distinction may be observed clearly in lines 333-335a, in which Wulfgar enumerates the offensive and defensive weapons of the Geats:

> 'Hwanon ferigeað ge   fætte scyldas,
> græge syrcan   ond grimhelmas,
> heresceafta heap? . . .'

This is an enumeration of different objects—shields, corselets, helmets, spears
—which stresses, individually, distinct details that, taken together, present the
total image of a company of splendidly armed men; but the several referents
are different things: there is unity of effect but complete diversity of detail.

This passage is part of a larger and well-integrated block of narrative; it
looks both backward and forward, and the whole of which it is a part reveals
the great skill of the poet in utilizing variations to create a texture. In the lines
closely preceding the last quoted the poet enumerates the weapons of the
Geats, and his enumeration contains variation of its partials:

> . . . . . .   Guðbyrne scan
> heard, hondlocen,   hringiren scir
> song in searwum,   þa hie to sele furðum
> in hyra gryregeatwum   gangan cwomon.
> Setton sæmeþe   side scyldas,
> rondas regnhearde   wið þæs recedes weal;
> bugon þa to bence,—   byrnan hringdon,
> guðsearo gumena;   garas stodon,
> sæmanna searo,   samod ætgædere,
> æscholt ufan græg; . . . (321b-330a)

These lines are separated from Wulfgar's opening words only by the poet's
announcement of his speech and identification of the speaker; the thread of
thought continues unbroken. The poet's enumeration of the details of Geatish
armament—corselets, shields, spears—has sketched the image of a gallant
band of men magnificently armed; now he communicates the effect of this
impression as conveyed to Wulfgar,—the total effect of this fine armament
upon a direct observer: 'that iron-clad company was well and worthily
equipped with weapons' (lines 330a-331b). For Wulfgar's first words, meaning
'Who are ye and whence do ye come?' are framed in terms which repeat the
poet's enumeration: 'Whence do ye bear the platebound shields, gray corselets
and masked helmets, a heap of warshafts?' In eleven words he pays compli-
ment to each of the kinds of arms mentioned by the poet, for he has been as
deeply impressed by the stately appearance of the Geats in their fine equipment as the poet's audience has been. This effect could not have been so
vividly produced upon the audience without the variations which the poet has
enclosed within his enumeration; for it is they which impart the excellence of
the weapons of the Geats.

There are three of these variations: *guðbyrne—hringiren; scyldas—rondas;*
garas—searo; the first of the three is reinforced by the terms *byrnan—*
guðsearo. Appropriate adjectives, which do not stand in variation, enhance the
effect by stressing typical and admirable qualities of corselets and shields: the
former are *heard, hondlocen, scir;* the latter are *side, regnhearde.* There is no
verb-variation: the various verbs denote different actions, each characteristic
of its subject: the corselets *shone;* the ringed iron *sang;* the warriors *set* the
shields against the wall, and themselves *bent* to the bench; the corselets *rang,*
the spears *stood* together in a clump. The martial effect of the arrival of the
Geats at Heorot, valiant men splendidly equipped, is presented dramatically,
in a vivid, moving image.

In the creation of this effect the poet has used not only enumeration and variation, but summation as well (once in his own words, lines 330b-331a, and once in the respectful words with which Wulfgar closes his salutation, 336-39), and back-reference. The back-reference also is double: Wulfgar's first words hark back to the poet's description of the weapons of the Geats; and his mention of their helmets (*grimhelmas*), which are not mentioned in the enumeration of lines 321 ff., is intended to recall the poet's comment in 303 ff.:

>. . . . . .   Eoforlic scionon
>ofer hleorber[g]an   gehroden golde,
>fah ond fyrheard,   ferh wearde heold . . .

In this whole block of narrative, variation, with its attendant devices of enumeration and back-reference, is important out of all proportion to its frequency. It lends emphasis to the description of the arms of the Geats and gives force to the impression which the men in their armor make upon Wulfgar. Wulfgar at once transmits this impression to King Hrothgar:

>'Hy on wiggetawum   wyrðe þinceað
>eorla geæhtlan . . .'   (368-369a)

And the martial appearance of the hero and his men helps to motivate the quality of Beowulf's reception by the Danes. Wulfgar's enumeration of the weapons of the Geats recalls and reinforces the poet's enumeration, within which much of the effect of military might and magnificence is communicated by the enclosed variations. The whole passage raises in high relief the quality of the Geats as valiant men armed in a manner worthy of their courage. The continuity of this whole section of the poem is maintained by the repeated emphasis upon this quality, from the moment that the Geats begin to march toward Heorot until they enter Hrothgar's presence. Its texture is close and rich, its structure firm; its movement and sound are conveyed by verbs of shining, hastening, gleaming, singing, marching, ringing.

There is also a close unity of effect between this passage and that which describes the interchange between Beowulf and the Captain of the Shore, in which the stately appearance of the hero and his men, in their fine equipment, and the impression made upon the Captain by both, are similarly conveyed (lines 237-238a, 247-250a, 292).

Variation is but one of the devices through which this effect is produced and sustained; but it is the variations which lie at its center. The centrality, the focusing power, of variation becomes more apparent as the narrative advances. And it is in the use of variation that the superiority of the poet of *Beowulf* over all others of his age is most manifest: in other Old English poems the device is too often conventional, flat, and trite; in *Beowulf* it is an instrument of power and beauty.

In passages of great solemnity (as in very formal speeches), or of special dramatic tension, variations of three or more members are apt to occur; e.g., *sawlberendra—niþða bearna—grundbuendra* (1004b-06a). In some of these there seems to be a deliberate climactic arrangement, as in *feo—ealdgestreonum— wundini golde* (1380-82a), in which the first term is the most abstract, the last the most specific and vivid. In one such triple variation each of three substantives is modified by an adjective: all three nouns have the same meaning, as do two of the adjectives: *stige nearwe—enge anpaðas—uncuð gelad.* Here it is the connotation of the last adjective—'uncanny'—which raises the sequence to its climax.

The threefold variation often communicates a sense of deep emotional tension; the most striking illustration appears in lines 1644b ff.:

> Ða com in gan   ealdor ðegna,
> dædcene mon   dome gewurþad,
> hæle hildedeor . . .

The second and third members of the substantive variation are modified by varying adjectives, *dædcene—hildedeor; dome gewurþad* stands outside the variation, but serves to add a further touch of stateliness. This variation conveys and emphasizes the exceptional dramatic height and tension of the situation. The poet has prepared most carefully for this scene. We recall how the Danes, seeing the blood of Grendel's dam staining the mere, assumed that it was Beowulf who had perished, and returned to Heorot; the Geats, though without hope that their lord still lived, remained behind. Their joy at Beowulf's triumphant reappearance with the spoils of victory, and the pride with which they bore the head of Grendel to the royal hall, have been presented briefly but with admirable power. Meantime the Danes sit despairing in Heorot, expecting that the coming of night will bring upon them further vengeful invasion by the she-troll. At this moment when the Danes think him dead, Beowulf strides into the hall, bearing Grendel's severed head. His appearance creates an instant and complete emotional reversal: grief and fear are succeeded first by stupefaction, then by joy once the shock of astonishment has been dispelled. The shock is momentarily intensified when the Danes see the head of Grendel—

> Ða wæs be feaxe   on flet boren
> Grendles heafod.   þær guman druncon,
> egeslic for eorlum   ond þære idese mid,
> wliteseon wrætlic;   weras on sawon. (1647-50)

Here is the structure of variation; but the elements *Grendles heafod—egeslic—wliteseon wrætlic* do not constitute a variation in fact: the second and third members are descriptive of the first. The manner of description is unusual: the head is, literally, terrible to look upon (*egeslic*); the poet, having made the point that it is as frightening to the earls as to the queen, then ironically calls it 'a wondrous spectacle of beauty.' Yet the ironic words (*wliteseon wrætlic*) contain a statement of literal truth: the terrifying sight of horror was also, in a very real sense, a pleasing spectacle for those whom the living Grendel had so cruelly persecuted.

The whole scene, from the moment of Beowulf's entrance—announced in the triple variation quoted above—is presented with extraordinary dramatic force and great solemnity. If its significance is fully appreciated, one may perceive how completely it justifies Hrothgar's long and often misjudged monologue, for which it provides the motivation. As the scene develops, the role of variation in the communication of its tensity and emotional temper becomes almost incalculable: nowhere else in Old English poetry is there anything to compare with it. Indeed, we can find few instances of so perfect a transmission of feeling through language before Shakespeare.

Beowulf reports his victory at once, before the Danes can recover from their astonishment that he lives. Wisely, the poet employs little variation in his speech. The hero's words lack the touch of ironic lightness which had marked his announcement of his earlier victory over Grendel; they are sober to the point of grimness. This is right, for the fight with the she-troll had almost cost Beowulf his life. The speech is solemn in the extreme—as it should be, for it announces the completion of the errand of mercy which had brought him to Denmark. Even the assurance, at its close, that Hrothgar has no further need to fear for his men's lives is as sober as it is forceful. The speech is as simple and direct as any in the poem.

The cumulative proofs of Beowulf's triumph—his appearance, his speech, even the display of the monster's head—only deepen the astonishment of the Danes, without dispelling their shock. The hero then presents the hilt of the magic sword to Hrothgar; and in the old king's contemplation of it his emotional tension is gradually relaxed. The terms in which its transmission is reported are dense with variation:

Ða wæs gylden hilt   gamelum rince,
harum hildfruman   on hand gyfen,
enta ærgeweorc;   hit on æht gehwearf
æfter deofla hryre   Denigea frean,
wundorsmiþa geweorc;   ond þa þas worold ofgeaf
gromheort guma,   Godes andsaca,
morðres scyldig,   ond his modor eac;
on geweald gehwearf   woroldcyninga
ðæm selestan   be sæm tweonum
ðara þe on Scedenigge   sceattas dælde. (1677-86)

The concepts expressed in substantive variations are 'sword,' 'Hrothgar,' 'Grendel,' in the following sequences: *gylden hilt—enta ærgeweorc—wundorsmiþa geweorc; gamelum rince—harum hildfruman—Denigea frean—woroldcyninga ðæm selestan; gromheort guma—Godes andsaca*. In addition, the whole proposition 'the sword-hilt was given to Hrothgar' is set forth in a clausal variation of three members: *wæs on hand gyfen—on æht gehwearf—on geweald gehwearf*; the substantival variations are enclosed within the larger frame of the clausal variation. Moreover, *æfter deofla hryre* is varied in sense by the clause *ond þa þas worold ofgeaf gromheort guma . . . ond his modor eac*. The appellation *Godes andsaca*, though it refers immediately to Grendel, also looks forward to the statement, in the immediately following account of God's destruction of the giants through the flood, *þæt wæs fremde þeod ecean Dryhtne*. Just as, after Beowulf's victory over Grendel, the monster's arm hung up in the hall, and later carried off by Grendel's dam, is a symbol of triumph and revenge, so now the golden hilt is a symbol of the final victory over monsters hateful to God: the symbolism becomes apparent in the account of the story of the Deluge inscribed on the hilt. Beowulf's victory is God's victory.

But that which is written on the hilt has another function: examination of it serves to give Hrothgar time to make the full transition from sorrow and shock to the joy that comes with the realization that all is gained rather than lost. This is obviously what the poet meant to convey by the wide separation of his first announcement of Hrothgar's speech (*Hroðgar maðelode,* line 1687a) from the actual utterance of his first words (1700), and by the quite exceptional parenthesis *swigedon ealle* (1699b). The other Danes are still gripped by emotional shock; Hrothgar has gained time, through his inspection of the hilt and the story engraved upon it, to recover and to formulate his thoughts. When words at last come to him, every thought expressed in his long monologue derives, with inexorable logic, from the circumstances which evoke the speech.

Moreover, the intensive and intricate variations in the account of Beowulf's gift of the sword-hilt to Hrothgar are so phrased as to communicate, fully and finally, the complete resolution of the central problem of Part I, and to mark the point of climax in the action. The monsters are slain, the Danes are safe; the hero has won matchless glory. From now on, although there are passages in which emotion is warmly and sensitively conveyed, the action slowly declines until it comes to rest in the last lines of the first part.

The scene we have been considering, the dramatic power of which is unmatched by any other in the literature of its age, illustrates certain of the larger aesthetic functions of variation. Paetzel, whose primary purpose was to establish a sound definition of the figure, and to examine and illustrate its structures and its formal characteristics, did not attempt to analyze its artistic effects; he tells us only that the psychological basis of variation is "Erregung der dichterischen Phantasie": "die Phantasie des Dichters ist so von einem Gegenstande erfüllt, dass sie ihn gar nicht aufgeben kann und sich in gewissen Abständen ihm immer wider zuwendet."[4] Now that which so fills the poet's imagination may be much more than an exciting concept: it may be a moving idea, a tragic situation, a clash of interest. Since out of tragic situations and clashes of interest dramatic action, and yet more tragic consequence, may develop, a poet who fully senses and deeply feels what he himself has to relate, and who participates sympathetically in the emotions of his personages, would inevitably find in variation a flexible and potent instrument. We have seen how, in the scenes we have examined, the poet of *Beowulf* transmits his own excitement to the listener through his variations, and how variation may carry the dramatic impact of an entire scene. It may indeed—as we shall see—carry over from scene to scene; even from one structural block of the poem to another. Our poet is given to comparatively heavy use of variation in passages charged with emotion; sometimes, indeed, in such contexts variation is reinforced by words and phrases which, not structurally members of the variations, yet attach themselves closely to the variational members, and load them so strongly as to become, in effect, part of them. The emotion thus communicated may dominate a long narrative passage; it may provide the point of departure for a new train of consequent action.

This may be observed in the development of the situation first introduced in lines 129b-131. After Grendel's first depredations, and their terrifying impact upon the Danes, have been reported, the poet imparts to us the grief of Hrothgar:

[4]Paetzel, *op. cit.,* pp. 11-12.

. . . . . . Mære þeoden,
æþeling ærgod,   unbliðe sæt,
þolode ðryðswyð,   þegnsorge dreah . . .

Mære þeoden—æþeling ærgod constitute a combination of adjective and sub-stantive variation; in line 131 there is verb-variation (*þolode—dreah*); the adjective *ðryðswyð*, used substantively, varies *mære þeoden—æþeling ærgod*. But semantically there is a third element in the verb-variation: *unbliðe sæt*. Without the adjective, the verb *sæt* would be too colorless to participate in a variation of verbs meaning 'suffer' and 'endure'; but 'sat unhappy' is, in all ways except pure structure, a sound variation of them.

This variation, giving forceful expression to the king's sorrow—a nobler emotion than the terror-stricken grief of his men,—is followed by an extended statement (lines 134b-164) of Grendel's savage and long-continued persecution: he haunts Heorot nightly for twelve years. Again and again, in and after this tragic account, the poet reverts to the king's sorrow; indeed, it is Hrothgar's grief for his thanes rather than their suffering that constitutes the major theme of this long section of narrative. And each time, the king's emotions are conveyed in variations, which express his feelings climactically as the monster's depredations increase the measure of his grief:

twelf wintra tid   torn geþolode
wine Scyldinga,   weana gehwelcne,
sidra sorga . . . (147-149a)
Þæt wæs wræc micel   wine Scyldinga,
modes brecða. (170-171a)

These revelations of Hrothgar's sufferings are presented each in turn as the consequence of each stage in the climactic ravages of Grendel; the second (lines 147 ff.) follows the second monstrous visitation, and is enclosed within the poet's exposition of Grendel's persistent and insatiable ferocity. This is followed by a summation containing a bitterly phrased triple variation:

Swa fela fyrena   feond mancynnes,
atol angengea   oft gefremede,
heardra hynða;   Heorot eardode,
sincfage sel   sweartum nihtum . . . (164 ff.)

Here, after the first variation (*feond mancynnes—atol angengea*), the second and third point an ironic contrast between the splendor of Heorot and the miseries which Grendel inflicts upon the Danes within it (*fyrena—heardra hynða; Heorot—sincfage sel*). The irony deepens in the following lines, in the magnificent, all too generally undervalued 'Christian Excursus,' which makes clear that in their heathenism the Danes have brought this tribulation upon themselves, and that there is no hope for them save in God's mercy—which, in the natural order of things, only Christians can expect (lines 168-188). Here is the sharpest tragic irony: in their efforts to gain deliverance through sacrifices to their pagan gods, the Danes not only increase their present affliction, but also hazard the penalty of eternal damnation.

This whole narrative of hopeless suffering and sorrow is keyed by the first statement of Hrothgar's grief, with its multiple variation. Variation is heavy throughout this whole tragic section of the poem; it recurs abundantly in every statement of emotion; every instance increases the weight of pity and terror. It reaches a thundering climax at the end of the Excursus, with its declaration of the hopeless condition of the Danes:

> . . . . . . Metod hie ne cuþon,
> dæda Demend, ne wiston hie Drihten God,
> ne hie huru heofena Helm herian ne cuþon,
> wuldres Waldend. (180b-183a)

These lines set forth the impelling cause of all the affliction undergone by Hrothgar and his people, the reason for its long and implacable continuance. The sentence is a massive clausal variation enclosing a fivefold substantive variation and a threefold verb-variation. The lines which immediately follow the conclusion of the Excursus contain the sharpest restatement of the misery of Hrothgar; the whole terrible story of the haunting of Heorot ends on this note:

> Swa þa mælceare maga Healfdenes
> singala seað; ne mihte snotor hæleð
> wean onwendan; wæs þæt gewin to swyð,
> lað ond longsum, þe on ða leode becom,
> nydwracu niþgrim, nihtbealwa mæst. (189-193)

Then, immediately, with that fondness for dramatic reversal which he frequently displays, the poet suddenly introduces the hero: the note of impending deliverance sounds like a trumpet. The sense of ineluctable tragedy has attained a tremendous climax, but it is instantly dispersed. The curtain has been lowered, as it were, upon a first act tense with terror, and swiftly rises upon a new setting, with new characters, who bring with them hope of happy consequence.

Throughout this first act of *Beowulf*, the cruel facts of Grendel's ravages have been narrated directly; but their impact has been imparted chiefly through their effect upon the emotions of Hrothgar. The primary vehicle of emotion is variation. Since variation, by its very nature, slows the pace of narrative,[5] and at the same time gives it specific force and sharpness, its use enables the author to communicate emotion with intensity and depth, and thereby impresses upon the listener the heroism and the tragic magnitude of the personages. The first part of *Beowulf* is heroic poetry so managed that it has the impact of drama: it gives the impression of a sequence of scenes upon the stage, connected by passages of transitional narrative. The first eighty-five lines are the Prologue to the play; in every ensuing scene the speeches are dramatic; the action falls naturally into several scenes, the tone of which is set by a dominant emotion. Thus the chief vehicle of emotion, variation, gives to each scene its quality and its continuity. Moreover the poet, in all the more tragic situations, is not content to convey the emotions of his characters in a single statement; he expresses them again and again, ever more forcefully, as

---

[5] Klaeber's edition, p. lxv.

the incidents of the action stimulate them afresh. In each restatement variation plays its central part. The consequences are, first, an increasingly developing awareness in the listener of the tragic situation; secondly, a deepening perception of the universality of its meaning; thirdly, appreciation of a continuous texture in the dramatic narrative.

Through variation, then, the representation of a dramatically significant emotion is emphasized and expanded; and its significance links together all the elements in a large narrative block. Yet, within the scene dominated by such an emotion, the poet, conscious of the complexity of human relationships, occasionally reveals cross-currents of interest, and uses their interactions toward that single effect which the character of the dominant emotion demands. Such a cross-current may make itself felt quietly and with subtle irony (as in the words of Wealhtheow to Hrothgar and to Beowulf, where emotion is controlled); or stormily, as in the interchange between Unferth and Beowulf.

That interchange, again, is the consequence of a powerfully felt emotion, the very quality of which is conveyed in variations. Its importance lies in the fact that it precipitates that very course of action toward which the dominant emotion of the scene—Hrothgar's passionate desire for Grendel's death—is directed. Beowulf has offered to venture his own life as Hrothgar's champion against Grendel; Hrothgar's reply is warmly friendly, but he does not immediately accept the offer. Near the close of his answer, Hrothgar expresses directly to Beowulf the horrors of the persecutions which the Danes have experienced, and the bloody outcome of the struggles of his thanes to defend the hall against the monster. This passage is the bitterest report of all: it communicates the sufferings of king and court far more sharply than the earlier statements of the king's grief; in it is focused, with terrible vividness, all the horror that has gone before:

> 'Ðonne wæs þeos medoheal   on morgentid,
> drihtsele dreorfah,   þonne dæg lixte,
> eal bencþelu   blode bestymed,
> heall heorudreore;   ahte ic holdra þy læs,
> deorre duguðe,   þe þa deað fornam.'   (484-488)

In this deeply passionate utterance, variation, dense and interlocked, is used to carry the force of the king's emotion.

The closing words of the king's speech imply—as he had said more explicitly in lines 381b-384a—that he sees in Beowulf's coming some prospect of deliverance. After he has spoken, the feasting and mirth in the hall are reported briefly; then, with explosive force, the conflict of interest declares itself. Unferth, a famous warrior and a favorite of the king's, is angered by the warm welcome given Beowulf, and envious of any man who presumes to undertake an exploit which he himself recognizes as beyond his powers. He directs against the hero a speech which—to the modern reader at least—seems shockingly insulting, and utterly out of harmony with the extreme courtesy which Hrothgar has shown Beowulf. This challenge, and Beowulf's vigorous reply, seem to interrupt the main narrative; but in actuality they advance it. For Unferth's words spur Beowulf to claim for himself the right to confront Grendel, and to prove his competence to do so; and when the hero has spoken, there is no longer any question that Hrothgar will grant his request.[6] Thus the clash between Unferth and Beowulf becomes the mechanism which triggers all the ensuing action of Part I.

The conflict between the two men, to be effective, must be charged with emotion. Unferth's challenge is emotional from first to last, pervasively bitter with the speaker's envy; Beowulf's reply is calm and dignified so long as he is explaining the actual course of events in his adventure with Breca, which Unferth has misrepresented. Beowulf's words become angry only when, rounding on Unferth, he accuses him of want of courage to face Grendel, and attributes the monster's successes to the military incompetence of Unferth himself and of the other Danes as well. It is therefore significant that, whereas Unferth's speech is filled with variations from beginning to end, Beowulf's reply contains only minor variations until the last sixteen lines,—and that these lines, edged with Beowulf's indignation and resolution, are heavy with variation. I need not discuss the variations in detail; the reader can see them for himself. Those in Unferth's speech are most marked in lines 513-518a and 520-522a. In lines 513-518, verb-variations predominate: they convey admirably the niggling scorn in Unferth's words. In 517-518 variation shifts from purely verbal to clausal; in 520-522a, lines in which Unferth asserts Breca's victory over Beowulf, the variation is substantival. Through much of the speech, the exciting, sneering misrepresentation is communicated chiefly through variation of verbs of action.

The more significant variations in Beowulf's retort appear in lines 590-606:

> 'Secge ic þe to soðe,   sunu Ecglafes,
> þæt næfre Grendel swa fela   gryra gefremede,
> atol æglæca   ealdre þinum,
> hynðo on Heorote,   gif þin hige wære,
> sefa swa searogrim,   swa þu self talast;
> ac he hafað onfunden,   þæt he þa fæhðe ne þearf,
> atole ecgþræce   eower leode,
> swiðe onsittan,   Sige-Scyldinga;
> nymeð nydbade,   nænegum arað
> leode Deniga,   ac he lust wigeð,
> swefeð ond sendeð,   secce ne weneþ
> to Gar-Denum.   Ac ic him Geata sceal
> eafoð ond ellen   ungeara nu,
> guðe gebeodan.   Gæþ eft se þe mot
> to medo modig,   siþþan morgenleoht
> ofer ylda bearn   oþres dogores,
> sunne sweglwered   suþan scineð!'

The concepts stressed in these variations are: the terror and humiliation wrought by Grendel; the insufficient courage of Unferth; the inadequate martial power of the Danes as a whole (with ironic emphasis on the first element of the compound *Sige-Scyldinga*); and, by contrast, the warlike might of the Geats; and the bright morning of the next day, which will shine upon the triumph of Beowulf. Those particular elements of the speech most effective in convincing

---

[6]This has been demonstrated convincingly by Adrien Bonjour, in "The Digressions in *Beowulf*," *Medium Ævum Monographs*, V (Oxford, 1950), pp. 20-22.

the Danes that they can expect Beowulf's victory are the concepts chosen for variation; and it is the variations which give Beowulf's words their bite and power. That they did carry conviction is demonstrated in the lines immediately following, which assert Hrothgar's joy over Beowulf's assurance, and his confidence that the hero will give him effective help. Those lines, quite appropriately, contain a threefold substantive variation, each member of which is the subject of its own clause; the referent of all three members is Hrothgar: he is king, with sole authority to appoint Beowulf champion of the Danes; and it is he whose state of mind is important at this point.

The scene is continued for some fifty-one lines, devoted to the pleasures enjoyed by Danes and Geats in the hall, the formal entry of Wealhtheow, Beowulf's vaunt that he will conquer or die, and Hrothgar's speech charging Beowulf with the defense of Heorot. These lines do not materially advance the action: they are partly setting, partly preparation for weighty matters to come; and they contain little variation. There is, however, one progression—a device admirably adapted to the conclusion of a scene—which sums up the account of the joys of the hall and serves as transition:

> Ða wæs eft swa ær   inne on healle
> þryðword sprecen,   ðeod on sælum,
> sigefolca sweg,   oþ þæt semninga
> sunu Healfdenes   secean wolde
> æfenræste. (642-46a)

The situation has been static since line 610, at which point the poet has established the complete emotional reversal experienced by Hrothgar. His sorrow and despair had received repeated emphasis from line 129b through line 488; now, filled with confidence and joy by the assurance contained in Beowulf's reply to Unferth, he is ready to entrust defense of the hall to Beowulf. Thus the dominant emotion—Hrothgar's suffering, lingering long, and suddenly transmuted into its joyful opposite—extends through, and unites, what we may call the first act of the drama. It is an act of two scenes, with two short narrative links, and one longer narrative passage which reports Beowulf's expedition to Denmark and his arrival at Heorot. The emotional cross-current set up by Unferth's challenge and Beowulf's reply precipitates the king's reversal of feeling, motivates his appointment of Beowulf as defender of the hall, and so makes possible all that follows. It is through the variations that the full force and acuity of these emotions is transmitted.

In one situation the poet uses variation with exceptional deftness and restraint, to suggest the tragedy impending over the House of the Shieldings. Wealhtheow's speech to Hrothgar, intended to remind Hrothulf of his obligations and ensure his loyalty (lines 1180b-87), contains very little variation: although her heart is filled with anxiety for her sons, her emotion is restrained. When, in the next moment, after giving gifts to Beowulf, she appeals to him to protect her sons, the depth of her feeling is disclosed in heavier variations (lines 1216-18; 1221b-24a; 1227).

Klaeber speaks of variation as "ubiquitous," and implies that it retards the action.[7] It is certainly pervasive; but in passages of vigorous action, such as the

---

[7]Edition, p. lxv. The retarding effect of variation accounts, of course, for its relative

accounts of the hero's combats with monsters, it is relatively rare in lines that
report the action itself, and heavier in those that communicate the feelings of
the participants. In the narrative of Beowulf's fight with Grendel, variations are
few and comparatively slight between the announcement of Grendel's advance
on the hall and the moment when Grendel feels the power of the hero's grip;
the first one of consequence occurs in lines 750 ff:

> Sona þæt onfunde   fyrena hyrde,
> þæt he ne mette   middangeardes,
> eorþan sceata   on elran men
> mundgripe maran;   he on mode wearð
> forht, on ferhðe;   no þy ær fram meahte.
> Hyge wæs him hinfus,   wolde on heolster fleon,
> secan deofla gedræg;   ne wæs his drohtoð þær
> swylce he on ealderdagum   ær gemette.

Here the variational pattern is remarkably complex; but it does not retard
the action at all; indeed, it conveys, with unique vividness and force, the
outstanding elements in that action, and the panic of Grendel. We have here
a group of variations enclosed in a larger one, which extends beyond the
bounds of a single sentence. The first of the enclosed variations is adverbial:
middangeardes—eorþan sceata—on elran men; the third member, though it
shifts from the sense 'anywhere' to that of 'in anyone,' nonetheless participates
in the general sense 'in any quarter.' The periodic structure enhances the force
of the whole, the most important member of the variation coming at the end.
The second variation is phrasal: *on mode—on ferhðe:* the first member suggests
a fear which fills the mind; the second, the sharp, sudden increase of that fear
till it overwhelms the heart. The positive assertion of Grendel's helplessness
(*no þy ær fram meahte*) is followed by a clausal variation declaring his
desperate eagerness to break free: *Hyge wæs him hinfus—wolde on heolster
fleon—(wolde) secan deofla gedræg.* Then the whole sequence is closed by the
same affirmation—though in more general terms—with which it opened: *ne
wæs his drohtoð þær swylce he on ealderdagum ær gemette* repeats the sense of
Sona þæt onfunde . . . þæt he ne mette middangeardes etc. The variations
convey Grendel's sudden, acute terror, contrasting with his earlier exultation
in the expectation of a full meal on human flesh, and anticipating his
anguished cries at the climax of his struggle to escape. If anything, the action
gains in power through this revelation of its progress by means of the
disclosure of Grendel's terror. Later the monster's lamentation is also set forth
in variation (lines 785-788a): *wop—sigeleasne sang; (gryreleoð) galan—sar
wanigean; Godes andsacan—helle hæfton.*

In narrating this combat the poet was confronted with a practical difficulty:
wishing to preserve the dramatic contrast between the ease with which
Grendel disposed of Hondscio and his helplessness in Beowulf's grip, and the
emotional contrast between the monster's hideous joy at the sight of so many
prospective victims and his agony of fear once the hero has laid hold on him,
the author found it necessary to convey the power and the menace of

infrequency in the passages of swift action in *Beowulf,* as Brandl pointed out (Paul's *Grundriss
der germanischen Philologie,* 2d ed., Strassburg, 1901-1909, II, I, p. 1014).

Grendel's gigantic strength without permitting him a moment's advantage over the hero. He accomplished this by making much of the noise of combat and the damage wrought upon the furnishings of the hall by the impact of the struggling contestants, and through the effect of these upon the onlooking Geats and the Danes who hear the tumult. The emotions of both Danes and Geats are sharply represented: the Geats make heroic, if vain, attempts to help their lord; and the Danes are filled with terror at the shaking of the house, the crashing of benches, and the hideous wails of Grendel. The feelings of both are set forth in variations. Each of the Geatish thanes

> wolde freadrihtnes   feorh ealgian,
> mæres þeodnes;

they all

> . . . on healfa gehwone   heawan þohton,
> sawle secan;

but they did not know that

> . . . . . .   þone synscaðan
> ænig ofer eorþan   irenna cyst,
> guðbilla nan   gretan nolde . . .

The three concepts chosen for variation are those most basic to the poet's meaning and purpose: the devoted loyalty of the Geats impelled them to defend their lord; they meant to kill his foe; but even the finest weapon would not penetrate the giant's hide. The less noble emotions of the Danes are represented in another periodic variation:

> . . . . . .   Denum eallum wearð,
> ceasterbuendum,   cenra gehwylcum,
> eorlum ealuscerwen. (767b-769a)

The irony of the situation—the fear of the Danes is excited not by any real peril, but by the din of the fight which is to deliver them—is underlined by the ironic term *ealuscerwen*.[8]

[8]All but the most recent interpretations of this word are discussed by J. Hoops (*Kommentar zum Beowulf,* Heidelberg, 1932, pp. 97 ff.; see also his "Altenglisch *ealuscerwen, meoduscerwen,*" *Englische Studien,* LXV, 1931, pp. 177-180). The translation 'deprivation of ale,' favored by Hoops and others, was long rejected by Klaeber: "-*scerwen,* related to **scerwan* 'grant,' 'allot' (*bescerwan* = 'deprive'). 'Dispensing of ale,' or, in a pregnant sense, of 'bitter or fateful drink' might have come to be used as a figurative expression for 'distress'. . . . It is to be noted that the author of *Andreas* (a better judge than modern scholars) understood the corresponding formation *meoduscerwen* (1526) in a sense which precludes the rendering 'taking away of (strong) drink'; to him it was 'plenty of (fateful) drink'. . ." (Klaeber's edition, p. 156). Now there is no evidence whatever that the simplex **scerwan* meant 'grant' or 'allot'; the prefix *be-* (*bescerwan*) does not negate the meaning of the simplex with which it is compounded. In *Ps. Cott.* 50, 98 the compound *bescerwan* means 'take away,' 'deprive' (*Ne ðinra arna me bescerwe*); the simplex must have had the same meaning as the compound—to deprive. I do not agree that the author of *Andreas* understood *meoduscerwen* as 'plenty of (fateful) drink'; that interpretation stems from a false association of the word with *biter*

The lines with which the combat with Grendel ends, converted by the poet into a kind of chant of triumph, contain a substantival variation which recalls the emphatic and repeated statements of the anguish suffered by the Danes under Grendel's repeated attacks:

> . . . . . .   Hæfde East-Denum
> Geatmecga leod   gilp gelæsted,
> swylce oncyþðe   ealle gebette,
> inwitsorge,   þe hie ær drugon,
> ond for þreanydum   þolian scoldon,
> torn unlytel. (828b-833a)

Thus the poet rounds out and places period to the first great stage of the action: in a clear statement that Beowulf has delivered the Danes from their long-endured persecution.

In this narrative of the first of Beowulf's three great adventures, the stages of the struggle, and its desperate nature, are communicated not so much by the direct statement of the action as through the revelation of emotions: of Beowulf's determination, Grendel's sudden and mounting fear once Beowulf has laid hold of him, and the emotions of Danes and Geats. In those lines which directly report the action there is very little variation, and that of the simplest; the variations are employed to express, explicitly and vividly, the emotions of the personages and of the onlookers. This revelation of emotion inspired by what happens, rather than the report of what happens, constitutes the active element in the management of the story.

In short, the author of *Beowulf* made use of the revelation of emotion as a major narrative principle; and perceiving the value of variation as a means of presenting emotion, he used it quite consistenty, both to express the dominant

---

beorþegu in line 1532; and it ignores the context in which the word occurs. The poet tells us that when the flood descended upon the Mermedonians, *meoduscerwen wearð æfter symbeldæge*—'deprivation of mead after a day of feasting.' Here is one of the typical contrasts so common in Old English poetry; the word *meoduscerwen* was chosen to contrast with *symbeldæge*. We have no right to interpret *meoduscerwen* in terms of *biter beorþegu*, which is neither a parallel nor a variation for it, but is rather a variation of *sorgbyrþen*. The author of *Andreas*, who knew *Beowulf*, simply imitated the Beowulfian *ealuscerwen* when he found himself in need of a word to contrast with *symbeldæg*. In both *Beowulf* and *Andreas* the term is figurative and ironic.

In the second supplement to his latest revision (1950), Klaeber (Edition, p. 466) cites Holthausen's view (*Anglia Beiblatt*, LIV-LV, 1943, pp. 27-30) that the first element in *ealuscerwen* is the same word *alu* "frequently met with in runic inscriptions and apparently meaning 'good luck,' 'safety.' Thus *ealuscerwen* 'taking away of good luck.' . . . Thus the annoying riddle of *ealuscerwen* . . . seems to be happily solved by a twofold misunderstanding: 1) (taking away of) good luck: ale; 2) dispensing (of ale, mead). The actual meaning of the noun in l. 769 is, most likely, 'disaster,' with a subaudition of 'terror.'"—Not at all: *alu* in the Prehistoric Norse runic inscriptions *may* mean 'good luck,' but there is no evidence that it does; it is found, for the most part, on bracteates in very short inscriptions. Its meaning is neither clear nor—apparently—uniform: on the stone of Orstad it seems to mean 'Denkmal,' 'Gedenkstein'; see A. Jóhannesson, *Grammatik der urnordischen Runeninschriften* (Heidelberg, 1923), pp. 76-77. Moreover there is no evidence that the word was used in Old English in the same sense as in Prehistoric Norse. I hold that *ealuscerwen* in *Beowulf* is used ironically: the Danes experience a terror such as they would have felt at deprivation of ale.

emotion of a scene or a sequence of scenes, and to give depth and force to a single poignant situation. He used the figure also to reveal the conflicting emotions of different personages, the clash of feeling which gives rise to action; and to emphasize moments of dramatic reversal.

I have not found such consciously artistic use of variation in any other Old English poem. As we should expect, the author of *Beowulf* does, not infrequently, employ the device in more conventional ways. Its use in formal speeches is too familiar to require much comment. Its value in such speeches is that it imparts stateliness and courtesy to what is said. For this very reason its ironic use in Unferth's challenging speech to Beowulf is all the more pungent. The most obvious instance of variation in formal address is, of course, the dialogue between Wulfgar and Beowulf. In less formal speeches, such as the dying hero's first words to Wiglaf—speeches in which the relation of speaker to hearer is so close as to make formality unnecessary,—there is very little variation, unless the words are uttered under stress of emotion. Thus Hrothgar's speech to Beowulf, committing Heorot to his care, and uttered after the friendship between the two has been established, is quite free from variation. On the other hand, the Danish king's parting words to Beowulf, colored as they are by his love for the hero and his regret at Beowulf's departure, contain a number of striking variations.

The poet also uses variation to mark transition between one major phase of the action and another. Thus we find variation increasing in incidence and in density at the point at which Beowulf and his men set out for Denmark (lines 210 ff.); when the Geats, having passed inspection by the Captain of the Shore, march toward Heorot (301 ff., 320 ff.); in the account of the jubilation of the Danes over Grendel's bloody tracks and the water stained with his blood (841-850); at the point of Beowulf's dramatic entry into Heorot with the golden hilt and the head of Grendel (1644 ff.); and the still more dramatic moment when Hrothgar receives the hilt (1677-86); and—most momentous of all—at the opening of the second part of the poem.

In Part II there is considerably less variation than in Part I. The action of Part II is concentrated in time and place: there are but two scenes, that of Beowulf's last combat and death and that of his cremation and burial. The settings are, first, the dragon's barrow and the region adjacent to it; and secondly, the place of Beowulf's burning. The action is focused upon the fight with the dragon and the hero's death; all else that is told—the circumstances which made the combat necessary, the summary of events over more than fifty years of Beowulf's regency and his quietly glorious reign, the accounts of the stages of the wars between Geats and Svear, and the fates of the Hrethling kings—all these are necessary background to the main action, and at the same time furnish the elements of the subplot, the decline and destruction of the Geatish nation. These things are unfolded partly through direct narrative by the poet, but chiefly in monologue placed in the mouths of Beowulf himself, of the Messenger, and in lesser degree of Wiglaf. Subsidiary as they are to the main action, their importance is none the less great; for the theme of Part II is double: the heroic death of Beowulf, and the overthrow of his people, who cannot long survive his fall.

The states of mind exhibited in Part II are, first and principally, those of

Beowulf himself: his grief at the thought that some offense of his against God has brought down the dragon's fury upon his people; his resolute and enduring courage; his tender and mournful recollections of his dead kinsmen; and his care for his people in his last moments. The poet is also concerned, though less deeply, with the feelings of the faithful Wiglaf and the cowardice of Beowulf's ten faithless thanes, and with the sorrow of the Geatish people at the king's death. At all points until the end, the actions and emotions of Beowulf are central: the grief of the Geatish warriors becomes a tribute to him; Wiglaf's importance lies in the help he could give Beowulf; the Messenger is a mere voice—a kind of Chorus—through whom the coming overthrow of his lordless people is forecast.

In Part II, moreover, there are virtually no dramatic reversals: the poet makes it clear to us, from the very opening lines, that his hero, and the Geatish nation, are doomed; and the action marches relentlessly on toward catastrophe. The mood is almost uniformly dark and melancholy; there are no major shifts in emotional tone. Part II is elegy, as Part I is drama.

As we should expect, we find variation in the transitional passage with which the second part opens:

> Eft þæt geiode   ufaran dogrum
> hildehlæmmum,   syððan Hygelac læg,
> ond Heardrede   hildemeceas
> under bordhreoðan   to bonan wurdon,
> ða hyne gesohtan   on sigeþeode
> hearde hildfrecan,   Heaðo-Scilfingas,
> niða genægdan   nefan Hererices—   (2200-06)

The variations are restricted to the most significant elements of the thought: the long lapse of time between the events of Part I and those about to be communicated (*eft—ufaran dogrum*); attack by the Svear (*hyne gesohtan—niða genægdan*); the slain Heardred (*hyne—nefan Hererices*), whose fall brings Beowulf to the throne. *Heaðo-Scilfingas* is rather an explanatory appositional to *hearde hildfrecan* than a variation of it. These seven lines are one long temporal clause; the circumstance which they place in time, Beowulf's accession, stands outside its scope. The next variation stresses the hero's advanced age: he was then *frod cyning, eald eþelweard* (lines 2209b-10). After this, so far as we can tell from the damaged text, there are no variations of much consequence until we come to the Lament of the Last Survivor (lines 2247-66). We might expect this speech, which sets forth the emotions of the lonely wanderer, to be heavy with variation; actually the variations are few: *guðdeað—feorhbealo frecne; fæted wæge—dryncfæt deore; æfter wigfruman— hæleðum be healfe; hearpan wyn—gomen gleobeames*. It should not be surprising, however, that variation should be so little in evidence in a speech which is really an elegiac set piece, not the expression of the actual emotion of any of the personages of the poem, nor in any way significant to the action. The value of the speech, apart from its intrinsic beauty, is the contribution which it makes to the prevailingly melancholy mood of Part II.

As in Part I, so here: variation has as its principal function the revelation and illumination of emotion. Even a dragon is permitted to feel passionately— as he must, if the tale of his ravages is to carry conviction:

Wæs þæs wyrmes wig   wide gesyne,
nearofages nið   nean ond feorran,
hu se guðsceaða   Geata leode
hatode ond hynde;   hord eft gesceat,
dryhtsele dyrnne   ær dæges hwile.
Hæfde landwara   lige befangen,
bæle ond bronde;   beorges getruwode,
wiges ond wealles;   him seo wen geleah.   (2316 ff.)

There is substantival variation in *wyrmes wig—nearofages nið;* the following clause repeats the sense in different structure. *Bæle ond bronde* varies *lige.* The other sequences are enumerations rather than variations.

These lines state the motivation for Beowulf's expedition against the dragon: he undertakes his last exploit, as he had ventured against the monsters of the mere, not from any selfish motive, but to defend a people. The burning of his hall would certainly supply a strong personal motive; but it is secondary. The terms *sylfes ham—bolda selest—gifstol Geata* (2325b-27a) are something less than a true variation: though they have the same referent, they really constitute an enumeration of the functions and qualities of the hall.

The first really complex variations in Part II appear in the lines which describe Beowulf's state of mind when he learns of the dragon's ravages, and makes his preparations for battle. In this passage the first variation is purely emotional: *hreow on hreðre—hygesorga mæst* (line 2328); the second is *Wealdende—ecean Dryhtne* (2329b-30b). The following lines, in which the death of both combatants is forecast, are rather heavy with variation: *leoda fæsten—eorðweard ðone; guðcyning—Wedera þeoden; wigendra hleo—eorla dryhten; holtwudu—lind; lændaga—worulde lifes* (2333-43). Beowulf's contempt for the dragon is likewise expressed in variations (lines 2345 ff.).

This exposition of Beowulf's emotions is followed by the second of four accounts of Hygelac's death, introduced as 'not the least' of Beowulf's experiences of perilous fights. Its immediate function is to account for the hero's want of fear; but—as I shall show in a later chapter—its role is one of much greater importance: Hygelac's significance in the poem is much larger than his single appearance in person would lead us to expect. Accordingly in these lines his name is followed by a threefold variation upon it: *Geata dryhten—freawine folca—Hreðles eafora.*

The explanation of Beowulf's fearlessness—his invariable success in battle— is stated again, briefly and in general terms, in another variation (lines 2397-99a):

Swa he niða gehwane   genesen hæfde,
sliðra geslyhta,   sunu Ecgðiowes,
ellenweorca,   oð ðone anne dæg . . .

It appears once more at the opening of Beowulf's first speech in Part II (lines 2426 ff.); but in Beowulf's mouth it ceases to be justification of confidence, and becomes occasion for reminiscence. For though he remains fearless, he is no longer confident: his change of mood is prepared for in the account of his progress with his men toward the scene of battle. Premonition of death has touched the invincible hero; its coming is foreshadowed in the lines which describe the advance upon the dragon's lair:

. . . . . . He [the guide] ofer willan giong
to ðæs ðe he eorðsele   anne wisse,
hlæw under hrusan   holmwylme neh,
yðgewinne;   se wæs innan full
wrætta ond wira.   Weard unhiore,
gearo guðfreca   goldmaðmas heold
eald under eorðan;   næs þæt yðe ceap
to gegangenne   gumena ænigum.
Gesæt ða on næsse   niðheard cyning,
þenden hælo abead   heorðgeneatum,
goldwine Geata.   Him wæs geomor sefa,
wæfre ond wælfus,   wyrd ungemete neah,
se ðone gomelan   gretan sceolde,
secean sawle hord,   sundur gedælan
lif wið lice . . .   (2409b-23a)

The referents of the variations here are: the dragon's lair (*corðsele—hlæw under hrusan*); the surging sea near which it stood (*holmwylme—yðgewinne*); the dragon lurking within it (*weard unhiore—gearo guðfreca*); Beowulf (*niðheard cyning—goldwine Geata*); the impending attack upon Beowulf's life by Fate, expressed in clausal variations. So far as we can judge, the shift in Beowulf's mood from confidence of victory to that state which can only be called feyness is induced by his contemplation of the scene itself, and his awareness of the terror lurking within the solitary mound by the sea. The oppression of the landscape, and understanding of the peril which it harbors, affect the hero's spirit. This is interesting: the ghastly scenery of the Haunted Mere had not so deeply shaken the young Beowulf; but now he has premonitions of doom. Behind these physical manifestations of danger lies the potency of Fate, which uses them to cast the shadow of death upon his spirit.

Throughout Beowulf's long monologue (lines 2426-2537), variations are scattered rather thinly; they appear in the opening lines slightly, in the brief account of Herebeald's death; and in the lines in which the hero recalls the vengeance he had taken upon Dæghrefn for the slaying of Hygelac (2501-27a). Two threads—one bright, one sombre—intertwine to form the fabric of this speech: that of Beowulf's valiant exploits in the past and his present resolution to confront the dragon bravely; and that of the deaths of his beloved kinsmen. The first flashes for a moment in lines 2426-27a, only to be overlaid by the second in 2427b; the second then prevails until line 2490; the intervening 64 lines recall with tender regret the tragic or heroic deaths of Herebeald, Hrethel, and Hæthcyn, and enclose the beautiful parable of the old warrior mourning for his hanged son. The two threads combine in a contrasting pattern in lines 2490-2508a, in which Beowulf's love and loyalty to Hygelac, and the vengeance which he exacted for his uncle's death, are equally stressed. His remembrance of the slaying of Dæghrefn brings the bright thread of valor into dominance:

'. . . . . . Nu sceall billes ecg,
hond ond heard sweord   ymb hord wigan';

and this thread remains dominant in the pattern to the end of the monologue. This speech is sentimental—in the best sense of the word—rather than emotional: the emotions recalled, however poignant when bitter events evoked them, are now recollected in tranquillity. It is not surprising, therefore, that variation is scattered and light; the more noteworthy instances cluster about these referents: Beowulf's early combats (*guðræsa—orleghwila*, lines 2426b-27a); the memory of Hrethel (*sinca baldor—freawine folca*, 2428b-29a); the dead Herebeald (*hyne—his freawine—his mæg*, 2437-39); the invasion of the Svear after Hrethel's death (*synn ond sacu—wroht—herenið hearda*, 2472-74a); Beowulf's vengeance upon Dæghrefn. The variations on this last theme express two referents: the necklace given to Beowulf by Wealhtheow and worn by Hygelac in his last fight (*ða frætwe—breostweorðunge*), and Dæghrefn himself (*Huga cempan—cumbles hyrde—æþeling*, 2502b-06a). From this point to the end of the speech variations are still fewer: they concern Beowulf's thanes; his sword; the impending combat with the dragon in its potentiality of death for the hero. If the speech is exceptional in the rarity of its variations, the concepts expressed in variational form are those most important in the mind of Beowulf and, for the audience, most evocative.

There is a sequence of rather simple variations in the speech in which Wiglaf exhorts his comrades to come to Beowulf's aid: nearly all are concentrated in lines 2633-48a. Their members emphasize the generous gifts which Beowulf had given his retainers, his own excellence as king and friend, and his need of help against the dragon—the essential elements in Wiglaf's appeal. The force of the young thane's feeling expresses itself admirably in his stress upon those considerations which should induce his companions to defend their lord to the death; and these are expressed in variations. On the other hand, Wiglaf's denunciation of the cowardly thanes after Beowulf's death contains very few variations: *maðmas—eoredgeatwe* (lines 2865b-66a); *healsittendum—þegnum* (2868a-69a); *God—sigora Waldend* (2874b-75a); *fleam—domleasan dæd* (2889b-90a). This is the only emotional passage in the poem in which expression of feeling is too intense for variation: Wiglaf's contempt bursts the bounds of form and erupts at the end in one of the most direct and passionate sentences in Old English poetry:

> '. . . . . . Deað bið sella
> eorla gehwylcum þonne edwitlif!'

There is much more variation in the speech of the Messenger. This is a singularly meaty passage: it brings together, in thoroughly explicit statement, all that has been implicit throughout the second part of the poem. It announces to the people Beowulf's victory and death; it predicts invasion by the Svear and the destruction of the Geatish nation; it motivates this forecast by recalling the fall of Hygelac and the war in which Hæthcyn and Ongentheow fell; and it gives instructions for Beowulf's funeral. All this is directly and vigorously set forth, and its significance is immediately apparent. Through much of the speech, and most obviously in its conclusion, there is both warmth of emotion and irony; and here (lines 3007-27) the variations eloquently reveal the feelings of the speaker.

The last considerable use of variation in the poem appears in lines 3110-33: a passage which introduces and reports Wiglaf's last speech and narrates the plundering of the hoard. Here we find the variations *byre Wihstanes—hæle hildedior; hæleða—boldagendra; hie—folcagende; gled—wonna leg; stræla storm —sceft; dracan—wyrm; wég niman—flod fæðmian.*

Some looser variations cluster near the end of the poem: *Hi on beorg dydon beg ond siglu—forleton eorla gestreon eorðan healdan; wordgyd wrecan—ymb wer sprecan; eahtodan eorlscipe—ellenweorc demdon* (3163-74a). These variations express naturally and warmly the deep grief of the Geats for their lord's death.

The praise bestowed upon Beowulf by his thanes in the last three lines of the poem is cast not in the form of variation, but in an eloquent enumeration of his virtues. Three of the four terms are very close to one another in meaning: *manna mildust, mon(ðw)ærust, leodum liðost.* I take the first superlative as meaning 'most liberal of men': although *milde* has the sense of 'liberal' only rarely in Old English texts, its Old Norse and Old High German cognates commonly have this meaning, which survives in Danish *gavmild,* Swedish *givmild.* The marked emphasis upon the hero's gentler qualities is significant: it is quite as much in his protectiveness and love for lord and people as in his valor that the heroic virtue of Beowulf resides.

In both parts of the poem there are many variations which have no other function than that of an ornament of style. Variation had become a conventional figure in Old English poetry; this accounts for its "ubiquity." But in *Beowulf,* to a degree and with a power and richness unmatched in any other poem, it becomes an instrument of vividness and beauty; it lends force and eloquence to the expression of emotion; it is used to emphasize those moments of feeling most productive of action, or those emotions or situations in themselves most dramatic. One has only to compare the variations in *Beowulf* with those in any other poem to see how consciously and imaginatively the epic poet manages the device. In Old Saxon poetry variation is so abundant that it becomes colorless; in *Brunanburh* it is almost constant and mechanical; in *Genesis* it rarely rises above the commonplace. Perhaps the author of *Andreas* comes closer to the poet of *Beowulf* in his variational effects; but he quite lacks the magnificence of *Beowulf,* and there is in his work none of that pervasive texture which variation achieves in the first part of the epic. The use of variation to mark the dominant mood, the salient and productive elements in a significant situation, and to link the situation with that which precedes or follows, is unique in *Beowulf.*

With respect to variation, then, the poet of *Beowulf* developed the inherited techniques of poetic convention in new and nonconventional directions. He did so, in a sense, under compulsion—the compulsion of a new and difficult task. He had to construct a heroic poem on the grand scale, in the traditional manner and with traditional matter. There were no sufficient native models from which he could learn how to create a structure, to organize and shape a long and moving narrative. He may have learned something from the *Aeneid;*[9] but not much in the matter of style, for the elements of his style descended to him from Germanic antiquity. Quite obviously he applied an original and powerful

[9]See T. B. Haber, *A Comparative Study of the Beowulf and the Aeneid* (Princeton University Press, 1931); R. W. Chambers, *Beowulf: An Introduction* (2d ed.; Cambridge University Press, 1932), pp. 121-128; Fr. Klaeber, "Die christlichen Elemente im *Beowulf,*" *Anglia,* XXXV (1911), pp. 111-136, 249-270, 453-482, XXXVI (1912), pp. 169-199; and Brandl's study in Paul's *Grundriss,* for the best discussions of the possible relationship between *Beowulf* and the *Aeneid.*

intelligence, and a rich sensitiveness, to the development of the potentialities of those traditional elements which, in the hands of older scops, had resembled the effects of "a worker in mosaic, placing in new combinations pieces ready to his hand."

*   *   *

The foregoing chapters have considered the major categories of content-words in the vocabulary of *Beowulf*, not as items in a glossary, but as the major stuff of the language of poetry. We have looked at them as the *specific* language of poetry, differing from that of prose now in dignity, now in figurative content, now in their connotations and associations. We have observed certain principles governing their use: notably, periphrasis, substitution, and variation. We have seen these words—simplices as well as compounds and combinations—functioning in connected lines and passages. We have, moreover, sought to look behind the word and the word-group to the image, the figure, to discover the poet's imagination at work. We have seen one thing clearly: the language of *Beowulf,* making heavy use of traditional formulas, is yet by no means "totally formulaic."

The formulaic element in *Beowulf* is indeed large: it extends beyond the selection or the formation of words into the patterns of word-groups, occasionally of verses, now and then of lines or short groups of lines. This is the inevitable consequence of the poet's undertaking to compose a heroic poem in the vernacular. We are grateful to Magoun for bringing to our attention the pervasiveness of this traditional and formal element in the language of the poem. But it is much more significant that, both quantitatively and qualitatively, the language of *Beowulf* is something other and more than formulaic: the majority of its compound content-words—the principal element of its poetic diction—are not to be found in any other poem.

It is equally significant that, as these words combine in the common figures of variation, enumeration, and progression, they assume power and beauty, and are used with a precision, a vividness, and an eloquence not to be discovered in other poems. In fine, the poet of *Beowulf*, like Homer, was by no means independent of formula, but was its master and not its servant. Nowhere else in Old English do we find such splendor of language; its wealth and sureness attest that *Beowulf* is the work, not of an illiterate 'singer,' but of a great literary artist, dominating, expanding, and transcending the limits of the form in which he elected to compose.

Beowulf—An Allegory of Salvation?

By M. B. McNamee, S.J.

When Beowulf's character is studied in the light of the Christian concept of magnanimity, the idea common amongst most modern scholars that his character and that of the poem in which he figures are substantially Christian in spirit is greatly strengthened.[1] Some few scholars have gone further and suggested that the story may possibly be read as an allegory of the Christian story of salvation. Klaeber has very tentatively hinted at that notion in the introduction to his edition of the poem.

That the victorious champion, who overcomes this group of monsters, is a decidedly unusual figure of very uncertain historical associations has been pointed out before. The poet has raised him to the rank of a singularly spotless hero, a 'defending, protecting, redeeming being,' a truly ideal character. We might even feel inclined to recognize features of the Christian Savior in the destroyer of hellish fiends, the warrior brave and gentle, blameless in thought and deed, the king that dies for his people. Though delicately kept in the background, such a Christian interpretation of the main story on the part of the Anglo-Saxon author could not but give added strength and tone to the entire poem.[2]

Gerald Walsh, in his provocative little book on Medieval Humanism, has stated forthrightly that the poem is a Christian allegory:

Beowulf is not a pagan poem; it is the creation of a Christian, possibly of a monk. The legends had come from Denmark and Sweden, but the Norsemen knew comparatively little of composition or literary creation. By the eighth century, these legends had become grist for the Christian poet's mill. They were welded together into a single allegorical song intimating the Divine Mystery of Redemption—a conception beyond the scope of the Viking's power.[3]

Professor Kennedy, although he denies in Beowulf any such liturgical echoes as occur in Christ I and any such reflection of theological dogmas as are evident in Christ II,[4] does concede that "the ancient tale of Beowulf's struggle with monster and dragon may well have lent itself to the uses of Christian allegory."[5] I wish to suggest in this study that as an allegory of the Christian

---

[1] I have made a detailed study of this aspect of Beowulf in Honor and the Epic Hero (New York, 1960), pp. 86-117.
[2] Frederick Klaeber, Beowulf and the Fight at Finnsburg (New York, 1950), pp. l-lii.
[3] Gerald G. Walsh, S.J., Medieval Humanism (New York, 1942), p. 45.
[4] Charles W. Kennedy, The Earliest English Poetry (New York, 1943), p. 91.
[5] Kennedy, p. 98.

Reprinted, by permission, from the Journal of English and Germanic Philology 59 (1960), 190-207.

story of salvation the *Beowulf* poem both echoes the liturgy and reflects New Testament theological dogma.

There is no doubt whatever that the *Beowulf*-poet has gone out of his way to exclude all the old pagan gods from an active place in his poem. The god referred to throughout by Hrothgar and Beowulf alike is the one, providential God of the Christians,[6] the Creator and Lord of the whole universe and the Creator and Final Judge of man as well. Idolatry and especially devil worship are looked upon as aberrations hateful to the true God and subject to divine punishment.[7] Man's whole life is represented as under the providential care of this one, true God. In estimating the effect of the new Christian revelation upon the poem, it is important to notice that the two most fundamental certitudes which that revelation provided—certitude about man's beginnings and about his end—play an important part in the poem. Professor Gilson has reminded us that no pagan philosopher ever arrived at a clear idea either of Creation as the beginning of life nor of the final judgment and man's destiny after death.[8] Both these ideas find a definite place in *Beowulf*. The joyful hymn which is sung at Hrothgar's court and which particularly enrages the jealous Grendel is a hymn of creation telling the story of the beginnings of all things, not unlike the Creation poem of Caedmon.[9] Besides this, God is referred to throughout the poem as the Creator and Lord of all and there is frequent reference to the judgment to come.[10] The human situation as a race fallen

[6]It is true that *Wyrd* or fate is also referred to frequently in the poem, but often in such a way as to suggest that *Wyrd* is subject to the decrees of a providential God. Professor Kennedy says of the relationship of these two ideas in the poem: "Examples of this incomplete fusion of pagan and Christian will be found in a parallelism of reference to the blind and inexorable power of *Wyrd*, or Fate and to the omnipotence of a divine Ruler Who governs all things well. But even in survivals of pagan material the modifying influence of Christian thought is often evident. In both instances in which there is reference to the curse upon the dragon's treasure the poet specifically excludes from the operation of the curse one who has God's favor. Elsewhere in the poem God and *Wyrd* are brought into juxtaposition in such a manner as to imply control of Fate by the superior power of Christian divinity" (Kennedy, pp. 87-88).

[7]See *Beowulf*, translated by Clark Hall, p. 29 [170-90], for a forthright condemnation of idolatry and more specifically of devil worship. "Sometimes they vowed sacrifices at the tabernacles of idols,—prayed aloud that the destroyer of souls would provide them help against the distress of the people. Such was their custom,—the hope of the heathen,—they remembered hellish things in the thoughts of their hearts. They knew not the Creator, Judge of deeds; they knew not the Lord God, nor, truly, had they learned to worship the Protector of the heavens, the glorious Ruler." [Note: All future references to *Beowulf* will be to the Hall translation newly edited and revised by C. L. Wrenn (London, 1950). The numbers in brackets in the references to the *Beowulf* refer to the pertinent lines of the original Old English edition of Frederick Klaeber.]

[8]Etienne Gilson, *The Spirit of Medieval Philosophy* (New York, 1936), pp. 68-69, 385-90.

[9]Hall, p. 25 [91-98]: "He who could recount the first making of men from distant ages, spoke. He said that the Almighty made the earth, a fair and bright plain, which water encompasses, and, triumphing in power, appointed the radiance of the sun and moon as light for the land-dwellers, and decked the earth-regions with branches and leaves. He fashioned life for all kinds that live and move."

[10]Note the reference to the Creator and Provident God of the Christians in the quotation in n. 6. But there are repeated references to this one true God, Creator and Judge, throughout the poem. See, for example, Hall, pp. 36 [318], 39 [384], 42 [442], 44 [478], 55 [687], 56 [700], 57 [707], 67 [932], 69 [978], 74 [1057], 85 [1270], 99 [1553], 108 [1725], 109 [1750], 111 [1778], 157 [2740], 160 [2794], 163 [2874], 171 [3054].

from grace is hinted at, too, in the fact that Grendel is represented as a monstrous offspring of the murderer Cain;[11] and the flood sent by God to destroy the sinful race is shadowed forth in the carvings of the flood on the hilt of the magic sword which Beowulf brings back from the mysterious mere.[12] All these Old Testament allusions, occurring, as it were, in asides in the poem, have led some scholars to say that all the Scriptural allusions in the poem are to the Old Testament and that they occur outside the events of the main story.[13] There is nothing from the New Testament, they claim, and nothing that expresses any specific dogma of Christianity in the main episodes of the poem. I wish to suggest here that that conclusion should not be reached too hastily.

Even more important than the idea of Creation and Final Judgment provided by divine revelation as a clue to the real meaning of life is the idea of a Redeemer sent by God to save man from the consequences of his own sins. The Christian story of redemption in its essentials is simply this: man has fallen from a state of innocence and happiness and is in the powerful grip of Satan. Utterly helpless to save himself, he is in dire need of a Savior. These bare facts about man's need and the historical advent of a Savior are as much a heart of the revelation of the New Testament as the story of Creation and the fact of the one true Lord and Final Judge of all were to the Old Testament.

I do not think that anyone perfectly familiar with the details of the Christian story of salvation can read *Beowulf* and not be struck by the remarkable parallel that exists between the outline of the *Beowulf* story and the Christian story of salvation. For the purpose of the comparison here, we may consider the poem as divided into two parts: part one concerned with the conflicts of the young Beowulf with Grendel and his dam, and part two with the mortal conflict of the aged Beowulf with the fire-dragon.

In part one we have a situation that parallels the story of salvation almost perfectly. In the first episode, dealing with the story of Hrothgar and his people, we have the spectacle of a people who are in the grip of a frightful monster who, jealous of their happiness in Heorot[14] has left woe and sorrow

[11]Hall, p. 25 [102-15].

[12]Hall, p. 106 [1687-95]. "Hrothgar discoursed; he scrutinized the hilt, the ancient heirloom, upon which was inscribed the rise of the primeval strife when the flood, the rushing deep, destroyed the brood of giants. They suffered terribly; that was a race alien from the eternal Lord, (and) for that the Sovereign Ruler gave them a final retribution by the surging water."

[13]Thus Klaeber (p. xlix): "Of specific motives derived from the Old Testament (and occurring in *Genesis A*, also) we note the story of Cain, the giants, and the deluge, and the song of Creation." And Kennedy (p. 88): "The Christian influence in the *Beowulf* is a matter of transforming spirit, rather than of reference to dogma or doctrine. And it is, in the main, an influence reflecting the Old Testament rather than the new. The poem contains specific references to Cain's murder of Abel, and to the stories of Creation, the giants, and the Flood. But we find no such allusions to New Testament themes as characterize, for example, the *Christ* of Cynewulf."

[14]That Grendel's envy of the happiness of Hrothgar's people in Heorot is the motive of his murderous raids is stated clearly in the poem itself. Hall, p. 24 [87-91]: "Then the mighty spirit who dwelt in darkness bore grievously a time of hardship, in that he heard each day loud revelry in hall;—there was the sound of harp, the clear song of the minstrel." This motive for Grendel's incursions into Heorot parallels the traditional motive of Satan's incursions into the Garden of Eden—envy of the happiness of our first parents in contrast to his own misery in hell.

in the wake of his destructive visitations. And it is emphasized in the story that neither the great and magnanimous Hrothgar himself nor anyone among his followers can do anything to save himself from the depredations of this monster.[15] Then, in the person of Beowulf, a savior, sent by God from outside, comes to them—a savior who has both the desire and the power to save them and who does actually free them from the ravages of Grendel by confronting and slaying the monster.

For an audience familiar with both the story of salvation and the ancient Nordic myths, all that would be needed to identify the story of Beowulf with that of the Christian Savior would be a clue. Miss Whitelock has rather convincingly argued[16] that the audience for which the poem was written was definitely Christian; there has never been any doubt that it was an audience familiar with the old, pagan, Nordic myths. Quite a sufficient clue for such an audience to make the identification, it seems to me, is the fact that Grendel is repeatedly identified throughout the first episode with the powers of darkness and described as an inmate of hell.[17] If the monster that has

[15]Hrothgar in his welcoming address to Beowulf is most emphatic in stating his own and his people's helplessness against Grendel: "It is grief to me in my heart to tell any man what Grendel with his thoughts of hate has wrought for me in Heorot of harm and sudden harassings. My troop in hall, my war-band is diminished" (Hall, p. 44 [474-477]). And when Beowulf has conquered Grendel, Hrothgar makes this public proclamation: "Many horrors and afflictions have I endured through Grendel: yet God, the King of Glory, can ever work wonder on wonder. It was but now that I despaired of ever seeing a remedy for any of my troubles, since the best of houses stood stained with the blood of battle,—an all-embracing woe for every one of the counsellors, of those who despaired of ever guarding the fortress of this people from foes, from demons and evil spirits. Now, through the might of the Lord, a warrior has done a deed which up to now we all could not accomplish by our schemings" (Hall, pp. 67-68 [927-943]).

[16]Dorothy Whitelock, The Audience of Beowulf (Oxford, 1951). Miss Whitelock's interest in the audience of Beowulf is motivated by her attempt to date the composition of the poem. Incidentally, she has this to say about its Christianity: "He [the poet] was composing for Christians, whose conversion was neither partial nor superficial. He expects them to understand his allusions to biblical events without his troubling to be explicit about them. He does not think it necessary to tell them anything of the circumstances in which Cain slew Abel, or when, and why, 'the flood, the pouring ocean, slew the race of giants.' He assumes their familiarity not merely with the biblical story, but with the interpretation in the commentaries—not necessarily at first hand, but through the teaching of the Church" (p. 5). See Chapter One, passim, for further discussion of the same point.

[17]Professor Tolkien in a note to his article "Beowulf: The Monsters and the Critics," Proceedings of the British Academy, XXII, 278-80, calls attention to the ambiguity that hovers about the titles of Grendel. It is not clear, he claims, that Grendel is conceived by the poet as a full-fledged medieval devil; he would seem to be a kind of transitional figure—half-ogre, half-devil. But whether the terms used unequivocally spell out a medieval devil or only a man-monster symbolizing the power of evil and the forces of hell makes little difference for the allegorical meaning of the poem. In fact, for the allegory a physical monster drawn from the old myths would serve the purpose better than a theologically accurate devil as long as the monster is associated with the powers of hell. And that the poet makes inescapably clear. See for instance Hall, p. 28 [164], p. 59 [755], and most striking of all, p. 60 [787]: "A din arose, strange and mighty; a horrible fear came to the North-Danes, to everyone who heard the shrieking from the wall,—heard the adversary of God chant his grisly lay, his song of defeat,—the prisoner of hell wailing over his wound." And again his retreat and death are described in the following terms: pp. 63-64 [841-853]: "His parting from life did not seem a cause of sorrow to any of the men who saw the trail of the inglorious one,—how he, weary in spirit and vanquished in the fight, bore the tracks of his failing life away from thence, fated

Hrothgar's kingdom in his grip is consistently associated with the powers of hell, it would take no great stretch of imagination for an audience familiar with the Christian story of salvation and with an innate taste for the allegorical and riddles in general to see in *Beowulf* an allegorization of Christ the Savior—especially since, as I have shown elsewhere, he so well exemplifies the virtues of humility and charity, which Christ Himself had come to preach. The first episode, then, could very readily have appeared to such an audience as an allegorization of the essential facts of the story of salvation.

And what would such an audience make of the second episode—the descent into the mysterious mere? A great deal more, it would seem to me, than some of the modern critics make of it. The facts of the story are again quite simply told: Hrothgar's people are once more in the power of a monster. Grendel's ghoulish dam comes to revenge the death of her son, and once more Hrothgar and his followers are helpless in the face of her murderous visitations. They once more look to Beowulf for succor from this new monster. Again the Geatish hero assures them that he will save them by subduing this new threat to their peace and happiness. He goes to the mysterious mere infested with serpents, plunges into the murky waters down to the fiery cave where the monster dwells. There, in a terrible struggle with the monster, he wounds her; and, as her blood bubbles to the surface, his followers on the shore are saddened at what they think is the death of their master. Meantime, when Beowulf is almost overcome by the demon, finding the sword of Unferth useless against her, he notices a great mysterious sword on the walls of the cave and, seizing it, does the monster to death. As her blood gushes out in fiery streams, the sword melts down to the very hilt in the hot blood. But the monster is dead. Then comes the climax to Beowulf's visit to this fiery cave at the bottom of the mere. He turns to the dead body of Grendel stretched out on the floor of the cave, triumphantly hacks off his head, and, with it and the hilt of the great sword, swims up through the waters of the mere, now purified of all its serpents, and rejoins his followers amidst their great rejoicing at his triumphal return. After being greeted and feted by the grateful Hrothgar, he returns home triumphantly laden with the gifts which the grateful Hrothgar has showered upon him.

A Christian can hardly read this second episode even today without hearing all sorts of Scriptural and liturgical echoes ringing in his ears; and those echoes would have been a great deal louder for members of the *Beowulf*-poet's audience, who were much more familiar with Scripture and the impressive contemporary ritualistic ceremonies of baptism than are most modern readers

and fugitive, to the lake of the water-demons. Then the water was boiling with blood, the frightful surge of the waves welled up, all mingled with hot gore,—with sword-blood; the death-doomed creature had hidden himself there, and then, deprived of joys, he gave up his life,—his heathen soul in the fen-refuge; there hell received him." For an allegory this is a much more effective way of dramatizing the defeat of Satan than if he were represented as the entirely spiritual entity of theology, where any suggestion of a body and soul in Satan would be absurd. Nor does this mean that the poet did not know his theology. It merely means that he chose to borrow some of the traditional Nordic monster-lore to allegorize the overthrow of the worst monster of them all, in much the same way that Milton later retained what he knew to be an obsolete cosmography and astronomy in *Paradise Lost* because it provided a more poetic stage for the action of his poem.

of the poem.[18] From the earliest times in the Church the symbolism of the baptismal ceremony by submersion was based on a passage in Saint Paul's Epistle to the Romans (6:3-4): "Know you not that we, who are baptized in Christ Jesus, are baptized in his death? For we are buried together with him by baptism into death; that as Christ is risen from the dead by the glory of the Father, so we also may walk in newness of life." In the old baptismal ceremony, which took place on Holy Saturday immediately after the blessing of the new baptismal water as a part of the Easter vigil service, the redemptive death and burial of Christ and the sinner's death to sin were symbolized by the submersion of the catechumen in the baptismal waters. Christ's triumphant resurrection and the sinner's new life of grace were in turn symbolized by his emersion from the waters. The fact that the waters represented death and sin and the power of Satan in this ancient baptismal ceremony[19] is suggested by the prayers that are still said on Holy Saturday at the blessing of the new baptismal water:

Therefore may all unclean spirits, by thy command, O Lord, depart from hence; may the whole malice of diabolical deceit be entirely banished: may no power of the enemy prevail here; may he not fly about to lay his snares; may he not creep in secretly; may

---

[18]Allan Cabaniss in an article entitled, "*Beowulf* and the Liturgy" (*JEGP*, LIV [April, 1955], 195-201), has called attention to the possible influence of the Holy Saturday Liturgy and the Harrowing of Hell tradition on the second episode of the *Beowulf*. In a concluding paragraph in the article he says: "However heathen the original story was, it is surely reasonable to suppose that the account of Beowulf's descent into the grim fen, his encounter with the demon-brood staining the water with blood, and his triumphant emergence from it into joyous springtime is, at the least, a reflection of the liturgy of baptism; at the most, an allegory of it. That this view is not on a priori grounds impossible is evident from the quite elaborate Christian allegories of Cynewulf and of the Cædmonian *Exodus*, both approximately contemporary with the *Beowulf*-poet. Indeed the *Exodus* shows precisely the influence of the same twelve Holy Saturday prophecies. And, interestingly enough, it reflects a knowledge of just that portion of *Beowulf* with which we are here concerned. Since it has been demonstrated that the *Exodus* shows the effect of the ancient liturgy of baptism and Holy Saturday, one goes not too far afield in presuming that a similar relationship exists in reference to *Beowulf*." I had come to the same conclusion myself before reading Mr. Cabaniss' article, and I believe that I provide further corroborative evidence for this interpretation of the second episode of *Beowulf* here and that I throw it into a broader allegorical context in the poem as a whole.

[19]A. Villien points out that the solemn symbolic ritual that surrounds the blessing of the baptismal water and the actual baptism of catechumens on Holy Saturday by immersion is amongst the most ancient in the Church, parts of it probably of Apostolic origin. See his *The History and Liturgy of the Sacraments* (London, 1932), p. 2. Besides the exorcism of Satan from the baptismal waters which occurs in the earliest *Ordo*'s and *Sacramentaries* very much as we find it in the present ritual for the baptism of adults, the symbolism of the anointing of the catechumen with sacred oil also is pertinent to *Beowulf*'s struggle with Grendel. Of this anointing Villien remarks: "As for the anointing of the breast and back (*inter scapulus*, as the Ritual says), we know what symbolism is represented by this. The *De Sacramentis* indicates it in a few words: the athlete of old anointed his body with oil in order that his adversary might not be able to get a grip on him; it is against the most formidable of all foes, the devil, that the catechumen is now taking up the struggle; the blessed oil of unction represents the power of Christ which will preserve him from defeat and lead him to eternal life" (pp. 34-35). This most ancient ritual, therefore, would have familiarized a Christian audience, which had witnessed it repeated dramatically each Holy Saturday, with the struggle against Satan as a hand-to-hand wrestling match. "*Unctus et quasi athleta Christi, quasi luctam hujus saeculi luctaturus*" are the words of the *De Sacramentis*, I, ii, 4 and 5, in this regard.

he not corrupt with his infection. May this holy and innocent creature be free from all the assaults of the enemy and purified by the removal of all his malice.[20]

To an audience familiar with this symbolic meaning of immersion into and emersion from waters infested by the powers of hell and purified by the powers of God, it would have been natural to see in Beowulf's descent into the serpent-infested mere and his triumphant ascent from those waters purified of their serpents a symbolic representation of the death and burial and of the resurrection of Christ, and, in the purification of the waters, a symbol of the redemption of man from the poisonous powers of evil. Again sufficient clue for such an interpretation would have been provided for such an audience by the explicit identification of Grendel's dam and Grendel himself with the powers of hell.

The description of the cave of Grendel and his mother as a fiery cavern under the sea corresponds, too, to what was, from the time of the apocryphal Gospel of Nicodemus on up to the heart of the Middle Ages, the traditional way of representing hell. A familiar subject of literary description and artistic representation, one that goes back to at least the ninth century, is what was called Christ's Harrowing of Hell.[21] These descriptions were meant to visualize the article in the Creed which states that Christ descended into hell. The minimum meaning of that tenet of the Creed is that Christ descended into Limbo to free the souls of the just from the Old Law and conduct them into their reward now that He had completed their redemption from the power of Satan. But, based on the apocryphal Gospel of Nicodemus, a tradition had grown up that Christ also descended into the very hell of Satan, where He made His victory over His old enemy felt in a very special way.[22]

[20]Dom Gaspar Lefebvre, O.S.B., *Saint Andrew Daily Missal* (Saint Paul, 1937), p. 609.

[21]The source of the Harrowing of Hell tradition is, of course, the Apocryphal Gospel of Nicodemus, the oldest manuscripts of which date back to the fifth century, and that work was tremendously popular in England from the earliest days of Christianity there. William Henry Hulme says of its history in England: "The influence of the *Evangelium Nicodemi* was felt in English literature long before the period of the religious drama. The Gospel was doubtless introduced into England in the Latin version not very long after Christianity began to flourish there. For early English writers like Bede show perfect familiarity with its contents. And the early Christian poets utilize the story and paraphrase it in a number of their productions. An extensive account of the descent of Christ is contained in the so-called Cædmonian poems, whilst the greatest of all Old-English religious poets, Cynewulf, refers to the Harrowing of Hell in several different connections, and he reproduces much of the description in his poem on Christ. Cynewulf, in fact, or one of his school of poets, devoted an entire poem to the subject, though only a fragment of it has been preserved [*The Harrowing of Hell*]. In the later centuries of Old-English literature the *Evangelium Nicodemi* was turned into the Old-English prose, which is preserved in at least three different manuscripts. Besides this the story of the descent was frequently employed by writers of Old-English homilies and lives of the saints. The Gospel probably reached the climax of its popularity in English during the thirteenth and fourteenth centuries." *Introduction to the Middle English Harrowing of Hell and Gospel of Nicodemus* (London [EETS, E.S., 100] 1907), pp. lxvii-lxviii. The seventh *Blickling Homily* on Easter Day is an excellent example of the assimilation of the Harrowing of Hell into the Old English literary tradition and provides the best background for the proper understanding of Beowulf's descent into the lake.

[22]This is the description of Christ's victory over Satan in hell as it occurs in one version of the Gospel of Nicodemus: "And, behold, suddenly Hades trembled, and the gates of death and the bolts were shattered, and the iron bars were broken and fell to the ground, and

In early book illuminations, especially of Anglo-Saxon and Germanic origins, Christ is frequently represented as leading souls out of fiery caverns or out of the flaming mouth of a dragon, and as making Satan, represented sometimes as a human monster and sometimes as a dragon or serpent, feel His complete triumph over him by transfixing him with a sword or spear, or by binding him in chains. Again, for an audience familiar with this ancient and rich tradition, the description of Beowulf descending into the fiery cave of Grendel, of his overcoming Grendel's dam with the magic sword, and of his climaxing his visit with the triumphal beheading of the dead Grendel himself, who had been repeatedly identified with the powers of hell, would almost certainly have been taken as an allegorization of Christ's descent into hell. In Beowulf's victorious ascent from the mere, carrying the symbols of his triumph over Grendel, they could also have seen an allegorization of Christ's triumphant resurrection and victory over death, and in his victorious return to his homeland, laden with gifts from Hrothgar, a representation of Christ's triumphal ascension into heaven.

I have long suspected that the mere in this second episode of the *Beowulf* represented to the Anglo-Saxon imagination hell itself, but have had no particular evidence for such a view. I have examined a large number of Anglo-Saxon illuminated manuscripts in the British Museum, and the Bodleian and Morgan libraries, but have been unable to find any illuminations picturing hell that date back as early as the presumed ninth-century date of the *Beowulf*. There are several from the eleventh century, however, which graphically represent hell as a lake infested with dragons and man-eating, man-shaped monsters. Several illuminations in an eleventh-century Psalter (Harley Manuscript, No. 603), for instance, consistently represent hell as a lake inhabited by serpents and a great man-monster, such as that seen in Fig. 1. This illustration accompanies Psalm XXV—which treats of the great mercy of God in sparing the psalmist from his enemies. Here the illuminator has definitely interpreted the enemy as Satan and has pictured him as a man-eating man-monster emerging from the surface of a serpent-infested lake and devouring souls.* In the illumination accompanying Psalm CII (not reproduced here) the souls are shown as being pitchforked into the maw of this same man-monster as it emerges from the lake. These illuminations for the Psalter of the Harley

everything was laid open. And Satan remained in the midst, and stood confounded and downcast, bound with fetters on his feet. And, behold, the Lord Jesus Christ, coming in the brightness of the light from on high, compassionate, great, and lowly, carrying a chain in His hand, bound Satan by the neck, and again tying his hands behind him, dashed him on his back in Tartarus, and placed His holy foot on his throat, saying: Through all ages thou has done many evils; thou has not in any wise rested. Today I deliver thee to everlasting fire. And Hades being suddenly summoned, He commanded him, and said: Take this most wicked and impious one, and have him in thy keeping even to that day in which I shall command thee. And he, as soon as he received him, was plunged under the feet of the Lord along with him into the depth of the abyss" ("The Gospel of Nicodemus," *The Ante-Nicene Fathers*, Translated by Rev. Alexander Roberts and James Donaldson [New York, 1908], VIII, 457). To an audience familiar with this and many other accounts of Christ's Harrowing of Hell, it would not have been difficult to see in Beowulf's climactic beheading of the dead Grendel in the fiery cave under the sea an allegorical representation of Christ's final victory over Satan.

*[The illustration that originally appeared with this article as Fig. 1 was of folio 9, which actually accompanies Psalm 17. With Father McNamee's kind permission an illustration of fol. 16ᵛ has been substituted. This does accompany Psalm 25, and also has a head of Hades in the lower right-hand corner, though there are no souls being devoured.—R.F.]

Manuscript, No. 603, could in general be used as illustrations for the second episode of the *Beowulf*. They show that, at least by the eleventh century, the mysterious serpent-infested mere of Anglo-Saxon saga had provided a means of making the story of Christ and Satan and Hell graphic to the Anglo-Saxon imagination. It is my suggestion that the *Beowulf*-poet had already begun to employ this means of representing Satan and Hell in the figure of Grendel and the mysterious mere.

As a matter of fact, the use of the traditional Nordic serpent and dragon motif for symbolizing the power of Satan over mankind became something of a tradition in Anglo-Saxon and Anglo-Norman art in general. The whole symbolical treatment of the theme of redemption in the famous Gloucester paschal candlestick (*ca.* 1110) preserved in the Victoria and Albert Museum in London employs this motif (Fig. 2). The condition of unredeemed man is symbolized in the candlestick, the base and stem of which are entirely made up of little human figures enwrapped in the coils of serpentine and dragonish creatures. Man's redemption from the toils of the evil one is symbolized by the signs of the four evangelists on the knob of the candlestick, by the candle itself (the symbol of the light of truth and the saving grace of Christ the redeemer), and most unmistakably by the inscription in Latin on the rim of the cup of the candlestick: LUCIS: ON[US]: VIRTUTIS: OPUS: DOCTRINA: REFULGENS: PREDICAT: UT: VICIO: NON: TENEBRETUR: HOMO (The duty of this light is a work of virtue, as a shining lesson it preaches that man be not darkened by sin). If my interpretation of *Beowulf* is correct, the poet had used, back in the ninth century, the Nordic material in very much the same way in which the designer of the Gloucester candlestick used it in the twelfth century—to symbolize the redemption of mankind by Christ from the grip of Satan.

If this was in any way intended by the *Beowulf*-poet, it might be asked why he was not more explicit. It might be countered that to have been more explicit would have spoiled the poem as an allegory—especially for an Anglo-Saxon audience which had such a taste for obscure allegory and the riddle of runes. All that would have been needed for such an audience is a clue sufficient to suggest the identification. The close parallel between the situation of Beowulf and the Savior would have been sufficient to fasten the allegory. And in many places the language employed by the *Beowulf*-poet is almost a direct paraphrase of the language of Scripture describing a situation in Christ's life parallel to that in which Beowulf finds himself.[23]

If this suggestion has any merit whatever, what the *Beowulf*-poet has done in the first two episodes of the poem is to tell the story of salvation twice in allegorical terms. In the first episode, he merely allegorizes the essential facts of the story—the need of a Savior and His advent. In the second episode, he

---

[23]Klaeber, in his notes to the poem, has pointed out many of the scriptural echoes which occur throughout the poem. Let me call attention here to just one typical example which subconsciously but inevitably makes one associate Beowulf with Christ. It occurs in Hrothgar's exclamation of thanks to Beowulf for having freed his people from the attacks of "demons and evil spirits." "Lo! That self-same woman who bore this child among the tribes of men may say, if she still lives, that the eternal God has been gracious to her in her child-bearing" (Hall, p. 68 [942-946]). This subtly echoes the woman's greeting of Christ in Luke 11:27: "Blessed is the womb that bore thee, and the paps that gave thee suck."

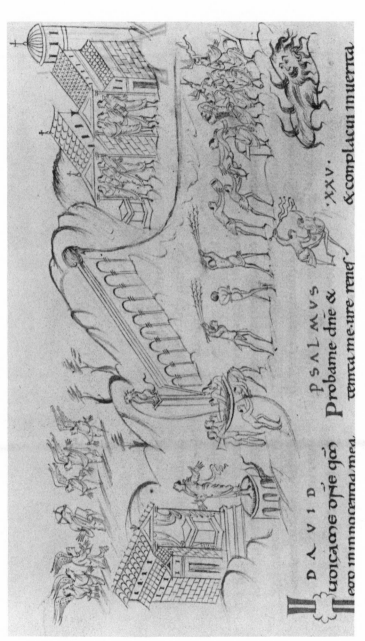

Fig. 1. Illustration for Psalm XXV. Eleventh Century, English.
Harley MS. 603 f. 16ᵛ. By permission of the British Library.

Fig. 2. Gloucester Candlestick (*ca.* 1110). By courtesy of
the Board of Trustees of the Victoria and Albert Museum.

repeats the story of man's need of a Savior from the powers of evil, but emphasizes the effects of redemption in the descent into and purification of the serpent-infested mere.

In the third and last episode of the poem, which tells of Beowulf's conflict with the fire-dragon, he allegorizes the story of salvation once again, this time dramatizing the price of salvation—the very life of the Savior Himself. The literal story is again quite simple. Beowulf's own people are being ravaged by a fiery dragon whose treasure-hoard has been disturbed by a fugitive from justice. They are powerless to save themselves from the havoc wrought by the dragon, and hence Beowulf goes out to do battle with the fire-drake. He is led out to the lair of the dragon by the guilty follower who enraged the dragon in the first place. When the monster comes forth belching fire, to meet his challenger, all Beowulf's followers flee in terror with one sole exception—the faithful Wiglaf, who stays with his master to the end. Beowulf succeeds in giving the dragon a mortal wound, but he himself has been mortally wounded by the beast in the struggle. He has saved his people and won for them the treasure hoarded by the dragon but at the price of his own life. He expires at the ninth hour of the day, and the poem ends with the picture of his twelve followers circling his funeral mound singing his praises to the four corners of the world.

Klaeber has observed, in his notes on this part of the poem, the close parallel between the circumstances that surround Beowulf in this last episode and those which surrounded Christ in the last hours of his life.[24] The number correspondence is exact. Beowulf is led out to his conflict by a guilty follower as Christ was betrayed into the hands of His executioners by His guilty disciple Judas. The poet notes that there are thirteen in the party going out to meet the dragon, thus paralleling Christ and His twelve apostles. When the dragon attacks, ten of Beowulf's followers flee in terror, leaving only Wiglaf, the one faithful follower, who remains to the end. This, too, corresponds to the situation of Christ in His last hours. Ten of His followers also deserted Him in His passion (Judas had deserted Him before the event), and only Saint John remained faithful to Him to the end. Beowulf is described, too, as expiring, like Christ, at the ninth hour. When his funeral mound has been built, his twelve disciples are described as circling it singing his praises to the four corners of the world. This again corresponds to the Apostles of Christ—twelve in number after the election of Matthias—who proclaimed the story of the Savior to the whole world after His death.

As the specific identification of the monsters in the first two episodes with

---

[24]Klaeber comments, regarding the third episode: "It is especially in the last adventure that we are strongly tempted to look for a deeper, spiritual interpretation. The duality of the motives which apparently prompt Beowulf to the dragon fight may not be as unnatural as it has sometimes been considered. Still, it is somewhat strange that the same gold which Beowulf rejoices in having obtained for his people before the hour of his death is placed by his mourning thanes into the burial mound; they give it back to the earth. Nay, Wiglaf, in the depth of his sorrow which makes him oblivious of all else, expresses the wish that Beowulf had left the dragon alone to hold his den until the end of the world. The indubitably significant result of the adventure is the hero's death, and, in the structural plan of the poem, the aim and object of the dragon fight is to lead up to this event—a death, that is, which involves the destruction of the adversary, but is no less noteworthy in that it partakes of the nature of a self-sacrifice. . . . Some incidents in the encounter with the dragon also lend themselves to comparison with happenings in the garden of Gethsemane" (p. li).

the powers of hell would have been sufficient clue to enable the *Beowulf*-poet's audience to identify the story with the Christian story of salvation, so the parallel between the circumstances surrounding Beowulf's last hours and those surrounding Christ's would also have sufficed for the identification of this third episode with the Christian story of salvation. But a climactic detail is added in this third allegorization of the story which emphasizes the kind of savior—a savior who saves by losing his own life. This, of course, was the most impressive feature of the Christian story of salvation—the unselfish generosity of a Savior Who lays down His life to redeem mankind. The use of the dragon as the adversary in this final conflict would also have served as a clue to the allegory for an audience familiar with the very ancient tradition representing the fiends of hell as fire-breathing dragons.[25]

But how much of this can be represented as the intention of the *Beowulf*-poet? I make no claim here of being able to answer that question. But this much at least is true: if one were to invent a story whose every detail was designed to allegorize the story of salvation, one could not improve very much on the Beowulf story as it stands. This fact suggests the possibility that the *Beowulf*-poet was writing in the spirit of Pope Saint Gregory, who had cautioned Saint Augustine in his zeal not to make a clean sweep of the old native Anglo-Saxon customs, myths, ceremonies, and traditions, but to adapt them to the expression of the new Christian message.[26] And if our interpretation of the poem is tenable, it would seem that the *Beowulf*-poet was proceeding in a manner exactly opposite to the procedure of the authors of poems like the *Andreas*. There an explicit Christian subject matter is told in the language and literary conventions of the old Nordic sagas; whereas in *Beowulf* the old pagan sagas are subtly reshaped and reorganized to shadow forth the essential facts of the new story of salvation. To an audience that was familiar with the substance of the Christian story of salvation, as well as with the traditional pagan myths, no more would be needed than the identification of Grendel and Grendel's dam with the powers of hell in part one, and the parallelism between the situations of Christ and Beowulf in part two to enable them to catch the allegory. It would be surprising, in fact, if this allegorical element were not present in Beowulf, when we see how much it permeated subsequent Anglo-Saxon and Anglo-Norman sculpture, and book illuminations.

---

[25]The tradition of representing Satan as a dragon, of course, is based on the following passage from the *Apocalypse* (21:2): "And he laid hold on the dragon the old serpent, which is the devil and Satan, and bound him for a thousand years."

[26]See The Venerable Bede, *The Ecclesiastical History of the English Nation* (Everyman Edition) (London, 1951), pp. 52-53: "When, therefore, Almighty God shall bring you to the most reverent Bishop Augustine, our brother, tell him what I have, upon mature deliberation on the affair of the English, determined upon, viz., that the temples of the idols in that nation ought not to be destroyed; but let the idols that are in them be destroyed; let holy water be made and sprinkled in the said temples, let altars be erected, and relics placed. For if these temples are well built, it is requisite that they be converted from the worship of devils to the service of the true God; that the nation, seeing that their temples are not destroyed, may remove error from their hearts, and knowing and adoring the true God, may the more familiarly resort to the places to which they have been accustomed." What St. Gregory is bidding St. Augustine do in the matter of pagan temples, purify them of their paganism and make them serve the purposes of Christianity, is parallel to what the *Beowulf*-poet has done with the old pagan myths, if our interpretation of the poem is defensible.

This allegorical intention would also help to explain why the poet combines the particular elements of the bear-man story and other sagas in the precise way in which he does. If our interpretation is reasonable, it was the story of salvation that was the principle of selection and arrangement for the poet. It was the outline of the story of salvation that dictated what he would take and what reject from the traditional tales to fit his allegorical intention. Thus the order of events in the cave, ending in the beheading of Grendel instead of the death of his mother, an order which differs from all comparable situations in similar traditional stories and which has consistently puzzled the critics,[27] is no puzzle at all if we see this episode as an allegorization of the Harrowing of Hell which must be climaxed by a dramatization of Christ's final victory over Hell and Satan.

This interpretation also reinforces the artistic unity and consistency of the poem as a whole. I have shown elsewhere in *Honor and the Epic Hero* how parts one and two are intimately woven together through the relationship of the characters of Hrothgar and Beowulf. They are also closely intertwined in the allegorical meaning. Part one tells the story of salvation, emphasizing the historical fact of the Savior; part two repeats the story but dramatizes the kind of Savior Who saved by yielding up His own life. This is also parallel to the relationship between parts one and two in the literal story in which the mature Beowulf of part two is a repetition of the mature Hrothgar of part one. Klaeber is right, then, in saying that if *Beowulf* can be interpreted as an allegory of salvation, a much fuller meaning and even greater artistic unity is discernible in the poem as a whole.

For the allegorical purposes of the poem, moreover, the conflict with the monsters is a far better vehicle than any either historical or fictional conflict on the battlefield could ever be. Historical battles are consistently kept in the background, and, as Chambers points out, we are continually given the impression that Beowulf's struggle has a far broader implication than any conflict of Odysseus with mere preternatural monsters like Polyphemus.[28]

---

[27]In discussing the parallel between the second episode of the Beowulf story and the *Samsonssaga*, Klaeber calls attention to the narrative shift in the position occupied by the beheading of Grendel. "Some noteworthy innovations in the *Beowulf* account—apart from the general transformation incident to the epic setting and atmosphere—are the following. The mother of the slain Grendel leaves her cave, appears in the hall, and avenges her son in heroic fashion—an evident amplification (including a partial repetition) of the narrative. Again, Grendel, though (mortally wounded by Beowulf and) found dead in the cave, is as it were slain again and definitely disposed of by beheading. In the original form of the story, it appears, the male demon had been merely wounded; when the hero made his way to the dwelling place of the monsters, he put the wounded enemy to death (and afterwards killed the mother)" (Klaeber, p. xviii). If the poet was here allegorizing the harrowing of hell, it would be clear why he puts the beheading of Grendel in the climactic position in this episode, and why he has Beowulf mount through the waters cleansed of the serpents that had infested it bearing triumphantly the severed head of Grendel.

[28]R. W. Chambers, "Beowulf and the 'Heroic Age' in England," *Man's Unconquerable Mind* (Philadelphia, 1953), p. 66. And Klaeber also suggests that the *Beowulf*-poet was content with the struggle with fabulous monsters precisely because that struggle may have suggested something far more significant. "It would indeed be hard to understand why the poet contented himself with a plot of mere fabulous adventures so much inferior to the splendid heroic setting, unless the narrative derived a superior dignity from suggesting the most exalted hero-life known to Christians" (Klaeber, p. li).

Beowulf's conflict with the monsters comes closer to that of Adam with Satan in *Paradise Lost*. It has some of the same universal implications. Although he made it in connection with specifically religious Anglo-Saxon poems, Professor Kennedy's remark is also applicable, it seems to me, to *Beowulf:*

It cannot be forgotten that there is constantly recurring evidence in Old English religious poetry that in many instances the central unity of these religious poems develops from theological, rather than from literary roots.[29]

---

[29]Kennedy, p. 190. Still another remark of Professor Kennedy's states generically of *Beowulf* what we have tried to show more specifically: "It was natural, then, that Old English poetry should reveal this blending of pagan and Christian culture. The pagan legend of *Beowulf* was reshaped into an unmistakably Christian poem. Conversely, Christian themes were versified and adorned in the spirit, and with the detail, of the pagan heroic lay" (p. 159).

The Christian Perspective in *Beowulf*

By Margaret E. Goldsmith

If I say that *Measure for Measure* is about chastity and charity, no one will suppose that I mean to imply that it is not a good play. When I say that *Beowulf* is about pride and covetousness, a simplification of roughly the same order, I can expect to be thought to say that it is not a poem at all, but a homily in verse. It is part of the purpose of this paper to show that *Beowulf* is a poem of the spirit, achieving its effects for the most part by poetic, not homiletic, techniques. To put this another way, *Beowulf* is not what Blake would call an Allegory, "formed by the daughters of Memory," but a poem of that greater kind which springs from Imagination, which he calls Vision.[1] Such poems stem directly from the poet's inbred beliefs about man and the universe, so that the work itself embodies his conception of reality. He may asseverate, as Blake did, that "Vision or Imagination is a representation of what Eternally Exists, Really and unchangeably," or affirm, less introspectively, that poetry can speak truth:

> hwilum gyd awræc
> soð ond sarlic, hwilum syllic spell
> rehte æfter rihte. (*Beowulf*, lines 2108-10)

This kind of poetry must be both "soð ond sarlic": true, as congruent with "what Eternally Exists"; sorrowful, because "Man being in the parlous state he is, vision for him is largely a question of seeing his aberrations reflected against the stainless mirror of the real."[2] Such a poet is more intensely aware than other men of human weakness and destitution: the ultimate nakedness of the rich, the ultimate helplessness of the strong. If he is also a Christian, he has a doctrine to explain human imperfection, a promise of help in weakness, a consolation for inevitable loss. His belief in the doctrine and the hope in no way dulls his awareness of these things—it often sharpens their poignancy; but it annihilates despair. So, the *Beowulf* poet, writing of strength and riches, is

---

[1] "Vision or Imagination is a representation of what Eternally Exists, Really and unchangeably. Fable or Allegory is Form'd by the daughters of Memory. Imagination is surrounded by the daughters of Inspiration, who in the aggregate are called Jerusalem." William Blake, "Notes on A Vision of the Last Judgment," in *The Complete Writings of William Blake*, ed. G. Keynes (London, 1957), p. 604.

[2] G. Wingfield Digby, *Symbol and Image in William Blake* (Oxford, 1957), p. 106.

This article first appeared in *Comparative Literature* 14 (1962), 71-90; and subsequently in *Studies in Old English Literature in Honor of Arthur G. Brodeur*, ed. Stanley B. Greenfield (Eugene: Univ. of Oregon Press, 1963), pp. 71-90. Reprinted by permission of the author and the University of Oregon Press.

synchronously aware, not only that strength and riches are transient, but that the greatest human strength is inadequate, and the greatest human wealth valueless, when the soul is in jeopardy. As an Anglo-Saxon Christian, he could lay the blame for man's parlous state upon Adam and Eve, who forfeited paradise "þurh heora gifernesse and oferhygde."[3] For him, self-sufficiency and love of the world would be the denial of man's natural service to God, for which he was created. These, therefore, are the primeval sins. Alienation from God begets envy and hatred of the good, as is told in the myth of Cain. These are the sins of the second generation. It follows that, if I say that *Beowulf* is about pride and covetousness in the first place, and about envy and hatred in the second place, I am asserting, in sum, that the Christian poet was writing about the human tragedy as he understood it.

Perhaps I may here rehearse some of the considerations which have led me to this view of the *Beowulf* poem. We read a story of fabulous adventures, peppered with general maxims about life, and the first question which forms in our minds is whether these maxims are necessary to the poem, or whether the author, or someone else, has scattered them broadcast, in order to lend an odor of sanctity to what might otherwise smack of heathenism. Since the publication of Professor Brodeur's book, *The Art of Beowulf* (Berkeley, 1959), this question of artistic unity need no longer be debated. Where we may still differ is over the emphasis to be given to those passages in which the poet speaks directly and not through the mouth of a character in the story. For me, these passages reinforce an impression, which grows stronger with study of the poem, that the poet was concerned with the minds and hearts of men *sub specie aeternitatis*, and only secondarily with wars and banquets and feats of swimming. One of the strongest reasons for this belief is the extraordinary way in which the poet has avoided writing an epic about a martial hero. If we compare *Beowulf* with the *Chanson de Roland*, it is plain that the earlier poet had the material, had he so wished, to write a poem of the *Roland* sort (granted some license in the matter of Beowulf's religious beliefs). It is not difficult to imagine an epic of a knightly Beowulf, the hero as the right arm of his uncle Hygelac as Roland was of Charlemagne, routing the Swedish companions with Nægling, fighting a desperate rear-guard action as the invading Geats are forced back to the Rhine, engaging in personal combat to the death with thirty of the attacking Franks, and so on. Yet, in spite of the promise of his opening lines, our poet seems to have very little interest in such battle poetry. He never allows Beowulf to move at the head of an army, or even to slay a human opponent, in any part of the main action. These features of his life story must be deliberately suppressed; we cannot say that the poet was constrained by his well-known story, since the poem as we have it contains somewhere all these heroic elements. For some purpose of his own, the poet has minimized all the battle scenes in which Beowulf might have displayed his prowess; though the vigorous treatment of the Battle of Ravenswood, in which Beowulf has no part, shows that he lacked neither the skill nor the temper to create battle-poetry.[4] It is noteworthy, too, that Beowulf's revenge on Onela

---

[3]*Blickling Homilies*, ed. R. Morris, EETS 58 (London, 1880), p. 24.

[4]The prominence given to the Battle of Ravenswood seems to call for some explanation, since its connection with Beowulf's life is very slight, and more significant battles are passed

for the slaying of his king Heardred is accomplished, as it were, by proxy, and his revenge on Dæghrefn for the death of Hygelac is not told as an exciting feat in itself, but as part of the history of the *breostweorðung* which was torn from Hygelac's dead body.[5] If a martial epic of Beowulf was known to our poet, he has taken pains to recast it in quite another mold. One feature which might find a place in a poem of either kind is the hero's pride. Beowulf, like Roland (and like Byrhtnoth), possesses that arrogant self-confidence which is the special trait of the supremely noble and courageous fighter. Roland's refusal to call for help destroys the flower of France; Beowulf's insistence on challenging the dragon alone destroys the Geats. Oliver's bitter reproach to Roland:

> Mielz valt mesure que ne fait estultie
> Franceis sont morz par vostre legerie . . .
> Vostre proecce, Rollanz, mar la veïmes,[6]

is matched by Wiglaf's words after Beowulf's death:

> Oft sceall eorl monig   anes willan
> wraec adreogan,   swa us geworden is.
> Ne meahton we gelæran   leofne þeoden,
> rices hyrde   ræd ænigne
> þæt he ne grette   goldweard þone. (Lines 3077-81)

If we regard his treatment of the disastrous pride of the traditional epic hero as a touchstone of the poet's Christianity, by this test *Beowulf* is revealed as a more fundamentally Christian poem than the overtly crusading poem of Roland. Beowulf's fatal pride is foreshadowed; it is treated as a sin which he must guard against when he comes to power.

This evidence of the poet's intention to put the wars into the background and the motives of men into the foreground led me to examine more closely his pointers to the meaning of the stories, both in the comments upon the action and in the emphases of the stories themselves. This approach revealed a coherence of inner design, which not only justified the sequel to the affairs at Heorot but also explained the relevance of several difficult passages.[7]

It may be in place to summarize briefly here my interpretation of the poem, as previously published,[8] since what I have to say now assumes a view of the work substantially in agreement with this interpretation.

Hrothgar, King of the Danes, builds a towering hall, in which he lives

over in a line or so. Are we intended to see in the cruel contest *wið Hrefnawudu* a particular example of the violence and hatred of the race of Cain, whose symbol, according to Bede, is the raven of the Ark? "significant homines in immunditia cupiditas teterrimos, ad illa quæ foris sunt in hoc mundo intentos," Beda, *In Pent. Comm., Gen.; P.L.*, XCI, col. 223. This passage is used by Huppé to elucidate lines 1446-48 of the OE *Genesis* (B. F. Huppé, *Doctrine and Poetry* [New York, 1959], p. 175). One might recall also the extraordinary raven that awakens the men of Heorot (line 1801) on the day of Beowulf's departure.

[5]See lines 2501-08.

[6]*La Chanson de Roland, laisse* 131 (Gröber's numbering).

[7]Notably, lines 175-188, 1002-08, 1059-60, 1722-81, 2291-93, 2329-32, 2764-66, 3058-60, 3074-75.

[8]M. E. Goldsmith, "The Christian Theme of *Beowulf*," *Medium Ævum*, XXIX (1960), 81-101.

prosperously, untroubled by enemies, until the terrible visitation of a hellish monster, of the race of Cain, who devours his men and parts him from his throne and treasure.[9] In retrospect, the old king recognizes this visitation as allowed by God because of his own pride in his power and his wealth. The tribulation of the Danes is brought to an end by the young champion Beowulf, whom Hrothgar hails as God-sent for their deliverance. Slowly the darker side of Heorot is revealed: it is to be destroyed, and the Scylding line cut off, through the workings of envy and murderous hatred within it. These are the sins of the generation of Cain, embodied in the destructive beast Grendel and his dam. The spiritual sons of Cain are all those who "build their cities" in this world, like Hrothgar at Heorot, pinning all their hope on a false good. God's mercy, working through Beowulf's selfless courage, reveals to Hrothgar his own folly; he then, in his new-found wisdom, warns the young hero of the dangers he will face when he comes to power. He may conquer his passions (unlike Heremod), and yet be corrupted insidiously, as Hrothgar was, by success and wealth. The second part of the poem is the realization of what Hrothgar's warning has foreshadowed, the old King Beowulf's mortal struggle with the dragon, who as a shape of the devil typifies pride, and as *goldweard* typifies covetousness. As young Beowulf's selflessness saved Hrothgar, so young Wiglaf's selfless love saves Beowulf from defeat, though it cannot save him from death. Beowulf, dying, puts off his royal adornments, and his spirit goes to face judgment among the just souls. Thus the poet uses the heroic combats of story to typify man's unending contest with the powers of darkness, an idea implicit in the Psalms, made explicit by Paul in his Epistles,[10] and elaborated by the Fathers, in particular by Gregory the Great: "Tentatio itaque ipsa militia est, quia dum contra malignorum spiritum insidias vigilat, in bellorum procinctu procul dubio exsudat."[11]

When I first formed this theory of the meaning of the poem some years ago, it looked a good deal more improbable than it does today. The recent spate of scholarly discoveries about the nature of Old English elegiac poetry is washing away many theories built upon the false impression that the Christian beliefs contained in them were not germane to the essential themes. The "paganism" of *Beowulf* died hard, chiefly because of widespread ignorance of what Anglo-Saxon Christianity was like. Professor Whitelock's book, *The Audience of Beowulf*, published ten years ago, showed that we have every reason to believe that the poet and his audience were grounded in the Christian faith and accustomed to listen to Christian poetry.[12] Some of the implications of this are suggested below.

Beowulf critics have been diffident in recognizing to the full that the stored mind of the hearer or reader is part of the poet's material. This fact, accepted

---

[9]I accept here the interpretation of lines 168-169 so convincingly argued by Brodeur, *The Art of Beowulf*, pp. 203-204, save that I should regard "ne his myne wisse" as a statement that Hrothgar did not enjoy God's favor at that time.

[10]*Ep. I Tim.* VI, 12; *Ep. ad. Eph.* VI, 10, 13-18.

[11]*Gregorius, Moralia; P.L.,* LXXV, col. 805.

[12]D. Whitelock, *The Audience of Beowulf* (Oxford, 1951), p. 7. This pioneer book has been followed by such consolidating studies as those of M. P. Hamilton, "The Religious Principle in Beowulf," *PMLA,* LXI (1946), 309-330, and A. G. Brodeur, *The Art of Beowulf, passim.*

as a truism by modern artists,[13] is none the less true for Anglo-Saxon poets, in spite of being ignored by the early manuals of poetic art, which concern themselves exclusively with formal structures. This critical diffidence is surprising when we consider the peculiar nature of the *Beowulf* narrative, which moves forward by "a subtle technique of allusion, reminder, and suggestion."[14] Where the allusions and reminders concern traditional heroic stories, research has always been busy, acknowledging the importance of finding the reference. Where the reminders concern Christian lore (with the exception of the explicit connection of Grendel with Cain and the giants of Genesis) scholars often silently assumed that these were out of keeping with the story of Beowulf, and hence not to be pressed. Now that scholars are accepting the importance of the Latin Fathers in the shaping of the Christian Anglo-Saxon's mental world, the critic has the task of sifting from these doctrines those which are poetically relevant.

Beowulf is not, Brodeur states, a religious poem.[15] Interpreted rather narrowly, this judgment is not to be questioned. This is not a poem of the same sort as *Crist* or *Andreas;* in essence it is neither devotional nor homiletic. Yet, as I am sure Brodeur would agree, it is by no means an irreligious poem or a wholly secular poem. It is a poem about the heroic life, written by a Christian poet, and such a theme could not be divorced from Christian faith and hope, save by a deliberate effort on the poet's part to recreate the past with the detachment of a scientific historian. There is no conceivable reason for the poet to adopt such a course. Nor should we expect him to chase from his mind the traditional Christian attitudes toward the Good Fight, when imagining a fight against monstrous creatures whose malice springs ultimately from the Ancient Enemy. Undeniably, *Beowulf* has a historical perspective, but even if the poet possessed the fictive power to create a wholly heathen Beowulf, he and his audience would still measure the hero's beliefs about life against their own.

Can we know what the poet's beliefs were? We can assume, without debate, that his intended audience would share them, since without this assumption his allusive method would please no one but himself. Can we guess at the subjects of the Christian poetry he knew and that they were accustomed to hear? I think we can. By common consent, *Beowulf* is placed later than Cædmon's poems. We know from Bede's list of them[16] that Cædmon's verse paraphrases covered the whole of the history of man: his Creation, Fall, Redemption, and his ultimate destiny. Because of the authority conferred on them by reason of Cædmon's miraculous gift of song, these poems were no doubt recited wherever Bede's tale was known. We shall see that they cover just those subjects which Bede would have required a Christian convert to know. We are not to suppose that there was ever an evangelical stage in the conversion of the English, when an audience of baptized Christians would have been familiar with the Gospel of Christ and yet unaware of the symbolic commentaries of

[13]E.g., J. M. Synge, Preface to *The Playboy of the Western World,* says "All art is a collaboration," and is quoted approvingly by modern critics.

[14]Whitelock, p. 2.

[15]Brodeur, p. 31.

[16]*Beda, Historia Ecclesiastica,* IV, lib. c. xxiv.

the Fathers. Professor Whitelock makes some general observations about the way missionaries teach the Faith,[17] but we can perhaps be more definite than this. It is relevant to note the evidence of Professor J. P. Christopher in the preface to his translation of *De catechizandis rudibus*:

Since St. Augustine composed this treatise on such sound principles of pedagogy and psychology, it is not surprising to find that upon it are based almost all subsequent works on catechetics. . . . In England, Bede and Alcuin, under whom the monastic schools reached their highest development, used *De catechizandis rudibus* and *De doctrina christiana* as textbooks.[18]

Though the reference here is to the use of these books in monastic schools, this formulation of the essentials of the Faith would spread from the priests to those whom they prepared for baptism or confirmation. The evidence of the surviving OE homilies is that in England, as elsewhere, the reverence for authority which is a dominant characteristic of the Roman Church showed itself in close repetition of patristic *sententiae* in popular sermons, so that even a lay audience might be expected to remember their chief doctrines and to recognize their favorite metaphors. For our purpose, however, we do not have to assume that every Anglo-Saxon knew his Gregory. There are signs in the secular interests of the poem that it was composed primarily for a cultured audience. Even if only a minority of the poet's hearers could have appreciated the richness of his allusions, they are there because the poet, himself an educated man, had been trained to see life like this, and expected his audience to share his attitude. It is no coincidence that Augustine's model form of instruction,[19] to be used by the priest in teaching the would-be Christian, begins, after an exhortation to think of the fleeting nature of this world's wealth and success, with the Creation, man's Fall, Cain and Abel, and the Flood, and follows the same course as the list of Cædmon's poems given by Bede. We shall recognize this approach in the *Beowulf* poem itself, with the difference that the poet, who is not instructing the ignorant, takes for granted the story of the Fall, and stops short of the Incarnation, since the characters in his story do not know Christ.

The other Christian teacher whose writings were particularly known to the Anglo-Saxons is of course Gregory the Great, whose mission established the Roman Church in England. It is not surprising, therefore, to find the major doctrines of both Gregory and Augustine alluded to, but never expounded, in *Beowulf.* The lines in which the most obvious Gregorian and Augustinian influence appears are suspect in the eyes of some editors,[20] chiefly on the grounds that their tone is "more Christianly homiletic than we could expect."[21] Professor Brodeur has gone a long way towards justifying the inclusion of these passages;[22] I hope to go even further in establishing their relevance.

[17]Whitelock, pp. 6-7.

[18]St. Augustine, *The First Catechetical Instruction* (in *Ancient Christian Writers,* Vol. II), translated by J. P. Christopher (Westminster, Md., 1946), p. 8.

[19]*De Catechizandis Rudibus,* c. xvi, §24; *P.L.,* XL, col. 328.

[20]See the edition by C. L. Wrenn (London, 1953), pp. 67-69.

[21]Wrenn, p. 67.

[22]Brodeur, pp. 182-219.

This, then, was my starting-point: the man who wrote Hrothgar's "sermon" was conversant with the teachings of Augustine and Gregory, and was familiar with Gregory's favorite image of the soldier keeping vigil against the onslaughts of the Enemy.[23] Suppose, therefore, that this sermon in the heart of the poem was no less carefully contrived than the rest of the narrative; we may look in the latter part of the poem for the poetic effect of the recalling of this image. Similarly, in other places, we may find reminders of commonly-held Christian ideas which are to be recollected later in the story. The "sermon" itself no doubt seemed to the poet completely appropriate for a pre-Christian king. As Brodeur says, it is "reminiscent of the Psalms,"[24] and this not only in its majesty and wisdom, but in its humility before the King of Kings. In speaking of its Augustinian or Gregorian modes of thought, we must not forget that these have roots in the Pentateuch and the Psalms; the attitude of Hrothgar here is that of the Psalmist who says, "Bonum mihi quia humiliasti me, ut discam iustificationes tuas. Bonum mihi lex oris tui super millia auri et argenti."[25] In just the same way the poet imputes to Beowulf thoughts which he finds in the Psalms, adding a little "local color" by also putting into his mouth some proverbial phrases about *Wyrd* which men would recognize as belonging to their ancestors. This seems to me the likely explanation of the feeling some readers have that Beowulf is portrayed as a Christian, and the belief of others that he is given a heathen character. As Brodeur says, "The hero is as much a Christian as Hrothgar—and no more. The question is: did the poet really conceive either of them as a Christian?"[26] It seems to me that he thought of them as living under the Old Covenant, to be judged according to the Old Law as the Israelites were, since they had had no Revelation of God.[27] In one important passage, which Tolkien has called the manifestation of "a heathen and unchristian fear"[28] and Brodeur has equated with the Christian state of "readiness for contrition,"[29] Beowulf grieves that he has incurred God's anger unwittingly.[30] Here again, the Psalter resolves the argument: "Delicta quis intelligit? Ab occultis meis munda me."[31] It is not surprising that this Psalm should be in the poet's mind, for the preceding verses speak of the judgments of the Lord as more to be desired than gold, "etenim servus tuus custodit ea; in custodiendis illis retributio multa." This recalls the general tenor of

[23]*Gregorius, Moralia; P.L.*, LXXV, cols. 805 ff., sections 244, 246, 399, etc. See also Whitelock for other examples, p. 7 and p. 81.

[24]Brodeur, p. 214.

[25]Psalm CXVIII, 71-72 (Vulg.).

[26]Brodeur, p. 196.

[27]This highly controversial point cannot be debated here. I interpret the Danes' idol-worship as a falling-away from the true God, *pace* Brodeur (p. 198 et seq.). The poet may have had in mind Psalm LXXVII (Vulg.), particularly 7, 8, 22, 34, and 58. If *Drihten God* (line 181) be taken as the Lord Jesus Christ, "ne wiston" (they knew not of) would be perfectly appropriate. "Metod hie ne cuþon" (line 180) might then be interpreted to mean that the Creator was not known to them (as a Person) because they did not know Christ. Line 182, "herian ne cuþon," surely means that they had no Church to guide their prayers? I offer these suggestions tentatively, to avoid the charge of having ignored this difficulty.

[28]J. R. R. Tolkien, "*Beowulf*: The Monsters and the Critics," *P.B.A.*, XXII (1936), 287.

[29]Brodeur, p. 193.

[30]Lines 2327-32.

[31]Psalm XVIII, 12 (Vulg.).

Hrothgar's sermon to Beowulf, as does the next verse of this Psalm, which reads, "Et ab alienis parce servo tuo. Si mei non fuerint dominati, tunc immaculatus ero; et emundabor a delicto maximo." With the difficult meaning of *alienis* here we need not concern ourselves;[32] it is the last phrase which once again reminds us of the warning against the great sin of pride: as Augustine explains, "Delictum magnum arbitror esse superbiam."[33]

It would be wholly wrong to suggest that because the characters of the story live under the Old Covenant the poet has adopted an outmoded moral law for the purposes of his tale. He and his audience have a knowledge denied to Hrothgar and Beowulf, and his hearers are not expected to suspend belief. Our sense of the *depth* of the poem comes not so much from its backward look into "a darker antiquity" as from its own Christian perspective, which gives the adventures another dimension. The reminders of another world, so far from being alien to the Beowulf stories, seem to me to have a special poetic result, demonstrating "the power of reducing multitude into unity of effect"[34] which Coleridge required of a great poet. Before I discuss more precisely some of the effects of this Christian perspective, I must digress shortly upon the general nature of the poet's narrative method. Its notable peculiarity is the device of foreshadowing the outcome of events—e.g., the burning of Heorot—which involves a conscious narrative structure and a carefully controlled management of dramatic irony. I believe that he has also contrived a thematic irony, which depends upon the Christian perspective of which I am speaking.

Simple contrast in *Beowulf* is common enough; the poet delights in antitheses. Simple allusion is obviously also a favorite device of his. The technique now under discussion might be described as a contrastive allusion. The writer makes us recall an image and simultaneously offers us a travesty of it. Through this "double focus," we become sharply conscious of an incongruity, to which we may respond in a variety of ways. By some writers we are moved to laughter through this process. So, Cervantes makes us laugh at Don Quixote, who would be merely a stupid creature if our stored minds did not already contain an image of gallant and impetuous knighthood. The anti-heroes of modern novels can be comic for the same reason, that we hold them in focus with their romantic predecessors. Or, with a shift of emphasis, they may be pitiable. When conceived for a serious purpose, this technique of the double focus on symbol and virtual counter-symbol can beget an irony which provokes scorn, or compassion, or the curiously potent stirring of both these feelings. A masterly use of the technique is to be found in *Hamlet*, IV.v, when Claudius, the usurper, draws about him the protective mantle of royalty, and thus, by invoking the image of sacred kingship, makes us sharply aware of his own sacrilege.

---

[32]Augustine understands *"ab alienis"* to mean "from the evil persuasions of others." *Enarr. in Ps.* XVIII; P.L. XXXVI, col. 162. He compares Ps. XXXV, 2, explaining *"Non veniat,* inquit, *mihi pes superbiæ,* hoc est, *Ab occultis meis munda me, Domine; et manus peccatorum non moveant me,* hoc est, *Ab alienis parce servo tuo.* Some commentators see in the following phrase, *"Si mei non fuerint dominati,"* an echo of Gen. IV, 7, *"tu dominaberis illius,"* where sin is imagined as waiting like a beast at the door to overcome Cain, or to be overcome by him.

[33]*P.L.*, XXXVI, col. 163, verse 15.

[34]*Biographia Literaria*, Ch. XV, §1.

There's such divinity doth hedge a king,
That treason can but peep to what it would,
Acts little of his will.

This sort of irony may inhere in a whole work. One naturally thinks of the many modern plays which retell stories from Greek mythology: Anouilh's *Antigone*, and T. S. Eliot's *Family Reunion*, for example. Perhaps the most self-conscious use of the double focus is in James Joyce's *Ulysses*. In all these instances, the contrastive myth lies in the mind of the audience or the reader, and the writer uses its latent power when and where he will. These modern examples are not so completely different from *Beowulf* as one might think. In each, the writer has used an outworn legend for a topical purpose: so, I believe, the writer of *Beowulf* has done.[35] And this technique is not a modern invention, as Chaucer's *Troilus* will bear witness. In that poem, the same narrative method is most delicately handled—so delicately, in fact, that the modern reader, lacking the proper background, is not certain, until he reaches the epilogue, that Chaucer intended him to focus on the real world as well as the world of romantic illusion.

In precisely the same way, I suggest, the undisguisedly moral discourse put into Hrothgar's mouth is there to assure us that *Beowulf* is no fabulous tale belonging to a world past and gone. It functions like the *Troilus* epilogue, keeping reality (as the poet saw reality) in focus with the legendary events of the story. The important difference between the two is that Hrothgar's sermon is not at the end of the work. It therefore colors all our view of the happenings treated subsequently by the poet. There are manifest indications throughout *Beowulf* that this author had a subtle and ironic turn of mind: his management of the story of Ingeld is an outstanding example.[36] We have no reason to expect his spiritual theme in general to be handled less subtly or without irony. In what follows, I shall point to some places in the poem where the use of a double focus seems intended, and I shall try to assess some of the consequences for our understanding of the poem as a whole. Such interpretations are in the nature of things unprovable; they will commend themselves only insofar as they throw light in some obscure places and reveal connections of ideas where before there appeared to be awkward juxtapositions. Most of what I have to say concerns the difficulties of the second half of the poem.

Consider first the atmosphere in which Beowulf sets out for his last adventure. At this point in the narrative we know nothing of Beowulf's life after his princely enthronement on his return from Heorot to Hygelac's court, except what the few intervening lines reveal: namely, that through the deaths of Hygelac and his son Heardred, Beowulf has become King of the Geats, and has ruled well for fifty years. Thus Hrothgar and Heorot are still fresh in our

[35]*Beowulf* presents a more complex situation than any of the modern works, since we have, in addition to the retelling of modernized legends of the past, the recall of the older myth of Genesis, and also its timeless interpretation. We cannot therefore press this analogy, but it seems to me useful for identifying the process by which at certain points in the narrative we respond to a symbol not directly described. The effect of the double symbolism is considered below.

[36]I here refer to Brodeur's original and convincing theory of the treatment of Ingeld's revenge, pp. 157-180.

minds, in spite of the long interval of years in the action, when we are told of the dragon's visitation and the burning of the royal hall. There can be no doubt that his effect is deliberately arranged, so as to place Beowulf in exactly the same plight as Hrothgar after his fifty years of prosperous and victorious rule. A less subtle storyteller would have told us more about the way in which Beowulf came to power and how he avenged his young lord, instead of keeping these facts until later. The very phrasing here echoes that of the earlier visitation,

> . . . oð ðæt an ongan
> deorcum nihtum   draca ricsian . . . (Lines 2210-12)

> . . . oð ðæt an ongan
> fyrene fremman   feond on helle;
> wæs se grimma gæst   Grendel haten. . . . (Lines 100-102)

When Beowulf takes the dragon's devastations as a sign of God's anger, Hrothgar's words are not forgotten:

> Swa ic Hring-Dena   hund missera
> weold under wolcnum . . . þæt ic me ænigne
> under swegles begong   gesacan ne tealde.
> Hwæt, me þæs on eðle   edwenden cwom,
> gyrn æfter gomene,   seoþðan Grendel wearð,
> ealdgewinna,   ingenga min. (Lines 1769-76)

If it were not for the existence of Hrothgar's sermon, this parallelism might be explained as an artless repetition of the "gyrn æfter gomene" motive, another example of the fleeting nature of human happiness. But the sermon gave Hrothgar's explanation of the cause of his misery, and by recalling now that other monstrous affliction, the poet also contrives to recall that explanation and Hrothgar's warning to Beowulf. We remember how he urged Beowulf to look to his spiritual armor, to shun pride, to seek eternal gain not earthly treasure, knowing that death must overcome him at last and another dispose of his wealth. With this in mind, we hear how Beowulf prepares to meet the dragon, the keeper of the treasure. Bluntly, Hrothgar, whose own spiritual sloth had let envy and murder into Heorot, has seen his error, and so could beg Beowulf to guard himself against pride and covetousness, when the testing time should come. Now is the testing time, when the Ancient Serpent, whose sins, like Adam's, are "oferhydo and gifernesse,"[37] tempts Beowulf to boast in his own strength and to covet the buried hoard. We must recognize that this is a physical fight with a snaky monster, whose tough hide turns the sword blade and whose grisly teeth inject venom, and that some of the *Beowulf* audience would be content with it so. Others who had taken note of old Hrothgar's warning might realize that in combating this serpent Beowulf was struggling with a creature whose shape was a shape of the Devil, the archetype of pride and greed. Here we have two possible levels of understanding. But this is not the "double focus" of my theme. Beowulf is a stubborn old king

---

[37]Cf. *Blickling Homilies*, p. 31, where Jesus, rebuking Satan, tells him that his pride and greed and empty boasting brought evil upon him.

who is burnt and gashed by a fearsome beast. Beowulf is also a man fighting his personal devil. And at the same time he reflects, and is a travesty of, the *miles Deo* of the Pauline image which Hrothgar's speech has brought to mind. As king, we admire his strength and fortitude. As man tempted, we share his agony of spirit. As soul aberrant from truth, "reflected against the stainless mirror of the real," we can only pity him. For he is supremely brave, supremely heroic in suffering, and supremely wrongheaded.

The poet's attitude of pity for the wrongdoing of the Danes who turn to false gods, so fully discussed by Brodeur,[38] prepares us for a similar but less openly expressed pity for Beowulf in his wrongheadedness concerning the affair of the dragon. To save himself and his people he has only to acknowledge his weakness and ask for divine aid. He recognized that God gave him victory when he overcame Grendel, and God intervened when he was in peril in the underwater fight. In this greater peril he heartens himself by boasting of his past victories, not by appeal to the God of Victories. He trusts in his own strength, and it is not enough.

> Nis þæt eower sið
> ne gemet mannes   nefne min anes
> þæt he wið aglæcean   eofoðo dæle,
> eorlscype efne.   Ic mid elne sceall
> gold gegangan,   oððe guð nimeð,
> feorhbealu frecne,   frean eowerne. (Lines 2532-37)

We hear this speech of defiance against the faint echo of Hrothgar's prophetic warning of what may happen to a powerful king:

> . . . him on innan   oferhygda dæl
> weaxeð ond wridað . . . (Lines 1740-41)

> þinceð him to lytel   þæt he lange heold,
> gytsað gromhydig. . . . (Lines 1748-49)

If the *Beowulf* poet had been a homilist, he might have turned the old hero into the wretched king of Hrothgar's *exemplum*, another cruel and grasping Heremod, destroyed by his own misuse of God's gift of strength and power and wealth. But for good reasons he does not do this. He shows us a Beowulf still generous and beloved, but spiritually unguarded because of his pride, as Hrothgar himself had been, so that the attacks of the Enemy take him unawares—"tentatio itaque ipsa militia est."[39] In the Good Fight, the soldier must rid himself of the impedimenta he might carry while journeying, cast off his worldly possessions, and then arm himself with faith and righteousness.

Sed videamus quod ille secundum Lucæ Evangelium gladius significare possit . . . Ille est nimirum verbum Dei, quem venditis omnibus sæcularis vitæ impedimentis nobis necesse est, et viriliter in eo pugnare contra omnes antiqui serpentis insidias.[40]

These words are Alcuin's, as he strives to explain to Charlemagne the hard

---

[38]Brodeur, p. 205.
[39]*Gregorius, Moralia.* See n. 11.
[40]*Ep. ad. Carolum* CLXIII; *P.L.,* C, col. 425.

saying of Luc. XXII. 36, in which the disciples are commanded to sell their garments and buy a sword. This verse must obviously be taken figuratively, and Alcuin labors to make the reader understand that a scriptural sword may signify many things, and that the sword Christ's follower cannot do without is the Sword of the Word of God, "ut dignus in gladio verbi Dei sectator Christi efficiatur miles."[41]

Before discussing the relevance of this passage I should like to quote alongside it some well-known words of Professor Tolkien's:

Beowulf's *byrne* was made by Weland, and the iron shield he bore against the serpent by his own smiths: it was not yet the breastplate of righteousness, nor the shield of faith for the quenching of all the fiery darts of the wicked.[42]

Tolkien's implication is that if the poet had lived a generation later, he could not have refrained from investing Beowulf's armor with spiritual significance: as things are, we are spared such allegorizing. But the case is not quite so simple. To accept Tolkien's statement we must also accept Tolkien's excision from the text of lines 1724-60, in which the metaphor of spiritual armor is used by the poet. For such excision we have no warrant, as Brodeur has convincingly argued,[43] since the only reason for rejecting the lines is their inappropriateness to a preconceived theory of the meaning of the poem and its date of composition. The date of *Beowulf*, I suggest, is not particularly important in this argument, for reasons already given above: exegetical symbolism is not absent from the Cædmonian poems; Bede certainly taught by the same methods as his predecessors Jerome, Ambrose, Augustine, Isidore, Gregory,[44] all of whom used these symbolic interpretations. Because of this continuity of Christian tradition, I need make small apology for quoting Alcuin in discussing the interpretation of *Beowulf*. I use his words, rather than similar passages by earlier writers, simply because he brings conveniently together the two symbols brought together by the *Beowulf* poet, the symbol of the *miles Deo* and the symbol of the Ancient Serpent. I have already said above that the poet's allusive treatment of the vigil of the *miles Deo* in Hrothgar's sermon indicates that he expected his audience to know what he was talking about. So, *pace* Tolkien, the significance of Beowulf's iron shield is that *it is not* the breastplate of righteousness, nor the shield of faith. Beowulf's special preparations to guard himself against the dragon are invested, in the light of Hrothgar's sermon, with a tragic irony. This huge shield

> . . . wel gebearg
> lif ond lice læssan hwile
> mærum þeodne þone his myne sohte. (Lines 2570-72)

His good sword betrayed him:

---

[41]*Ibid.*
[42]Tolkien, p. 266.
[43]Brodeur, pp. 208 ff.
[44]See P. C. Spicq, *Esquisse d'une histoire de l'exégèse latine au Moyen Age* (Paris, 1944), pp. 29-32.

> Nægling forbærst,
> geswac æt sæcce   sweord Biowulfes,
> gomol ond grægmæl.   (Lines 2680-82)

He is trying to fight with the wrong weapons, and moreover, he is impeded by the love of worldly possessions, which he has not cast off. But the old king's arrogance and desire for the treasure are offset by Wiglaf's love and loyalty. Wiglaf, armed in love, helps his kinsman to overcome the beast.

It may be objected that the poet is here showing some confusion of thought, if I have interpreted him aright. Beowulf is not, and cannot be *sectator Christi*. Is it just, to blame him for his ignorance? The answer, I think, lies in the poet's portrayal of Hrothgar as a kind of Old Testament prophet, to whom God has revealed that pride and greed are the prime causes of man's afflictions. He might have found this idea in *De catechizandis rudibus*:

Neque tunc sane defuerunt justi qui Deum pie quærerent, et superbiam diaboli vincerent, cives illius sanctæ civitatis, quos regis sui Christi ventura humilitas per Spiritum revelata sanavit. . . . Erant ibi autem pauci futuram requiem cogitantes et cœlestem patriam requirentes, quibus prophetando ralevabatur futura humilitas Dei regis et Domini nostri Jesu Christi, ut per eam fidem ab omni superbia et tumore sanarentur.[45]

Or he may have been content to use the Psalms as pointers to pre-Christian moral law. Either way, Hrothgar's *andgyt*, his understanding of divine truth, is used to reveal to Beowulf the danger of accepting this world's values. Because Beowulf has not heeded the warning, he is not prepared for death. "Dol bið se þe his Dryhten nat, to þæs oft cymeð deað unþinged."[46] He faces death unflinchingly when his sword stroke fails to harm the dragon, but the pull of the world upon him is strong. At this point in the narrative the poet's Christian attitude to death is openly contrasted with Beowulf's own:

> Ne wæs þæt eðe sið
> þæt se mæra   maga Ecgðeowes
> grundwong þone   ofgyfan wolde;
> sceolde ofer willan   wic eardian
> elles hwergen,   swa sceal æghwylc mon
> alætan lændagas.   (Lines 2586-91)

If these lines are taken as a litotes for "Beowulf did not wish to die," they are intolerably verbose and clumsy. Who, one asks, would find the journey from this world to a home elsewhere an easy one to take? Once posed in this context, the question is answered. The man who leaves the world willingly is the man who puts his hope in "ece rædas," not in earthly possessions. He is the man, of the sons of Abel, who knows that this world is not his true home; he is on a journey elsewhere, and this world to him is an inn where he sojourns for a while. This image of the spiritual *peregrinus* journeying to his heavenly home is Augustine's,[47] and it was widely known. The *Seafarer* and

---

[45]*P.L.*, XL, col. 334.
[46]*Ex. Gnomic Verses*, 35. Cf. *Seafarer*, line 106.
[47]"Iter agis, attende ad quem venisti . . . stabuli est ista conditio." *Aug. Serm. in I Tim.*

Exodus poets knew it;[48] Cynewulf knew it, and used it almost casually at the end of *Crist II*:

> Forþon ic leofra gehwone   læran wille
> þæt he ne agæle   gæstes þearfe,
> ne on gylp geote,   þenden god wille
> þæt he her in worulde   wunian mote,
> somed siþian   sawel in lice,
> in þam gæsthofe. (*Crist II*, lines 815-820)

Once again the poet has contrived a contrastive allusion. Beowulf, it would seem, has aligned himself with the sons of Cain, like Hrothgar before him. But suffering saved Hrothgar, and there is still hope for Beowulf's soul, though none for his body. The link between the two metaphors, of the *miles Deo* and the *peregrinus*, is their rejection of *cupiditas*, the love of this world's goods. Beowulf, in his fight to win the hoard, is held in antithesis with both.

The poignancy of Beowulf's last hours is made greater by the hearer's knowledge that in bartering his life for the gold, he has committed the dire folly of buying what is worthless at the greatest price. This is the supreme irony, that Beowulf, blinded by arrogance and desire for the treasure, exchanges the remainder of his length of days for short-lived possession of the dragon's gold. The deluded old man finds comfort in this preposterous bargain. Again the values of the world are shown to be topsy-turvy, when we hold up this barter against the Divine Trade of a memorable sermon of Augustine's, which appears also in *Guthlac* (probably through some intervening Latin homily):

> Swa þas woruldgestreon
> on þa mæran god   bimutad weorþað
> þonne þæt gegyrnað   þa þe him godes egsa
> hleonaþ ofer heafdum. (*Guthlac*, lines 70-73)

The godfearing man barters his worldly wealth for the heavenly treasure of eternal life—a good bargain, as Augustine points out—"Non ergo simus pigri in ista mutatione rerum, in ista mercatura optima et ineffabili."[49] A similar irony is briefly hinted in the single phrase "secean sawle hord," used when Beowulf first comes in sight of the dragon's mound. We are told that he is soon to die:

> Him wæs geomor sefa,
> wæfre and wælfus,   wyrd ungemete neah
> se þone gomelan   gretan sceolde,
> secean sawle hord,   sundur gedælan
> lif wið lice. . . . (Lines 2419-23)

VI; *P.L.,* XXXVIII, col. 954. Here he is discussing the right and wrong use of treasure on earth. Cf. *Beda, Comm. in Gen.; P.L.,* XCI, col. 219: "Impiorum progenies in ipsa mundi origine civitatem construxit, quia omnes impii in hac vita fundati sunt, ubi habent thesauros; sancti vero hospites sunt et peregrini."

[48] I. L. Gordon, ed. *The Seafarer* (London, 1960), pp. 4 ff., and *Exodus*, lines 534 ff.

[49] *Aug. Serm. ad. Pop.* CLXXVII; *P.L.,* XXXVIII, col. 959. It would seem to be more than a coincidence that the text of this sermon is I Tim. VI, the chapter which I offered in my previous paper as the ultimate source of the ideas which govern the structure and values of *Beowulf*. See also n. 47. This provides the link beween lines 2586-91 and lines 2799-2800.

As Beowulf moves to attack (*gretan*) the guardian of the treasure, seeking the hoard, death (*wyrd*) is moving to attack the old man's life, seeking the treasury of the soul.[50] Here, as in the image of the barter, the poet has used stock phrases ironically so as to produce a Christian counter-image. Here the word *hord* reminds the hearer that Beowulf, facing death, should be occupied with spiritual treasure, his soul's need, instead of the earthly treasure which fills his thoughts. This wealth, because of God's decree (*wyrd* is God's instrument) can never be his—"Dixit autem illi Deus: Stulte, hac nocte animan tuam repetunt a te: quæ autem parasti, cuius erunt? Sic est qui sibi thesaurizat, et non est in Deum dives."[51]

When the dragon is dead, Beowulf, mortally wounded, desires to see the gold he has bought with his life. His arrogance is now gone, his thought is for those to whom he will leave this wealth. Yet his values are still awry; he gives thanks to God for the treasure that he has won for his people, ignorant that his death will deprive them of any profit from it. He is concerned about his earthly memorial. But, at the last, he himself puts off the golden symbols of his wealth and rank and gives them to Wiglaf, and faces the inevitability of death. In carefully chosen words, the poet tells us that his soul has gone to judgment among the souls of the just.

There is no hint here, or in his dirge, that Beowulf was the savior of his people. On the contrary, it is emphasized that they are doomed by his death to enslavement, and that they will have no good from the dragon's hoard. Why, then, have some critics gone so far as to suggest that the poem is an allegory with Christ the Savior as its true hero? The reason is not far to seek. At several points in the narrative the poet uses language which recalls the gospels. Most of these resemblances are of so general a sort as merely to indicate that biblical language filled the poet's mind.[52] The most striking of these reminders perhaps asks a better explanation. I refer to Hrothgar's praise of Beowulf, that it may truly be said that his mother was blessed by God in her childbearing.[53] This is extraordinarily like the words shouted by a woman in the crowd to Jesus as he was preaching,[54] as has been pointed out by Klaeber and others. If the reminiscence is deliberate, it recalls Christ's rebuke to the woman who shouted, and his rejoinder:

---

[50]The word *hord* itself is ambiguous, being used both for treasure and for the treasure-house. I am not clear whether *wyrd*, as God's agent, could be thought to attack a man's soul; lines 1057-59 of *Guthlac* suggest that *wyrd* has power over the soul, but here the context, as well as the genitival phrase itself, makes "body" more likely. The image appears to be that of the robber breaking into the treasurehouse, as in the similar lines in *Guthlac*:

> Deaþ nealæcte,
> stop stalgongum, strong ond hreðe
> sohte sawlhus. (Lines 1139-41)

Cf. also the compound *feorhhord* (*Guthlac*, line 1144), which undoubtedly means "body," since the despoilers use keys to unlock it.

[51]Luc. XII, 20.

[52]Such are lines 1707 ff., 2419 ff., 2596 ff. See Klaeber's notes on these lines in his edition.

[53]Lines 942 ff.

[54]Luc. XI, 27.

At ille dixit: Quin imo beati, qui audiunt verbum Dei, et custodiunt illud. Turbis autem concurrentibus, coepit dicere: Generatio hæc, generatio nequam est.[55]

So, if any weight is to be attached to these words of Hrothgar's, they form a reminder that the Scyldings have not in fact been saved by Beowulf;[56] the neglect of God's law by the evil generation within Heorot will be their bane.

The destruction of Heorot by fire and the burning of the treasure on Beowulf's funeral pyre make a fitting consummation of the two halves of the story. This is the end of the cities of earth; this is the end of the wealth of kings. To those accustomed to sermons and poems on the Last Days, the prophecy of the burning of Heorot might be seen in double focus with the burning of Sodom and Gomorrah, the cities of Cain's race, a conflagration which itself prefigures the universal burning of the wealth of the kingdoms of earth in the Apocalyptic fire. This eschatological relationship concludes the spiritual theme, as the hall-burning and the funeral pyre conclude the secular themes of the poem. The double funeral of Beowulf, by cremation and interment of his ashes, has been regarded by archaeologists as historically unlikely.[57] The poet has been accused of ignorance of the proper rites, or of attempts to harmonize pagan cremation with Christian burial. But he is not writing a history, nor yet a homily, and in terms of poetry this splendid funeral is undeniably right. The pyre hung with useless gold and unavailing armor puts the achievements of the legendary hero into Christian perspective, and accomplishes imaginatively what a didactic Christian poet attempts like this:

> Brond bið on tyhte,
> æleð ealdgestreon   unmurnlice,
> gæsta gifrost,   þæt geo guman heoldan
> þenden him on eorðan   onmedla wæs.
> (*Crist II*, lines 811-814)

And what is left? A mound of earth on a headland, burying while earth lasts the treasure of the dead; a landmark to symbolize the earthly *dom* of King Beowulf of the Geats. But to the Christian onlooker it speaks of a more enduring *dom*, that which

> lifge mid englum
> awa to ealdre,   ecan lifes blæd
> dream mid dugeþum. (*Seafarer*, lines 78-80)

This is the memorial of all good men who fight "wið feonda niþ," and this shall last when earth itself crumbles—"in memoria æterna erit justus."[58] This is the consolation for inevitable loss. And more than this, the royal grave brings to our poet, as to the writer of *The Seafarer*, the solemn thought that earth will sink into nothingness before the face of its Creator in the day of ineluctable *Dom*.

---

[55]Luc. XI, 28, 29.

[56]Thus the allusion here would serve the same purpose as lines 1002-08, 1018-19.

[57]See R. W. Chambers, *Beowulf: an Introduction*, rev. ed. (Cambridge, 1959), pp. 124 ff., and the further information added by C. L. Wrenn, p. 513.

[58]Psalm CXI, 6 (Vulg.), a verse familiar through its liturgical use in masses for the dead.

The conclusion of the poem thus completes the vision in its three aspects. We have here interpreted the fights of Beowulf in the same three ways: historically, with giant and serpent; morally, with envy, hate, pride, and greed; eschatologically, with the race of Cain and the Ancient Serpent, who is the Enemy till Doomsday. It will be recognized that these descriptions correspond to three familiar mediaeval kinds of interpretation of biblical story: literal, tropological, anagogical. The recognition will not come as a surprise to those who admit that the poet of *Beowulf* was, after the manner of his time, a learned man. For it is not strange that a man trained during his early years to contemplate truth in three aspects should see the life of man reflected in a triple mirror.

Geatish History: Poetic Art and
Epic Quality in *Beowulf*

By Stanley B. Greenfield

Although the digressions in the second part of *Beowulf* have been fruitful material for historically-oriented students of the poem, they have been somewhat unyielding to literary critics. The former have found ample sustenance in Hygelac's Frisian expedition, the poem's one historically verifiable fact; and with the aid of archaeological evidence and the testimony of Scandinavian saga they have drawn the battle lines between Swedes and Geats. The latter, concerned with structural unity and aesthetic decorum, have too frequently felt constrained to denigrate the second part of *Beowulf*. They find the fight with the dragon too much encumbered with "history", with retrospection and prognostication, as if the poet had not found his dragon combustible enough and needed more fuel for his poetic fire. These critics are more apt to perceive an aesthetic rationale in the digressions and episodes of Part I: in the tragic dramas of Finn and Ingeld, in the comparisons of Beowulf to Sigemund and Heremod, in the poignant foreshadowings of Danish downfall. Even favorable criticism of Part II has largely relegated the historical material to a background or framework role, viewing it in approving but rather general terms. For example:

. . . . the whole elaborately investigated matter of the Geatish-Swedish wars, which seem to play so relatively large a part in the later *Beowulf*, is really significant from the point of view of the poem, as part of a lively and most moving framework or setting in which the rising tragedy of the hero can the more effectively be brought home—not only the tragedy of Beowulf, but the temporal tragedy of men in this world. Or one might say that these allusions and digressions, like so many others, help to give something of universal quality and meaning to the poem.[1]

That the *Beowulf*-poet has handled the events of Geatish history with insight and poetic power the recent researches of Adrien Bonjour and Arthur G. Brodeur[2] clearly demonstrate, and the observations which follow are designed, for the most part, to supplement their perceptions. First let us consider in certain historical passages the poet's selection of events from the totality of "history" in the poem, the themes he seems to emphasize in the different selections, and some aspects of the diction in these accounts.

[1] C. L. Wrenn, ed., *Beowulf* (London, 1953, 1958), p. 73.
[2] Adrien Bonjour, *The Digressions in Beowulf* (Oxford, 1950); Arthur G. Brodeur, *The Art of Beowulf* (Berkeley and Los Angeles, 1959), esp. Chap. III.

Reprinted, by permission, from *Neophilologus* 47 (1963), 211-17.

Three passages in Part II of *Beowulf* conjoin Hygelac's Frisian raid and the Swedish-Geatish wars: lines 2349*b*-2399*a*, 2425-2515, and 2910*b*-3000. (There is a fourth reference to the wars which stands by itself, accounting for the provenience of Wiglaf's sword. This passage structurally balances an earlier reference to Hygelac's death in Part I of the poem.) The circumstances of the Frisian Fall come easily to mind: Hygelac's at-first-successful foray and ultimate defeat by the Hetware, Beowulf's revenge on Hygelac's slayer, and the champion's escape over the sea with thirty suits of armor. The Northern wars offer more trouble to the memory. As Miss Whitelock remarks, "The poet's account of these matters is scattered, and out of chronological order, so that modern readers find it difficult to gather the sequence of events without the aid of pencil and paper".[3] It may not be amiss, therefore, to set down briefly the dramatis personae and chronology of events in these wars, that we may see the historic totality plain.

On the Geatish side, the principal actors are King Hrethel and his sons Herebeald, Haethcyn, and Hygelac; Hygelac's wife Hygd and son Heardred; and Beowulf, Hygelac's nephew. On the Swedish side are King Ongentheow and his sons Ohthere and Onela, and Ohthere's sons Eanmund and Eadgils. The wars begin after Hrethel's death from sorrow over the unavenged and unavengeable death of his eldest son. With Haethcyn on the Geatish throne, an attack is made, but as to who dared first presume, critics still debate (see note 13). The upshot is the battle at Ravenswood in Sweden, where Ongentheow kills Haethcyn and threatens to exterminate his followers. But when Hygelac comes to the aid of his brother, Ongentheow prudently retreats into his fortress. But retreat is insufficient, and there he is killed by the Geat brothers Wulf and Eofor, whom Hygelac rewards handsomely. The first phase of the feud is ended, with the Geats victorious.

Ohthere rules in Sweden when Hygelac, now King of the Geats, makes his fatal raid on the Franks. He rules, too, during the period of Beowulf's regency. But when Heardred reaches maturity and occupies his rightful place as king, Onela, much to the wintry discontent of Ohthere's son Eanmund, occupies the Swedish throne. Eanmund and his brother Eadgils, revolting against their uncle, are forced to flee; they take refuge with Heardred in Geatland. Onela pursues, and having killed Eanmund and his Geatish protector, he departs, leaving Beowulf to rule the Geats. In *uferan dōgrum* Beowulf supports Eadgils against Onela, avenging Heardred's death when Onela falls. Finally, with Beowulf's own death in the fight with the dragon, it is predicted that the Swedes will again attack, and this time destroy the Geats as a nation.

So much for a chronological reconstruction. But how do we actually learn about the historic events? How may we construe their segmented presentation in the three passages under consideration? We may first note, with Brodeur,[4] that the three accounts are presented from different points of view: the poet's, Beowulf's, and Wiglaf's Messenger's. Passage I (lines 2349*b*-2399*a*) is the poet's choralistic commentary, which provides a bridge between the two parts of the poem. It recapitulates the engagements Beowulf has lived through since he cleansed Heorot of the Grendel clan. These events move chronologically, from

---

[3]Dorothy Whitelock, *The Audience of Beowulf* (Oxford, 1951), p. 54.
[4]Brodeur, *op. cit.,* pp. 83-85.

the Fall of Hygelac, through the Fall of Heardred, to Beowulf's succor of Eadgils against Onela. Nothing is mentioned here of the early wars between Ongentheow and Hrethel's sons most fittingly, Bonjour believes,[5] because the poet wants to laud Beowulf's heroic accomplishments and Beowulf had been too young for deeds at that time. But where Bonjour finds the poet's recitation to be in the heroic mode, serving to glorify Beowulf as he approaches his final fight, I find an elegiac strain. Beowulf is about to take up arms against the dragon. The poet first warns the audience that the encounter will be fatal to both beast and man; but Beowulf, he adds, was not afraid, because he had survived many cruel hostilities since he had liberated Heorot, not the least of which was that expedition of his uncle Hygelac's. The formulaic expression "forðon hē ǣr fela / nearo nēðende nīða gedīgde, / hildehlemma", heralds this summary, a formulaic counterpart, "Swā hē nīða gehwane genesen hæfde, / slīðra geslyhta, sunu Ecgðīowes, / ellenweorca", concludes it. The theme of this entire passage, the "envelope pattern"[6] suggests, should be *survival,* providing an ironic contrast to the present situation: Beowulf will *not* survive his confrontation of the dragon. The emphasis and details of the passage sustain, it seems to me, the ironic contrast. What is notable in the poet's presentation of the Fall of Hygelac is that Beowulf was a lone, wretched survivor (*earm anhaga,* a formula used principally in elegiac poems), who escaped only by swimming from the scene. In his reference to the Swedish-Geatish wars, the poet likewise gives the champion a curiously passive role as survivor of Onela's pursuit of his nephews and as recipient of Onela's bestowal of the Geatish throne. Onela, not Beowulf, receives the poet's praise, and for his magnanimity is awarded the time-honored "þæt wæs gōd cyning". And in recounting Beowulf's aid to Eadgils, the poet underplays heroics; we cannot even be sure that Beowulf was present in person at Lake Väner, but context suggests he was, and survived. It is true that we are shown, in the course of the poet's summary, something of Beowulf's strength (the Hetware who opposed him in the Frisian battle did not return home, and he carried thirty suits of armor with him in his dash across the sea); we are also given a glimpse of Beowulf's moral decency (he refuses the offer of crown and throne from the widow Hygd, preferring to act as counselor to the young Heardred); and we are presented with Beowulf's loyalty (he supplies an army for Eadgil's match with Onela). The chronology of these affairs pictures the hero maturing from warrior to king. But these insights into Beowulf's character do not prevail over the elegiac atmosphere of the report; they are concomitants to the theme of survival and wretchedness, a theme accentuated by the elegiac diction applied to others as well as to the hero: to Hygd and Heardred who, after Hygelac's death, are called *fēasceafte*; to the rebellious sons of Ohthere who, seeking refuge with Heardred, are called *wræcmæcgas;* to Eadgils alone, epithetized as *fēasceaft.* In brief, the poet from his choral eminence has so colored his historical picture that he depicts Beowulf's career as one of survival in a world in which even the best must fall, friend and foe alike: the great Geat Hygelac, the helpful Heardred,

---

[5]Bonjour, *op. cit.,* p. 42.

[6]The phrase is Adelaide C. Bartlett's, *The Larger Rhetorical Pattern in Anglo-Saxon Poetry* (New York, 1935), p. 9.

the aggressive but admirable Onela. *Sic transit gloria mundi*—and Beowulf goes to fight the dragon.

Before the hero engages his adversary, however, we hear his own voice on these matters. In the second passage (lines 2425-2515), Beowulf himself takes us chronologically from his seventh year, through Haethcyn's accidental killing of his elder brother, through Haethcyn's own death and Hygelac's revenge therefor, to the time he (Beowulf) crushes Daeghrefn to death. The champion's recollections thus cover a period of time prior to and up to the point at which the first passage began: the Fall of Hygelac.

Beowulf speaks his piece because he feels wyrd immeasurably nigh. He harks back to earlier days: "Fela ic on gioguðe guðræsa genæs, / orleghwīla", he begins. While there is a similarity here to the opening formula of the first historical passage, there is a new element in the word *youth;* Beowulf, now an aged king, vividly sees the contrast between age and youth. And he makes of this contrast a framework for the main theme of this passage, the theme of revenge. He first recalls an event in which revenge could not be taken: the old King Hrethel could not avenge the accidental death of Herebeald upon his second son. So, too, in the famous elegiac comparison Beowulf makes at this point to an old man whose son hangs on the gallows, revenge cannot be taken. Old age and deaths unavenged thus are prominent in this earliest of the hero's memories. In contrast, the following delineations of both the Swedish-Geatish wars and the Fall of Hygelac emphasize youthful vengeance: young Hygelac on Ongentheow, young Beowulf on Daeghrefn. Beowulf concludes his speech by introducing a parallel to his opening formula: "Ic genēðde fela / guða on geoguðe", and appropriately vows vengeance on the dragon. Although Beowulf feels his death is imminent, he cannot view himself and his history from the perspective of the poet. His goal is revenge, a laudatory concern in a Germanic hero.[7] Interestingly enough, a key word in Beowulf's speech is *fæhð(o)*—lines 2465, 2480, 2489, 2513*a*—a word absent from passage I; on the other hand, though *sorh* is plentiful—lines 2447*a*, 2455, 2460*b*, 2468*a*—the words denoting wretchedness and exile in the first passage do not appear here.[8]

Beowulf's speech affords some further points of interest. It explicitly blames the sons of Ongentheow for beginning the Northern hostilities; it strongly intimates that Hygelac personally avenged Haethcyn (the actual killer, Eofor, is the grammatical object of the Swedish King's enmity in a subordinate clause: "þær Ongenþēow Eofores nīosað"); and it suggests in its reference to the death of Hygelac that the Frisians did not get the king's war-gear and the famous *Brōsinga mene.* Now these three points are controverted elsewhere in the poem. In Part I of the poem, the poet comments that all of Hygelac's equipment passed into the enemy's power; in the Messenger's speech, the

---

[7]Recently, some critics have attempted to find a tragic flaw in Beowulf's character, in his desire to acquire earthly treasure instead of the heavenly variety that will not rust—see, for example, Margaret E. Goldsmith, "The Christian Perspective in *Beowulf*", *CL*, XIV (1962), 71-90, esp. p. 88. But Beowulf's express concern about obtaining the dragon's gold is a muted one, quite secondary to his acceptance of the necessity for vengeance, until after he knows he is dying—and his concern for the gold is obviously not for himself.

[8]Although *fæhð(o)* does not appear in Passage I, the semantically related *gewraec* does at the very end of the passage (line 2395); in addition to the *sorh* words in Passage II, the elegiac *geōmorlic* appears in line 2444.

commencement of hostilities is attributed to the Geats themselves, and the killing of Ongentheow by Eofor and Wulf is detailedly described. But let us hold in abeyance for the moment these contradictions.

Passage III (lines 2910*b*-3000), the third point of view on the wars, is part of the speech of Wiglaf's Messenger. Unlike the first two passages, it does not move chronologically. First the Messenger alludes to the Fall of Hygelac; then he moves back in time to give the longest exposition of the first phase of the wars between Swedes and Geats, supplying the needed details in the Ongentheow-Haethcyn-Eofor battles. This order of events stresses the conflict in the North as the ultimate source of Geatish destruction. Thematically, the Messenger's speech has a double concern: presumption and rewards. Whereas the poet, in referring to the Fall of Hygelac, had focused on Beowulf's survival, and Beowulf had emphasized revenge, the Messenger views the outcome of the action as a result of Hygelac's arrogance[9] in making the raid; and in his account of the Swedish-Geatish feud, he finds the Geats presumptuous and the *causa belli*.[10] He dwells on Hygelac's inability to give treasure when he was killed in Frisia, contrasting with his largess in rewarding Eofor and Wulf for their dispatching of Ongentheow. The Messenger minimizes the concept of revenge until he begins his prophecy of doom: "Þæt ys sīo fæhðo ond se fēondscipe, / . . . ðe ic / wēn / hafo". His emphasis on arrogance vs. humbling and on treasures paid and unpaid suits the context of his speech very well: the death of Beowulf and the renewal of feud begun in arrogance and ending in loss of treasure to all—the maiden who will tread a foreign land deprived of gold, the reburial of the cursed and useless treasure, and the ultimate loss of *glēodrēam* to all the Geats.

The apparent contradictions between Passages II and III (and the earlier reference to Hygelac's Fall) may best be viewed, I think, in terms of their speakers and contexts. Since Beowulf, in Passage II, is intent on revenge as he prepares his attack on the old night-flyer, it is aesthetically suitable and psychologically proper that he single out his revenge on Daeghrefn in talking about Hygelac's Fall, that he blame the sons of Ongentheow for starting the Northern feud, and that he give credit obliquely to Hygelac *in propria persona* for avenging Haethcyn's death. It is understandable, too, that he should intimate that he prevented the famous necklace from passing into the hands of the Franks. He is a Germanic warrior uttering his *gylp*, however subdued and elegiac the tone of that boast may be. The Messenger, on the other hand, has another axe to grind. As a result of Beowulf's Fall, the Geats themselves will fall; and he is determined to locate the responsibility for the imminent disaster in the Geats: in their aggression against the Frisians, in large measure already paid for, and in their aggression against the Swedes, not yet fully paid for.[11] He by-passes the more recent phase of the wars, involving the sons of

---

[9]Most edited texts read *genǣgdon* "attacked" in line 2916*b* to avoid alliteration on the fourth stress of the line; but the MS. has *ge hnǣgdon* "humbled". Cf. the poet's account in Part I of the poem, in the earliest reference to Hygelac's raid, lines 1206-07*a*: "syddan hĕ for wlenco wēan āhsode, / fæhðe tō Frȳsum."

[10]The passage is, I am aware, subject to differing interpretations. I follow Klaeber (*Beowulf*, 3rd ed.) here, p. xxxviii: "It is started by the Swedes, who attack their Southern neighbors. . . ."

[11]The Messenger's emphasis on the Geats' past aggressiveness contrasts ironically with

Ohthere and their uncle Onela—more a Swedish civil war, anyway, as Bonjour has pointed out,[12] in which the Geats got accidentally involved—in favor of the ruin and destruction the Geats in their arrogance carried to Ongentheow. Even if we accept Dobbie's reconciliation of the two different accounts of the start of hostilities, that "we are probably to understand that the first invasion was made by the Swedes . . . and that shortly thereafter Haethcyn initiated a war of retaliation and invaded Sweden",[13] the difference in emphasis in Beowulf's and the Messenger's speeches remains and is, I believe, aesthetically effective. Also, the Messenger, like the poet in Passage I and unlike Beowulf, achieves a fine balance of sympathy between the Geats, of whom he is one, and the Swedes, the traditional enemy, broadening our perspective once again as the epic draws toward its appointed end. If the passages are thus viewed, no real contradictions exist; we are presented rather with refractions of historical truth seen through the prisms of the speaker's perspectives and states of mind.

The *Beowulf*-poet's artistry is amply revealed in these three prismatic views of Geatish history. Where Olympian detachment sustains a theme of survival, heroic purpose lingers on revenge, and vatic admonition, in turn, sees beyond heroic presumption. The totality of such views and themes may well lead to the universal quality that Wrenn and others have noted. Perhaps it also contributes to the epic quality of the Old English poem.[14]

Coleridge has defined what seems to me to be a central attribute of epic: in epic, he says, Fate subordinates human will to its purposes; human will, in effect, subserves the larger ends of destiny.[15] Such a Fate-controlled universe we find in Homer, in Vergil, in Milton. Odysseus's will, for example, in a sense serves the purposes of Poseidon and Athena, and Hector stands before Troy's gate because Fate will have it so; Aeneas leaves his Dido to fulfill his destiny and Rome's; and Adam and Eve, though acting freely, are clearly attuned to God's providence. In *Beowulf,* epic effect is achieved differently. Wyrd and God may be repeatedly mentioned, but their force is less personal, less directive, than the Olympian and Heavenly decrees. The poem gives us no sense that Beowulf moves through his heroic deeds in accord with a higher will. Rather, Beowulf's is an historic destiny, as are all the doom-laden movements of the poem. The Scylding dynasty will fall—because historically it fell; the Geats will lose their national independence—because history records the loss. Wyrd will no longer grant Beowulf unalloyed victory when he fights the dragon—because the doom of the Geats is nigh. There is no "higher" destiny in *Beowulf;* and yet there is epic sweep. If there is a distinction and withal a similarity between

their unheroic behavior in the dragon fight. It is not just Beowulf's death that will precipitate the Geats' downfall, but report of their cowardly conduct, as Wiglaf had made clear to them. After all, Beowulf was old and would have died soon anyway; but there is bitter irony in the fact that the circumstances of his death gave the Geats the opportunity to show their cowardice, thus inviting their neighbor's attack. The Geats are responsible for their own destruction. Not enough emphasis is placed on this point, it seems to me, in discussions on the "tragedy" of Beowulf's death.

[12]Bonjour, *op. cit.*, p. 42.

[13]E. V. K. Dobbie, ed., *Beowulf and Judith*, ASPR IV (New York, 1953), p. xxxix.

[14]For some indication of critical hesitancy to call *Beowulf* an epic, see note 6 of my article, "*Beowulf* and Epic Tragedy", *CL,* XIV (1962), 92.

[15]Samuel T. Coleridge, *Shakespearean Criticism*, ed. Thomas M. Raysor (London, 1960), I, 125.

other epics and *Beowulf*, it is in the kinds of destiny manifest; and it is precisely in the accretion of historical material—the many-viewed repetitions of the Swedish-Geatish wars in particular—that we are made epically aware. While the universal quality of other epics may reside in the assimilation of human motives and forces to suprahuman though basically anthropomorphic purposes, in *Beowulf*, it would appear, history subsumes the hero as an individual. This historic destiny, in a centrally significant way, universalizes and makes epic this Old English heroic poem.

Him sēo wēn gelēah: The Design for Irony in
Grendel's Last Visit to Heorot

BY RICHARD N. RINGLER

I

Students of *Beowulf*, pondering the hero's encounter with Grendel, have had two serious doubts about the poet's procedures. The first stems from the (supposed) disruption of narrative tension that results from the author's concentration on Grendel's mental processes almost as much as on the fight itself. Although penetrating psychological analysis is now recognized to be a characteristic of the poet, and in fact one of the elements of his genius,[1] still it is felt that he ought to have restrained his subjective bent in passages of intense narrative action.[2]

The second problem seems at first to be unrelated to the first: Why does the poet repeatedly announce the outcome of the fight in advance, thereby ignoring the most elementary rules for creating suspense?[3] A lengthy critical discussion of the relationship between surprise and suspense and of the possibility of suspense without surprise[4] has not rendered any less remarkable the author's perfect indifference to the element of surprise, nor has an appeal to the epic and narrative precedent (where it is not unusual to find a certain amount of prophecy)[5] served to exonerate a poet who is "so eager to have us know what is going to happen that he . . . takes care to tell it no less than three or four times in advance."[6] Still another argument—that since the story was familiar in advance to the poet's audience, he considered it wasted effort to try to develop the kind of suspense that rests on ignorance of the future[7]— runs into two objections: first, the poet did not seem to think it wasted effort in his account of Grendel's mother, where we can probably assume equally great audience familiarity;[8] second, many narrators, in all sorts of genres, have

---

[1] See for example F. Klaeber, *Beowulf and the Fight at Finnsburg*, 3rd ed. (New York 1950), p. lviii f. *Beowulf* citations in this paper are from this edition.

[2] *Ibid.*, p. 154 (note to 710 ff.)

[3] *Ibid.*, p. lvii.

[4] See especially James R. Hulbert, *"Beowulf" and the Classical Epic*, MP, XLIV (1946-47), 71, and Arthur Gilchrist Brodeur, *The Art of Beowulf* (Berkeley 1960), p. 89.

[5] Hulbert, p. 71.

[6] Adrien Bonjour, "The Use of Anticipation in *Beowulf*," RES, XVI (1940), 292.

[7] So William Witherle Lawrence, *Beowulf and Epic Tradition* (Cambridge, Mass., 1928), p. 113, and the oral-formulaic school would perhaps tend to support this view. For my present purpose, it is perfectly indifferent whether or not the audience knew the stories in advance.

[8] See below, p. 145, for an attempt to explain the poet's use of a different technique in the episode with Grendel's mother.

Reprinted, by permission, from *Speculum* 41 (1966), 49-67.

found it convenient to assume a fictive ignorance on the part of the audience, even when they are telling a story that the audience already knows.

Another approach to the problem is to deny the forecasts as much weight as is accorded to the context in which they are embedded. A. G. Brodeur's theory of the "design for terror," posited as it is on the mounting suspense of the whole Grendel episode, cannot accommodate the forecasts, hence he (in effect) tries to get rid of them: they are "so blanketed by the oppressive sense of fear that the brief release from tension which each affords only increases the hearer's responsiveness to each succeeding shock."[9] Elsewhere Brodeur claims that "the poet used the several forecasts of Beowulf's victory to nourish a degree of hope, so that the listener might experience with more vivid excitement each new effect of fear."[10] But the prophecies do not merely "nourish a degree of hope": they instill absolute certainty. Not only does this explanation seem to me psychologically unsound, but I feel that it misrepresents the effect of the first climax of *Beowulf*: the poet's allusions to the outcome of the battle are not momentary and insignificant ebbs in the rising tide of terror, but rather rocks upon which the sea of terror breaks.

With the single exception of Adrien Bonjour, critics of *Beowulf* have hitherto tried to "account for," or minimize, or neutralize the forecasts, not to justify them. And clearly, if the Grendel episode was intended to be only a simple heroic narrative cast in a pattern of rising suspense, this critical discomfort is to some degree justified. But what if it was intended to be more? What if there is a pattern into which the forecasts will fit without apology or sterilization? What if there is "one main theme which is capable of bearing more emphasis, of being more elaborately worked out if the scheme of anticipation is adopted instead of the technique of surprise"?[11] It is my contention, in brief, that the design for terror is only half the design, the warp in the pattern. The woof is an elaborate and quite explicit group of dramatic ironies which attend Grendel's reversal. The mechanism of this irony is precisely the two elements in the poem that have most puzzled the critics: the reiterated forecasts of Beowulf's success and the author's intense preoccupation with Grendel's thoughts.

II

The central and most highly wrought irony stems from the contrast between Grendel's expectations, on the night of the battle, and his actual experience.[12] The background for this irony is the length of his hitherto unchallenged regimen in Heorot, a point which the poet is at great pains to emphasize: *Wæs sēo hwīl micel; / twelf wintra tīd* [146b-147a]. In fact it had become widely known to men

---

[9]Brodeur, p. 89.

[10]*Ibid.*, p. 102.

[11]Bonjour, p. 292.

[12]The contrast has been noted by R. E. Kaske in his article, "*Sapientia et Fortitudo* as the Controlling Theme of *Beowulf*," *SP*, LV (1958), 423-456: "there is a continual contrast between what Grendel hopes or expects and what actually happens, a sort of ὕβρις in him that contributes to poetic effect even if, logically, he could not be expected to foresee the outcome."

þætte Grendel wan
hwīle wið Hrōþgār,   hetenīðas wæg,
fyrene ond fæhðe   fela missēra,
singāle sæce.   (151b-154a)

Later a present participle stresses the continuity of Grendel's visitations
(*ǣglǣca ēhtende wæs,* / *deorc dēaþscua, duguþe ond geogoþe* [159a-60b]), and
their frequency finds yet further statement:

Swā fela fyrena   fēond mancynnes,
atol āngengea   oft gefremede,
heardra hȳnða;   Heorot eardode,
sincfāge sel   sweartum nihtum;—(164a-167b)

where *eardode* makes the ironic suggestion that visitation has become resi-
dency. And although all this was a great sorrow and humiliation to Hroðgar,
he could do nothing about it—partly because *þæt gewin* was *tō swyð* and *lāþ*,
but also partly because it was too *longsum* (191b-192a).

A counter current sets in when news of Grendel's depredations reaches
Beowulf in Geatland. As Brodeur puts it, "with that fondness for dramatic
reversal which he frequently displays, the poet suddenly introduces the hero:
the note of impending deliverance sounds like a trumpet":[13]

sē wæs moncynnes   mægenes strengest
on þǣm dæge   þysses līfes,
æþele ond ēacen.   (196a-198a)

Grendel still thinks he reigns supreme in Heorot, but this description of
Beowulf and the triumphant accounts of his voyage and reception which follow
suggest that the monster's dominion will not last much longer. Soon Beowulf
makes a speech to Unferð in which he predicts Grendel's reversal: Grendel,
says the hero, has learned not to fear the Danes. His long experience of the
Sige-Scyldinga [597b]—no doubt Beowulf intends this ironically—has shown him
that they will not fight back:

nymeð nȳdbāde,   nǣnegum ārað
lēode Deniga,   ac hē lust wigeð,
swefeð ond snēdeþ,   secce ne wēneþ
tō Gār-Denum.   (598a-601a)

The last two lines emphasize Grendel's well-defined expectations when he visits
Heorot: notice the metrical stress on *wēneþ*. He has never been given any
reason to anticipate a counter-attack *tō Gār-Denum*. "But," says Beowulf,

ic him Gēata sceal
eafoð ond ellen   ungeāra nū,
gūþe gebēodan.   (601b-603a)

The carefully contrived antithesis, reinforced by alliteration, of what Grendel

---

[13]Brodeur, p. 51.

may expect from the *Gār-Denum* and receive from the *Gēatum*, suggests in a nutshell the ironies of Grendel's reversal which the poet will soon be working out in all their detail.

After this *bēot* of Beowulf's, mead is served in the most elegant, courtly fashion by Wealhþeow, and revelry mounts in the hall

> oþ þæt semninga
> sunu Healfdenes sēcean wolde
> æfenræste; wiste þǣm āhlǣcan
> tō þǣm hēahsele hilde geþinged,
> siððan hīe sunnan lēoht gesēon meahton,
> oþ ðe nīpende niht ofer ealle,
> scaduhelma gesceapu scrīðan cwōman
> wan under wolcnum. (644b-651a)

This passage suggests[14] that the haunting of Heorot has become Grendel's *raison d'être*, that he thinks about little else during the day than holding sway in the meadhall the next night and causing Hroðgar even more *gryre* and *hȳnðu*. The successful and unopposed haunting of Heorot has become Grendel's way of life, his routine, his *drohtoð*.

So far I have collected evidence of the *Beowulf*-poet's emphasis on the fact that for a long time Grendel has had his own way. Now it is time to assemble a few of the forecasts. Even as Hroðgar leaves Heorot to seek Wealhþeow among the *būras*, the poet indulges himself in an oblique prediction of Grendel's forthcoming debacle:

> Hæfde Kyningwuldor
> Grendle tōgēanes, swā guman gefrungon,
> seleweard āseted. (665b-667a)

There is a natural presumption that a *seleweard* appointed by *Kyningwuldor* will be successful. A more explicit statement follows the poet's poignant description of the apprehension—on the part of Beowulf's retainers—that they will never again see their homes:

---

[14]Klaeber is surely right in refusing to emend l. 648 (by introducing a *ne* before *meahton*). He interprets the passage: "In other words, the king knew that fight had been in Grendel's mind all day long; Grendel had been waiting from morning till night to renew his attacks in the hall. . . ." (p. 152). Grendel spends his nights haunting Heorot and devotes his days to fiendish anticipations of the pleasures of the forthcoming night. That he operated only at night is explicit (*Heorot eardode . . . sweartum nihtum* [166b, 7b]; *sinnihte* [161b]); that he could not remain in the hall during the day is perhaps implied (Klaeber, p. 465) by the critical lines:

> nō hē þone gifstōl grētan mōste
> māþðum for Metode, nē his myne wisse. (168a-9b)

Hroðgar knows from bitter experience that twilight (*nīpende niht ofer ealle*) was the time to vacate Heorot, since it was then that the *scaduhelma gesceapu scrīðan cwōman*, among them Grendel, who had been planning his next regular attack on Heorot ever since the last dawn had freed men temporarily from his ravages—*siððan hīe sunnan lēoht gesēon meahton*. This seems much the simplest interpretation of the lines, it saves an emendation, and it fits in with what we can deduce about Grendel's habits.

Ac him Dryhten forgeaf
wīgspēda gewiofu,   Wedera lēodum,
frōfor ond fultum,   þæt hīe fēond heora
þurh ānes cræft   ealle ofercōmon,
selfes mihtum.   Sōð is gecȳþed,
þæt mihtig God   manna cynnes
wēold wīdeferhð.   (696b-702a)

Grendel is now about to enter onto a stage that has been carefully set to
receive him. He will come on assuming, *for his wonhȳdum* [434a], that the
conditions of the past twelve years still obtain: after a day's anticipation he will
be looking forward to another night's *geweald* in Heorot. *Secce ne wēneþ / tō
Gār-Denum.* He does not know that God has set a hallguard against him and
that the hallguard's victory is assured. The audience's superior knowledge—
both of Beowulf's presence and his destined victory—combines with Grendel's
erroneous assumptions to produce a typical situation of dramatic irony.

Cōm on wanre niht
scrīðan sceadugenga.   Scēotend swǣfon,
þā þæt hornreced   healdan scoldon,
ealle būton ānum.   Þæt wæs yldum cūþ,
þæt hīe ne mōste,   þā Metod nolde,
se s[c]ynscaþa   under sceadu bregdan;—
ac hē wæccende   wrāþum on andan
bād bolgenmōd   beadwa geþinges.   (702b-709b)

The first brief announcement that Grendel is on the march is immediately
followed by the statement that Beowulf was awake, by another strong assertion
of the disappointment that is in store for Grendel tonight, and by yet further
elaboration of Beowulf's wakefulness. One can hardly agree with Brodeur that
the poet's concentration on the result of the battle in 696b-702a and 705b-
707b is "blanketed by the oppressive sense of fear"; on the contrary, it is the
statement about Grendel on his journey that is blanketed by the assertions
about the satisfactory outcome. Grendel's slow and determined advance must
be seen against the ironic background of his imminent discomfiture and the
fact that in the meadhall which he has controlled for so long, now, unbeknownst to him, someone is *wæccende wrāþum on andan*. Pathetically ignorant of all this, wrapped up (we may assume) in gloating anticipations of
the night's satisfactions, Grendel continues his progress:

Ðā cōm of mōre   under misthleoþum
Grendel gongan,   Godes yrre bær;
mynte se mānscaða   manna cynnes
sumne besyrwan   in sele þām hēan.   (710a-713b)

Mynte gives us our first sudden flash of insight into Grendel's mind: he is full,
as he advances, of what he intends to do. He assumes that this evening will
follow the usual pattern. It is noteworthy that in the passage upon which we
are now embarking, the verb *mynte* appears three times within fifty lines,
always applied to Grendel. It appears nowhere else in the poem. There can

be no clearer demonstration of the poet's concern, in these lines, with Grendel's purposes.[15]

We see him again now, advancing with characteristic evil vigor:

> Wōd under wolcnum   tō þæs þe hē wīnreced,
> goldsele gumena   gearwost wisse
> fǣttum fāhne.   (714a-716a)

Mr George Clark, in his analysis of "The Theme of the Traveler's Arrival in Anglo-Saxon Poetry,"[16] has called attention to the typical features of this theme in its many Anglo-Saxon occurrences: a traveller approaches a shining destination and the tone is one of triumph. There have already been two quite typical appearances of the theme in *Beowulf* (306b-311b, 569b-572a), so the ironic effects of this third appearance have been set up within the context of the poem itself. The chief irony resides in the fact that this usually cheerful *motif* should be applied to anything so ominous as Grendel's arrival at Heorot. But there is a further irony: since the theme of arrival so often implies rejoicing in its other occurrences in Anglo-Saxon verse, and since this is indubitably its tone in the earlier two occurrences in *Beowulf*, it is entirely pertinent to, and even symbolic of, Grendel's own state of mind as he arrives at the hall, and it thus becomes woven into the larger pattern of dramatic irony of the episode as a whole.

The poet now indulges in a few lines of reflection which introduce yet another of the ironies he will exploit. *Ne wæs þæt forma sīð* (this is litotes, since we remember the emphasis hitherto on Grendel's *nightly* haunting of Heorot)

> þæt hē Hrōþgāres   hām gesōhte;
> nǣfre hē on aldordagum   ǣr nē siþðan
> heardran hǣle,   healþegnas fand!   (716b-719b)

Grendel has made many trips to Heorot, but this is to be his last. That in itself is ironic, and the poet of *Beowulf* will exploit the irony in much the same way as the poet of *Judith* exploited a similar irony in his story.[17] *Aldordagum* is ironic (this will be Grendel's *dēaðdæg*), but the latent irony of *aldordagum ǣr* is swallowed up in the splendid ironic contradiction of *aldordagum . . . siþðan*. The overall ironic intent of this passage is underscored by the syllepsis in the last line (*heardran hǣle, healðegnas*), and the way in which *fand*, suggesting Grendel's reversal in an ironic nutshell, caps everything off.

Now Grendel arrives at the hall and for a few lines (720a-727b) the poet concentrates on the design for terror. Even in this passage, however, the design for irony is not neglected: *bealohȳdig* keeps the attention of the audience focussed on Grendel's thoughts and their dramatic irony, as to a lesser extent does *yrremōd*. And though it would be folly to deny the "suspense" and terror of these lines, yet our foreknowledge of the outcome of the battle, and the

---

[15]Like the trinal *cōm* (which is so central to the design for terror), the *mynte* triad is a sophisticated and purposeful use of the "echo-word" technique discussed by John O. Beaty in "The Echo-Word in *Beowulf*. . . .," *PMLA*, XLIX (1934), 365-373.

[16]Forthcoming in *JEGP* (1965). [Appeared as "The Traveler Recognizes His Goal: A Theme in Anglo-Saxon Poetry," *JEGP* 64 (1965), 645-59—R.F.]

[17]Cf. *Judith* 69b-73a.

contrast between Beowulf's alert quiescence and Grendel's reckless tumult, suggest that there may be something just a little amusing about the huffings and puffings of a monster who is unaware that in a few moments he will be quelled. Though Grendel is *drēamum bedǣled* in the Christian sense, he is always capable of *Schadenfreude*, and tonight he experiences a moment of Satanic mirth when he discovers that the meadhall, long empty, is once again occupied:

> Geseah hē in recede   rinca manige,
> swefan sibbegedriht   samod ætgædere,
> magorinca hēap.   Þā his mōd āhlōg;   (728a-730b)

it is *hleahtor* of the *mōd*: Grendel's mind is illuminated by a bright burst of anticipation and purpose, the mental state that has been crescent in him ever since he set out from his *unhēore* pool:

> Þā his mōd āhlōg;
> mynte þæt hē gedælde,   ǣr þon dæg cwōme,
> atol āglǣca   ānra gehwylces
> līf wið līce,   þā him ālumpen wæs
> wistfylle wēn.   (730b-734a)

Mynte echoes the earlier *mynte* and brings us back sharply to the irony of Grendel's intentions on what is to be his last visit; his arrogant plans for thorough-going ravage deepen this irony, and *wēn* punctuates it with an exclamation point.

Further clarification of the author's ironic purpose—in fact an almost point-blank announcement of it—follows immediately, and the ironic antithesis is reinforced by the rhyming of *gēn* with *wēn* in the preceding halfline:

> Ne wæs þæt wyrd þā gēn,
> þæt hē mā mōste   manna cynnes
> ðicgean ofer þā niht.   (734b-736a)

This passage and its predecessor offer a striking juxtaposition of Grendel's intentions and his actual fate: we see one of the much maligned anticipations operating to underpin the irony of the scene as a whole.[18]

---

[18]The tactics of the author of *Judith* are very similar. At the very outset of the fragment we are promised Judith's triumph (1b-7a), and against our foreknowledge is subsequently counterpointed the ignorance of Holofernes and the irony of what we see to be his false assumptions and futile purposes. The ambiguity of *weagesiðas* (16b) is resolved by this irony: at present his generals are his comrades in crime (BT *wēa* II), but we know that shortly they will be his comrades in woe (BT *wēa* I).

The fact that Holofernes' men, in the midst of their lively revelry, are actually *fǣge*—and his inability to imagine such a contingency (19b-21a)—constitute irony of a type with which we are familiar from *Beowulf*, where the author's prophecies serve the same purpose as the outright announcement of *feigð* in *Judith*. But the technique employed by the *Beowulf*-poet in the last two passages cited in the text—his immediate juxtaposition of a malign intention and the assurance that the intention will be frustrated—is also used by the *Judith*-poet:

> Þa wearð se brema on mode
> bliðe, burga ealdor,   þohte ða beorhtan idese
> mid widle ond mid womme besmitan.   Ne wolde þæt wuldres dema

The poet's statement as to what *wyrd* has in store for Grendel leads him, naturally enough, to another source of irony: Beowulf's silent scrutiny of the monster's pyrotechnics.

> Þrȳðswȳð behēold
> mǣg Higelāces, hū se mānscaða
> under fǣrgripum gefaran wolde. (736b-738b)

Wolde returns us once again to Grendel's mental processes and purposes, and the poet pursues this theme for a moment (with the litotes, *yldan þōhte*) as he moves into his account of the appropriately anonymous retainer:

> Nē þæt se āglǣca yldan þōhte,
> ac hē gefēng hraðe forman sīðe
> slǣpendne rinc. (739a-741a)

After Hondscioh has been polished off (*gefeormod* [744b]), Grendel advances on Beowulf. If, as Brodeur suggests, the description of Hondscioh's death was the climax of the design for terror, Grendel's stealthy assault on Beowulf—and its wholly unexpected result—is the climax of the design for irony:

> Forð nēar ætstōp,
> nam þā mid handa higeþīhtigne
> rinc on ræste, rǣhte ongēan
> fēond mid folme; hē onfēng hraþe
> inwitþancum ond wið earm gesæt. (745b-749b)

It is a pity, of course, that this climactic moment should be so notable a crux. C. L. Wrenn's explanation has the advantage of doing away with the curious hysteron proteron (*nam þā mid handa . . . rǣhte ongēan*) and also of suggesting how the ironic climax is contrived:

The pret. forms *nam* and *rǣhte* are progressive or continuous tenses: Grendel was doing these things, but did not complete them. Bēowulf lay quite still as if asleep, allowing Grendel to stretch out his hand to seize him, and then suddenly sat up.[19]

> geðafian, þrymmes hyrde, ac he him þæs ðinges gestyrde,
> dryhten, dugeða waldend. (57b-61a)

With these lines from *Judith* should also be compared *Beowulf* 1055b-57a, cited below, p. 141.
    Note also, later in *Judith*, that the audience's knowledge that Holofernes is dead sets up the ironies of the scene in which his generals stood outside his tent and *hogedon* to tell him of the battle (250b), *mynton* ("imagined, assumed") that he and Judith were still together (253b), *hogedon* to wake him up (273b), until one of their number finally ventured inside and *funde* (278a) the true circumstances. (The citations from *Judith*, along with all other non-*Beowulf*ian citations in this paper, are from *The Anglo-Saxon Poetic Records*, ed. George Philip Krapp and Elliott Van Kirk Dobbie, 6 vols. [New York 1931-53].)
    [19]*Beowulf with the Finnsburg Fragment*, ed. C. L. Wrenn, revised and enlarged edition (London 1958), p. 198. What Wrenn calls a "progressive or continuous tense" may also be thought of as the imperfective usage of a normally perfective verb. Klaeber finds this usage twice in *Beowulf*, certainly in 1511b and probably in 2854a (see his notes to these lines). The puzzling *nam* in the present passage could thus be translated: "was in the act of seizing," "tried to seize." Whichever nomenclature one prefers, Wrenn's interpretation of the passage is supported by the language used later in the poem to refer to this incident. There is no

On this interpretation, the suspense of the passage is unbearable, and it is wholly an ironic suspense, since we are never in any fear for Beowulf. Beowulf's misleading stillness and our certainty as to how everything is going to end are the background against which we see Grendel, transported by gluttony, sure of what he is doing, heedlessly confident as to the outcome, reaching out in deliberate and exaggerated slow-motion towards his next victim. Little does he imagine, in his *wonhȳdum*, that anyone else may have a counter-purpose: but Beowulf is *higepīhtig*. The monster is on the razor's edge. And then Beowulf *wið earm gesæt*—whatever its exact meaning may be, it clearly indicates that Beowulf's offensive, Grendel's reversal, has begun. Painfully, and with shattering irony, the master of *fǣrgripum* himself experiences a *fǣrgripe*.[20]

But if the contrast between Grendel's objective experience in Heorot hitherto and the events of tonight is a masterstroke of irony, so is the closely related contrast between his subjective crescendo of anticipation as he approaches Heorot, and his sudden realization (*sōna* [750a]) of disaster.[21] All along we have been concentrating on his state of mind: what is it like now, in the crisis? Here too the reversal is complete:

> Sōna þæt onfunde   fyrena hyrde,
> þæt hē ne mētte   middangeardes,
> eorþan scēa*t*a   on elran men
> mundgripe māran;   (750a-753a)

the adverbial genitives (*middangeardes,* / *eorþan scēa*ta) suggest Grendel's

---

evidence that Grendel actually laid hold of Beowulf. Speaking of the kin of Cain, the hero observes:

> wæs þǣra Grendel sum,
> heorowearh hetelīc,   sē æt Heorote fand
> wæccendne wer   wīges bīdan;
> þǣr him āglǣca   ætgrǣpe wearð;   (1266b-1269b)

Grendel "was grasping towards him"—no more. And again, telling the story to Hygelac, Beowulf relates how, after killing Hondscioh, Grendel *mīn costode, / grāpode gearofolm* [2084b-85a]. Gear*o*folm suggests the incompleteness of the action, as also, probably, does the poet's use of *grāpian* (cf. ModE. *grope*) rather than *grīpan*.

[20]The quotations in the preceding note support my interpretation of the climax of the Grendel episode by showing that when the author recurs to it, later in the poem, the central ironies are still in his mind. According to the first quotation, Grendel *fand* (this word by itself suggests the ironic reversal) not the sleeping victims of his earlier experience but *wæccendne wer wīges bīdan*. Grendel was in fact actually "grasping towards him" when Beowulf went into action. It is impressive how strongly and succinctly all the earlier ironies are revived in these few lines. The *costode* and *gearofolm* of the second quotation strike me as having the same effect—particularly *gearofolm*, which suggests Grendel's suppressed excitement as he reaches out.

The oral-formulaist would perhaps argue that if/since the groping monster and the overall ironic scheme had become an integral part of the singer's version of "Grendel's last visit to Heorot," they would be likely to reoccur with any appearance of that theme, no matter how abbreviated.

[21]Brodeur calls attention to "the emotional contrast between the monster's hideous joy at the sight of so many prospective victims and his agony of fear once the hero has laid hold of him" (p. 57 f.), but he does not note that the contrast is subservient to a controlling ironic purpose.

recognition of the hopelessness of his present position. What has become of his plans to spend his usual unopposed night in Heorot?

> hē on mōde wearð
> forht on ferhðe;   nō þȳ ǣr fram meahte.   (753b-754b)

The last halfline shows that, in this highly ironic situation, opportunities for new departures of irony are opening right and left. But the notable thing here is the author's triple assertion that Grendel's mind and the change which has come over it are his present area of observation: *on* mōde *wearð* / *forht on* ferhðe,

> *Hyge* wæs him hinfūs,   wolde on heolster flēon,
> sēcan dēofla gedræg.   (755a-756a; my italics)

The authorial aside which follows is very revealing:

> ne wæs his drohtoð þǣr
> swylce hē on ealderdagum   ǣr gemētte.   (756b-757b)

His *drohtoð*: his routine, his accustomed way of doing things—that pleasurable, unopposed *gryre* that he had been indulging in for twelve years. The design for irony was premised on the audience's awareness, and Grendel's ignorance, that the *drohtoð* was about to end. In this statement of the poet, his ironic purpose becomes perfectly explicit. And there is further irony implicit in the reappearance of *ealderdagum*. It is interesting that there should be only two occurrences of this compound in the poem, and that they should be within hailing distance of each other.

Now Beowulf intensifies his offensive tactics. Fingers burst. Grendel's wishes become half-translated into action: *eoten wæs ūtweard* (761a).

> Mynte se mǣra,   (þ)ǣr hē meahte swā,
> wīdre gewindan   ond on weg þanon
> flēon on fenhopu;   (762a-764a)

the final echo of *mynte* is poignant and pathetic, of course, but still ironic, since although Grendel *mynte* to flee, at the very same time he *wiste*

> his fingra geweald
> on grames grāpum.   (764b-765a)

The ironic confrontation of what Grendel *mynte* and what he *wiste* is precisely what we might expect at this point. The author now sums it all up with a characteristic ironic aside: Grendel's last visit to Heorot was not the pleasurable trip he had anticipated, quite the contrary,

> Þæt wæs gēocor sīð,
> þæt se hearmscaþa   tō Heorute ātēah!   (765b-766b)

Now the poet concentrates for twenty lines on the noise and violence of the fight and the terror of the Danes. These features are (among other things) an index of the strength of Grendel's desire to get away.[22] It is ironic that the monster who had performed so much *gryre* should now himself begin *gryrelēoð galan* (786a), and his pathetic struggles to escape, accompanied by so much violent dislocation of furniture, lead nowhere—ironically—but to the climactic paean:

> Hēold hine fæste
> sē þe manna wæs   mægene strengest
> on þæm dæge   þysses līfes.   (788b-790b)

No doubt we are intended to recall that these identical two lines had been used to describe Beowulf on his first appearance in the poem; the echo is very appropriate.

After an ironic assertion that Beowulf did not intend

> þone cwealmcuman   cwicne forlǣtan,
> nē his līfdagas   lēoda ǣnigum
> nytte tealde,   (792a-794a)

and a few lines of attention to Beowulf's retainers milling around and hewing with their useless swords, the poet indulges in another forecast of Grendel's fate:

> Scolde his aldorgedāl
> on ðǣm dæge   þysses līfes
> earmlīc wurðan,   ond se ellorgāst
> on fēonda geweald   feor sīðian.   (805b-808b)

It is remarkable how *on ðǣm dæge þysses līfes* echoes—ironically—the application of the same phrase sixteen lines earlier.

Now the poet introduces a new and terrifying aspect of Grendel's awareness:

> Ðā þæt onfunde   sē þe fela ǣror
> mōdes myrðe[23]   manna cynne,
> fyrene gefremede   —hē [wæs] fāg wið God—,
> þæt him se līchoma   lǣstan nolde,
> ac hine se mōdega   mǣg Hygelāces
> hæfde be honda;   (809a-814a)

and now Grendel's arm is wrenched from its socket:

---

[22]Many critics feel that "Grendel does not give Beowulf a really good fight" (Brodeur, p. 114; see also Klaeber, p. lii): since Beowulf throughout the struggle *hēold hine fæste* (788b), "the issue is not really in doubt after Grendel feels the power of Beowulf's grip" (Brodeur, p. 94). It seems to me that this situation results from the fact that once Beowulf grabs Grendel, much of the poet's attention shifts to an ironic consideration of Grendel's mounting panic and realization that hard as he may struggle, *ūtfūs* as he may be, he is doomed. The poet's concern with this aspect of Grendel's predicament is indicated by the echo-word *fæste* in 760a, 773b (applied to Heorot) and 788b.

[23]Though it is hardly a demonstrable point, the fact that there are so many ironies in the present scene, and that a reference to Grendel's earlier *Schadenfreude* would furnish an appropriate ironic antithesis (at this juncture) to his recent and terrible discovery (*onfunde* etc.), suggest to me that it would be in many ways preferable to follow the older editors—in their equation of *myrðe* with *myrhðe* ("joy")—than Klaeber or Wrenn.

Bēowulfe wearð
gūðhrēð gyfeþe;   scolde Grendel þonan
feorhsēoc flēon   under fenhleoðu,
sēcean wynlēas wīc.   (818b-821a)

The wheel has come full circle, and perhaps we are justified in hearing in
these lines about Grendel's despairing retreat an ironic echo of the earlier
lines about his confident advance:

Ðā cōm of mōre   under misthleoþum
Grendel gongan. . . .

However that may be, there is an evident irony in the fact that he who *mynte*
so confidently when he *cōm* to Heorot, who subsequently *fand* such reversal,
should now *flēon* in a desperate certainty of mind:

wiste þē geornor,
þæt his aldres wæs   ende gegongen,
dōgera dægrīm.   (821b-823a)

III

"The sharp and imminent sense of contrast is persistent in the thought of
Anglo-Saxon poets," writes Brodeur.[24] And he goes on to say:

Contrast is not only the essence of tragedy; it also serves to convey the sense of dramatic irony. When the poet suggests to his listeners an impending catastrophe, of
which the personages to be involved have neither awareness nor expectation, but which
will plunge them from prosperity and power into misery and ruin; when, in their ignorance of what is to come, they continue in their joy and pride, the contrast between
their present and future states communicates the tragic irony to the audience.[25]

There is considerable outside support for the suggestion that an Anglo-
Saxon reader or hearer of the poem would have immediately responded to the
ironies of the Grendel story. They are, in fact, deeply rooted in two aspects
of Anglo-Saxon thought: first, man's ignorance of the future (*Is seo forðgesceaft
/ digol ond dyrne*),[26] second, and closely related, a thoroughgoing belief in the
reversal which comes to men *þonn*[e hy] *læs*[t] *wenað.*[27] *Swiðe oft se micla
anwald ðara yflena gehrist swiðe færlice.*[28] Both aspects find frequent mention
in the literature of the Anglo-Saxons,[29] and they have a corollary which is

---

[24]Brodeur, p. 228.
[25]*Ibid.*, p. 230.
[26]*Maxims II*, 61b-62a, whose poet continues: *drihten ana wat, / nergende fæder* (62b-63a).
[27]*King Alfred's Old English Version of Boethius* De Consolatione Philosophiae, ed. Walter
John Sedgefield (Oxford 1899), p. 15. The full quotation: 'Ic ongiete genoh sweotule þ þa
woruldsælða mid swiðe monigre swetnesse swiðe lytelice oleccað þæm modū ða hie on last
willað swiþost beswican; 7 þonne æt nihstan, þonn[e hy] læs[t] wenað, hi on ormodnesse for-
lætað on þæm mæstan sare.'
[28]*Ibid.*, p. 117.
[29]For the first, see *The Fortunes of Men* 14b, *Maxims I* 29b-30b, *Seafarer* 69. The *Beowulf*-
poet is firmly within this tradition in 3062b-64a, and 3067b-68a can perhaps (despite Klaeber's

often, if somewhat more obliquely, expressed: it behooves men to be wary, to regard the future with a kind of negative capability, bearing its possible alternatives in mind. For example, when Beowulf fought the dragon, his retinue waited all day long,

> bēga on wēnum,
> endedōgores   ond eftcymes
> lēofes monnes.   (2895b-97a)

When Beowulf left Denmark, Hroðgar was very distressed:

> Him wæs bēga wēn
> ealdum infrōdum,   ōþres swīðor,
> þæt h[ī]e seoðða(n) [nō]   gesēon mōston,
> mōdige on meþle.   (1873b-76a)

Beowulf's followers, sitting at the pool's edge *mōdes sēoce*,

> wīston ond ne wēndon,   þæt hīe heora winedrihten
> selfne gesāwon.   (1604a-05a)

We find in *Waldere* and the OHG *Hildebrandslied* the same controlled refusal to anticipate the invisible event.[30] Observe that, according to the Beowulf quotations, it is precisely *wēn* that must be restrained: a man must refuse to commit himself to a single unguarded expectation, since any mortal *wēn* is likely to be deceptive, nothing but *vana spes*. "Quae nequent fieri, spondet fiducia cordi," is the ominous warning of the *Waltharii poesis*.[31]

As a result of this attitude, it is not surprising that the discomfiture of heedless *wēn* is a perennial source of irony. King Oswald and his troops

> alédon heora fynd
> þone modigan cedwallan . mid his micclan werode .
> þe wende þæt him ne mihte nan werod wiðstandan.[32]

Bede, in his account of the fire at Coldingham, tells us that the wicked there were restrained from evil for a time by Adamnan's vision of destruction, but soon returned to their old ways, *7 mid ðy cwædon: Nu is sib 7 orsorhnes: hi ða instepe, ða hie læsest wendon, mid ðy wiite ðæs foresprecenan wræces slægene wæron.*[33] Waldere mocks Guðhere in the Old English fragment:

note, which wishes to limit the *hwæt* to the curse on the treasure) be taken as another statement of the same principle.

The second is of course one of the most familiar of all medieval commonplaces. "Hwæt singað þa leoðwyrhtan oðres be ðisse woruld buton mislica hwearfunga þisse worulde?" (Boethius, p. 18). The contrast of prosperity and adversity is frequent in *Beowulf*, from compact expressions like *gyrn æfter gomene* (1775a) to careful alliterating antitheses like *þā wæs æfter wiste wōp up āhafen* (128).

[30]*Waldere I*, 8a-11a, *Hildebrandslied* 53 f.

[31]L. 1099. See *Waltharii Poesis*, ed. Hermann Althof, 2 vols. (Leipzig 1899-1905).

[32]*Ælfric's Lives of Saints*, ed. Rev. Walter W. Skeat, EETS, 4 vols. (1900 [O.S. 114]), II, p. 126.

[33]*The Old English Version of Bede's Ecclesiastical History of the English People*, ed. Thomas Miller, EETS (1891 [O.S. 96]), I, 356.

"Hwæt! Đu huru wendest,   wine Burgenda,
þæt me Hagenan hand   hilde gefremede
and getwæmde [. .]ðewigges." (II, 14a-16a)

Many other passages in Old English literature stress the ironic disparity between purpose and discomfiture.[34] The first part of *Genesis B*, for example, is a dramatic revery on the contrast between Satan's intentions[35] and their frustration. In fact, the disconfiture of heedless *wēn* is so native to Old English verse that we find its ironies crystallized into a frequently-recurring formula: *him sēo wēn gelēah*.[36] The dragon in *Beowulf*, for instance,

beorges getruwode,
wīges ond wealles;   him sēo wēn gelēah. (2322b-23b)

The formula is used with the same effect to describe the discomfiture of the Myrmedonians in *Andreas*, who [*w*]*endan and woldon* that in a moment they would be enjoying a cannibalistic feast (1072a-74b); also in *Genesis A* to describe the discomfiture of the rebel angels who arrogantly

Cwædon þæt heo rice,   reðemode,
agan woldan,   and swa eaðe meahtan.
Him seo wen geleah. . . . (47a-49a)

There are other occurrences of this and similar formulas.[37]

In the last few pages I have tried to suggest how deeply rooted, in the thought and poetry of the Anglo-Saxons, is an appreciation of the ironic reversal that is in store for heedless *wēn*. In the light of this evidence, we should not be surprised to find the ironic patern, foolish *wēn* > reversal, writ large in the career of Grendel—a character who approaches Heorot in a dangerously unalert frame of mind (*him . . . wæs wistfylle wēn* [733b, 4a]), and who is constantly reported as "intending" to direct events over which, from a wider point of view, he is seen to have no real control. I see him, throughout his appearance in the poem, as a dramatic *exemplum* of the dangers of total commitment to an expectation.[38] In the end, *him sēo wēn gelēah*. The ironic formula might almost serve as his epitaph. I would suggest all this as a slight but necessary qualification of Kaske's view: "[L]ogically [Grendel] could not be expected to foresee the outcome."[39] This is quite true. Even so, he should

[34]See, *inter alia*, *Exodus* 197a-202b.
[35]See especially 265a, 268a, 272b, 274b, 276b, 279b, 283b.
[36]There is a counter-formula in the Latin literature of the period, a direct inversion of *him sēo wēn gelēah*, which is used to express the solidity of *wēn* directed towards God. In the *Vita Sancti Guthlaci* we are told that Æðelbald, on the advice of Guðlac, "*spem* suam *in Domino pos*uit, *nec vana spes* illum *fefellit.*" *Felix's Life of Saint Guthlac*, ed. Bertram Colgrave (Cambridge, 1956), p. 150. Æðelbald "fidemque inseducibilem in vaticiniis viri Dei defixit; nec illum fides fefellit" (p. 166).
[37]The same formula in *Genesis A* 1446b; similar ones, also used to underline the ironic reversal of *wēn*, in *Guðlac* 665b (*Eow þær wyrs gelomp*) and *Andreas* 1393b (*Hit ne mihte swa!*).
[38]Clearly this is an aspect of his overall lack of *sapientia*, a matter that has been canvassed by Kaske, pp. 438-440. Observe that he is called a *dolsceaða* (479a) and that reference is made to his *wonhȳdum* (434a).
[39]See above, note 12.

not have been so confident. If it should be objected that he has been conditioned to be confident, and cannot help himself—why, that is precisely the point of the whole pattern that I have been discussing: the heedless confidence generated by prosperity is just what is shattered so ironically by the reversal which comes when men *læs*[t] *wenað. Eadig byð se mann þe simle byð forhtigende*, says Ælfric, *7 soðlice se heardmode befeolð on yfele*.[40]

Furthermore, these remarks on the cautious Anglo-Saxon attitude toward *seo forðgesceaft* and *wēn* suggest the purpose of a passage in *Beowulf* which has hitherto been regarded as somewhat problematical. When Hroðgar is distributing his lordly gifts to Beowulf the day after the battle, he incidentally pays the *wergild* on Hondscioh,

> þone ðe Grendel ær
> māne ācwealde,— swā hē hyra mā wolde,
> nefne him wītig God wyrd forstōde
> ond ðæs monnes mōd. Metod eallum wēold
> gumena cynnes, swā hē nū gīt dêð.
> Forþan bið andgit æghwær sēlest,
> ferhðes foreþanc. Fela sceal gebīdan
> lēofes ond lāþes sē þe longe hēr
> on ðyssum windagum worolde brūceð! (1054b-62b)

According to Klaeber, the "earlier dissecting critics" regarded the last lines of this passage as an interpolation,[41]—one of the Christian redactor's typical, unhappy additions. More recently Marjorie Daunt, puzzled to know what help *andgit* and *forþonc* will be to a man if *Metod* rules all and fate is determined in advance, proposed giving *Forþan* in 1059a the adversative meaning that has been postulated for it in *The Seafarer*.[42] Unless some such adjustment is made, the last four lines of gnomes seem, at first, to spill out as irrelevantly as do similar gnomic bursts in *The Wanderer*.

But actually the entire passage is perfectly coherent as it stands. When the poet says that Grendel criminally slaughtered Hondscioh,

> swā hē hyra mā wolde,
> nefne him wītig God wyrd forstōde
> ond ðæs mannes mōd,

he alludes to and, for a moment, reawakens all the earlier ironies: Grendel intended to do such-and-such, but God (and Beowulf) prevented him.[43]

[40]*Early English Homilies from the Twelfth-Century MS Vesp. D. XIV*, ed. Rubie D-N. Warner, EETS (1917 [O.S. 152]), p. 30 f. As the poetry has it: *Dol bið se þe him his dryhten ne ondrædeþ: cymeð him se deað unþinged (Seafarer* 106). Or: *Dol bið se þe his dryhten nat, to þæs oft cymeð deað unþinged (Maxims I*, 35).

[41]Klaeber, p. 170.

[42]Marjorie Daunt, "Some Difficulties of 'The Seafarer' Reconsidered," *MLR*, XIII (1918), 478.

[43]The citations and references at BTS *forstandan* II.1c, where this passage is listed, attest to the meaning "to stand in the way of (something [acc.] for someone [dat.])," "to forbid (it) to them." This idiom usually follows (4 cases out of 5) a verb of intention, *willan* or *þencan*, and signals the frustration of the intention in question. Hence Dobbie's argument that *him* is d. pl. referring to Beowulf's men and that the line may be translated "if wise God and the

Grendel proponit, Deus disponit: it is an ancient irony. Immediately the poet elaborates on the fact the God has always had and always will have this authority to govern what happens to a person [*wyrd*]:

Metod eallum wēold
gumena cynnes,   swā hē nū gīt dêð.

But, as I have pointed out above, man is ignorant of God's plans for *seo forðgesceaft*, hence it behooves him to make no easy assumptions about it and to exercise *andgit* and *foreþanc*, precisely those qualities which had been so lacking in Grendel as he advanced on Heorot for the last time.[44]

Forþan bið andgit   æghwær sēlest,
ferhðes foreþanc.

The point is not that *andgit* and *foreþanc* can forestall *wyrd*—it is of course impossible for a man *ðæs Wealdendes wiht oncirran* (*Beowulf* 2857)—rather that they make a man ready for *wyrd*, mentally resilient in the moment of crisis, unliable to the terrible ironies of Grendel's predicament. *Geara is hwær aræd* (*Maxims I*, 191). The most pregnant comparison here is between Grendel's attitude as he approaches Heorot, and Beowulf's as he approaches the dragon: Beowulf has a clear apprehension of the alternatives. Consequently he is not "surprised" by disaster and his mind thrown into confusion and panic. Grendel, on the other hand, reminds us forcibly of Ælfric's words:

þ þwyre mod, þone hit geheapð yfel ofer yfele, 7 þwyrnysse ofer þwyrnysse, hwæt deð hit bute swylce hit lecge stan ofer stane?   Ac þone seo sawle byð to hire witnunge gelædd, þonne byð eall seo timbrung (7) hire smeagunge toworepan, for þan þe heo ne oncneowen þa tid hire geneosunge.[45]

Andgit and *foreþanc*, in any event, represent the only viable attitude, since, as the Middle Ages knew so well, and as the *Beowulf*-poet now concludes the passage in question,

Fela sceal gebīdan
lēofes ond lāþes   sē þe longe hēr
on ðyssum windagum   worolde brūceð!

IV

If we can take Grendel, like Satan, as an example of the *ofermōd* or *fortrūwung* which was held suspect by both Germanic instinct and Christian doctrine, and if we can regard his career in *Beowulf* as having been carefully

courage of the man had not averted fate from them" is untenable. Had the poet wanted to convey that idea, he would probably have written *nefne hī wītig God wyrde forstōde*: see BTS *forstandan* II.2a.

[44] And which are so characteristic of Beowulf himself, whose "wise foresight is shown by his preparations for combat, his arrangements for the management of his affairs in case of his death (1474-91), his clear realization of the possible outcome of his own actions (440-455), and his ability to predict accurately in the affairs of others (974-77, 1674-76, 2029-69)" (Kaske, p. 429).

[45] *Early English Homilies*, p. 32.

designed to highlight the ironies of heedless *wēn* in its confrontation with the unexpected; then Hroðgar's sermon may be regarded as the logical conclusion of the entire business in Denmark. It is a more or less abstract discussion of the dangers of the kind of *ofermōd* which results from heedless *wēn*. This fact is partly obscured—as is the coherence of the sermon as a whole—by certain distortions of emphasis which stem from the poet's use, in a Christian sermon on the Christian sin of pride, of Heremod as an *exemplum*. For this traditional figure quite clearly embodies, not the cardinal sin of Christian theology, but the unforgivable sin of Germanic kingship: that state of *nīðing*hood which is characterized chiefly by niggardliness and the irrational destruction of one's retainers. Heremod represents a complete moral inversion, since the *summum bonum* is the lord's generosity towards and protection of his men (*bēaggyfa* and *helm*). The result of this collision between Germanic and Christian ethics is that the sermon—from the more familiar Christian point of view—seems to confuse *superbia*, *avaritia*, and their respective symptoms.[46]

First Hroðgar praises Beowulf for his steadiness, the fact that awareness of his fame and physical prowess does not unbalance him:

> Eal þū hit geþyldum healdest,
> mægen mid mōdes snyttrum. (1705b-06a)

It was otherwise with Heremod, whom God had also exalted above other men. He cultivated a *brēosthord blōdrēow* and came to a bad end. As Hroðgar continues to talk, we become forcibly reminded of Grendel: not only are the symptoms which Hroðgar discusses perfectly descriptive of the monster, but the now familiar ironic pattern, a mounting crescendo of heedless *wēn* punctuated by reversal, is repeated:

> Wundor is tō secganne,
> hū mihtig God   manna cynne
> þurh sīdne sefan   snyttru bryttað,
> eard ond eorlscipe;   hē āh ealra geweald.
> Hwīlum hē on lufan   lǣteð hweorfan
> monnes mōdgeþonc   mǣran cynnes,
> seleð him on ēþle   eorþan wynne
> tō healdanne   hlēoburh wera,
> gedēð him swā gewealdene   worolde dǣlas,
> sīde rīce,   þæt hē his selfa ne mæg
> his unsnyttrum   ende geþencean.
> Wunað hē on wiste;   nō hine wiht dweleð
> ādl nē yldo,   nē him inwitsorh
> on sefa(n) sweorceð,   nē gesacu ōhwǣr
> ecghete ēoweð,   ac him eal worold
> wendeð on willan;   hē þæt wyrse ne con—,
> oð þæt. . . . (1724b-40a)

---

[46]It is possible, of course, that the ambiguity is deliberate: that the poet is attempting to synchronize the cardinal sins of Christianity and Germanic kingship, and that Hroðgar's sermon is another example of the Christian-pagan syncretism which many scholars feel characterizes the poem. See on this point Kaske, p. 433; also his paper, "The Sigemund-Heremod and Hama-Hygelac Passages in *Beowulf*," *PMLA*, LXXIV (1959), 489-494.

The ominous *oð þæt*,[47] as so often in *Beowulf*, heralds the reversal. It is a reversal analogous to, but not equivalent with, Grendel's: Hroðgar is not talking of monsters but of kings—and specifically Heremod. Nonetheless, much of what Hroðgar says *can* remind one of Grendel, and in the lines which follow these parallels are noteworthy: an *oferhygda dæl / weaxeð ond wrīdað* (1740b-41a) in Grendel; his *weard swefeð* (1741b) in that he fails to exercise *andgit* and *foreþonc*; as he approaches Heorot, all unbeknownst to him is *bona swīðe nēah* (1743b); Beowulf seizes him and he *him bebeorgan ne con* (1746b); in the end his *līchoma læne gedrēoseð* (1754) (Grendel during the fight had in fact recognized *þæt him se līchoma læstan nolde* [812]); and of course in the end *dēað oferswȳðeð* (1768b) Grendel. I am not claiming that Grendel is an allegorical embodiment of the statements in this part of Hroðgar's sermon, only that Grendel's *ofermōd* naturally suffers a reversal quite analogous to that which Hroðgar says is always in store for *ofermōd*.

Hroðgar concludes his sermon with a personal application, probably intended to give his moral propositions greater immediacy and impact. He, too, is an *exemplum* of *ofermōd* and *edhwyrft*, hybris and nemesis. Once again the familiar ironic pattern opens before us. He first describes his hybris:

> Swā ic Hring-Dena   hund missēra
> wēold under wolcnum   ond hig wigge belēac
> manigum mægþa   geond þysne middangeard,
> æscum ond ecgum,   þæt ic mē ænigne
> under swegles begong   gesacan ne tealde. (1769a-73b)

The ironic crescendo here is the soaring description of Hroðgar's Danish *imperium* in time *(hund missēra)* and space *(under wolcnum, geond þysne middangeard, under swegles begong)*, and it mounts to the familiar climax of heedless *wēn* with its verb, stressed and in final position, *ne tealde*.

> Hwæt, mē þæs on ēþle   edwenden cwōm,
> gyrn æfter gomene,   seoþðan Grendel wearð,
> ealdgewinna,   ingenga mīn. (1774a-76b)

The irony of reversal is beautifully underscored by the "geographical" irony: Hroðgar, with his far-reaching authority, could not imagine an enemy *under swegles begong*—lo! reversal comes *on ēþle*, in his own native land! And notice how inevitably the reciprocal ironies of *edwenden* and *on ēþle* are linked by alliteration.

I have spoken of the "familiar ironic pattern," and perhaps I can most clearly state my views on the relationship between Grendel's last visit to Heorot and Hroðgar's sermon by saying that the former is a full dramatic

---

[47]*Oðþæt* introducing a subordinate clause is sometimes capitalized in MSS (*e.g. Genesis* 715a, 2750a), and on three occasions occurs as the first word of a "fit" (here, *Beowulf* 2039a and *Genesis* 1248a). Sir Israel Gollancz suggests that these curious procedures "can be explained as emphasizing a critical change in time or condition" (*The Cædmon Manuscript* [Oxford 1928], p. xxx). I would go farther and suggest that they are followed quite deliberately by the scribes and that their purpose is to emphasize the contours of the rising-falling pattern that I have been discussing, by throwing into strong relief the moment of *edhwyrft*. In all three cases where *oðþæt* begins a fit, it marks a transition from prosperity to disaster; it does this also at *Genesis* 715a. In *Genesis* 2750a the transition is from disaster to prosperity.

realization of, and the latter an abstract reverie on, this pattern. The sermon attacks the kind of pride and heedless *wēn* which Grendel represents dramatically, and in this sense the two are not only complementary and mutually illuminating, but between them lend a unity to the first part of the poem.

V

In the foregoing pages I have tried to suggest that the *Beowulf*-poet's reiterated assertions that his hero will triumph over Grendel, as well as his concentration during the fight on Grendel's state of mind, far from being errors of judgment or taste which serve to cancel, respectively, the suspense and excitement of the encounter, are in fact premises of an elaborate structure of irony. Many of the ironies of Grendel's predicament had been implicit in the traditional structure of the folktale which underlies the first part of *Beowulf*, and our poet, keen as he always was on understatement, anticipation, and contrast, was not the man to miss opportunities of this sort. Finally, as I have tried to suggest, he has made of Grendel's last visit to Heorot a dramatization of the classical Germanic notion of the hybris and nemesis of heedless *wēn*—a notion that appears elsewhere in Anglo-Saxon literature and elsewhere in *Beowulf*, notably in Hroðgar's sermon.

One question, perhaps, remains—though by this time its answer is probably obvious: why does the poet make only one prophecy when he tells the story of Grendel's mother, and why does he reserve it until the moment when it is prophecy no longer, but leads directly into the account of the last seconds of the struggle? Throughout the raid of the *brimwylf* on Heorot, the discussions of the next day, the journey to the mere, and most of the fight, we are ignorant as to the future. Indeed, we are made to live through a terrible moment when Beowulf is stretched out on the floor and the troll-wife, squatting on his chest, is whipping out her *seax* to finish him off. Disaster is very near here, yet the poet does not see fit to unlock his *wyrdhord*.[48]

It seems likely to me that the reason why, on this occasion, the poet chooses to be reticent about the future, is that he now really *is* concerned with building up the effects of suspense pure and simple. The habitual terror, nearing its unimagined end, had been a source for ironic comment; the *fǣrsceapa* is not. She is an unknown quantity, her attack sudden and unexpected. If there is any irony, it is that the Danes themselves had not exercised sufficient *andgit* and *foreþanc*—hence to them in their turn comes ironic *edhwyrft* (1281a). No one knows what Grendel's mother is capable of, or in fact much about her. Though we are sometimes told what she thinks, her thoughts are never lifted into ironic prominence, and she is presented altogether more objectively. Beowulf must descend into her pool in almost total ignorance of what to expect. Clearly the whole situation is fraught with uncertainty, suspense and alarm in a way that the Grendel fight was not. Wisely, this time, the poet lets us share the ignorance and worry of his characters.

---

[48]One can hardly accuse him of *always* revealing everything in advance. If his overall strategy calls for suppression of information, he does not hesitate for a moment. A fine example of this is the way in which the very existence of Grendel's mother is kept a closely-guarded secret. Telling the audience all about her far in advance of her first appearance would upset the careful equilibrations of the Grendel episode, which depends for some of its terrors and ironies on his supposed uniqueness.

The Interlace Structure of *Beowulf*

By John Leyerle

In the time since Norman Garmonsway* died I have reflected about what I could say that would not embarrass the spirit of the man I wish to honour. He was reticent about himself and I shall be brief. I rarely heard him refer to his distinguished career at King's College, London, for when he spoke of his work, it was always of what lay ahead. His characteristic manner was understatement, like that of the early literature of the north that he knew so well and loved. He was a man who preferred to listen rather than to talk, but he was quick to praise and encourage. He had the virtues of Chaucer's Clerk of Oxenford mixed with a gentle humour.

> Noght o word spak he moore than was neede,
> And that was seyd in forme and reverence,
> And short and quyk and ful of hy sentence;
> Sownynge in moral vertu was his speche,
> And gladly wolde he lerne and gladly teche.

Toronto is a better place for his having lived and worked among us. This paper concerns material he was teaching this year, the relation between early art and poetry in England. I should like to dedicate it to his memory.

I

Beowulf is a poem of rapid shifts in subject and time. Events are fragmented into parts and are taken with little regard to chronological order. The details are rich, but the pattern does not present a linear structure, a lack discussed with distaste by many.[1] This lecture will attempt to show that the structure of *Beowulf* is a poetic analogue of the interlace designs common in Anglo-Saxon art of the seventh and eighth centuries. *Beowulf* was composed in the early eighth century in the Midlands or North of England, exactly the time and place where interlace decoration reached a complexity of design and skill in execution never equalled since and, indeed, hardly ever approached. Interlace

---

*On February 28, 1967, Norman Garmonsway, Visiting Professor of English at University College in the University of Toronto, died suddenly. This paper, in a slightly different form, was read on March 30 in West Hall of the College in place of a lecture on Canute that Professor Garmonsway was to have delivered on that day.

[1]For example, see F. P. Magoun, Jr., "*Beowulf A'*: A Folk-Variant," *ARV: Tidskrift för nordisk folkminnesforskning*, XIV (1958), 95-101, or *Beowulf and the Fight at Finnsburg*, ed. Fr. Klaeber, 3rd edition (Boston, 1950), li-lviii. All quotations are from this edition.

Reprinted, by permission, from the *University of Toronto Quarterly* 37 (1967), 1-17.

designs go back to prehistoric Mesopotamia; in one form or another they are characteristic of the art of all races.[2]

The bands may be plaited together to form a braid or rope pattern, a design that appears, for example, on borders of the Franks Casket, a whalebone coffer made in Northumbria about the year 700. Interlace is made when the bands are turned back on themselves to form knots or breaks that interrupt, so to speak, the linear flow of the bands. The south face of the Bewcastle Cross from Cumberland has three panels of knot work: this cross is dated before 710.[3] The bottom panel (Plate I) has two distinct knots formed by two bands and connected together, a pattern that is identical to that on folio 94[v] of the Lindisfarne Gospels (Plate VIII).[4] There are about a thousand separate pieces of stone surviving from pre-Norman Northumbrian crosses. One need only leaf through W. G. Collingwood's *Northumbrian Crosses of the Pre-Norman Age* (London, 1927) to be struck by the appearance of one interlace design after another, despite the fact that such patterns are relatively difficult to execute in stone, especially when there is any undercutting.

When the bands are cut, the free ends are often elaborated into zoomorphic heads, seen in a very simple stage of development on the Abingdon Brooch (Plate II), dated in the early seventh century.[5] In more complex designs the stylized heads take on a pronounced zoomorphic character, often derived from eagles or wolves; the bodies of these creatures extend into curvilinear ribbon trails that form the interlace design. The heads often bite into the bands or back on to a free end, as on the seventh-century Windsor dagger pommel which has an open design with clear separation betwen the bands (Plate III). When the bands are drawn together more tightly, the pattern becomes harder to follow, as on the great gold buckle from Sutton Hoo, also of the seventh century (Plate IV). The interlace on the buckle is not symmetrical. The weave is drawn tighter and the zoomorphic heads are less prominent than on the Windsor dagger pommel.

In further development of the zoomorphs, the ribbon trails develop limbs on their serpentine bodies. These limbed lacertines have a coiled and woven appearance and look very like dragons even when they have no wings and have canine heads. The abundant appearance of lacertines in early Anglo-Saxon design may well have reinforced belief in the existence of dragons, thought of as uncommon creatures not met with every day, much as we might think of a hippopotamus or iguana. An example of vigorous treatment of such lacertines may be seen on folio 192[v] of the Book of Durrow (Plate V); this manuscript is generally dated in the middle or the second half of the seventh century and is often ascribed to Iona. The design is similar to that found on

[2]For an account of the origin of these designs, see Nils Åberg, *The Occident and the Orient in the Art of the Seventh Century*, Part I, The British Isles, Kungl. Vitterhets Historie och Antikvitets Akademiens Handlingar, Del 56:1 (Stockholm, 1943). An admirable account of such designs is given by R. L. S. Bruce-Mitford in *Codex Lindisfarnensis*, ed. T. D. Kendrick, *et al.* (Olten and Lausanne, 1956-60), II, iv, vii-x, 197-260.

[3]Lawrence Stone, *Sculpture in Britain* ([London], 1955), 13.

[4]I wish to thank Professor Michael Sheehan of the Pontifical Institute of Mediaeval Studies at Toronto for helping me assemble the slides used in the lecture and Miss Ann Hutchison of the University of Toronto for help in assembling the prints used to make the plates.

[5]Ronald Jessup, *Anglo-Saxon Jewellery* (London, 1950), 116.

the hilt of the Crundale sword, found in Kent; it dates from the early seventh century (Plate VI*a*). A detail from the seventh-century pins from Witham, Lincolnshire (Plate VI*b*), shows a similar design, although the zoomorphs are distinctly canine. In the lacertine design on folio 110ᵛ of the St. Chad Gospels, which were probably written between the Severn and the Welsh marches in the late seventh or early eighth centuries (Plate VII), the zoomorphs are clearly derived from birds, despite the ears. Designs over an entire folio are called carpet pages after their resemblance to woven tapestries. Perhaps the finest carpet pages are found in the Lindifarne Gospels of about 700; in the later years of the Anglo-Saxon period it was thought to have been the work of angels since no mortal could execute such complex designs so faultlessly. Folio 94ᵛ is reproduced in Plate VIII. The entire design of the knot work is done with only two ribbons. The generally circular pattern is elaborated with intricate weaving, but the circular knots—which might be thought of as episodes, if I may look forward for a moment—are tied with relatively long straight bands that bind these knots together in the total pattern of the page. With patience and a steady eye one can follow a band through the entire knot-work design of this page. Occasionally the lacertines become recognizable dragons as on the Gandersheim Casket. It is carved from walrus teeth and probably was made at Ely in the second half of the eighth or early ninth century (Plate IX). The casket is small and the skill shown in carving on such a miniature scale is impressive.

From the early Anglo-Saxon period there are thousands of interlace designs surviving in illuminations of manuscripts, in carving on bone, ivory and stone, and in metal work for weapons and jewellery. They are so prolific that the seventh and eighth centuries might justly be known as the interlace period. In one artifact after another the complexity and precision of design are as striking as the technical skill of execution. Recognition of this high level of artistic achievement is important for it dispells the widely held view, largely the prejudice of ignorance, that early Anglo-Saxon art is vigorous, but wild and primitive. As the interlace designs show, there is vigour to be sure, but it is controlled with geometric precision and executed with technical competence of very high order. Apart from such direct analogies as the one presented in this lecture, study of Anglo-Saxon art is most useful as an aid to the reassessment of early English literature because it is an important reminder that the society was capable of artistic achievements of a high order which can be looked for in the poetry as well.

II

The pervasive importance of interlace designs in early Anglo-Saxon art establishes the historical possibility that a parellel may be found in poetry of the same culture. The historical probability for the parallel, a rather more important matter, can be established from seventh- and eighth-century Latin writers in England. There is ample evidence that interlace design has literary parallels in both style and structure.

Stylistic interlace is a characteristic of Aldhelm and especially of Alcuin. They weave direct statement and classical tags together to produce verbal braids in which allusive literary references from the past cross and recross with the present subject.[6] The device is self-conscious and poets describe the technique with the phrases *fingere serta* or *texere serta*, "to fashion or weave intertwinings." *Serta* (related to Sanscrit *sarat*, "thread" and to Greek σειρά, "rope") is from the past participle of *serere*, "to interweave, entwine, or interlace." The past participle of *texere*, "to weave, braid, interlace," is *textus*, the etymon of our words text and textile. The connection is so obvious that no one thinks of it. In basic meaning, then, a poetic text is a weaving of words to form, in effect, a verbal carpet page.

The passage in *Beowulf* about the scop's praise of Beowulf describes a recital in which a literary past, the exploits of Sigemund and Heremod, is intertwined with the present, Beowulf's killing of Grendel. This episode is extended and might equally be considered as an example of simple structural interlace. The scop is said to *wordum wrixlan*, "vary words" (874); the verb *wrixlan* is found elsewhere in this sense, for example in Riddle 8 of the Exeter Book. Klaeber calls such variation "the very soul of the Old English poetical style" (lxv); it involves multiple statement of a subject in several different words or phrases, each of which typically describes a different aspect of the subject. When variation on two or more subjects is combined, the result is stylistic interlace, the interweaving of two or more strands of variation. This may be what Cynewulf refers to in *Elene* when he writes *ic . . . wordcræftum wæf*, "I wove words" (1236-7). An example from *Beowulf* will serve to illustrate stylistic interlace:

No þæt læsest wæs
hondgemot[a] þær mon Hygelac sloh,
syððan Geata cyning guðe ræsum,
freawine folca Freslondum on,
Hreðles eafora hiorodryncum swealt,
bille gebeaten. [2354-9]

Although awkward in modern English, a translation following the original order of phrases shows the stylistic interlace.

That was not the least
of hand-to-hand encounters where Hygelac was killed,
when the king of the Geats in the rush of battle,
the beloved friend of the people, in Frisia,
the son of Hreðel died bloodily,
struck down with the sword.

Hygelac, Geata cyning, freawine folca, and *Hreðles eafora* make one strand; *mon . . . sloh, hiorodryncum swealt*, and *bille gebeaten* make a second strand; *þær, guðe ræsum*, and *Freslondum on* make the third. The three strands are woven together into a stylistic braid. This feature of style is familiar to readers of Anglo-Saxon poetry and is the literary counterpart for interlace designs in art that are decorative rather than structural. Designs on a sword, coffer or cross are decoration applied to an object whose structure arises from other considerations.

[6]See Peter Dale Scott, "Alcuin as Poet," *UTQ*, 33 (1964), 233-57.

At a structural level, literary interlace has a counterpart in tapestries where positional patterning of threads establishes the shape and design of the fabric, whether the medium is thread in textile or words in a text. Unfortunately cloth perishes easily and only a few fragments of Anglo-Saxon tapestry survive although the early English were famous for their weaving and needle work which was referred to on the continent simply as *opus Anglicum* with no other description. Since tapestry examples are lost, decorative interlace must serve here as graphic presentation of the principle of structural interlace, a concept difficult to explain or grasp without such a visual analogue.

Rhetoricians of the classical period distinguished between natural and artificial order, but emphasized the former as being especially effective for oral delivery since they were chiefly concerned with the orator. In the *scholia Vindobonensia*, an eighth-century commentary on the *Ars Poetica* of Horace, there is a passage on artificial order of great interest to the subject of interlace structure in Anglo-Saxon poetry. The authorship of the *Scholia* is unknown, but its editor attributes it to Alcuin or one of his school.[7] The passage is a comment on four lines of the *Ars Poetica*.

> Ordinis haec virtus erit et venus, aut ego fallor,
> ut iam nunc dicat iam nunc debentia dici,
> pleraque differat et praesens in tempus omittat,
> hoc amet, hoc spernat promissi carminis auctor. [42-5]

Of order, this will be the excellence and charm, unless I am mistaken, that the author of the long-promised poem shall say at the moment what ought to be said at the moment and shall put off and omit many things for the present, loving this and scorning that.

The commentator was particularly interested in the last line, which he regards as having the force of an independent hortatory subjunctive; he takes *hoc . . . hoc* in the strong sense of "on the one hand . . on the other" which would have been expressed by *hoc . . . ille* in classical Latin.

Hoc, id est, ut nunc dicat iam debentia dici quantem ad naturalem ordinem; *amet auctor promissi carminis,* id est, amet artificialem ordinem. *Hoc,* id est, contrarium ordinis artificialis, id est, ordinem naturalem *spernat auctor promissi carminis*; hoc breviter dicit. Nam sententia talis est: quicunque promittit se facturum bonum carmen et lucidum habere ordinem, amet artificialem ordinem et spernat naturalem. Omnis ordo aut naturalis aut artificialis est. Naturalis ordo est, si quis narret rem ordine quo gesta est; artificialis ordo est, si quis non incipit a principio rei gestae, sed a medio, ut Virgilius in Aeneide quaedam in futuro dicenda anticipat et quaedam in praesenti dicenda in posterum differt.[8]

Hoc, that is, he should say now what ought to have been said before according to natural order; *amet auctor promissi carminis,* that is, should love artificial order. *Hoc,*

---

[7]*Scholia Vindobonensia ad Horatii Artem Poeticam*, ed. Josephus Zechmeister (Vienna, 1877), iii. I wish to acknowledge my considerable debt to Paula Neuss of the University of Kent at Canterbury for research assistance in eighth-century Latin authors and for constructive criticism throughout the work for this lecture.
[8]Zechmeister, 4-5, repunctuated.

that is, the opposite of artificial order, that is *spernat auctor promissi carminis* natural order; Horace says this briefly. For the meaning is as follows: whoever undertakes to make a good poem having clear order should love artificial order and scorn natural order. Every order is either natural or artificial; artificial order is when one does not begin from the beginning of an exploit but from the middle, as does Virgil in the *Aeneid* when he anticipates some things which should have been told later and puts off until later some things which should have been told in the present.

This comment extends the source into a doctrine on the suitability of artificial order for poetry concerned with martial material (*res gesta*) and takes an epic (the *Aeneid*) as an example. What I have called interlace structure is, in more general terms, complex artificial order, with the word complex in its etymological sense of woven together. Interlace design is a dominant aspect of eighth-century Anglo-Saxon visual art and the *Scholia Vindobonensia* present convincing evidence that the same design principle was applied to narrative poetry.

Alcuin's two lives of St. Willibrord provide instructive examples of natural and artificial order.[9] The prose version begins with an account of Willibrord's parents and gives a chronological account of the Saint's life, death, and the subsequent miracles at his tomb. The poem, on the other hand, plunges *in medias res* with an account of Willibrord's visit to Pippin; the details of the Saint's early life are placed at the end. The poem is in simple artificial order, and in the Preface Alcuin states that it is for private study but that the prose version is for public reading. The same logic is followed in Alcuin's *Disputatio de Rhetorica* which deals only with natural order since it is intended for instruction in public oral discourse.[10] On the basis of this preference for natural order in work intended for oral delivery, an argument might be made that *Beowulf* was meant for private study since it has complex artificial order.

Before I turn to the poem, a brief summary of my argument thus far might be helpful. In the visual arts of the seventh and eighth centuries interlace designs reached an artistic perfection in England that was never equalled again. Interlace appears so regularly on sculpture, jewellery, weapons, and in manuscript illuminations that it is the dominant characteristic of this art. There is clear evidence that a parallel technique of word-weaving was used as a stylistic device in both Latin and Old English poems of the period. Finally there is the specific statement of the *Scholia Vindobonensis* that artificial order was preferred for narrative poetry. Such artificial order I have called interlace structure because the term has historical probability and critical usefulness in reading *Beowulf*.

III

Beowulf is a work of art consistent with the artistic culture that it reflects and from which it came, eighth-century England. It is a lacertine interlace, a complex structure of great technical skill, but it is woven with relatively few strands. When *Beowulf* is read in its own artistic context as an interlace

---

[9]*De Vita Sancti Willibrordi Archiepiscopi*, ed. B. Krusch and W. Levison, *MGH, Scriptores Rerum Merov.* (Hannover and Leipzig, 1919), VII, 113-41; this is the prose version. *De Vita Willibrordi Episcopi*, ed. E. Dümmler, *MGH, Poetarum Latinorum Medii Aevi*, I (Berlin, 1881), 207-20.

[10]Ed. and trans. Wilbur S. Howell (Princeton, 1941), Section 22.

structure, it can be recognized as a literary work parallel to the carpet pages of the Lindisfarne Gospels, having a technical excellence in design and execution that makes it the literary equivalent of that artistic masterpiece.

Examples of narrative threads, intersected by other material, are easy to perceive in the poem once the structural principle is understood. The full account of Hygelac's Frisian expedition is segmented into four episodes, 1202-14, 2354-68, 2501-9 and 2913-21, in which chronology is ignored. The poet interlaces these episodes to achieve juxtapositions impossible in a linear narrative. In the first episode the gift of a precious golden torque to Beowulf for killing Grendel is interrupted by an allusion to its loss years later when Hygelac is killed. Hygelac's death seeking Frisian treasure foreshadows Beowulf's death seeking the dragon's hoard. The transience of gold and its connection with violence are obvious. In the second episode Beowulf's preparations to face the dragon are intersected by another allusion to Hygelac's expedition; each is an example of rash action and each ends in the death of a king. The third episode comes as Beowulf recalls how he went in front of Hygelac

> ana on orde,   ond swa to aldre sceall
> sæcce fremman,   þenden þis sweord þolað.   (2498-9)
>
> alone in the van and so will I always
> act in battle while this sword holds out.

He had needed no sword to crush Dæghrefn, the slayer of Hygelac; against the dragon his sword Nægling fails. The pattern is the same as for the fights with Grendel whom he had killed with his hands and with Grendel's mother against whom the sword Hrunting fails. Beowulf's trust in a sword against Grendel's mother had nearly cost him his life; against the dragon it does. The last episode comes in the speech of the messenger who states that the fall of Beowulf will bring affliction to the Geats from their enemies. Among them, the messenger warns, are the Frisians seeking revenge for Hygelac's raid years before. Hygelac's death led to the virtual annihilation of his raiding force; Beowulf's death leads to the virtual annihilation of all the Geats. The four Hygelac episodes, like all the narrative elements in the poem, have positional significance; unravel the threads and the whole fabric falls apart. An episode cannot be taken out of context—may I remind you again of the etymology of the word—without impairing the interwoven design. This design reveals the meaning of coincidence, the recurrence of human behaviour, and the circularity of time, partly through the coincidence, recurrence, and circularity of the medium itself—the interlace structure. It allows for the intersection of narrative events without regard for their distance in chronological time and shows the interrelated significances of episodes without the need for any explicit comment by the poet. The significance of the connections is left for the audience to work out for itself. Understatement is thus inherent in interlace structure, a characteristic that fits the heroic temper of the north.

The Hygelac episodes contribute to what I believe is the major theme of *Beowulf*, "the fatal contradiction at the core of heroic society. The hero follows a code that exalts indomitable will and valour in the individual, but society requires a king who acts for the common good, not for his own glory."[11] Only two periods in Beowulf's life are told in linear narrative; they are the few days, perhaps a week, when he fights Grendel and his mother and the last few days when he fights the dragon. This treatment emphasizes Beowulf's heroic grandeur, his glorious deeds, and his predilection for monster-fighting. However, this main narrative is constantly intersected by episodes which present these deeds from a different perspective. The Hygelac episodes show the social consequences of rash action in a king and they become more frequent as the dragon fight develops. Hygelac's Frisian raid was a historical event; the history of this age provides many parallels. In 685 Ecgfriŏ, King of Northumbria, led a raiding party against the advice of his friends deep into Pictish territory. Caught in mountainous narrows at a place called Nechtanesmere on May 20, he and most of his army were killed, a disaster that ended English ascendancy in the north. The main theme of *Beowulf* thus had relevance to a major recent event in the society that most probably produced it. Ecgfriŏ's brother Aldfriŏ, a man famed for his learning and skill as a poet, ruled from 685 to 704; Bede says that he re-established his ruined and diminished kingdom nobly,[12] a stable reign that made possible the learning and scholarship of eighth-century Northumbria, the golden age of Bede and Alcuin.

At first the episodes give little more than a hint that Beowulf's heroic susceptibility may have calamitous consequences for his people. The references to Sigemund and Heremod after Beowulf kills Grendel foreshadow Beowulf's later career as king. He kills a dragon, as Sigemund did, and leaves the Geats to suffer national calamity, as Heremod left the Danes to suffer *fyrenŏearfe* (14), "terrible distress."[13] In the second part of the poem Beowulf's preparations to fight the dragon are constantly intersected by allusions to the Swedish wars, ominous warnings of the full consequences to the Geats of Beowulf's dragon fight. In this way the poet undercuts Beowulf's single-minded preoccupation with the dragon by interlacing a stream of more and more pointed episodes about the human threats to his people, a far more serious danger than the dragon poses. Beowulf wins glory by his heroic exploit in killing the dragon, but brings dire affliction on his people, as Wiglaf quite explicitly states.

Oft sceall eorl monig   anes willan
wræc adreogan,   swa us geworden is. [3077-8]

Often many men must suffer distress
For the willfulness of one alone, as has happened to us.

Of particular interest to my subject is the way in which the interlace design, in and of itself, makes a contribution to the main theme. Because of the many lines given to the monsters and to Beowulf's preparations to fight them, they are the largest thread in the design, like the zoomorphs on the Windsor dagger pommel or the dragons on the Gandersheim casket. Monster-fighting thus pre-empts the reader's attention just as it pre-empts Beowulf's; the reader gets

---

[11]John Leyerle, "Beowulf the Hero and the King," *Medium Ævum*, 34 (1965), 89.
[12]*Historia Ecclesiastica*, ed. C. Plummer (Oxford, 1896), IV, xxiv, Vol. I, 268.
[13]See "Beowulf the Hero and the King," 101.

caught up in the heroic ethos like the hero and easily misses the warnings. In a sense the reader is led to repeat the error, one all too easy in heroic society, hardly noticing that glorious action by a leader often carries a terrible price for his followers.

The monsters are the elongated lacertine elements that thread through the action of the poem making symmetrical patterns characteristic of interlace structure. Beowulf's fights against Grendel's mother and against the monsters in the Breca episode are clear examples. During the swimming match Beowulf, protected by his armour, is dragged to the ocean floor. Fate gives him victory and he kills *niceras nigene* (575), "nine water monsters," with his sword; this prevents them from feasting on him as they intended. After the battle, light comes and the sea grows calm. This is almost a *précis* of the later underwater fight against Grendel's mother; the pattern is the same, though told in greater detail.

Once the probability of parallel design is recognized, the function of some episodes becomes clearer. The Finnesburh lay, for example, is probably a cautionary tale for the Danes and Geats. Beowulf and his Geats visit Hroðgar and his Danes in Heorot to assist in defending the hall against an *eoten*, Grendel. During the first evening they share the hall Unferð issues an insulting challenge to which Beowulf makes a wounding reply stating that Unferð had killed his own brothers. This deed associates him with Cain, the archetypal fratricide, and Cain's descendant, Grendel. The defence of the hall is successful and Grendel is killed. At the victory celebration the scop recites a lay about the visit of Hnæf and his Half-Danes to Finn and his Frisians in Finnesburh. They fall to quarrelling and slaughter each other. In this episode the word *eoten* occurs three times in the genitive plural form *eotena* and once in the dative plural *eotenum*. These forms are often taken as referring to the Jutes, although no one can say what they are doing there or what part they play. More likely the references are to monsters. At line 1088 the Frisians and Danes surviving from the first battle are said each to control half of the hall *wið eotena bearn*, which probably means "against the giants' kin." Quite possibly the Half-Danes go to Finnesburh to help the Frisians hold their hall against monsters, a situation which would explain why Finn did not burn out the Half-Danes when the fighting started. The hall was their joint protection against the monsters. After the lay Wealhþeow makes two moving pleas (1169-87 and 1216-31) for good faith and firm friendship in Heorot, especially between the Geats and the Danes. She clearly takes the scop's lay as a warning and fears being afflicted like Hildeburh. Just before she speaks, Unferð is described as sitting at Hroðgar's feet; he is a figure of discord as shown by his name, which means "mar-peace," and by his behaviour. The queen might well be concerned lest insults between Dane and Geat be renewed and lead to fighting. From all this emerges an interesting connection. In *Beowulf* monsters are closely associated with the slaying of friends and kinsmen.[14] They function in part as an outward objectification and sign of society beset by internecine slaughter between friend and kin.

The Finnesburh episode and the situation in Heorot are part of another theme that forms a thread of the interlace design of *Beowulf*—visits to a hall.

---

[14]Heremod's story fits this context, too, for he kills his table-companions and dies *mid eotenum* (902).

A guest should go to the hall with friendly intent and be given food and entertainment of poetry by his host. Grendel inverts this order. He visits Heorot in rage, angered by the scop's song of creation, and makes food of his unwilling hosts. Hroðgar cannot dispense men's lives in Heorot, but Grendel does little else. He is an *eoten*, or "eater," and swallows up the society he visits almost as if he were an allegorical figure for internecine strife. In a similar way Grendel's mother visits Heorot and devours Æschere; in return Beowulf visits her hall beneath the mere, kills her, and brings back the head of Grendel. The Heaþobard episode concerning Ingeld and the battle that breaks out when the Danes visit his hall is another appearance of this thematic thread. Hroðgar gives his daughter Freawaru to Ingeld in marriage, hoping to end the feud between the two tribes, but an implacable old warrior sees a Dane wearing a sword that once belonged to the father of a young Heaþobard warrior. He incites the youth to revenge and the feud breaks out again; in the end the Heaþobards are decimated and Heorot is burnt. Other hall visits may be noted briefly. A slave visits the hall of the dragon and steals a cup; the dragon burns halls of the Geats in angry retribution, a token of the fate in store for Geatish society soon to be destroyed by war. Beowulf attacks the dragon who dies in the door of his hall fighting in self-defence.

Another theme of the poem is that of women as the bond of kinship. The women often become the bond themselves by marrying into another tribe, like Wealhþeow, Hildeburh, and Freawaru. This tie often has great tension put on it when the woman's blood relations visit the hall of her husband and old enmities between the tribes arise, as happens in the Finnesburh and Heaþobard episodes. The marriage then gives occasion for old wounds to open, even after an interval of years, and produces a result exactly opposite to its intent. On the other hand, women can be implacable in revenge as Grendel's mother is. Þryð (or Modþryð) is also implacable at first in resisting marriage; she causes her would-be husbands to be killed. Afterwards her father sends her over the sea as wife to Offa who checks her savage acts and she becomes a *freoðuwebbe*, "peace-weaver," knitting up her kinsmen rather than refusing all ties. In general the women are *cynna gemyndig*, "intent on kinship," as the poet says of Wealhþeow (613). They preserve the tie of kin or revenge it when given cause.

Another tie that binds society is treasure, especially gold; but, like kinship, it is also a cause of strife. Treasure is not sought for selfish avarice, but to enable a hero to win fame in gaining treasure for his lord and his lord to win fame dispensing it as a *beaga brytta*, a "dispenser of treasure," from the *gifstol*, "gift throne." The gift and receipt of treasure are a tie between a lord and his retainer, an outward sign of the agreement between them. The strength and security of heroic society depend on the symbolic circulation of treasure. A lord offers support and sustenance to his retainer who agrees in turn to fight unwaveringly for his lord, a bond of contractual force in heroic society. Injury or slaughter of a man had a monetary price and could be atoned by *wergild*, "man payment." The monsters are outside this society; for them treasure is an object to be hoarded under ground. They receive no gifts and do not dispense them. The poet states ironically that none need expect handsome recompense for the slaughter that Grendel inflicts. Hroðgar is the one who pays the *wergild* for the Geat, Hondscioh, killed by Grendel in the Danish cause. The relation of the monsters to *gifstolas* presents an interesting parallel in the interlace design. The dragon burns the *gifstol Geata* (2327), an act that implies his disruption of the entire social order of Beowulf's *comitatus*. The full extent of this disruption appears when all but one of Beowulf's chosen retainers desert him in his last battle. Grendel, on the other hand, occupies Heorot, but he is not able to cause complete disruption of Hroðgar's *comitatus*, however ineffective it is against him. The sense of lines 168-9, a much disputed passage, thus seems likely to be that Grendel cannot destroy Hroðgar's *gifstol* (168), thought of as the objectification of the Danish *comitatus*.

The poem is also concerned with a society's gain of treasure as well as its loss. When a king seeks treasure himself, the cost may be ruinous for his people. Hygelac's Frisian raid and Beowulf's dragon fight are examples. Although Grendel's cave is rich in treasure, Beowulf takes away only a golden sword hilt and the severed head of Grendel; his object is to gain revenge, not treasure. Hroðgar's speech to Beowulf after his return contains warnings on pride in heroic exploits and on the ease with which gold can make a man stingy, hoarding his gold like a monster; either way the *comitatus* is apt to suffer. Heremod, who ended *mid eotenum*, is an example. When treasure passes outside the society where it is a bond, it becomes useless. The treasure in Scyld's funeral ship, the golden torque lost in Frisia, the lay of the last survivor, and the dragon's hoard buried with Beowulf are examples. Treasure had some positive force in heroic society, but it casts a baleful glitter in the poem because it is associated with monsters, fighting, the death of kings, and funerals.

These various themes are some of the threads that form the interlace structure of *Beowulf*. Often several are presented together, as in the Finnesburh episode or in the final dragon fight. The themes make a complex, tightly-knotted lacertine interlace that cannot be untied without losing the design and form of the whole. The tension and force of the poem arise from the way the themes cross and juxtapose. Few comments are needed from the poet because significance comes from the intersections and conjunctions of the design. To the *Beowulf* poet, as to many other writers, the relations between events are more significant than their temporal sequence and he used a structure that gave him great freedom to manipulate time and concentrate on the complex interconnections of events. Although the poem has to be lingered over and gives up its secrets slowly, the principle of its interlace structure helps to reveal the interwoven coherence of the episodes as well as the total design of the poem in all its complex resonances and reverberations of meaning. There are no digressions in *Beowulf*.

The structural interlace of *Beowulf*, like the visual interlace patterns of the same culture, has great technical excellence, but is not to be regarded as an isolated phenomenon. The term is specifically applied to literature in the late middle ages. Robert Manning states in his *Chronicle* (1338) that he writes in a clear and simple style so that he will be readily understood; others, he says, use *quante Inglis* in complicated schemes of *ryme couwee* or *strangere* or *enterlace*.[15] *Entrelacement* was a feature of prose romances, especially those in the Arthurian tradition, as Eugène Vinaver has recently shown.[16]

[15]Ed. F. J. Furnivall (London, 1887). See lines 71-128.
[16]"Form and Meaning in Medieval Romance," The Presidential Address of the Modern Humanities Research Association (1966).

The term interlace may be taken in a larger sense; it is an organizing principle closer to the workings of the human imagination proceeding in its atemporal way from one associative idea to the next than to the Aristotelian order of parts belonging to a temporal sequence with a beginning, middle, and end. If internal human experience of the imagination is taken as the basis, the Aristotelian canon of natural order as moving in chronological progression is really *ordo artificialis*, not the other way around as the rhetoricians taught. The human imagination moves in atemporal, associative patterns like the literary interlace. *Don Quixote* provides a useful illustration. The Don, supposedly mad, is brought home in a cage on wheels at the end of Part I. He could be taken as the interlacing fecundity of the associative mind, caught in the skull-cage, reacting with complex atemporal imagination, weaving sensory impressions with literary experience. The Canon of Toledo who rides along outside mouthing Aristotelian criticism of romances is, as his name suggests, an uncomprehending set of external rules, or canons, sent to bedevil and torment the poetic imagination.

There is a substantial amount of literature having interlace structure, if I may extend the term without presenting evidence here. Mediaeval dream poetry, such as *Le Roman de la Rose* and *Piers Plowman*, is largely a mixture of literary and imaginative experience with an atemporal interlace structure as are many complex romances, especially those with allegorical content like the *Faerie Queene*. The allegorical impulse in literature is often presented with an interlace structure because it is imaginative, literary and atemporal. Stream-of-consciousness novels frequently have something like interlace structures as well, for the same reasons.[17]

Like the poem, this lecture will make an end as it began. Scyld's glorious accomplishments and ship funeral at the opening of the poem mark the start of a dynasty and a period of prosperity for the Danes after the leaderless affliction they suffer following the death of Heremod. The funeral in the Finnesburh episode begins the period of affliction of the Half-Danes and presages the destruction of Finn's dynasty. At the end of the poem Beowulf's death begins a period of affliction for the Geats. The poem ends as it began with a funeral, the return of the interlace design to its start. The sudden reversals inherent in the structure as one theme intersects another without regard to time give to the whole poem a sense of transience about the world and all that is in it as beginnings and endings are juxtaposed; this is the much-remarked elegiac texture of *Beowulf*. Scyld's mysterious arrival as a child is placed beside his mysterious departure in death over the seas. A description of Heorot's construction is followed by an allusion to its destruction. The gift of a golden torque, by its loss. Beowulf's victories over monsters, by his defeat by a monster. With each reversal the elegiac texture is tightened, reminding us of impermanence and change, extending even to the greatest of heroes, Beowulf, a man mourned by those who remain behind as

> manna mildust   ond mon(ðw)ærust,
> leodum liðost   ond lofgeornost. [3181-2]

---

[17]Interlace structure in later texts will be the subject of a larger work now in preparation. I wish to thank Mrs. Medora Bennett of the University of Toronto for help in the final preparation of this article for press.

the most gentle and kind of men,
most generous to his people and most anxious for praise.

A bright and golden age of a magnanimous man vanishes, even as it seems hardly to have begun.

> The jawes of darkness do devoure it up:
> So quicke bright things come to confusion.
> [*Mids.* I. i. 148-9]

PLATE NOTES

PLATE I. The Bewcastle Cross stands where it was erected about the year 700 in the churchyard of St Cuthbert at Bewcastle in Cumberland. The top is broken away leaving a truncated shaft 14 feet 6 inches high. The width at the base of the south face is 1 foot 9 inches. For a full discussion and many plates of the cross, see G. Baldwin Brown, *The Arts in Early England*, V (London, 1921), *passim*.

PLATE II. This jewel, now in the Victoria and Albert Museum, is one of two composite disc brooches found at Milton near Abingdon, Berkshire, in 1832. It is 3.1 inches in diameter; the detail shown here is about 1.9 inches wide. See Ronald Jessup, *Anglo-Saxon Jewellery* (London, 1950), 116 and Plate XXV (1).

PLATE III. The Windsor dagger pommel, now in the Ashmolean Museum, is one of the finest pieces of Anglo-Saxon gold work known. It is only 1.7 inches wide and is shown here greatly enlarged. The panel of gold interlace is .72 inches high by .61 inches wide. See G. Baldwin Brown, *The Arts in Early England*, III (London, 1915) 311 and Plate LVI.

PLATE IV. The great gold buckle from Sutton Hoo is 5.5 inches long and weighs nearly 15 ounces. Its value as gold bullion exceeds that of any other object yet dug up in England. See Ronald Jessup, *Anglo-Saxon Jewellery* (London, 1950), 139-40 and Plate XL and Charles Green, *Sutton Hoo* (London, 1963), 79-80 and Plate XX.

PLATE V. The Book of Durrow is in Trinity College Dublin Library. The leaves measure about 9.5 by 6.25 inches. During the later middle ages it was at Durrow in Ireland and was thought to have medicinal value. Water was poured over it and given to sick cattle; whatever this treatment did for the livestock it impaired the manuscript, especially the early leaves which were badly damaged. For a full account and facsimile of the manuscript, see *Codex Durmachensis*, ed. A. A. Luce, *et al.* (Olten, Lausanne, and Freiburg, 1960).

PLATE VI*a*. This sword hilt, found near Crundale in Kent, is 2.4 inches wide. See G. Baldwin Brown, *The Arts in Early England*, III (London, 1915), 330 and Plate LXIII (4) and T. D. Kendrick, *Anglo-Saxon Art* (London, 1938), 86 and Plate 33; figure 17, XXII, page 82, is a schematic drawing of the hilt.

PLATE VI*b*. The Witham Pins, a group of three silver, linked discs, were found at Fiskerton near Lincoln in the River Witham. The detail shown here is about 1.4 inches wide and is greatly enlarged. See the British Museum *Guide to Anglo-Saxon Antiquities* (London, 1923), 98 and T. D. Kendrick, *Anglo-Saxon Art* (London, 1938), 170-1.

PLATE VII. The manuscript containing the St Chad Gospels is in the Lichfield Cathedral Library. The Bishop of Lichfield, the Dean and the Canons swear an oath on this volume to maintain the rights of the Church when they take office. The leaves of the manuscript measure about nine by 12 inches; the detail shown here measures about 2.25 by 3 inches. Folio 110 was originally the first leaf of the manuscript, but

Plate I. The south face of the cross shaft at Bewcastle, Cumberland.

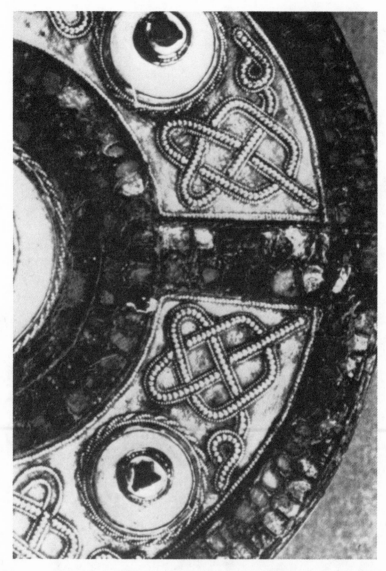

Plate II. Detail from the Abingdon Brooch. By courtesy of the Board of Trustees of the Victoria and Albert Museum.

Plate III. The Windsor dagger pommel. Courtesy of the Ashmolean Museum.

Plate IV. The great gold buckle from Sutton Hoo. Reproduced by Courtesy of the Trustees of the British Museum.

Plate V. Folio 192^v of the Book of Durrow. Courtesy of The Board of Trinity College Dublin.

Plate VIa. The Crundale Sword hilt. Reproduced by Courtesy of the Trustees of the British Museum.

Plate VIb. Detail from the centre disc of the Witham Pins. Reproduced by Courtesy of the Trustees of the British Museum.

Plate VII. A detail from folio 110^v of the St. Chad Gospels. Courtesy of the Conway Library, Courtauld Institute of Art.

Plate VIII. Folio 94ᵛ of the Lindisfarne Gospels. By permission of the British Library.

Plate IX. The front of the Gandersheim casket. Courtesy of the Herzog Anton Ulrich-Museum, Braunschweig.

was placed in its present location as early as the ninth century, as is shown by the arrangement of marginal notes. The manuscript is discussed by Canon L. J. Hopkin-James, *The Celtic Gospels* (Oxford, 1934), *passim*. See also *Codex S. Ceaddae Latinus*, ed. F. H. A. Scrivener (Cambridge, 1887) and H. E. Savage, "The Story of St. Chad's Gospels," *Transactions of the Birmingham Archaeological Society*, XLI (1915), 4-21.

PLATE VIII. The excellent facsimile of the Lindisfarne Gospels (British Museum MS. Cotton Nero D IV) shows this folio, which measures about 9.6 by 13.5 inches, in colour. See *Codex Lindisfarnensis*, ed. T. D. Kendrick, *et al.* (Olten and Lausanne, 1956-60).

PLATE IX. The Gandersheim casket, also called the Brunswick casket, in the Herzog Anton Ulrich-Museum, Braunschweig, Germany, is 4.8 inches tall by 2.6 inches wide and is carved from walrus teeth. See M. H. Longhurst, *English Ivories* (London, 1926), 127-8 and Plates 13-14 and August Fink, "Zum Gandersheimer Runen-kästchen," *Forschungen zur Kunstgeschichte und christlichen Archäologie*, Vol. III, *Karolingische und ottonische Kunst* (Wiesbaden, 1957), 277-81.

The Text of Fate

By Edward B. Irving, Jr.

Everything, however, is what it is, and in the moral world leans for its existence on its contrary, as courage upon the possibility of cowardice, magnanimity on that of meanness.[1]

In one very important sense the Old English poem *Beowulf* is the product of centuries. Much of its meaning is directly traceable to the traditional style itself, especially to those rhetorical patterns inherited by the poet and used by him almost unconsciously. Such patterns tend to give shape to the events he describes and largely determine the nature of his comments on those events— largely but of course not entirely, for it would be unwise to deny originality to the *Beowulf* poet or to see him as merely a mechanical producer of verses. Yet before we move on to the evidence for his individual genius in later chapters it would be advisable to look first at some of the habitual constructions that in themselves create so much of the atmosphere of the poem. A great deal of what we see here in miniature will be exemplified on a larger scale in the poem as a whole.

Since a study of all the rhetorical patterns would be a book in itself, we must limit ourselves to examining a few important patterns. Most of this chapter will be concerned with negative constructions, since they have always been recognized as a striking feature of Germanic rhetoric. They surely play a major role in creating the impression of a persistent tone of irony and understatement that modern readers receive from this poetry, and they also have much to do with the usual representation of behavior in extreme terms. Particular attention will be given to that form of rhetorical heightening which is provided by the frequent combination of a negative clause or phrase with the adversative conjunction *ac* or with other words such as *hwæðre* or *swa þeah*, with the general meaning usually something like: "It is by no means A; on the contrary it is B."[2]

---

[1]W. Macneile Dixon, *Tragedy* (2d ed. London, C. Arnold & Co., 1925), pp. 110-11.

[2]Some remarks by Randolph Quirk in the introduction to his book, *The Concessive Relation in Old English Poetry* (New Haven, Yale University Press, 1954), probably suggested this general subject to me originally. I should make clear that the study here means to be suggestive rather than statistically exhaustive. Not all negatives in the poem are included, for example, although those negatives that are made more emphatic by the addition of some intensifier (e.g. *nealles, no, ne . . . wiht*) have all been examined. Enough examples will be cited to point to a pattern, but examples that are of no special rhetorical interest will sometimes be omitted.

This essay is Chapter One of the author's *A Reading of 'Beowulf'* (New Haven: Yale Univ. Press, 1968), pp. 1-42. Reprinted by permission.

Defining the Ideal Hero

The poet may use negative terms to state or amplify his conception of what a true hero should be in two different ways. He may mention what a true hero is not or does not do (namely, bad things), or he may mention what a nonhero is not or does not do (namely, good things).

Let us begin by looking at some examples of the second kind of statement, in which characters or behavior more or less sharply defined as being the opposite of heroic are typically described. Two such examples occur in the passage in Hrothgar's sermon where the wicked king Heremod is described. Heremod is, to be sure, an antitype of the ideal king rather than of the ideal hero, but the passage illustrates the principle of the construction especially well.

> Ne wearð Heremod swa
> eaforum Ecgwelan,   Arscyldingum;
> ne geweox he him to willan,   ac to wælfealle
> ond to deaðcwalum   Deniga leodum.[3]   (1709b-12)

Heremod was not so [helpful] to the descendants of Ecgwela, to the honorable Scyldings; he did not grow up to be what they wished—far from it, he grew into the slaughter and violent death of the Danish people.

In such a passage we can sense the full rhetorical effect of this adversative form of statement. Here we have the energetic clash of powerful opposites: growth, potentiality for good, and the people's will on one hand; murder and destructiveness on the other. On one side of the *ac* fulcrum is stated (in negative terms) one ideal of true kingship: that the king grow into what his people wish him to be, or that he grow to become loved by his people. On the other side of the *ac* the two tautological compounds *wælfealle* and *deaðcwalum* put particularly heavy stress on the anarchic violence we actually find in this king. Heremod's brutality leads to alienation from humanity, as we see in the following lines:

> breat bolgenmod   beodgeneatas,
> eaxlgesteallan,   oþþæt he ana hwearf,
> mære ðeoden,   mondreamum from.   (1713-15)

In furious anger he cut down his table-companions and comrades in arms, until at last he went off alone, that famous prince, away from men's joys.

Keeping two opposites alive simultaneously in the hearer's mind (in this instance, attributes of good and bad kings) may be the most important function of this form of rhetoric.

What we find here, and in many similar passages, is a form of statement in terms of extremes, where poetic energy may originate in the violent oscillation

---

[3]The text quoted here and throughout (unless otherwise indicated) is basically that of E. V. K. Dobbie, *Beowulf and Judith,* Anglo-Saxon Poetic Records, 4 (New York, Columbia University Press, 1953). Dobbie's text has been somewhat simplified for the purposes of this book by the omission of his brackets and italics in those cases where he is indicating readings from the Thorkelin transcripts. I do use brackets and italics in the customary way to indicate emendations of the manuscript, however, and I occasionally modify Dobbie's punctuation.

of sense from one extreme to another. Our second example, from the passage immediately following the lines we have quoted, shows just such an effect.

> Ðeah þe hine mihtig god   mægenes wynnum,
> eafeþum stepte,   ofer ealle men
> forð gefremede,   hwæþere him on ferhþe greow
> breosthord blodreow.   Nallas beagas geaf
> Denum æfter dome;   dreamleas gebad
> þæt he þæs gewinnes   weorc þrowade,
> leodbealo longsum.   (1716-22a)

> Even though mighty God had favored him and exalted him beyond all men
> in joys of might and strength—still a bloodlust grew in his secret heart. He
> gave no rings to any Danes to gain glory; no, he lived to be joyless and to
> suffer pain for his violence, and longlasting affliction.

Here *hwæþere* serves as the rhetorical fulcrum. We are told that, on the one hand, God, by giving Heremod the same gift of heroic strength he has given Beowulf, has encouraged him and raised him above other men. But Heremod suddenly turns to evil, and to a particular form of evil (stinginess, not giving rings) that is peculiarly ironic in view of God's generosity toward him. The very willfulness of his behavior is signaled by the abrupt adversative transitions *hwæþere* and *nallas*. The expression "not giving rings" is in fact here a notable understatement, since Heremod apparently murders his subjects. We see the same expression later in Hrothgar's sermon, in the exemplum of the man corrupted by pride and the devil's arrows, a man much resembling Heremod:

> Þinceð him to lytel   þæt he lange heold,
> gytsað gromhydig,   nallas on gylp seleð
> fædde beagas,   ond he þa forðgesceaft
> forgyteð ond forgymeð,   þæs þe him ær god sealde,
> wuldres waldend,   weorðmynda dæl.   (1748-52)

> What he has held for so long now seems to him too little; he covets
> fiercely—never any longer does he proudly bestow ornamented rings; and
> he then ignores and scorns the created world, the great share of honors
> which God, Ruler of glory, had given him.

Even if we leave murder out of the picture, avarice itself is always something more serious than mere stinginess in Germanic heroic poetry; it represents the immoral violation of a personal relationship that happens to be symbolized by the exchange of material wealth. In this light we may with some justice regard avarice as a form of extreme behavior.

Unferth, the Dane who insultingly challenges Beowulf when he arrives at the great Danish hall of Heorot, is in some respects another antitype of the hero. One negative phrase of the type we are examining is applied to him:

> Gehwylc hiora his ferhþe treowde,
> þæt he hæfde mod micel,   þeah þe he his magum nære
> arfæst æt ecga gelacum.   (1166b-68a)

Each of them trusted his spirit, that he had a great heart, even though he had not been honorable to his kinsmen in the play of sword-edges.

The past history of Unferth and his position at Hrothgar's court are by no means clear and may never be, but this remark by the poet, couched as it is in the habitual ironic mode of understatement, can hardly mean anything other than that Unferth has murdered his kinsmen.[4]

Again, the cowardly retainers who retreat from the dragon's attack and hide in the forest are certainly pictured as nonheroes:

> Næs ða lang to ðon
> þæt ða hildlatan   holt ofgefan,
> tydre treowlogan   tyne ætsomne.
> Ða ne dorston ær   dareðum lacan
> on hyra mandryhtnes   miclan þearfe,
> ac hy scamiende   scyldas bæran,
> guðgewædu,   þær se gomela læg,
> wlitan on Wilaf. (2845b-52a)

It was not long before those slow in battle came out of the forest, ten cowardly faith-breakers together; they had not dared to make play with their spears in their lord's moment of great need; on the contrary, in shame they bore shields and armor to where the old man lay, and they looked at Wiglaf.

Now that the dragon is dead and the danger over, they come forward quickly, although when they were needed they did not come at all.[5] But the negative clause here (2848-49) serves to define very plainly their primary obligation as retainers: to come to their lord's help when he has need of them. The clause with *ac* that follows presents a minor problem in interpretation, however. Precisely what is being opposed to what? If the emphasis in the preceding clause is on *scamiende,* is the chief contrast then between the retainers' previous shamelessness in flight and their present feelings of mortification? More interesting is the possibility of an ironic contrast between the help they did not bring when it was so urgently needed and the useless shields and corselets they now officiously carry to the place where Beowulf lies dead.

Another passage in which the retainers' duty is stated flatly and unequivocally by means of a negative phrase is the following:

> Nealles him on heape   handgesteallan,
> æðelinga bearn,   ymbe gestodon
> hildecystum,   ac hy on holt bugon,
> ealdre burgan. (2596-99a)

In no way did those war-comrades, those sons of noblemen, take their stand around him in formation as fighting-men should; no, they fell back into the forest and took care of their own lives.

---

[4] The reader will find in Chapter Four [of Irving's book] a more extensive discussion of the larger context of this scene, the Great Banquet in Heorot.

[5] The phrase *næs ða lang to ðon* or its equivalent seems at times to be a half-ironic way of describing a noticeably rapid sequence of events, as, for example, in *Beowulf* 2591 or *Guthlac* 903 ff.

This is again rhetorical statement in terms of the polarizing of possible behavior into two extreme kinds. The alliteration here of *hildecystum* and *holt* draws our attention to the alternatives: to stand in military formation or to go hide in a forest. As so often in Old English poetry, and in Germanic literature generally, this kind of statement vividly dramatizes a character's free choice of action, at the same time that a phrase like *aeðelinga bearn* reminds us of his hereditary aristocratic obligations. Heroic life is consistently presented as a series of such radical choices.

Another possible violation of heroic decorum, though in this instance certainly a venial one, may be the storm of emotion that overwhelms King Hrothgar when he says farewell to Beowulf, as the hero takes leave of Denmark and returns home.

> Wæs him se man to þon leof
> þæt he þone breostwylm   forberan ne mehte,
> ac him on hreþre   hygebendum fæst
> æfter deorum men   dyrne langað
> beorn wið blode. (1876b-80a)

> That man was so dear to him that he could not hold back the surge in his breast; on the contrary, a secret longing in his bosom for the dear man strained against rational restraints, burned in his blood.

Beowulf's feelings on this occasion are not described. Assuming that he too feels some measure of grief, one may perhaps see a contrast between his stoical behavior and Hrothgar's yielding to the expression of emotion (a moment before we were told of Hrothgar's tears). But the more important contrast here is between youth and age (often referred to in this part of the poem[6]) rather than between heroic self-restraint and emotionalism. Hrothgar's long experience in disappointment has taught him that they will probably never see each other again; Beowulf is still too young to see the world this way. The rhetorical structure of this sentence differs somewhat from the structure of the previous examples, in that here we have a parallel rather than the usual contrast, for the ideas of the dearness of the man, the fight for self-control, and the hot wave of emotion are really to be found here on both sides of the *ac* fulcrum. Possibly the *ac* construction in this instance may serve simply to emphasize in a general way the strength of Hrothgar's feelings, since such a construction ordinarily suggests some form of emotional tension.

Let us turn now to some examples of the more common way of defining the heroic ideal by negations, this time by negating or denying the nonheroic. It goes without saying that courage is the most important heroic attribute; consequently there are a number of negative expressions that allude to the hero's courage in terms of his "not fearing" or not showing other signs of cowardice.[7] Not only phrases but compounds like *unforht* or (in *The Battle of Maldon*) *unearg* (uncowardly) fall into the same category.

[6]For example: *ealdum infrodum* 1874; *oþþæt hine yldo benam / mægenes wynnum* 1886b-87a.

[7]For example: *nis þæt seldguma* 249 (that is no hanger-about in the hall [but a fighter]); not being frightened but . . . 2967b-69; not fleeing a step but . . . 2524b-27a; not dreading battle 2345-49a; not flinching from violence 1537; not caring about life 1442, 1536.

In *Maldon*, as I have suggested elsewhere, constant reminders of the possibility of flight from battle do much to increase the dramatic tension of the poem.[8] There, of course, such verbal reminders operate in the context of a narrative that in fact describes mass flights. While the flight of the cowardly retainers does of course take place in *Beowulf*, it does not have as much relative importance in the poem; it is merely one dark background stroke in the tremendous heightening and brightening of the figure of Beowulf. Even though they are used less intensively than in *Maldon*, such formulas probably serve to keep alive at the edge of the audience's consciousness the thought that it is after all normal behavior to be frightened under such conditions.

From an assortment of negative phrases describing other nonheroic attributes, we might construct an interesting model of the Anglo-Saxon nonhero: a man who kills his companions over drinks and secretly weaves an ensnaring net of malice for others; who has a ferocious temper and the bad manners to find fault with gift swords.[9] Behavior like this may well have been common in England in the seventh or eighth century, perhaps even common enough to be called a realistic norm. But, since such speculation takes us beyond the bounds of our poem, it would be more profitable to examine these expressions in context. Three of them happen to occur in the same scene.

The final lines (2101-62) of Beowulf's report to Hygelac after he has returned to Geatland project an image of Hrothgar as ideal king, stressing as they do the grief Hrothgar had to suffer under the oppression of Grendel, the warmth of his affection for Beowulf, and, above all, his great generosity. The speech comes to its climax when Beowulf orders Hrothgar's splendid gifts to be brought into the hall and presents them formally to his uncle Hygelac. Hrothgar's magnanimity is used here (as nearly everything in the poem is used sooner or later) to reveal to us Beowulf's own virtues: in this instance, his love, generosity, and loyalty.

The occurrence of three of our negative expressions in this triumphant scene is of interest partly because it reveals what comes into the poet's mind as he contemplates uncle and nephew. A central theme all through this passage is fidelity, symbolized as usual by the exchange of gifts, and, again as usual, we are urged to think both of the affection that inspires the gifts and the obligations they entail. It is entirely characteristic of Old English poetic style that fidelity must be defined or set off or deepened in meaning by strong hints of its opposite.

In his presentation speech to Hygelac, Beowulf mentions that the arms Hrothgar has given him once belonged to Heorogar, Hrothgar's older brother, and that Hrothgar had not wished to give them to Heorogar's son Heoroweard. We are not told what Hrothgar's reason for this last decision may have been, but later versions of the story in Saxo Grammaticus and in the saga of Rolf Kraki make it seem at least possible that Heoroweard, like his cousin Hrothulf, may also have been eying his uncle's throne.[10] In any event the

---

[8]Edward B. Irving, Jr., "The Heroic Style in *The Battle of Maldon*," *Studies in Philology*, 58 (1961), 457-67.

[9]Respectively: *nealles druncne slog / heorðgeneatas* 2179b-80a; *nealles inwitnet oþrum bregdon / dyrnum cræfte* 2167-68a; *næs him hreoh sefa* 2180b; *nales wordum log / meces ecge* 1811b-12a.

[10]See R. W. Chambers, *Beowulf: An Introduction* (3d ed. with a supplement by C. L. Wrenn, Cambridge, The University Press, 1959), pp. 29-30.

reference to the Scylding royal family must at least have reminded the poet of some plotting nephew, whether Heoroweard or Hrothulf, for otherwise the ensuing description of Beowulf as a nephew loyal to Hygelac would have had little point.

> Swa sceal mæg don,
> nealles inwitnet   oðrum bregdon
> dyrnum cræfte,   deað ren[ian]
> hondgesteallan.   Hygelace wæs,
> niða heardum,   nefa swyðe hold,
> ond gehwæðer oðrum   hroþra gemyndig.   (2166b-71)

This is how a kinsman should behave—and not be secretly weaving a treacherous net for others or laying a deathtrap for a comrade. His nephew [Beowulf] was indeed very loyal to war-toughened Hygelac, and each of them was attentive to the happiness of the other.

This passage is a good example of the rhetorical effect we have been discussing. The semantic rhythm here is positive (*swa sceal mæg don*)—negative (the *nealles* clause)—positive (Beowulf's own loyalty). From a different point of view one could see it as constructed in another way: the first two parts are statements of ethical alternatives, while the third is a specific instance of choice. Beowulf has chosen one of the two possible modes of behavior.

What is done in miniature in this brief passage is done on a larger scale in the scene as a whole. Into this scene of absolute and dedicated fidelity in Hygelac's hall the poet introduces a flood of dark reminders of treachery in Heorot, chiefly through references to Hrothgar (2155), to Hrothgar's queen Wealhtheow and the marvelous necklace she gave Beowulf at the great banquet, and to an unnamed hypothetical nonhero who bears some resemblance both to Unferth and to the evil Danish king Heremod, as we can see in the following passage:

> Swa bealdode   bearn Ecgðeowes,
> guma guðum cuð,   godum dædum,
> dreah æfter dome,   nealles druncne slog
> heorðgeneatas;   næs him hreoh sefa,
> ac he mancynnes   mæste cræfte
> ginfæstan gife,   þe him god sealde,
> heold hildedeor.   (2177-83a)

Thus Ecgtheow's son [Beowulf], a man known in battles, showed his bravery in heroic deeds, lived to gain glory; never was he the one to strike comrades over drinks by the hearth; his temper was never savage. No, with the greatest strength of mankind this valorous man kept safe the abundant gifts which God had given him.

Strength and courage are essential to the hero but they are not enough. Heremod and Unferth, both fatally undisciplined, showed their aggressiveness in the violent disruption of social order; Beowulf, while assuredly a veteran warrior, a *guma guðum cuð*, saved his fighting for the battlefield. The negative image of the nonhero is needed here for clearer definition of the moral requirements of true heroism, as they are embodied in Beowulf.

Elsewhere and in somewhat different ways, negative phrases are used to differentiate Beowulf from other men. The Danish coastguard's awed reactions to his first sight of Beowulf, for example, are largely conveyed in a rapid series of expressions that define the nature of the hero by excluding the expected, the normal, the usual, by saying what he is not:

> No her cuðlicor   cuman ongunnon
> lindhæbbende;   ne ge leafnesword
> guðfremmendra   gearwe ne wisson,
> maga gemedu.   Næfre ic maran geseah
> eorla ofer eorþan   ðonne is eower sum,
> secg on searwum;   nis þæt seldguma,
> wæpnum geweorðad,   næfne him his wlite leoge,
> ænlic ansyn. (244-51a)

Never have shield-bearers arrived here in a more open way, yet you were not sure of the permission of our fighting-men or the consent of our kinsmen. I never saw a bigger man on earth than one of you, that fighter in armor. He is certainly no hall-lounger, unless his looks belie him, his noble face.

How can the puzzled coastguard establish the identity of these strange visitors? He can do it only by excluding them from successive categories. Their behavior is entirely different from that of previous visitors to Denmark, who apparently have come either as deferential guests or as furtive spies. But these men come openly and confidently; they walk as if they already had the password. Indeed all the password they need walks among them in the person of Beowulf. And so at the end of this passage the coastguard singles out Beowulf from the rest of the band: he is bigger, braver, of a more resolute and heroic appearance. Yet it is interesting to see how such a luminous and compelling image is constructed out of negative expressions.

Later Wulfgar, who keeps the door of Hrothgar's hall, further distinguishes Beowulf and his men from other visitors. After a moment's inspection, he concludes that these men are not only brave men but that they are responsible and honorable volunteers rather than *wreccan*, that type so common in Germanic literature, roving professional adventurers or refugees from foreign vendettas.

> Wen ic þæt ge for wlenco,   nalles for wræcsiðum,
> ac for higeþrymmum   Hroðgar sohton. (338-39)

I believe that you have come to see Hrothgar out of sheer pride and greatness of spirit, certainly not as adventurers in exile.

Another negative construction (if we may take *forhicge* as expressing an essentially negative idea) sets Beowulf apart from ordinary warriors in respect to his method of fighting:

> Ic þæt þonne forhicge . . .
> þæt ic sweord bere   oþðe sidne scyld,
> geolorand to guþe,   ac ic mid grape sceal
> fon wið feonde   ond ymb feorh sacan,
> lað wið laþum. (435-40a)

I have no intention on that occasion . . . of carrying any sword or wide yellow-bordered shield to battle; on the contrary, I will be obliged to grapple with the fiend with my hands and fight for life, one enemy against another.

Other warriors in heroic poetry make much of the process of assembling their weapons for battle, but Beowulf is different. The difference is most clearly dramatized in the half-ironic "disarming of the hero" scene just before the fight with Grendel, in the course of which Beowulf methodically divests himself of all the traditional accouterments of the epic fighter in order to meet the monster with his bare hands.

Finally, as king, Beowulf differs from others in his response to Queen Hygd's offer to him of the throne of the Geats:

> No ðy ær feasceafte   findan meahton
> æt ðam æðelinge   ænige ðinga,
> þæt he Heardrede   hlaford wære
> oððe þone cynedom   ciosan wolde;
> hwæðre he hine on folce   freondlarum heold,
> estum mid are,   oððæt he yldra wearð,
> Wedergeatum weold.[11]   (2373-79a)

None the sooner could the destitute Geats prevail on the prince in any way to become Heardred's lord or willingly to accept the kingdom; no, he [Beowulf] went on to maintain Heardred in his proper place in the nation by his friendly advice and respectful affection, until he [Heardred] grew up to rule over the Storm-Geats.

Placed in a situation of this kind, where the king is only a child, most men would yield readily to the reasonable pleas of their people to assume power. Many men would be only too glad to seize the royal authority. But Beowulf goes to the other extreme: far from plotting to seize power for himself, he devotes himself to keeping young Heardred in power by his friendly counsels. He will not accept a position that he thinks he does not deserve, even when it is freely (and probably legally) offered to him by a majority of the Geats and by their queen.

Defining the Monstrous

Just as the hero can be effectively defined by the use of negatives, so negatives can serve to describe the hero's chief antagonist Grendel, especially in his relation to some familiar human norm. In fact it may well be that the essential reality of Grendel is best understood in terms like these, for in many ways Grendel could be called an instance of Negative Man. As a fighter and as a "visitor" to the Danish hall that he devastates, he is often treated ironically as a peculiar kind of human warrior. But he is set off from ordinary warriors in one respect, for example, because, as Beowulf points out, for all his courage and ferocity he does not even know how to fight with a sword:

---

[11]In line 2377 Dobbie reads *him*, most other editors *hine*, for MS *hī*.

Nat he þara goda   þæt he me ongean slea,
rand geheawe,   þeah ðe he rof sie
niþgeweorca;   ac wit on niht sculon
secge ofersittan. (681-84a)

He has no knowledge of how to fight properly, to swing sword against me
and hew at my shield, even though he is brave in his savage attacks; no,
tonight we must do without swords, the two of us.

Not only is Grendel cut off from the normal concerns of a Germanic warrior
by his ignorance of the use of weapons, but he is further excluded from the
ranks of noblemen because he has no father, or at least his father's name is
not known by men.

þone on geardagum   Grendel nemdon
foldbuende.   No hie fæder cunnon,
hwæþer him ænig wæs   ær acenned
dyrnra gasta. (1354-57a)

People named him Grendel in the old days. They knew nothing of any
father, whether any such mysterious spirit had ever been born for him.

Since, in all epic poetry, a patronymic is at least as necessary to a hero as a
sword, Grendel's title to heroic identity is wholly obscured.

Unlike normal men, Grendel does not pay the Danish people the honor
they surely deserve, but instead he obeys his own fierce impulses in disposing
of them:

Nymeð nydbade,   nænegum ara ð
leode Deniga,   ac he lust wigeð,
swefeð ond sendeþ,   secce ne weneþ
to Gardenum.   Ac ic him Geata sceal
eafoð ond ellen   ungeara nu,
guþe gebeodan. (598-603a)

He extorts toll, and honors no man of the Danish nation; quite the
contrary, he does just as he pleases, butchers and sends to death (?),
expecting no resistance from the Spear-Danes. But I am the one who will
show him very soon now the strength and courage and fighting-power of
Geatish men.

In this passage we see Grendel beyond the control of any of the Danes and
equally beyond the control of any code of conduct that would be binding on
noblemen.[12]

Grendel and his mother of course live somewhat beyond the pale, in a
lake-bottom home which no human being has ever seen:

[12]In the latter part of this passage we may note another use of the *ac* comstruction that
Beowulf happens not to illustrate very impressively. Here the *ac* is an expression of the heroic
response, signaling the deliberate placing of Beowulf's will (or Geatish will, since the
alliteration in line 601 surely reinforces the contrast between Geats and Danes) against this
wildy careening force of evil. Cf. also lines 1269-70. *Beowulf* has no other good examples,
but this "heroic adversative" can be found in other poems; several of Juliana's speeches have
this form (*Juliana* 105-16, 147-57, for example).

No þæs frod leofað
gumena bearna,   þæt þone grund wite. (1366b-67)

No one of the sons of men lives so old and wise that he knows the bottom
[of that lake].

The range of human experience and wisdom cannot even reach the place
where Grendel lives.

As was already suggested, several negative expressions of this kind are
closely related to the poet's consistent and ironic presentation of Grendel as
a mock thane, and serve to provide particularly compact and vivid statements
of the irony. Grendel is first shown to us as a wretched exile from the human
race, living in the darkness of social disgrace and spiritual isolation, perpetually
bearing God's anger. Infuriated by the harmonious sounds of human joy in
Heorot, he comes first as a "guest" to visit the hall; perhaps he is even viewed
ironically as the good neighbor paying a social call on the new arrival (Heorot
has just been completed and occupied). When the Danes abandon Heorot,
Grendel "rules" there; it is in the context of a passage describing the whole-
sale evacuation of the hall by the terrified Danes that Grendel is called a
"hall-thane" (142). But Grendel's authority in Heorot has limits.

Heorot eardode,
sincfage sel   sweartum nihtum;
no he þone gifstol   gretan moste,
maþðum for metode,   ne his myne wisse. (166b-69)

He lived in Heorot, that treasure-bright hall, in the black nights; but he
was never permitted to draw near the gift-throne or the treasure because
of the Lord, and did not know pleasure in it.[13]

Even though Grendel seems to be living in the hall, he cannot (perhaps has
no wish to) approach the gift-throne—that is to say, make proper use like an
ordinary retainer of the treasure for which Heorot is so famous. While the
much-discussed phrase *for metode* might possibly mean in the presence of a
secular lord (who is distributing treasure to his men), more likely it refers to
God and hence suggests that a supernatural order in the world must finally set
limits to the outrages of such creatures as Grendel.

In another well-known passage, the same kind of irony is used to bring out
Grendel's distance from mankind. It is almost as if the Danes in the poem (or
at least the audience listening to the poem) were being invited to try to bring
Grendel into some meaningful and familiar pattern of reference, some relationship to the structure of human society. In this case the frame of reference
is the Germanic wergild system of monetary compensation for wrongs done.

Sibbe ne wolde
wið manna hwone   mægenes Deniga,

[13]See the note in the second supplement of Fr. Klæber, *Beowulf and the Fight at Finnsburg*
(3d ed. Boston, D. C. Heath, 1950), p. 465, and John C. Pope's remarks on this passage in
his review of Arthur G. Brodeur's *The Art of Beowulf* (*Speculum*, 37 [1962], 415), where he
paraphrases line 169b as "he feels no gratitude for gifts (or, as I prefer to think, no affection
for treasure)."

feorhbealo feorran,	fea þingian,
ne þær nænig witena	wenan þorfte
beorhtre bote	to banan folmum,
[ac se] æglæca	ehtende wæs,
deorc deaþscua,	duguþe ond geogoþe,
seomade ond syrede,	sinnihte heold
mistige moras;	men ne cunnon
hwyder helrunan	hwyrftum scriþað.	(154b-63)

He wished no peace-settlement with any man of the Danish force, and he
refused to remove the deadly evil or to compound by making payment. No
wise man had any cause to hope for the bright remedy from that butcher's
hands! Far from it—that terrifying creature, the dark death-shadow, kept
on plaguing them, young and old, tirelessly lying in wait and ambushing
them, ruling the misty moors in endless night. Men do not know where
such mysterious hellions go in their roamings.

The lines just preceding this passage have strongly emphasized the violence
of Grendel's feud with Hrothgar (*heteniðas, fyrene, fæhðe, sæce*). But, as we
see later in the poem in the story of Beowulf's own father Ecgtheow, human
feuds can be resolved and peace can be restored, if the participants in feuds
want peace. But *sibbe ne wolde*—Grendel does not want peace, nor indeed
relationship of any sort with any human being, no matter how such relationship
is (ironically) extended to him. Denied here emphatically is the (ironic) hope
that he will abide by human laws and pay the fine for his murders, even
though the idea is toyed with almost humorously for a few lines.

The verses that follow (here I assume that the *ac se* supplied by most recent
editors in line 159 to replace letters lost from the manuscript is almost certain)
move us abruptly, in the usual way of an *ac* construction, away from this temporary accommodation with mankind, this way of seeing Grendel as somehow
human. A man as well as a monster could be called an *æglæca*, an inspirer of
fear—Beowulf himself is called one in line 2592—but no man is a *deorc
deaþscua*, a dark shadow of death. And then we move out quickly even further
from the human center into perpetual night, the misty moors, all those areas
beyond any ordering powers of the human imagination. As we cannot know
his motives, so we cannot know Grendel's dwelling-places: *men ne cunnon*.

An ironic transaction of a somewhat similar kind is described by Beowulf
in his report to Hrothgar on the fight with Grendel. In order to save his life,
Grendel had left his arm behind when he fled. The act of leaving his arm
seems to be represented as some kind of involuntary offering (and, if we take
feasceaft literally, all he could pay) but this down payment nets him nothing.

No þær ænige swa þeah
feasceaft guma	frofre gebohte;
no þy leng leofað	laðgeteona,
synnum geswenced,	ac hyne sar hafað
mid nydgripe	nearwe befongen,
balwon bendum.	Ðær abidan sceal
maga mane fah	miclan domes,
hu him scir metod	scrifan wille.	(972b-79)

But the destitute man did not purchase any comfort by this action; the horrible plunderer, crippled by sin, lived none the longer for it; on the contrary, pain had seized him tight in an inescapable grip, in the bonds of death. And in that place he must wait, that man branded with crimes, to see how bright God will wish to judge him at the Great Judgment.

Perhaps it is significant that the words *guma* and *maga*, common words for man, are applied to Grendel in this passage, for what is stressed here is Grendel's sinfulness (*synnum geswenced, mane fah*) and his ultimate responsibility for his actions in the face of the Last Judgment. However badly Grendel may seem to fit the usual patterns of human society and behavior, he is not an animal; in some higher scheme of order he is seen as human and therefore responsible. Yet, just as the sacrifice of his arm gains him no respite, his suffering and death gain him no pity. A total failure as hero, he wins no glory or reputation in the eyes of others; he does not even win their momentary sympathy:

> No his lifgedal
> sarlic þuhte   secg ænegum
> þara þe tirleases   trode sceawode. (841b-43)

His parting from life did not seem pitiable in any way to any of the men who looked at the trail of one devoid of glory.

These curious ironic expressions, constantly bringing as they do the possibility of Grendel's humanity into the periphery of our consciousness even in the act of emphatically denying it, have considerable importance in the meaning of the poem, as we shall see when we look more closely at Grendel in Chapter Three. For, despite all his inhuman and monstrous attributes, it is ultimately Grendel's human ancestry that makes him the kind of monster he is—the renegade who has deserted humanity to live in the wilds of exile, the frantic destroyer of the society he was once symbolically driven from in his ancestor Cain, the bearer always of the mark of murderer, and the bearer too of the mark of man.

The Defeat of Expectation

The emphatic negative or negative-plus-adversative is often used in the poem to express a conflict of wish, hope, or intention with actuality, a conflict, that is, where what someone expects to happen does not happen.[14] In *Beowulf*

[14]The formula survives into early Middle English literature. Two examples from Laȝamon:
> He wænde mid his crucche us adun þrucche.
> Ah tomærȝe, wæne hit dæi buð, duȝeðe scal arisen
> and oppenien ure castel-ȝæten; . . .
> Þus him ispac Octa wið his iuere Ebissa,
> ah al hit iwrað oðer þene heo iwenden.

(Quoted from *Selections from Laȝamon's Brut*, ed. G. L. Brook [Oxford, Clarendon Press, 1963, pp. 58-59].)
    I had completed this chapter before reading Richard N. Ringler, "*Him Seo Wen Geleah*: The Design for Irony in Grendel's Last Visit to Heorot," *Speculum*, 41 (1966), 49-67, which parallels my own arguments in this section at an extraordinary number of points and which goes into this particular device of rhetorical irony at even greater length. I have chosen to

the expectations of the evil characters are most often frustrated. Since Grendel is the only evil character whose mental processes we are told much about, it is not surprising that we are frequently told of his intentions and what happens to them. R. E. Kaske has already called attention to this pattern in speaking of Grendel's lack of *sapientia*: "There is a continual contrast between what Grendel hopes or expects and what actually happens, a sort of öbriq in him that contributes to poetic effect even if, logically, he could not be expected to foresee the outcome."[15] In a footnote to this passage Kaske adds a list of six passages of this type. Three of them contain the word *mynte* (intended):

> 1. mynte se manscaða   manna cynnes
> sumne besyrwan   in sele þam hean. (712-13)

The evil attacker intended to entrap some human being in that high hall [but he soon meets a rough reception from Beowulf, lines 718-19].

> 2. mynte þæt he gedælde,   ærþon dæg cwome,
> atol aglæca,   anra gehwylces
> lif wið lice,   þa him alumpen wæs
> wistfylle wen. (731-34a)

The atrocious demon intended, before day came, to separate the life from the body of each one of them, when his hope of eating his fill came true.

But here the poet immediately denies Grendel any possibility of the fulfillment of his expectation:

> Ne wæs þæt wyrd þa gen
> þæt he ma moste   manna cynnes
> ðicgean ofer þa niht. (734b-36a)

It was not then destined that he be allowed to devour more human beings after that night.

> 3. Mynte se mæra,   [þ]ær he meahte swa,
> widre gewindan   ond on weg þanon
> fleon on fenhopu. (762-64a)

The renowned creature intended, if he could, to get farther away and flee from there into the depths of the fen.

Grendel wants to make his escape from Beowulf's crushing grip but is prevented from doing so by the hero until he finally breaks away mortally wounded. Lines 791-94a, describing Beowulf's unwillingness to let Grendel escape alive, seem to me to be the appropriate second element in this pattern of defeated expectation, although Kaske suggests lines 805a-08, a more general statement of destiny.

---

leave my own version unrevised on the grounds that an important point is even more effectively established by our two independent approaches.

[15]"*Sapientia et Fortitudo* as the Controlling Theme of *Beowulf*," *Studies in Philology*, 55 (1958), 439.

While these *mynte* formulas are quite remarkable in their similarity, other rhetorical patterns of the same kind appear in the account of Grendel's attack on Heorot. The passage, for example, that describes Grendel first reaching toward Beowulf after he has entered the hall is not free from difficulties of interpretation, but what is perfectly clear is that Grendel expects to find another succulent meal in the man he is about to pick up and that instead he encounters the wholly unexpected:

> Forð near ætstop,
> nam þa mid handa   higeþihtigne
> rinc on ræste,   ræhte ongean
> feond mid folme;   he onfeng hraþe
> inwitþancum   ond wið earm gesæt.
> Sona þæt onfunde   fyrena hyrde
> þæt he ne mette   middangeardes,
> eorþan sceata,   on elran men
> mundgripe maran.[16]   (745b-53a)

He stepped up closer, seized then with his hand the brave man in his bed, the enemy reached toward [him] with his hand; he [Beowulf] quickly seized [him] hostilely and sat up against his arm. At once the shepherd of crimes discovered that he had never met on earth, anywhere in the world, a greater handgrip.

Frustrated in his attack, Grendel instantly formulates a new intention—to run.

> He on mode wearð
> forht on ferhðe;   no þy ær fram meahte.   (753b-54)

He became terrified in his heart; he could not get out of there any the sooner for that.

In spite of the extra strength his terror has presumably given him, even his hope of escape is blocked by Beowulf's strength.

The rhetoric of another sentence in this same scene is of interest:

> Ða þæt onfunde   se þe fela æror
> modes myrðe   manna cynne,
> fyrene gefremede   (he [wæs] fag wið god),
> þæt him se lichoma   læstan nolde,
> ac hine se modega   mæg Hygelaces
> hæfde be honda;   wæs gehwæþer oðrum
> lifigende lað.   (809-15a)

Then he suddenly realized—he who in the past, murderous [or: joyous?] in heart, had committed many crimes against mankind, being in a state of feud with God—that his body would simply not hold up any longer; but the bold kinsman of Hygelac had him by the hand. While alive each was the deadly enemy of the other.

---

[16]This puzzling passage may very well demand emendation, but here I have tried to make some sense of the text as it stands.

The long five-verse relative clause between the verb *onfunde* and its object clause describes the past history of Grendel's malevolent will and the crimes to which it has driven him, or the successes it has had. By delaying mention of what it is that Grendel discovers, the syntactical construction delays for the audience, as well as for Grendel, the shocking realization of his antagonist's power. Grendel discovers that his own body fails him. It is almost as if his body were some trusted retainer, half-personified here, now no longer willing (*nolde*) to stand by him in crisis. Physical strength collapses in the face of the adversary's adversative: *ac* Beowulf had him by the hand, naked will against will, as the final phrase of the quoted passage suggests in its balancing of hatred against hatred.

Expressions juxtaposing Grendel's expectations with the actual event occur several times in Beowulf's own later accounts of the fight with Grendel. We are told, for example, that Grendel had no intention of leaving *idelhende*, empty-handed, when he came to Heorot (the temptation to see irony in the word *idelhende* in view of the murderous handclasp that is to follow is hard to resist); he hoped to put Beowulf in his *glof*, his food-container. But *hyt ne mihte swa*, things couldn't turn out that way, as Beowulf laconically puts it, *syððan ic on yrre uppriht astod*, after I stood up in anger.[17]

Mention was made earlier of Grendel's final desperate hope of surviving by leaving his hand and arm behind, as some kind of payment or sacrifice that would save the rest of his body. This hope is quickly frustrated; he lives none the longer for his sacrifice but is locked inexorably in a prison of pain, death, and damnation, as the emphatic negatives point out:

> no þy leng leofað   laðgeteona
> synnum geswenced,   ac hyne sar hafað
> mid *ny*dgripe   nearwe befongen,
> balwon bendum. (974-77a)

The horrible plunderer, crippled by sin, lived none the longer for it; on the contrary, pain had seized him tight in an inescapable grip, in the bonds of death.

Later Grendel is described as having a brief moment of life's joys, but the very hand that was left behind to ensure him such a respite is soon the cause of his miserable death:

> He on weg losade,
> lytle hwile   lifwynna bre[a]c;
> hwæþre him sio swiðre   swaðe weardade
> hand on Hiorte,   ond he hean ðonan
> modes geomor   meregrund gefeoll. (2096b-2100)

He got away, enjoyed life's pleasures for a short time; but his right hand remained behind him in Heorot, and from that place, humiliated and grieving in heart, he fell to the bottom of the mere.

The phrase *swaðe weardade* cannot be easily translated into modern English

---

[17]The passage referred to here is 2081-92, in Beowulf's long speech to Hygelac.

but literally, of course, it means "guarded [his] track" and I think it possible here that Grendel's right hand is represented as serving as a rear guard to cover his retreat.

Taken as a group, these passages amply illustrate one aspect of Grendel's lack of *sapientia:* all his guesses about the future are wrong. In this he is certainly in contrast to Beowulf, who never makes guesses about the future in this way. Instead he is likely to sketch out the possible alternatives and then cheerfully commit the issue to God.[18]

More important may be the impression that the audience receives through these formulaic expressions of intention first of the tremendous and indefatigable will—properly called demonic—which drives this rough beast onward and then of the successive forcible, even brutal, defeats inflicted on his expectations. One effect of such an emphasis on intention is to cast the whole struggle of Beowulf and Grendel into clear-cut terms of the direct conflict of willpower. Grendel's will (if we may indeed apply such a term to an animal drive) is furious, tremendous, terrifying, yet we see it ultimately blocked, deflected, and finally destroyed by the only force capable of meeting it, a will even stronger and more determined. When the struggle is seen in such terms, the actual physical encounter can be reduced to an almost symbolic minimum, a touching of hands, in order to make clear the moral nature of this conflict.

There are other evil creatures in the poem besides Grendel who meet frustrations. Grendel's ancestor Cain was looking forward to enjoying the pleasures stemming from the murder of his brother Abel but found himself suddenly exiled far from mankind by God's power.[19] Grendel's mother was confident that she could pierce Beowulf's armor when she seized him under the water, but his ring-mail protected him.[20] The sea-monsters Beowulf encountered after he was separated from Breca in the great swim had made elaborate plans for enjoying dinner on the sea-bottom, but in the morning they lay dead instead.[21] While the dragon's peculiar mentality is scarcely explored

---

[18]See Beowulf's various formal vows: 442-55; 632-38; 677-87; 1474-91; 2529-37.

[19]
> Ne gefeah he þære fæhðe,   ac he hine feor forwræc,
> metod for þy mane,   mancynne fram. (109-10)

He [Cain] gained no enjoyment from that violent act; on the contrary the Lord hurled him off into exile for that crime, far from mankind.

[20]
> Grap þa togeanes,   guðrinc gefeng
> atolan clommum.   No þy ær in gescod
> halan lice: hring utan ymbbearh,
> þæt heo þone fyrdhom   ðurhfon ne mihte,
> locene leoðosyrcan laþan fingrum. (1501-05)

Then she reached for him and gripped the warrior in her frightful claws. But none the sooner did she manage to pierce that uninjured body. Rings formed a barrier on the outside so that she could not penetrate that war-covering, the metal-linked shirt which guarded his limbs, with her cruel fingers.

[21]
> Næs hie ðære fylle   gefean hæfdon,
> manfordædlan,   þæt hie me þegon,
> symbel ymbsæton   sægrunde neah;
> ac on mergenne   mecum wunde
> be yðlafe   uppe lægon,
> sweo[r]dum aswefede,   þæt syðþan na

in the poem, it is logical to assume that he had the intention of deriving some advantage from the gold he was guarding; if so, he was not a bit the better for it.[22] In any event it is indisputable that the dragon expected his barrow to protect him when he returned to it after ravaging the land of the Geats, but this expectation is not fulfilled:

> Hæfde landwara   lige befangen
> bæle ond bronde,   beorges getruwode,
> wiges ond wealles;   him seo wen geleah. (2321-23)

He had enveloped the inhabitants in flame, fire, and burning; he trusted in his barrow, in his fighting-power and his wall; that expectation deceived him.

The reader may notice that several of these passages contain marked elements of humor at the expense of the evil characters and the disappointments they suffer.

Finally one special instance of the double negation of expectation, something like a one-two punch, ought to be recorded. Beowulf tells his men how he killed Dæghrefn, the Frankish warrior who had slain King Hygelac.

> Nalles he ða frætwe   Frescyning[e],
> breostweorðunge,   bringan moste,
> ac in compe gecrong   cumbles hyrde,
> æþeling on elne;   ne wæs ecg bona,
> ac him hildegrap   heortan wylmas,
> banhus gebræc. (2503-08a)

Never was he allowed to bring those valuables, that breast-ornament, back to the Frisian king; on the contrary, the guardian of the standard, brave and noble, fell in battle. And the sword did not kill him; no, my fighting grasp crushed his bone-house and the surges of his heart.

Since the Geatish landing force has been defeated, Dæghrefn certainly expects to carry loot to his king, but he has not counted on the power and opposing will of Beowulf. Dæghrefn falls in battle, as perhaps any warrior might expect to fall some day; but his presumable expectation that the sword will be the cause of his death is not fulfilled, for Beowulf simply crushes him in a

---

> ymb brontne ford   brimliðende
> lade ne letton. (562-69a)

Those wicked destroyers did not have the joy of eating their fill, of partaking of me as they sat about their sea-bottom banquet; no, in the morning, gashed and pacified by swords, they lay stranded on the beach, and never afterwards kept any sailors from their voyages on the high seas.

For a discussion in another context of the lively irony involved here, see James L. Rosier, "The Uses of Association: Hands and Feasts in *Beowulf*," *PMLA*, 78 (1963), 9-10.

[22]
> He gesecean sceall
> [ho]r[d on] hrusan,   þær he haeðen gold
> warað wintrum frod,   ne byð him wihte ðy sel. (2275b-77)

He is obliged to seek out a hoard in the earth, where, ancient in years, he will guard heathen gold; he will profit by it in no way.

bear-hug. To put this another way: that the great hero Dæghrefn is killed is remarkable; that he is killed in this way is incredible. Again, Beowulf's unique and "unexpectable" powers are set off.

Other examples of this same rhetorical pattern of defeated expectation appear throughout the poem, although most of them are of less interest in themselves. Still they add to the almost incessant reinforcement of certain themes important in the poem as a whole. Taken together such patterns, by their stress on intention and determination, keep before us the typical preoccupation of epic poetry with the will. Usually they offer a perspective on "fate" as being fundamentally a will-blocking force indifferent to the wishes of the characters, and often they bring out the complex role of the hero in cooperating with fate or serving as fate's agent.

The Pattern of "Until"

That Tolkien's famous essay on Beowulf ends with the phrase "—until the dragon comes" is appropriate, for the phrase reminds us of many such expressions with "until" that constitute a major theme pattern in the poem.[23] These expressions are generally similar in their implications to the negative phrases in the preceding section. Both rhetorical constructions place one kind or quality of human experience (usually success or the hope of success) in sharp and dramatic contrast with another kind of experience (usually failure or disaster). Here only those sentences that actually contain the words *oð* or *oððæt* (until) will be studied.[24]

There are thirty-six instances of these words in *Beowulf*. For purposes of this study we can discard some thirteen as being "neutral," that is, carrying no specific emotional charge, serving merely to describe journeys or movements in space or the passage of time.[25] It should be added immediately, however, that some of these are much less neutral than others; the term is quite relative. In a sentence like this, which describes the Geats' arrival at Heorot, the construction seems straightforward:

> Guman onetton,
> sigon ætsomne,   oþþæt hy [s]æl timbred,
> geatolic ond goldfah,   ongyton mihton. (306b-08)

The men hastened on, marching together, until they could see the well-constructed hall, stately and gold-bright.

But the following sentence, on the other hand, contains a perceptible suggestion of suspended terror:

[23]J. R. R. Tolkien, "*Beowulf:* the Monsters and the Critics," *Proceedings of the British Academy*, 22 (1936), 295.

[24] A great many other sentences of course express the same concept without using words for "until." See, for example, the well-known description of how Heorot towers high when first built, awaiting the fire that will destroy it (81b-85).

[25]Under the heading of "spatial" are included the occurrences of the word in lines 219, 307, 622, 1414, 1640; under "temporal" the occurrences in lines 296, 1801, 2303, 2782, 2791, 3069, 3083, 3147. One can see how this division reflects the greater concentration on time in Part II of the poem and on "space" (i.e. action) in Part I.

Hordweard onbad
earfoðlice   oððæt æfen cwom. (2302b-03)

The guardian of the hoard [the dragon] waited in impatient misery until
evening came.

The more interesting rhetorical uses of the construction, however, can be
broken down into simple descriptive categories. For our purposes we may use
the naive terms "good" and "bad" to describe events or situations that, in
their context, are either desirable or undesirable from the point of view of the
poet or his human characters. The pairs of events described in an "until"
phrase may then be roughly classified as follows in these terms:

> good follows good—4
> good follows bad—3
> bad follows bad—6
> bad follows good—10

In the first category, good follows good, three of the four passages are
concerned with some form of hereditary succession. The Danish king Beow
rules well in Denmark until Healfdene is born to succeed him (53-57a);
Hrothgar prospers in war until a new generation of warriors grows to maturity
(64-67a); Weohstan keeps the arms given him by Onela until his son Wiglaf
is old enough to use them (2620-22). The fourth passage is similar in that it
describes Beowulf's friendly protection of young Heardred until he is old
enough to rule the Geats (2377-79b). The theme here is obvious: in the heroic
world, strong rulers are the sole source of order. Social stability and continuity
consists in the orderly succession of strong rulers.

In two of the three instances of "good follows bad," we can see that the
change is the result of heroic character and initiative. Scyld is at first a
destitute child in Denmark, but he lives to see consolation for that suffering
and to exact obedience from all his neighbors (6b-11). Grendel rules Heorot
until at last death comes to him at Beowulf's hands (1253-55a). In the third
passage spring follows winter, melting the fetters—of ice, as Hengest sits
unhappily in Finn's hall (1131b-36a); Hengest and the Danes are then free to
carry out their delayed vengeance against Finn.[26]

Few generalizations can be ventured about the category of "bad follows
bad." Persistence in a course of violence is sometimes stressed. In the Ingeld
episode, this passage occurs:

> Manað swa ond myndgað   mæla gehwylce
> sarum wordum,   oððæt sæl cymeð
> þæt se fæmnan þegn   fore fæder dædum
> æfter billes bite   blodfag swefeð,
> ealdres scyldig. (2057-61a)

In this way he will remind and admonish him on every occasion with words
of pain, until the time comes that the woman's retainer will sleep

---

[26]In reality the effect and implications of this image are too complex to fit our simple-
minded categories here; see the discussion of the Finn Episode in Chapter Four [of Irving's
book], pp. 169-74.

bloodstained from the sword's bite, forfeiting his life for the deeds of his father.

The old retainer's rekindling of hatred in the young man is seen almost as the normal fulfillment of natural process. So, in Germanic literature generally, feuds once set in motion tend to grind on to their conclusion. Other events in a career of violence are connected with *oððæt* constructions: Grendel kills some of the Danes and rules until Heorot stands unusable for Hrothgar and his men (144-46a); Heremod slaughters his subordinates in fury until at last he goes away into "exile" (1713-15); Ongentheow attacks the Geats and then pursues them into a trap at Ravenswood (2928-35).[27]

We come now to the largest of these categories. That most of these "until" constructions should be "bad follows good" is in perfect keeping with the grim tone of the poem as a whole, its emphasis on tragic unawareness and unpreparedness, and its long perspective over several generations of men.

The passage in this category that happens to occur first in the poem may be taken as representative of this pattern; it deserves attention besides because it is one of the most elaborate rhetorical structures of the poem. The *oððæt* construction is at its very center, but the context should be quoted at some length.

> Đa se ell*or*gæst[28]   earfoðlice
> þrage geþolode,   se þe in þystrum bad,
> þæt he dogora gehwam   dream gehyrde
> hludne in healle;   þær wæs hearpan sweg,
> swutol sang scopes. (86-90a)

Then that alien spirit suffered longlasting misery, the one who lurked in darkness, because every day he heard joy loud in the hall, there where the harp's song was, and the clear voice of the minstrel.

Then, after the scop's song of the creation of the world, which offers its own brief and memorable impressions of light and vitality, the poet continues:

> Swa ða drihtguman   dreamum lifdon
> eadiglice,   oððæt an ongan
> fyrene fre[m]man   feond on helle.
> Wæs se grimma gæst   Grendel haten,
> mære mearcstapa,   se þe moras heold,
> fen ond fæsten. (99-104a)

That was how those noble men lived in luck and joy—until one fiend from hell began to commit crime. That fearful creature's name was Grendel, a

---

[27]If it is of any real importance to classify all these passages, I include tentatively under this heading two more examples. The Last Survivor wanders in misery over the grave of his nation until death's wave touches his heart (is death "good" or "bad" for him?) (2267-70a): the waves in the Grendel mere move up out of their proper place until the air becomes wet (1373-76a).

[28]MS *ellengæst*, a jejune reading preserved by editors too ready to accede to scribal vagaries; the compound *ellorgæst* is used elsewhere four times of Grendel and his mother. Not that courage might not fairly be attributed to Grendel, but in this context what is poetically stressed is his alien, outsider aspect, his habitation *in þystrum*, away from the light.

well-known prowler of the borders, ruling over moor, fen, and wild country.

Then there follows the account of Grendel's descent from Cain and the origin of the race of monsters. Finally Grendel comes to Heorot.

> Gewat ða neosian, syþðan niht becom,
> hean huses, hu hit Hringdene
> æfter beorþege gebun hæfdon. (115-17)

> He came then, after night fell, to visit that lofty house, to see how the Ring-Danes had settled into it after the pouring of beer.

Note first the paralleling, for purposes of strictest contrast, of *earfoðlice* 86 with *eadiglice* 100, and of *þrage geþolode* 87 with *dreamum lifdon* 99. The formal antithesis suggested on a small scale by such verbal patterns extends of course to much larger contrasts. The explanation in the scop's song of how the universe was created, following as it does upon the description of the building of Heorot and the establishment of the great Danish civilization it represents (its light gleams over many lands), has its complement in the explanation of Grendel's origin—how dark evil came into being in the midst of a universe of sunlight and green leaves. On one side of this great opposition we have human society in harmony with the divine plan, dazzling in images of light, song, and joy; on the other side we have Grendel-Cain, the individual who has freely chosen to rebel against human society and who is now outcast in a world of darkness, misery, and violence. We will examine this mythic pattern at greater length in Chapter Three.

At the very center of this opposition is the *oððæt* phrase, which, by introducing the element of time into the static opposition, sets the active conflict of the poem in motion. They lived in joy until. . . . The construction here (perhaps partly because of its semi-formulaic use in similar contexts) points both to human capacities for happy unawareness of the darkness outside and to the nature of a world that sooner or later always brings in on us its merciless "until," where time, change, and disaster operate outside man's powers of control.

The particular "good" broken in on by such ominous untils is, as this Heorot-Grendel contrast implies, most often a social good. Social order is to be succeeded by social chaos. At one extreme, the social good may take the form of a friendly, if rivalrous, community of two: Breca and Beowulf stay together in their swim (partly for mutual protection) until a storm drives them apart.[29] At the other end of the range, it may take the form of the peace and order of an entire nation over a long period of time: Beowulf ruled the Geats well for fifty years, until a dragon began to gain power on dark nights.[30]

---

[29]
> Ða wit ætsomne on sæ wæron
> fif nihta first, oþþæt unc flod todraf,
> wado weallende, wedera cealdost, . . . (544-46)

Then the two of us were together in the sea for five nights, until the waters, swelling waves, the coldest of storms, drove us apart.

[30]
> He geheold tela
> fiftig wintra (wæs ða frod cyning,

The reference to dark nights suggests that most primitive, durable, and effective of all poetic dichotomies, the opposition of light and dark, and images of light and dark are often associated with these constructions.[31] We see this contrast used to good effect, for example, in this sentence from Beowulf's report to Hygelac:

> Swa we þær inne   ondlangne dæg
> niode naman,   oððæt niht becwom
> oðer to yldum.   (2115-17a)

In this way we enjoyed ourselves indoors the whole long day, until another night arrived for men.

The poet combines the idea of being *inne*—inside, warm, and secure—with what seems to be suggested by *ondlangne dæg,* namely, the possession of a long space of time for relaxed enjoyment free from interruption, and thrusts against this combination the contrasting image of night (both darkness and time itself) arriving among men as an assailant or intruder.

Attention to such patterns of imagery may even provide some help in reaching satisfactory interpretations of such passages as the following, taken from the poet's account of the first night in Heorot, when Hrothgar decides to retire to sleep. Beowulf has just made his resolute vow to Queen Wealhtheow and the hall resounds with joy and new confidence.

> Þa wæs eft swa ær   inne on healle
> þryðword sprecen,   ðeod on sælum,
> sigefolca sweg,   oþþæt semninga
> sunu Healfdenes   secean wolde
> æfenræste;   wiste þæm ahlæcan
> to þæm heahsele   hilde geþinged,
> siððan hie sunnan leoht   geseon meahton,[32]
> oþ ðe nipende   niht ofer ealle,
> scaduhelma gesceapu   scriðan cwoman,
> wan under wolcnum.   Werod eall aras.   (642-51)

Then once more as before powerful words were spoken inside the hall. The people were happy, and a sound went up from both victorious nations, until suddenly Healfdene's son [Hrothgar] decided to go to his bed for the night. He knew well that the monster had determined on attack on the high hall from the time they could make out the sun's light until gathering darkness and shapes of shadow raced up, dim under the clouds. The company stood up.

> ealde eþelweard),   oððæt an ongan
> deorcum nihtum   draca rics[i]an, ...   (2208b-11)

[31]These images are examined further in Chapter Three [of Irving's book]. For an extended discussion of them see Herbert G. Wright, "Good and Evil; Light and Darkness; Joy and Sorrow in *Beowulf," Review of English Studies* (n.s.), 8 (1957), 1-11.

[32]This is the MS text of line 648. Most editors, including Dobbie, insert *ne* after *geseon,* so as to make the line refer to the coming of night, and hence they usually read *oþ ðe* as *opðe,* "or" rather than "until."

Like many others, this passage reveals the heavy emphasis that the poem places on the cyclic rhythms of joy and sorrow in human experience. The feast here is really a great outburst of joy and hope, which follows twelve long years of anxiety and despair for the Danes. But the sound of merriment is no sooner heard than a change is signaled, within the very space of a single alliterative line: *sigefolca sweg, oþþæt semninga*. . . . Hrothgar's sudden decision to retire is not in itself occasion for alarm except insofar as it marks the end of communal joy, but the poet seems to touch here, as often, on such simple but profound primitive fears as the child's reluctance at bedtime to leave the warm safe circle. The next few lines are not clear beyond dispute, but we seem to be told that Hrothgar knew that Grendel had been waiting all day (or possibly all evening, from the beginning of sunset until total darkness) to make his assault on Heorot. Perhaps this knowledge on Hrothgar's part is offered as a kind of reason for his retirement from the scene; at night it is now Grendel's hall, as it has been for twelve years—or else it may now be Beowulf's hall, for Hrothgar's last act before leaving Heorot is to deed over the hall to Beowulf: *hafa nu ond geheald husa selest* (658).

In a more strictly poetic way, several effective contrasts are made here. In the final lines of the passage, through the channel of Hrothgar's imagination, the outside world of darkness is permitted to come into our consciousness; it comes rushing in—*scriðan cwoman*—on the heels of the *oþ* phrase, after having been staved off and held at a distance for those brief moments of light. The similarity in the language here to that used to describe Grendel when he actually comes (*com on wanre niht / scriþan sceadugenga* 702b-03a) points to the close identification of Grendel, who indeed is later described as *æfengrom* (2074) (evening-ferocious), with darkness itself. Yet he is no more than a conspicuously energetic pseudopod of that darkness. Here and throughout the poem we are to think of the ultimate darkness of chaos and nonbeing which hangs first over this proud and splendid civilization of Denmark (if only because we are so often reminded of the destructive feuds in prospect) and which, beyond that, hangs over all human institutions and all men. Against a background of this immensity the hall becomes a crucial symbol, and the defender of the hall the embodiment of a profound kind of courage even beyond ordinary heroism.

Old age and death figure in two instances of the "until" construction. Beowulf survives many battles until that one day when he is obliged to face the dragon.[33] And great Hrothgar was always blameless, especially in his generosity, until age took the joy of his strength from him, as it has often injured many a man.[34] These are the universal untils that come to all.

[33]   Swa he niða gehwane   genesen hæfde,
sliðra geslyhta,   sunu Ecgðiowes,
ellenweorca,   oð ðone anne dæg
þe he wið þam wyrme   gewegan sceolde. (2397-2400)

In this way he had survived every battle, violent conflict, act of courage, until that one day when he was obliged to fight against the dragon.

[34]   Þæt wæs an cyning,
æghwæs orleahtre,   oþþæt hine yldo benam
mægenes wynnum,   se þe oft manigum scod. (1885b-87)

Weapons that outlast their owners are used as symbols of the pathos of · human existence more than once in the poem, as we shall see in our examination in Chapter Five [of Irving's book] of the second part of the poem. One "until" phrase gives expression to this idea. The weapons and armor worn by the Danes in the Ingeld episode were once the property of the Heathobeards, who (it is im-plied) had rejoiced in the excellent qualities of these arms until they lost their comrades in battle, and afterwards lost their own lives.[35]

Finally, in the partially Christianized sermon that Hrothgar preaches to Beowulf, there is a passage containing both the kind of negative we examined earlier and an *oððæt* construction. Hrothgar is speaking of the fortunate man who can see no end to his prosperity.

> Wunað he on wiste;   no hine wiht dweleð
> adl ne yldo,   ne him inwitsorh
> on sefan sweorceð,   ne gesacu ohwær
> ecghete eoweð,   ac him eal worold
> wendeð on willan   (he þæt wyrse ne con),
> oðþæt him on innan   oferhygda dæl
> weaxeð ond wridað.   (1735-41a)

Life for him is a feast. Disease and old age never block his path; evil sorrow never darkens his mind; no quarrels bring the savage attack of swords. No, for him the whole world goes as he wishes—he has no knowledge of something worse—until within him an enormous pride grows and puts forth shoots.

In its allusions to the common lot of human suffering from which this man thinks himself exempt, the rhetorical series of negative phrases leads us toward the "until" climax of unrealistic pride. But it is worth observing that the "until" construction here suggests something different from what is suggested by other examples in the poem. There such external forces as death, old age, or attack by evil creatures, all aspects of what we call fate and all beyond human control, are seen as arriving from outside to disrupt or destroy human happiness. That the "until" here is clearly internalized and placed in a pattern of moral cause and effect significantly reflects the Christian thinking of this sermon. It is important to recognize, however, that such a pattern is exceptional in Beowulf.

In summary, the methodical scrutiny of items on such arbitrarily selected lists as these can direct our attention to important poetic habits that might otherwise have been overlooked. In the passages cited in this chapter, we have seen the persistent tendency to present character and behavior in terms of

---

[35]
> On him gladiað   gomelra lafe,
> heard ond hringmæl   Heaðabear[d]na gestreon
> þenden hie ðam wæpnum   wealdan moston,
> oððæt hie forlæddan   to ðam lindplegan
> swæse gesiðas   ond hyra sylfra feorh.   (2036-40)

On them will gleam the heirlooms of old fighting-men, once the treasured arms, keen and ring-marked, of Heathobeards while they were still capable of using weapons, until that time that they led their much-loved comrades and themselves to destruction in the play of linden-shields.

opposites and to set off a positive by a negative wherever possible, and we have noticed how such polarization of value keeps the idea of the constant heroic choice alive in our minds. On a larger scale, we see how the monsters that the hero must encounter are at the same time greatly distanced from normal humanity and yet related to it. In the sequence of events in time a similar clash of opposites often occurs, where the outcome shows an extreme divergence from the expectation.

Even from this brief glance at the inherited rhetoric of Germanic poetic style, the reader should be able to gain some sense of what this style does best and most expertly—or, to view it another way, what it can scarcely help doing, being what it is. Any story that such a style sets out to tell will be in very large measure cut to fit its capabilities and limitations. Unless we make some initial effort to see through these rhetorical lenses we will inevitably misunderstand much about the poem.[36]

[36]Two recent general discussions of the poem touch (in different ways) on correspondences of style and meaning; see Stanley B. Greenfield, *A Critical History of Old English Literature* (New York, New York University Press, 1965), pp. 85-91, and E. G. Stanley, "Beowulf," in *Continuations and Beginnings: Studies in Old English Literature* (London, Nelson, 1966), especially pp. 120-26.

The Ironic Background

By T. A. Shippey

The *Finnsburg Episode* centres on a painful 'moment of truth'. Outside it, though, in the rest of *Beowulf*, is the more normal side of the *eorla lif* [life of nobles], a happy immersion in the present. To this the poet returns with the triumph of Hengest's men and the resumption of the banquet in Heorot:

> Leoð wæs asungen,
> gleomannes gyd.   Gamen eft astah,
> beorhtode bencsweg;   byrelas sealdon
> win of wunderfatum   (1159-62)

[The song was sung, the minstrel's melody. Mirth rose again, talk brightened along the benches, the chamberlains gave out wine from wondrous bowls]

But is it possible for any reader or listener to return without suspicion to such a state? Very soon after this the poet, preparing for the sudden attack of Grendel's mother, will be inviting us to see the pleasure of the Danes as dangerous, vulnerable:

> Wyrd ne cuþon,
> geosceaft grimme,   swa hit agangen wearð
> eorla manegum,   syþðan æfen cwom   (1233-5)

[They did not know their fate, grim destiny, as it had happened to many men, once evening came]

Yet has this change not already been made by the pain and sacrifice of the *Episode*, accepted by its Danish audience as *entertainment*? Many would argue for an even closer connection than that, suggesting that even while the Danes applaud heroism and Hengest, we are meant to see that some of those present are already cast in the roles of Finn, Hnæf, or Hildeburh.

For as the *Episode* ends with the recapture of Hildeburh, another queen is moved into the foreground with six most ominous lines, put in a longer measure, one might imagine, to give them more emphasis:

> Þa cwom Wealhþeo forð
> gan under gyldnum beage,   þær þa godan twegen
> sæton suhtergefæderan;   þa gyt wæs hiera sib ætgædere,
> æghwylc oðrum trywe.   Swylce þær Unferþ þyle
> æt fotum sæt frean Scyldinga;   gehwylc hiora his ferhþe treowde,

---

This selection represents a portion of Chapter Two, "The Argument of Courage," of the author's *Old English Verse* (London: Hutchinson, 1972), pp. 30-43 and 196-7. Reprinted with the permission of Unwin Hyman Ltd.

194

þæt he hæfde mod micel,   þeah þe he his magum nære
arfæst æt ecga gelacum.   Spræc ða ides Scyldinga . . . (1162-8)

[Then Wealhtheow came out, going under her golden coronet to where the
two good men sat, uncle and nephew. Then their kinship was still together,
each true to the other. There as well sat Unferth the 'þyle', at the feet of the
lord of the Scyldings. Each of them trusted his spirit, that he had great courage,
though he was not faithful to his kin in the play of swords. Then the woman of
the Scyldings spoke . . .]

Nowadays the interpretation of this passage is all but universally agreed.
Present at that moment in the hall are the *suhtergefæderan* [uncle and
nephew], Hrothgar and Hrothulf, with the former's sons and latter's cousins,
Hrethric and Hrothmund. The last name is unknown to Scandinavian legend,
and the fate of King Hrothgar is at least dubious. But the twelfth-century Latin
historian Saxo Grammaticus tells quite clearly of the killing, by Rolvo, son of
Helgo, son of Haldanus (= O.E. Hrothulf, son of Halga, son of Healfdene),
of a certain Røricus (= O.E. Hrethric); and the assertion is supported to some
extent by other sources. Furthermore, in Saxo again the eventual killer of
Rolvo himself is given as one Hiarwarthus, paralleling yet another character
mentioned in *Beowulf* but notably not present at this time, Heoroweard, son
of Heorogar, son of Healfdene, again a cousin involved in the internecine
Scylding feud.[1] It sounds as if, in history or legend, the family present in
Heorot was known to dissolve in treachery, murder, and final extinction; to
such knowledge the six longer lines presumably refer. Still, since all this comes
from outside the text, one can never be sure how far to take the theory.
Would a shudder have gone down the spines of an Anglo-Saxon audience as
soon as it heard of this gathering of father and sons, uncle and nephew, posed
(one might think) in almost symbolic groupings? Would Anglo-Saxons have
seen immediately that Wealhtheow was like Hildeburh in that she too would
wake one morning to *morþorbealo maga* [the killing of kinsmen] and the loss
of all her hopes? The answer from most quarters is unhesitatingly 'Yes!' But
if this is true, it causes some revaluation of Old English poetic technique.
    It has to be admitted that if these complex and reverberating ironies have
in fact been created, then the job has been done with exceptional economy.
The poet after all tells us nothing whatever of the Scyldings' future. Nearly all
his remarks could be taken as observations of the peace and joy of that
evening in the hall. He writes earlier:

Heorot innan wæs
freondum afylled;   nalles facenstafas
þeodscyldingas   þenden fremedon (1017-19)

[Heorot was filled inside with friends; the Scylding people did not then by any
means carry out treacherous deeds]

We may feel that he protests too much; a great deal depends on the stress on

---

[1]See references to Saxo in *Beowulf and its Analogues*, trans. G. N. Garmonsway and
Jacqueline Simpson, London and New York 1968; or Saxo Grammaticus, Books I-IX, trans.
O. Elton with comentary by F. Y. Powell, London 1894.

þenden [then], as it does on *þa gyt* [still] in the passage introducing Wealhtheow.[2] But on the face of it the remark is thoroughly approving, meaning no
more in its typically negative form than the praise of Beowulf himself:

> nealles druncne slog
> heorðgeneatas;   næs him hreoh sefa (2179-80)

[not at all did he strike his hearth-companions drunkenly; his mind was not fierce]

One could be forgiven for thinking that if Saxo Grammaticus had not survived,
then this interpretation of *Beowulf* would never have been considered. So, is
the poem self-contained, an artistic success? Is there anything present in the
text that should sensitise us—and also an Anglo-Saxon audience without
libraries or cross-references—to the possibilities of this scene, with its thoughtful opposition of insight (in Hengest) and ignorance (in the feasters)?

Something can indeed be gained if one makes the further assumption that
Old English poetry can express a state of mind delicately through speech, and
(as in the *Episode*) by what is left out as well as by what is put in. For the
next speech by Wealhtheow seems to be amazingly precise. It conveys hesitation, worry, suspicion against everyone on behalf of her sons; but it does so
within the conventions of a speech of encouragement. Speaking to Hroth-gar,
Wealhtheow begins with a series of cheerful imperatives; *'Onfoh þissum fulle'*,
she says, *'þu on sælum wes . . . to Geatum spræc mildum wordum . . . Beo wið
Geatas glæd'* ['Take this cup . . . be happy . . . speak to the Geats with kind
words . . . be gracious to the Geats']. But then one sentence changes the
mood. She refers back (some 250 lines) to Hrothgar's joyful praise of Beowulf
after the death of Grendel:

> 'Nu ic, Beowulf, þec,
> secg betsta,   me for sunu wylle
> freogan on ferhþe' (946-8)

['Now, Beowulf, best of men, I will take you for my son and cherish you in my
heart']

It was accepted then, perhaps, as hyperbole, and forgotten. Wealhtheow takes
it literally, and comments on it in one sentence with cautious indirection:

> 'Me man sægde   þæt þu ðe for sunu wolde
> hererinc habban' (1175-6)

['Someone told me that you wished to have the warrior for your son']

And though that subject is immediately dropped, the next two imperatives are
not outgoing, but restrictive:

> 'bruc þenden þu mote
> manigra medo,   ond þinum magum læf
> folc ond rice   þonne ðu forð scyle' (1177-9)

[2] See Kenneth Sisam, *The Structure of 'Beowulf'*, Oxford 1965, pp. 339, 80-2.

['enjoy while you may the praise of many, and leave to your kin the people and kingdom, when you must go forth']

The 'and' in that sentence cries out to be replaced by 'but', for she is making several distinctions at once: 'Give away what you like but not the succession, reward the Geats as a whole but do not exalt one of them, live while you can but leave a chance for others'. Still, it is typical that any overt sign is avoided. Though the two imperative series oppose each other over the vital words *for sunu* [for your son], the audience is left to make out what it can. A further startling leap marks the rest of the speech. Turning from the possible adoption of Beowulf and the risks involved, Wealhtheow addresses Hrothulf. Twice she makes assertions about past and future:

> 'Ic minne can
> glædne Hroþulf, þæt he þa geogoðe wile
> arum healdan, gyf þu ær þonne he,
> wine Scildinga, worold oflætest;
> wene ic þæt he mid gode gyldan wille
> uncran eaferan, gif he þæt eal gemon,
> hwæt wit to willan ond to worðmyndum
> umborwesendum ær arna gefremedon' (1180-7)

['I know my gracious Hrothulf, that he will maintain the young ones in honour if you, friend of the Scyldings, leave the world before him; I expect that he will repay our sons with good, if he remembers all the honours we did him as a child, for his desire and his glory']

'I *know* . . . I *expect*, that he *will* help our sons, *if* . . .' The pattern itself implies vulnerability. Wealhtheow's connection of Hrothulf with Beowulf, her unexpected vision of the latter as a rival—these reveal movingly a state of mind, without any necessity of statement. The absence of connections is characteristic, but in no sense vague.

Though this speech has admittedly been considered with every advantage of outside knowledge, it still looks as if it might, on its own, provide good reason for thinking twice about the joyful scene of the banquet. To do so is to add a new dimension to *Beowulf*—especially if one assumes that the poet is in full control of these subtleties. His next four or five sentences open up the history of the Geats even more clearly than has been done for the Danes, as he mentions the giving of a great torque to Beowulf, and then suddenly flashes years into the future to remark:

> Þone hring hæfde Higelac Geata,
> nefa Swertinges, nyhstan siðe,
> siðþan he under segne sinc ealgode (1202-4)

[Hygelac of the Geats, Swerting's grandson, had that ring on his last journey, when he defended treasure under his banner]

Up to this moment, Beowulf has been presented consistently as reliant on his uncle;[3] now in the midst of Beowulf's triumph the reader is forced to glimpse

[3]A. G. Brodeur gives a good account of this passage in *The Art of Beowulf*, Berkeley and Los Angeles 1959, pp. 78-87.

an unhappy future, though he does not know exactly how it will come about. Possibly in the circumstances there is something additionally pathetic in Wealhtheow's second speech, this time to Beowulf, with mingled and twice-repeated appeal and blandishment:

> 'cen þec mid cræfte, ond þyssum cnyhtum wes
> lara liðe; ic þe þæs lean geman . . .
>   . . . Beo þu suna minum
> dædum gedefe, dreamhealdende' (1219-27)

['know your strength, and be good in your counsel to these boys; I will remember a reward for you for that . . . Be gracious in your deeds to my son, you who possess joy]

As we can now see, it is only one character doomed to unhappiness calling on another. Her hopeful summary of the situation in the hall is followed immediately by the poet's pitying one:

> Þær wæs symbla cyst:
> druncon win weras. Wyrd ne cuþon,
> geosceaft grimme . . . (1232-4)

[There was the best of feasts, men drank wine. They did not know their fate, grim destiny . . .]

He makes the careless sleep of the thanes, from which one of them will never awake, seem representative of the life of man.

The poetic results are unmistakable. They cannot be fortuitous. But are we to think that the poet, casually introducing nine or ten references to Hygelac before this point, did it all in full knowledge of the effect he was going to produce in this scene and nowhere else? That the *Finnsburg Episode* was chosen from all other legends precisely to create the right kind of ironic gap between its audience and that of *Beowulf*? These things are possible; the difficulty with this poem is, always, knowing where to stop. But to agree with such a reading is to declare *Beowulf* a work at least as subtly handled as, say, the *Aeneid*—a poem from a much higher level of culture. Nor is the Old English poem at all *like* any Classical one in these effects, having apparently no visible model.[4] But could any poet have invented a whole ironic technique, involving contrast, allusion, interpolation and the use of 'authorial voices', all by himself? If he did, who could have understood him without prolonged study? Once again, we are driven back to considering the credible limits of an Anglo-Saxon audience's responses. And once again—since the ironic intention is (almost) undeniable—we must conclude that in his background of irony as in his foreground of incident, the *Beowulf*-poet was able to rely on that community of

---

[4]Fr. Kläeber made an early attempt to relate *Beowulf* to the *Aeneid* in his 'Aeneis und Beowulf', *Archiv* 126 (1911), 40-8, 338-59. The idea was given powerful but indirect support by E. R. Curtius, *European Literature and the Latin Middle Ages*, trans. Willard Trask, London 1953, pp. 167-76. But for all his deserved influence, Curtius does not seem to have read *Beowulf* for himself; and if the Anglo-Saxon poet did know the Latin epic, it is curious that he followed its letter only occasionally, and its spirit not at all.

author and audience we have discussed on p. 19, developing methods, and concepts already familiar, at least in their essentials.

We cannot expect much of this presumed tradition of story-telling to survive in any very obvious form, there being no other secular poem in Old English or any related language on anything like the same ambitious scale as *Beowulf*. What can still be seen is something of the state of mind, the habitual turns of thought which may have contributed to the *Beowulf*-poet's ironic development. We can see these in the smallest and best-preserved units of Old English verse, the characteristic syntax and even the individual words which do so much to signalise and define this type of narrative. It does not do to underestimate the importance of words and word-orders, though they may evade the nets of scholarly method. Considerable evidence now exists to suggest that even something as natural and apparently physiological as the apprehension of colour is affected by the words that exist, in any particular language, to describe it, and of course abstract concepts must be even more readily affected.[5] A rather similar study of the specialised vocabulary of Homer has led one scholar to declare: 'Since Homer also gave to the Greeks their lingua franca of literature, we must acknowledge that it was Homer—using his name in the broad sense which scholarly practice has sanctioned—who *created* [my italics] the intellectual world of the Greeks, their beliefs and their thoughts.'[6] The claim may seem ambitious, but is justified. Words codify men's understanding of events.

To turn from the general to the particular, one essentially ironic device can be seen in several of the passages already quoted. It is the use of the conjunction *sippan*, a word varying its meaning between 'since', 'when', 'after' and 'because'.[7] We have met it at three important moments—Hildeburh's awakening:

> Nalles holinga   Hoces dohtor
> meotodsceaft bemearn,   syþðan morgen com   (1076-7)

[Not without reason did Hoc's daughter lament fate, once morning came]

Hygelac's raid:

> Þone hring hæfde   Higelac Geata,
> nefa Swertinges,   nyhstan siðe,
> siðþan he under segne   sinc ealgode,
> wælreaf werede;   hyne wyrd fornam,
> syþðan he for wlenco   wean ahsode   (1202-6)

[Hygelac of the Geats, Swerting's grandson, had that ring on his last journey, when he defended treasure under his banner; fate took him, when he sought out woe, out of recklessness]

---

[5]Laurence Lerner makes the point about Old English ideas of colour in 'Colour Words in Anglo-Saxon', *MLR* 46 (1951), 246-9, an article which could be compared with Stephen Ullmann's description of an aphasic patient in *Language and Style*, Oxford 1964, pp. 207-12. With his usual understated brilliance J. R. R. Tokien uses the point in his description of the cloaks of Lorien in *The Fellowship of the Ring*, London 1954, p. 386.

[6]Bruno Snell, *The Discovery of the Mind*, trans. R. G. Rosenmayer, Cambridge, Mass, 1953, p. 37. Snell's qualification means that he does not consider 'Homer' to have been one individual; 'Homer' means the shared style of Greek epic in general.

[7]See Klaeber's edition of *Beowulf*, Glossary, p. 399, and also Introduction, p. lvii.

and the Danes asleep in Heorot:

Wyrd ne cuþon,
geosceaft grimme,   swa hit agangen wearð
eorla manegum,   syþðan æfen cwom   (1233-5)

[They did not know their fate, grim destiny, as it had happened to many, once evening came]

Each of these passages centres on human ignorance, and each expresses it in a similar way. Which came first, the thought or the expression? That question is hardly answerable, but we should note here one of *Beowulf*'s marked grammatical peculiarities. Subordinate clauses beginning with *siþþan* can naturally come before or after their main clauses, and there is no reason to expect one order to be more common than the other. But, in fact, of the 57 *siþþan*-clauses in the poem, all but one follow the pattern, main clause first, subordinate clause second.[8] It may appear a conclusion of interest only to pedants, but the poetic effect of many of these passages is very strong. The fact comes first, the explanation, cause, or time-indication trailing loosely behind. As a result the reader is often left momentarily in a condition of surprise or ignorance parallel to that of the characters inside the poem. Consider, for example, this brilliant transition in a 'digression' towards the end of the poem, when a beaten Geatish army is trapped in 'Raven's Wood', the fierce old Swedish king Ongentheow drawing his forces round them in the darkness, promising the survivors a painful death in the morning:

cwæð, he on mergenne   meces ecgum
getan wolde,   sum on galgtreowum
fuglum to gamene. // Frofor eft gelamp
sarigmodum   somod ærdæge,
syððan hie Hygelaces   horn ond byman,
gealdor ongeaton,   þa se goda com
leoda dugoðe   on last faran   (2939-45)

[he said that in the morning he would cut them with the edge of the sword, some on gallow-trees as sport for the birds. // Relief then came to the dispirited, with the dawn, once they heard the sound of Hygelac's horn and trumpets, when the good man came on the track of his people's army]

How much of the effect depends, not on vocabulary, but on word-order! In that situation *frofor* [relief] is for a moment inconceivable; dawn seemed to promise only death. Then, in the subordinate clause, the trumpets of Hygelac explain it. Clearly the sound is simultaneous with the relief, but its

[8]The figure is necessarily based on Klaeber's edition, the only one to provide a completely itemised glossary. Comparison with other usages is not easy, since the word is not commonly used as a conjunction in prose, its functions being taken over by *þa* and *þonne*. Thus in the first 10 of Ælfric's *Catholic Homilies*, 1st series, ed. B. Thorpe, London 1844, it occurs twice (in over 80 pages), and both times the order is the reverse of the Beowulfian one, i.e. the subordinate clause precedes the main one. If one considers the more frequent *gif*-clauses, the figures are, for *Beowulf*, 26 examples of main + subordinate and 3 of sub + main, for the first 10 *Catholic Homilies*, 33 of main + sub and 50 of sub + main—quite a convincing reversal. See, however, R. Quirk and C. L. Wrenn, *An Old English Grammar*, London 1967, p. 95.

postponement creates a momentary shock for the reader, paralleling that of the dispirited Geats. Naturally, the meaning of *siþþan* then varies between a time-word 'once', and a cause-word 'since'; but what is important is the change from despair to triumph within a single line, *frofor* alliterating with *fuglum*, the birds of death. In all, the reader or listener experiences similar effects 56 times in *Beowulf*. The *siþþan*-clauses finely exemplify what Coleridge called 'quick reciprocations of curiosity still gratified and still re-excited . . . too slight indeed to be at any one moment objects of distinct consciousness, yet . . . considerable in their aggregate influence'.[9] Implicit in the type of pleasure they provide is a sense of irony, of the sudden reversals of time. Though this sense might never, for most Anglo-Saxon listeners or poets, have attained to 'distinct consciousness', the familiarity of constructions expressing it cannot but have strengthened their sensitivity to the ironic possibilities of history. The grammar of *siþþan* is part of the same continuum as the hints and prophetic glimpses of the banquet in Heorot, whether or not it helped to form them.

Similar examples are not hard to find in the syntax of *Beowulf*. Clauses beginning with *gif* [if] follow much the same pattern as *siþþan* ones, reaching for effects of afterthought and menace. More interestingly, *oþðæt* clauses produce what has been called the 'pattern of until',[10] in a way the reverse of the *siþþan* pattern in that it deals with the long periods between and leading up to moments of sudden insight. Twice the *Beowulf*-poet (or scribe) uses this conjunction to begin a section in the manuscript, and it starts off both main adventures.[11] The warriors live happily in Heorot *oððæt an ongan fyrene fremman feond on helle* [until a hell-fiend began to commit crimes], while after Grendel's destruction Beowulf reigns happily for fifty years *oððæt an ongan deorcum nihtum draca ricsian* [until on dark nights a dragon began to rule]. Probably the parallelism is not deliberate. For poets of this type it is natural to see joy growing into sorrow, and to pull the two opposites together, carefully linked within a sentence.

Only subsidiary to these syntactic habits is the question of vocabulary. Did Anglo-Saxons have words for the specialised concepts of the heroic life which this chapter is trying to isolate? Without any Old English 'philosophical tractate' it is impossible to say for sure. But some words, in poetry, do stand out. The 'moments of reversal' which bring sudden insight to heroes appear to be expressed, in *Beowulf* and elsewhere, by the word *edwenden* [a change back], or by similar forms such as *edcyr, edhwyrft, edsceaft*.[12] *Edwenden* is used forcefully and dramatically in several places, but has overall a curious neutrality. It can be seen as a good, for Beowulf assumes that Hrothgar's unhappy subjection to Grendel would be saved,

'gyf him edwenden   æfre scolde,
bealuwa bisigu   bot eft cuman' (280-1)

---

[9]Coleridge, *Biographia Literaria*, ch. 18.
[10]This has been discussed by Edward B. Irving jr, *A Reading of Beowulf*, New Haven 1968, pp. 31-42. Here, as elsewhere, I owe a great deal to this exceptionally stimulating author.
[11]See the comments of E. Van K. Dobbie in the Introduction to vol. IV of *The Anglo-Saxon Poetic Records*, 'Beowulf and Judith', New York and London 1953, pp. xxv-xxvi.
[12]Once again, this idea is mentioned by Irving, op. cit, pp. 147-50.

['if a change should ever again come to him, a cure for the turmoil of evils']¹³

But later Hrothgar is to use the same word, not for his deliverance, but for the shock of Grendel's first attack:

> 'Hwæt, me þæs on eþle   edwenden cwom,
> gyrn æfter gomene'   (1774-5)

['From this indeed a change came on me in my home, sorrow after pleasure']

Edwenden is again a consolation when the poet remarks on Beowulf's recovery of a bad early reputation; but a similar word is applied to the killing of Æschere:

> Þa ðær sona wearð
> edhwyrft eorlum,   siþðan inne fealh
> Grendles modor   (1280-2)

[Then soon there was a change for men, once Grendel's mother forced a way in]

Clearly the idea of surprise and reversal is present for this Old English poet in *any* situation; the only places where there is no change are Heaven and Hell. The concept's neutrality is reminiscent of that other neutral word already mentioned (on p. 28), *wlenco*, the quality of a hero—or of a meddler? Perhaps this should be translated, at least in heroic verse,¹⁴ neither as 'arrogance' nor as 'courage', but as 'a man's readiness to risk *edwenden*' (which he knows may be a change for the better or for the worse). This is something which Beowulf does share with Hygelac and Saint Guthlac¹⁵—he goes outside his own boundaries (and he succeeds while his uncle fails). It is also notably a quality he does not share with his thanes, even if to a modern mind their courage is equal to his own. They stay in Heorot, though 'none of them thought that he would ever go from there to seek his loved home again' (lines 691-2); still, though brave, they are not heroes, since they are not ultimately responsible for their own presence in the hall. The Old English attitude is the reverse of fatalistic. It exalts individual decision.

Other words could be drawn into this discussion. The qualities of the hero are pre-eminentiy *andgit* and *foreþanc* [sense and forethought], for it is these virtues which help the hero to perceive the inevitable changes of time and to prepare for them. One might look especially at the total *non sequitur* of lines

---

¹³I have departed here from the *ASPR* edition to the extent of making a noun, *edwenden*, from what might be a verb, *edwendan*. The case for this (fairly unimportant) change is put by Klaeber in his note to the passage cited, op. cit., p. 139.

¹⁴In *An Anglo-Saxon Dictionary*, Ed. J. Bosworth and T. N. Toller, London 1898 (with supplement by Toller 1921), *wlencu* is given in several contexts. In prose it is generally unfavourable, being used even for the stubbornness of a strayed animal; it can also mean 'pomp' or 'wealth', no doubt because connected with the attitudes which prosperity engenders. These uses only show up the strangeness of the favoured poetic contexts. The word is illuminated by its use to translate the Psalms' *abundantia*, and by its collocations with *orsorgnesse* [carelessness] and *geogoðe* [youth].

¹⁵*Guthlac*, lines 206-9. The devils complain that St. Guthlac has done them the greatest of harms, *siððan he for wlence on westenne beorgas bræce . . .* [once in his daring he disturbed the mounds in the wilderness . . .].

1057-62, where the poet curiously relates Christian trust in God's power with a suspicious awareness of change rather similar to the advice of the Old Norse *Hávamál!* Another word loaded with a sense of ultimate responsibility is *bana*, meaning not always 'the physical killer' (since Hygelac is named as the *bona Ongenþeowes* in line 1968, whereas the man who struck the actual blow was Eofor son of Wonred), but more generally 'the causer, the man responsible'. But the most obviously significant word peculiar to Old English philosophy is that ancient stumbling-block of translators, *wyrd* or Fate.

The ubiquity of this concept in Old English verse may seem to refute the earlier suggestion that a passive and fatalistic attitude was by and large not admired by Anglo-Saxons. Yet though the word was used on occasion to translate Latin *Fata* or *fortuna*, it still seems probable that most of the time a modern reader would be misled by the 'false friend', the easy translation by 'fate' or 'destiny' (used so far in this book to avoid premature explanation). *Wyrd* is at least remotely related to *weorþan*, 'to become', and an acceptable translation is often 'what becomes, what comes to pass, the course of events', not a supernatural and wilful Power, but more simply, the flow of Time.[16] Only some such rendering avoids giving an oddly (and wrongly) pagan turn to what might be fairly unpretentious statements, as when Beowulf observes cheerfully *'Wyrd oft nereð unfægne eorl, þonne his ellen deah'* ['often events turn out to save the undoomed man, as long as his courage holds'], or when the poet explains that Grendel would have killed more men *nefne him witig god wyrd forstode ond ðæs mannes mod* [if God's wisdom and the man's courage had not prevented that turn of events]. In both cases the more impersonal translation saves one from strange conflicts between Fate and Doom, or God and Fate. The question is, how can what is to us a relatively weak concept have gathered its obvious associations, in Old English, with death, fear, the ultimate challenge? Perhaps the answer lies in the connection of 'events' with 'change'. As so many characters in Beowulf find out, men cannot predict their lives, and often in the midst of success come upon disaster. To know this is to be aware of *wyrd*, 'the way things turn out', the way results do not follow intentions. Still, though it is foolish not to recognise the possibility of disaster—like Hygelac attacking the Frisians, or the Danes asleep in Heorot who *wyrd ne cuþon*—the true hero is nevertheless not prevented from trying to force his personality on events when they are amenable to human will.[17] Indeed, this is his glory. The concept of *wyrd*, then, more chaotic and less irresistible than the Classical one of Fate, exists, like many other Old English words, in intimate relation with the idea of the ironies brought about by Time.

To take it no further, it could be claimed that a strong and consistent outlook on life, honour, and courage lurks in the very syntax and vocabulary

---

[16]There is a very thorough article by B. J. Timmer, '*Wyrd* in Anglo-Saxon Prose and Poetry', *Neophil.* 26 (1941), 24-33, 213-28. This marks the word's transitions of meaning very clearly. However, Timmer never questions that the 'outlook on life of the Germanic peoples was fatalistic' in some unrecorded era; more far-reaching is the discussion of the word in *The Wanderer*, Ed. T. P. Dunning and A. J. Bliss, London 1969, pp. 71-4. See also A. H. Roper, 'Boethius and the Three Fates of *Beowulf*', *PQ* 41 (1962), 386-400.

[17]It has been pointed out that even the metaphor of the 'weaving of fate' is not as passive and deterministic a one as we might think, see R. B. Onians, *The Origins of European Thought*, Cambridge 1954, pp. 347-57.

of the epic style; and that this attitude acts as a preparation for the great contrasts underlying that banquet in Heorot, where the heroes' achievements are simultaneously acknowledged, and shown to be impermanent by hints and allusions. It goes with the frequent rhythms of *wop æfter wiste, gyrn æfter gomene* [lament after feasting, sorrow after joy]; it underlies the repeated metaphors of debt and payment (*lean, gyldan, forgyldan*); above all it explains how a delicate irony could be created and recognised without any overly subtle context. One speech may finally be taken as a coherent, if partial statement of this philosophy.

The speech is, of course, Hrothgar's 'sermon' of lines 1700-84, delivered to Beowulf at the poem's second point of rest, in the trough between the action-peaks of Grendel's mother and the dragon. The time is long gone when anyone would venture to call it irrelevant. But it certainly has no point in the story; Beowulf needs the old king's speech neither as warning for the future nor reprimand for the past.[18] The analysis of the *monnes modgeþonc mæran cynnes* [mentality of a man of famous race] is a detailed, but general, rounding-off of themes till then present, but submerged.

The speech is given one immediate motive—Beowulf's recovery of a sword-hilt with curiously appropriate carvings from the submarine hall:

> on ðæm wæs or writen
> fyrngewinnes,   syðþan flod ofsloh,
> gifen geotende,   giganta cyn (1688-90)

[on it was written the origin of that far-off fight, when the Flood, the pouring ocean, killed the giants' race]

He presents this to Hrothgar, and the king speaks from it as from a text. Professor Irving has acutely pointed out that both the capture of the hilt and what was written on it express the theme of 'the sudden and extreme shift of power, a lesson implicit both in the frequency with which the hilt has changed hands and in the calamitously sudden overthrow of the arrogant giants. To warn Beowulf now of such a change is precisely the chief purpose of Hroth-gar's sermon'.[19] It is not just a warning, though, but also an explanation of how this change occurs.

The utterly typical feature of what Hrothgar has to say is his grounding of all evils in ignorance, short sight, over-confidence. Heremod is picked as an example, one feels, because he fell from a situation in which everyone's opinion was in his favour; but popularity leads through complacence to disaster. Generalising, and also making a striking attempt to penetrate to inner psychology, Hrothgar forces on us the insight that both the immediate causes of disaster, pride and avarice [*oferhygd, gytsung*], come from the fool's idea (and desire) that things will last for ever, without change. The mind of the stupid, or sinful, man—Hrothgar makes no distinction between the two—dwells on present happiness,

---

[18]The attempt to relate this speech closely to Beowulf leads insidiously to arguments that the hero is meant to be condemned, or seen as increasingly weak and sinful, as for instance in H. L. Rogers, 'Beowulf's Three Great Fights', *RES NS* 6 (1955), 339-55. There is a more cautious statement by A. G. Brodeur, *The Art of Beowulf*, pp. 212-15.

[19]E. B. Irving jr, op. cit., p. 147.

'Þæt he his selfa ne mæg
for his unsnyttrum   ende geþencean.
Wunað he on wiste;   no hine wiht dweleð
adl ne yldo . . .
                    (he þæt wyrse ne con),
oðþæt him on innan   oferhygda dæl
weaxeð ond wridað.   Þonne se weard swefeð,
sawele hyrde;   bið se slæp to fæst,
bisgum gebunden,   bona swiðe neah'   (1733-43)

['so that he himself, in his unwisdom, cannot think of ending. He lives in joy; sickness and age do not disturb him at all . . . (he does not know the worse side), until within him a measure of pride grows and spreads. Then the watcher sleeps, the soul's guard; the sleep is too firm, bound with cares, the killer very close']

No doubt the attempt to analyse the soul owes something to the developments of theology.[20] But the stress on ignorance, lack of experience, the dangers that mere lapse of time must bring, are all part of the attitude expressed in *Beowulf* at least from the *Finnsburg Episode*. Like the Danes asleep in Heorot, the soul is proud not from malice, but because it lacks foresight; it suffers from what one might call the 'young man's disease'. It is this failure in philosophy of which Hrothgar accuses himself and warns Beowulf, not the crude and (for them) unbelievable temptations of *Superbia* and *Avaritia*. Grendel was not called up by sin; yet Hrothgar rebukes himself for somehow not expecting something like it, twelve years before:

'Hwæt, me þæs on eþle   edwenden cwom,
gyrn æfter gomene,   seoþðan Grendel wearð,
ealdgewinna,   ingenga min'   (1774-6)

['From this indeed a change came on me in my home, sorrow after pleasure, once Grendel became, that old enemy, my invader']

Great labour has been spent on relating this speech to homiletic commonplace. It is not commonplace; it is in some ways a masterpiece of abstract thought. Yet it grows out of an attitude one can, and must, see everywhere in Old English heroic verse, from vocabulary to narrative structure. No one should be surprised to find less impressive analogues of it in half a dozen other poems, not only in *Christ* and *Daniel* (the ones most commonly cited), but also in *Guthlac*, *The Gifts of Men*, *Judgement Day I*, and the Proem to King Alfred's verse *Boethius*.[21] Not that the authors of all these had necessarily read *Beowulf*. The sense of time's ironies and human insecurity must have been familiar enough to Anglo-Saxons for many of them independently to recognise it, express it, and develop it artistically.

[20]There is a fine summary of learned Christian material similar to Hrothgar's 'sermon' in Margaret E. Goldsmith's *The Mode and Meaning of Beowulf*, London 1970, pp. 183-209. See also R. E. Kaske, '*Sapientia et Fortitudo* as the Controlling Theme of *Beowulf*', *SP* 55 (1958), 423-56, an attractive and judicious article, but one reminiscent of Curtius (see note 21).

[21]The parallels with *Christ* (lines 660ff.) and *Daniel* (lines 488ff.) are discussed by Goldsmith, loc. cit., and Klaeber in his edition of *Beowulf*, pp. cx-cxiii. The passages in the other poems mentioned are *Guthlac* 495-504, *Gifts* 18-29, *Judgement* 73-80, and Proem to *Boethius* 3-10.

Artful Avoidance of the Useful Phrase in *Beowulf*, *The Battle of Maldon*, and *Fates of the Apostles*

By Geoffrey R. Russom

In recent years, several scholars have attacked the claim that Old English poets composed "not word by word with deliberation and at leisure but rapidly in the presence of a live audience by means of ready-made phrases."[1] It now seems clear that the *Beowulf* poet used ready-made phrases less persistently than did Homer,[2] and there is reason to believe that formulaic composition could take place in written works.[3] Critics are accordingly free to speculate about artistic effects which oral-formulaic theory had seemed to rule out. Unfortunately, they have been given no positive justification for doing so. Deliberate artistry in the composition of verses seems likely; but, as Ann Watts points out, such artistry has so far proved impossible to demonstrate conclusively in any particular case.[4] Nor is everyone impressed by the number of synonymous expressions in *Beowulf*: William Whallon and G. S. Kirk ascribe that to an immature tradition or a lack of prosodic strictness,[5] not to any deliberate search for variety. Moreover, the very poems which show the clearest signs of literacy are often quite unoriginal in their diction. Larry Benson acknowledges that *The Meters of Boethius* uses a high proportion of alliterative "filler," and Frank Whitman cites other examples of literate composition which he describes as "mechanical."[6] Apparently, the literate poet could remain the slave of his diction even when freed from the demands of live, improvisational performance. To say that a poet was literate is to say very little about the quality of his work.

In this paper I would like to investigate the poet's control of diction directly, setting aside the question of oral vs. written composition. To this end, I will inspect passages of the type supposed, according to oral theory, to be most

---

[1]Francis P. Magoun, Jr., "Bede's Story of Cædmon: The Case-History of an Anglo-Saxon Singer," *Speculum*, XXX (1955), 52.

[2]See William Whallon, *Formula, Character and Context* (Cambridge, Mass., 1969), pp. 71-116. In "Variation and Economy in *Beowulf*," *MP*, LXV (1967), 353-6, Donald K. Fry pointed out that this difference between Greek and Old English epics must be due in part to the characteristically Germanic device of variation.

[3]See Larry D. Benson, "The Literary Character of Anglo-Saxon Formulaic Poetry," *PMLA*, LXXXI (1966), 334-41.

[4]*The Lyre and the Harp* (New Haven and London, 1969), pp. 115, 119, 197.

[5]"The Diction of *Beowulf*," *PMLA*, LXXVI (1961), 318; *The Songs of Homer* (Cambridge, England, 1962), p. 89.

[6]Benson, "Literary Character," p. 337; Whitman, "The Meaning of 'Formulaic' in Old English Verse Composition," *NM*, LXXVI (1975), 533.

Reprinted, by permission, from *Studies in Philology* 75 (1978), 371-90.

heavily formulaic. This approach reveals a stark contrast between Homer and the best Old English poets—not merely a difference in the amount of formulaic repetition, but an absolute difference in kind. Homer is most dependent on the repeated phrase just where oral theory would predict, but some Old English poets introduce maximum *variety* of diction in exactly comparable circumstances. In such passages, the *scop* shows unmistakably his ability to express a given idea in as many ways as he likes.

A characteristic feature of formulaic poems is the sequential repetition of small compositional units which are similar in structure and content. In *The Iliad*, there is the well-known Catalogue of Ships (B 494-759); in Serbo-Croatian poetry, the familiar letter-writing theme.[7] Many similar passages can be found in the Anglo-Saxon poetic corpus. I have chosen for analysis the sequential death scenes of *Maldon* and *Fates*, and the genealogy of Scylding kings in *Beowulf*.[8] Formulaic theory clearly predicts that passages of this type will show the largest quantity of repetitive diction. Oral poets are supposed to repeat useful phrases whenever the need arises, providing fresh language only when they encounter unfamiliar material, or when memory proves faulty. According to Albert Lord, what looks at first glance like an innovative phrase or an elegant variation can always be assigned to one of these two causes.[9] Where the same type of scene occurs again and again, there can of course be little question of unfamiliar material or forgetfulness. The poet may provide some variety by adding or omitting a given essential idea; but, according to oral theory, he will not alter its form unless special circumstances force him to do so.[10] This persistent adherence to the useful phrase is called "economy."[11]

In the Catalogue of Ships, Homer avoids monotony through the kind of craftsmanship that oral theorists acknowledge.[12] He embellishes individual

[7]See Albert Lord, *The Singer of Tales* (Cambridge, Mass., 1960), pp. 82-6. In his chapter on the formula, Lord deliberately excluded the letter-writing theme from consideration "with an eye to making the experiment as valid as possible and to anticipating any objection which might be brought that the passage is of a sort which would be more formulaic by the very nature of its position or contents" (p. 45).

[8]The long sequences of *Fates* and *Maldon* have an interesting critical history. Some have found them repetitious, others somehow "varied." Summaries of the disputes may be found in James L. Boren, "Form and Meaning in Cynewulf's *Fates of the Apostles*," *PLL*, V (1969), 115-22; O. D. Macrae-Gibson, "*Maldon*: The Literary Structure of the Later Part," *NM*, LXXI (1970), 192-6; and Geoffrey R. Russom, Sequential Repetition of Similar Narrative Units as Proof of the Scop's Originality, Diss. State Univ. of New York at Stony Brook, 1973, pp. 20-7. The most recent article on the subject is Constance B. Hieatt "*The Fates of the Apostles*: Imagery, Structure and Meaning," *PLL*, X (1974), 115-125.

[9]"If the singer knows a ready-made phrase and thinks of it, he uses it without hesitation, but he has, as we have seen, a method of making phrases when he either does not know one or cannot remember one. This is the situation more frequently than we tend to believe" (*Singer*, p. 45).

[10]Thus in his discussion of the letter-writing theme, Lord observes that the poet avoids monotonous repetition by varying the length of the letters (p. 85). Any variation in the form of repeated ideas is apparently accidental (see p. 52, where the term "variation" is assigned a special, technical sense).

[11]See Milman Parry, "Studies in the Epic Technique of Oral Verse-Making. I. Homer and the Homeric Style," *HSCP*, XLI (1930), 80; "The Homeric Gloss: A Study in Word-Sense," *TAPA*, LIX (1928), 242.

[12]R. F. Lawrence takes several Old English scholars to task for their apparent belief that

passages with special details pertinent to the city or warrior whose contribution to the fleet is being assessed, and the necessary copiousness of his formulaic language adds an additional measure of variety. As William Whallon puts it, "the great number of names, or other special nouns, provides amplitude; the great number of epithets, color."[13] On the other hand, concepts which recur from one passage to another do show the fixity postulated by oral theory. The poet is quite willing to repeat useful phrases, even where close proximity threatens to lay bare the mechanical devices of his art.[14] In *Iliad*, II, 563, for example, Homer tells us that the leader of the towns around Argos was "Diomedes of the great war-cry" (βοὴν ἀγαθὸς Διομήδης). Four lines later, the whole phrase is repeated in the same position, filling the space from the feminine caesura to the end of the line. Then, nineteen lines later, we meet "Menelaus of the great war-cry" (βοὴν ἀγαθὸς Μενέλαος).

The poet's adherence to a single verse-making strategy can be observed most clearly in his whole-line formulas and systems. Homer says of the Cretans in 650 that "spear-famed Idomeneus led them" (τῶν μὲν ἄρ' Ἰδομενεὺς δουρικλυτὸς ἡγεμόνευε). Seven lines later, the leader of the Rhodians appears in an identical type of line (τῶν μὲν Τληπόλεμος δουρικλυτὸς ἡγεμόνευεν). The two formula frames differ only with respect to ἄρα, a meaningless verse-filler necessary for the first name, but not the second. Verbatim repetition occurs at 703 and 726, where the poet says of two contingents that "they were not leaderless, though they missed their [former] leader" (οὐδὲ μὲν οὐδ' οἳ ἄναρχοι ἔσαν, πόθεόν γε μὲν ἀρχόν). These lines serve to avoid any appearance of conflict between the catalogue, which refers back to the sailing of the fleet, and the story proper, which takes place in the ninth year of the siege. Such details testify to a concern with overall structure and at the same time to a complete lack of interest in elegant variation.

Surely the most striking examples of whole-line formula repetition are those in which Homer specifies the number of ships in a given contingent.[15] This is a frequently recurring essential idea in the catalogue, and it is perhaps the most fixed in form, just as oral theory postulates. The poet mentions three contingents having thirty ships and provided with more than one leader (516, 680, 733). The same formula serves on all occasions: three times Homer tells us that "thirty hollow ships advanced with them," where "them" refers to the leaders (τοῖς δὲ τριήκοντα γλαφυραὶ νέες ἐστιχόωντο). At line 602, the same formula is adapted to the number "ninety" (ἐνενήκοντα) by contraction of the particle δέ (δ'). If the number of ships is forty, fifty or eighty, the ships are "black" rather than "hollow" (e.g., τῷ δ' ἅμα τεσσαράκοντα μέλαιναι νῆες ἕποντο, 534, 545, 630, 710, 737, 759). The number "sixty" occurs twice (587, 610); it appears in the same type of verse on both occasions. Homer also lists

oral theory rules out artistry of all sorts. See "The Formulaic Theory and Its Application to English Alliterative Poetry," in *Essays on Style and Language*, ed. Roger Fowler (London, 1966), pp. 173-4.

[13]*Formula, Character and Context*, p. 58.

[14]Even Parryite critics have found this sort of repetition offensive. See Kirk, *Songs*, pp. 166, 361; Lord, *Singer*, p. 85.

[15]This important group of formulas is discussed in M. Parry, *L'Épithète traditionelle dans Homère* (Paris, 1928), pp. 135-9; trans. in Adam Parry, ed., *The Making of Homeric Verse* (Oxford, 1971), pp. 109-13.

contingents of eight, nine, ten, eleven, twelve, twenty-two, and one hundred ships. Since each number is represented only once, no violation of economy can occur. Within this efficient network of useful phrases there are two anomalies. The number "fifty," which fits the "black ships" formula, appears twice in a different type of line (509, 685). There is no violation of economy, however. The usual formula asserts that so many black ships followed him or them, where the pronoun must refer to the leader(s). In 509, the leaders are not present in the immediate context; in 685, the leader has not been introduced, and the line specifying the number of ships is used to introduce him. Such unique lines show that Homer's themes are "flexible and within limits adaptable to special circumstances (Lord, *Singer*, p. 93). When such circumstances are absent, however, the poet resorts time and again to his standard devices.

Some Old English poets show a willingness to repeat stock phrases much as did Homer. In *Caedmon's Hymn*, for example, the common formula *eci dryctin* "eternal lord" appears in 4a and again in 8a when conditions allowing its employment recur.[16] The repetition is directly comparable to that of the phrase βοὴν ἀγαθὸς Διομήδης in Homer's catalogue (B 563, 567). Repetition of whole-line formulaic patterns with only those changes absolutely required can also be found, even in works supposed to show signs of literate composition. In *Meters of Boethius*, 10, the following three verses occur within nine lines:

> 33   Hwær sint nu þæs wisan   Welandes ban
> [Where now are wise Weland's bones?]
> 35   Forþy ic cwæð þæs wisan   Welandes ban
> [Thus I have said, etc.]
> 42   Hwa wat nu þæs wisan   Welandes ban
> [Who knows now, etc.]

Here a difference between Greek and Germanic poetry becomes evident. Since in Anglo-Saxon verse the number of light syllables is not strictly regulated, a poet can change unstressed function words and pronouns with great facility. A given formulaic pattern can therefore be adapted to a much wider variety of uses than can Homeric formulas. Fully stressed words can also be exchanged where their position makes alliteration unnecessary. In *Dream of the Rood*, for example, the poet can keep the useful part of the line and introduce a new verb with little effort:

> 137   þe ic her on eorðan   ær *sceawode*
> [which I *saw* here on earth before]
> 145   se ðe her on eorþan   ær *þrowode*
> [he who *suffered* here on earth before]
>
> 109   on þyssum lænum   life *geearnaþ*
> [in this fleeting life *earns*]
> 138   on þysson lænan   life *gefetige*
> [from this fleeting life *may fetch*]

[16]Citations of this and all other Old English poems refer to *The Anglo-Saxon Poetic Records,* 6 vols., ed. George Philip Krapp and Elliott Van Kirk Dobbie (New York, 1931-53).

Although non-alliterating words can replace one another freely, it is clearly more difficult to alter the alliterative pattern. The order of alliterating elements can seldom be changed without a complete reworking of the syntax, and a change in the number of such elements (there can be two or three) tends to be just as involved. Where lines like those above are concerned, it would be hard to imagine any such changes. Of course, if the poet introduces a new alliterating word, he has essentially started afresh, since the most difficult requirement is to find a word that alliterates. In some cases, however, it is possible to substitute one word for another with the same linguistic root, leaving the alliterative pattern intact. This procedure may be illustrated with examples from *Seasons for Fasting*, a poetic calendar comparable in structure to Homer's Catalogue of Ships:

108	he þæt fæsten heold feowertig daga
	[he kept that fast for forty days]
125	to gefæstenne feowertig daga
	[to fast for forty days]
27	þæt hie fæstenu feower heoldon
	[that they should keep four fasts]
79	on þissum fæstenum is se feorþa dæg
	[on this fast the fourth day]

In the a-verse, the poet interchanges the OE word for "fast" and its derived verb; in the b-verse, we find related words for "four," "forty," and the derived adjective "fourth." Other repeated patterns in the poem show the same type of substitution. Lines 103, 159, 177, and 181 have *feowertig* in the a-verse and *fæsten* in the b-verse; line 71 has *feorþe* in place of *feowertig*. The poet clearly saved some effort by exchanging cognate words within the same alliterative pattern, but it is hard to say just how much. Lines 108 and 125 are very nearly the same formula, but the relation between 27 and 79 is much more remote.

The sequential units of *Seasons for Fasting* contain many more examples of repeated alliterative patterns, including verbatim repetition of whole lines (109, 126) and repetition with necessary changes in inflection only (e.g., 159, 181). Here, as in Homer's catalogue, the most frequently repeated concepts are the most fixed in poetic form. If oral theory is correct, the same principle should hold true for all sequential structures in Old English formulaic verse. Wherever repeated ideas cluster most thickly, we should observe an especially heavy concentration of repeated formulas. In *Beowulf, Maldon,* and *Fates,* however, we find exactly the contrary. The heaviest concentration of repeated concepts is accompanied by a total elimination of useful repetition. There are no repeated formulas, and no repeated alliterative patterns. Essential ideas recur time and again, but each expression of a given concept is achieved with a fresh act of verse-making. Such perfect consistency can hardly be due to chance. We have to deal here with deliberately varied diction.[17]

---

[17]I would like to distinguish between varied diction and the more familiar sort of variation, since these two devices differ in their relation to economy. A true variation violates economy only if it duplicates another expression with the same meaning and alliterative value. In some cases, as for example in *Caedmon's Hymn,* variations can serve as useful line-fillers. Varied diction, on the other hand, always involves at least one violation of economy.

Let us look at just a few of the numerous violations of economy in these passages.[18] In line 31 of *Beowulf*, the poet says *leof landfruma lange ahte* "the beloved lord of the land ruled for a long time"; in line 54 describing the long reign of the succeeding king, we find *leof leodcyning longe þrage*. The pattern has been varied by replacing *landfruma* with the synonymous *leodcyning*. Interestingly enough, both these compounds are *hapax legomena*, a fact which lends support to Brodeur's claim that the *Beowulf* poet used compounding with special skill.[19] The b-verse *longe þrage* "for a long time" also varies *lange hwile* (16a). In line 30, there is a reference to the time "when the Scyldings' friend ruled with words" (*þenden wordum weold wine Scyldinga*); at 79, Hrothgar is described as one "who widely possessed the power of his word" (*se þe his wordes geweald wide hæfde*). The poet could have used *þenden his wordes geweald wide hæfde* at line 30 without change in essential idea, or at 79 he might have said *se þe wordum weold, wine Scyldinga*. Concerning Hrothgar we are told in lines 80-1 that after Heorot was built "He did not fail in his boast, he gave away rings, treasure at the feast" (*He beot ne aleh, beagas dælde, / sinc æt symle*). We might have expected *ond þær on innan eall gedælde* instead, on the analogy of line 71, *ond þær on innan eall gedælan* "and there inside to give away everything." Such a verse would follow without awkwardness from the preceding discourse, and it would anticipate *sinc æt symle* in a way perfectly consistent with the poet's usual practice. One could interpret *eall* as modifying *sinc*, since both are neuter forms (for the syntax, cf. 1796-7); or *eall* could be regarded as a pronominalized adjective ("everything"), with *sinc* serving as a variation (cf. 2042-3, where *eall* is neuter and *garcwealm* masculine). A particularly conspicuous violation of economy involves the familiar concept of kingly glory. In describing Scyld's growing fame (8b), the poet uses the half-line *weorðmyndum þah* "he throve in honors." Nine lines later, we learn of Beowulf Scylding that to him "the lord of glory gave worldly honor" (*wuldres wealdend woroldare forgeaf*). The expected repetition would be *weorðmynd forgeaf*, since in *Beowulf weorðmynd* is the term most commonly associated with such contexts. The word appears in the passage devoted to Hrothgar's prosperity (65) and in a later scene, where Hrothgar discusses the perils of kingly success (1752). Here the old ruler criticizes one who becomes arrogant "because God, ruler of glory, has previously given him a share of honors" (*þæs þe him ær god sealde / wuldres waldend, weorðmynda dæl*). When the poet was choosing for line 17b a word meaning *honor* which alliterated with *wuldres wealdend* in 17a, he must have noticed instantly that *weorðmynd* would do. It was the word he used regularly to express that concept, and he had used it just nine lines earlier in the same type of situation. Instead he chose *woroldar*, a word rare in poetry and one which occurs nowhere else in *Beowulf*. The verse *woroldare forgeaf* was not chosen primarily for its alliterative value, as Magoun's theory would postulate.[20] It was created to provide contrast as part of a systematic effort to eliminate repetitive diction.

---

[18]Complete lists of alliterative patterns can be found in my dissertation (cited in note 8, above).

[19]*The Art of Beowulf* (Berkeley and Los Angeles, 1959), pp. 6, 11.

[20]See "The Oral-Formulaic Character of Anglo-Saxon Narrative Poetry," *Speculum*, XXVIII (1953), p. 455.

Numerous similar alterations occur in *Fates.* Here the concept of seeking out a place on earth or in heaven recurs frequently. In 32a we have *siðe gesohte* "sought in journeying"; in 62a, *sawle gesohte* "the soul sought"; in 77a, *sohton siðfrome* "sought journey-bold." The expected repetitions would be *siðe gesohte* at 62a and *siðe gesohton* at 77a, or *sohte siðfrom* at 32a and 62a. No change in essential idea would result from these substitutions. The soul need not be mentioned in 62a, since it was not mentioned in 32a, where the spirit's journey to heaven is similarly described. Nor do we need to be told that the apostles Simon and Thaddeus were bold as they journeyed. The bravery of all these adventurous thanes has been duly noted before (3-6), and it will be noted again (86-7). A rather different manifestation of the poet's search for variety occurs in lines 27 and 74. In one case the compound *wuldorcining* is employed; in the other, we find the genitive expression *wuldres cyning.* Both mean "king of glory," and serve as distinctive epithets reserved for God. Homer never tinkers with the form of such expressions in this way.

The constraint against repetition in *Fates* is not limited to the sequence of martyrdoms; it applies to the whole poem. Compare, for example, the description of the apostles' glory in the opening passage with that of God's glory at the close:

6   Lof wide sprang,
miht ond mærðo,   ofer middangeard
[The glory spread widely, the power
and the fame, over middle-earth]
120   Nu a his lof standeð
mycel ond mære,   ond his miht seomaþ,
ece ond edgiong,   ofer ealle gesceaft
[Now his glory stands eternal, great and
famous, and his power stands, everlasting
and ever-young, over all creation]

Line 7 could replace 121 with no difference in meaning, since *seomaþ* merely varies *standeð* in this context, and *mycel* adds nothing to *mære.* In fact, the poet might have omitted line 121 altogether with little semantic loss. It was by his own choice that he repeated the essential idea of line 7 while varying its form. By the same token, *mycel ond mære* would have served at 7a; but Cynewulf is not one to use formulas "without ever thinking of employing other words to express the same idea."[21] From first to last, *Fates* is a painstaking search for variety in diction.[22]

The parallel death scenes of *Maldon* are particularly rich in recurrent essential ideas which receive varied expression. In 268, the poet says of a warrior that "he did not turn aside during the war-play" (*He ne wandode na æt þam wigplegan*). In 316, Byrhtwold curses "anyone who thinks to turn aside from this war-play" (*se ðe nu fram þis wigplegan wendan þenceð*). The verbs

[21]M. Parry, *L'Épithète,* p. 17; A. Parry, *Making,* p. 14.
[22]Additional arguments showing violations of economy could readily be contrived for the following line-pairs: 12/58, 17/43, 43/50, 35/70, 89/108, and 93/110. Of course, the total number of violations must be considerably greater than the number of those which are easy to demonstrate. In view of the poet's total consistency in avoiding useful repetition, it is reasonable to claim that economy is actually violated every time an essential idea is repeated.

wendan and *wandian* mean exactly the same thing in these contexts: to flee from battle. Another recurrent concept is that of a warrior brandishing a weapon as he begins to speak. In 230, the poet says, "Offa spoke, shook the ash-wood" (*Offa gemælde, æscholt asceoc*); in 310, he tells us that Byrhtwold, the old retainer, "vibrated the ash" (*—se wæs eald geneat—æsc acwehte*). The b-verses are interchangeable; both mean simply that the warrior brandished his spear. Again, in line 292, a warrior boasts that he will achieve victory "or fall in the troop" (*oððe on here crincgan*); in 324, the poet observes that another warrior wreaked havoc among the enemy "until he fell in battle" (*oðþæt he on hilde gecranc*). There is no need to distinguish between falling in the troop and falling in battle; in both cases the essential idea is simply that of dying. The phrases *on hilde* and *on here* doubtless help fill out the line and satisfy the prosodic requirement of alliteration. To that extent they function somewhat like Homeric epithets; but the *Maldon* poet does not use these added phrases with the persistence of Homeric epithets: he finds different means of fulfilling the same requirements. Thus the resemblance to the epithet is quite deceptive.

Maldon contains two pairs of lines which look at first glance like re-used alliterative patterns:

> 209   Swa hi bylde forð   bearn Ælfrices
> [Thus the son of Ælfric urged them on]
> 311   he ful baldlice   beornas lærde
> [he full boldly instructed the men]

> 216   Ic wylle mine æþelo   eallum gecyþan
> [I shall declare my lineage to all]
> 320   Swa hi Æþelgares bearn   ealle bylde
> [Thus the son of Æþelgar urged them all on]

It has been suggested that *beorn* "man" might be related to *bearn* "child," though the word is probably related instead to Norse *björn* "bear" (see OED s.v. *berne*). If *beorn* and *bearn* are in fact related, then 311 does repeat the pattern of alliterating roots in 209. The relation would not have been perceptible to the poet, however. Obviously, there must be some awareness of an etymological relation if it is to be counted as a useful repetition. From a synchronic point of view, *bearn* and *beorn* are simply two different words. Where the relation can be recovered, however, the poet provides variety. Consider the second pair, 216 and 320. They share the root *æþel-*, which occurs in the one case as a de-adjective noun and in the other as the first element in a compound name. The relation is inconspicuous, but recoverable. Accordingly, we can say that the pattern *æþel- / eall-* has been exploited in both cases to satisfy the alliterative requirement. The repeated pattern could have saved little effort, however. The lines are different in structure and convey different essential ideas: there is no question of deriving one from the other by simple substitution. A more significant resemblance is that between 320 and line 209, which conveys the same essential idea of "urging forth":

> 209   Swa hi bylde forð   bearn Ælfrices
> [Thus the son of Ælfric urged them on]
> 320   Swa hi Æþelgares bearn   ealle bylde
> [Thus the son of Æþelgar urged them all on]

Line 320 actually contains the alliterative constituents of 209, in reverse order. Since the names Ælfric and Æþelgar are metrically equivalent, the poet could have re-used the *bylde* / *beam* pattern when the same need arose. Instead, he shifted these constituents away from the alliterating positions and added another collocation. The result is a unique pattern of *abab* alliteration: *æþel-* / *beam* / *eall-* / *bylde*, like verse one of *Beowulf*, which has *Gar-* / *dena* / *gear-* / *dagum*.[23] J. B. Hainsworth has shown that Homer uses formulas on occasion even where metrical conditions are unfavorable, splitting and reordering the formula constituents as necessary to adapt the old phrase to the new position.[24] This skill seems to Hainsworth evidence of considerable creative power. What happens in *Maldon* 320 is analogous, with one important difference. According to Hainsworth, Homer seldom or never alters a formula unless he must (*Flexibility*, p. 104). The *Maldon* poet does so purely for the sake of variety.

Conspicuous changes in the manner of expression would doubtless appear even more frequently if the poets who composed these passages did not also vary the matter. Thus the *Beowulf* poet says of Scyld in lines 8-10 that he grew (*weox under wolcnum*) and throve in honors (*weorðmyndum þah*), until all the neighboring kingdoms obeyed him (*oðþæt him æghwylc þara ymbsittendra* / . . . *hyran scolde*). Similar statements are made in the description of Hrothgar's success (64-6), and many of the same words appear, but everything is presented from a different point of view, and the formulas are unlike in structure. This time the glory is specifically that of military success (*wiges weorðmynd*). The growth is that of the retainers (*oðð þæt seo geogoð geweox*), and it is their obedience which is stressed (*þæt him his winemagas* / *georne hyrdon*). Such shifts in perspective may involve different essential ideas, in which case no true violation of economy can occur; but they are also of obvious help to the poet in his effort to avoid repetitive diction.

The contrast between Homer and these three poets could not be clearer. In the Catalogue of Ships, as far as we can tell, Homer always adheres to the principle of economy, whereas, in exactly comparable circumstances, the Old English poets cannot once be shown to have done so. Lord's theory does not allow for oral poets with such talents. It also rules out genuine transitional texts.[25] Therefore, according to the theory, *Beowulf*, *Maldon* and *Fates* must be post-oral. Yet they are also totally unlike the post-oral works described by Parryite critics. Such works are supposed to be "weakly imitative, clumsy or fantastic in language, unobservant of the true oral conventions, eccentric in subject, and pretentious in their straining for dramatic, emotional or rhetorical

---

[23]In "Alliterative Patterns as a Test of Style in Old English Poetry," *JEGP*, LVIII (1959), 434-440, Robert Le Page argues that "extra-alliteration has no stylistic significance in Old English poetry" and that "lack of it indicates a higher degree of conscious artistry" (p. 439). Le Page's statistical analysis does not take into account any differences between one type of passage and another. A poet who displaces expected collocations for the sake of variety will naturally produce lines of a rather unusual type.

[24]*The Flexibility of the Homeric Formula* (Oxford, 1968), pp. 60, 89, 90.

[25]According to Lord, the process of abandoning formulas and systems can already be observed in oral, dictated texts (*Singer*, p. 130). When a singer has learned to use writing as an aid in composition, the process is supposed to be so far advanced that one cannot speak of a mixture of the two styles: the result is purely literary (p. 129). Moreover, an oral poet would never revise his work, even if a dictated text should provide the opportunity (p. 128).

effects" (Kirk, *Songs*, p. 98). Dissatisfied with the old-fashioned diction of their forefathers, post-oral poets make "pretentious attempts to alter and improve the fixed language of the past" (p. 205). Now, to be sure, the effect of varied diction may seem striking to one who has studied the normal use of formulas; but it is not pretentious, and it indicates no dissatisfaction with ancient expressions. Magoun found many such expressions in the very passage of *Beowulf* which we have just analyzed, and Robert Diamond found numerous others in *Fates*.[26] Because they considered only one or two narrative units, Magoun and Diamond overlooked the massive violations of economy; but their lists of "supporting evidence" do serve to demonstrate the traditional character of both poems.

This curious Old English mixture of creativity and tradition is particularly evident in the notion of fighting "while one can wield weapons," an essential idea which occurs frequently in *Maldon*. Within the sequence of deaths, it is always varied; but there does exist a formula which the poet is willing to re-use, provided that the distance between occurrences makes repetition inconspicuous:

> 83 þa hwile þe hi wæpna   wealdan moston
> [while they could wield weapons]
> 272 þa hwile ðe he wæpna   wealdan moste
> [while he could wield weapons]

The formula also occurs in *Beowulf* (2038, *þenden hie ðam wæpnum wealdan moston*). It may therefore be regarded as part of the inherited diction. Obviously, the *Maldon* poet had no objection to such expressions, in and of themselves. He would use them where he could do so unobtrusively, but he clearly did not wish to be dependent on them. Hence, within the sequence of deaths, the traditional expression is altered:

> Us is eallum þearf
> þæt ure æghwylc   oþerne bylde
> 235 wigan to wige,   þa hwile þe he wæpen mæge
> habban and healdan,   heardne mece,
> gar and godswurd.
> [For all of us it is needful that each should
> embolden the other, the warrior to battle,
> while he can retain and hold a weapon, a
> keen blade, a spear and a fine sword.]

Line 235 could have been replaced by the standard formula:

> þæt ure æghwylc   oþerne bylde
> *235 þa hwile ðe he wæpna   wealdan moste,
> habban and healdan   heardne mece,
> gar and godswurd.

[26]In "Oral-Formulaic Character," Magoun analyzes *Beo* 1-25, all within Scyld's portion of the genealogy. In "The Diction of the Signed Poems of Cynewulf," *PQ*, XXXVIII (1959), 228-41, Diamond confines his study to lines 1-29 of *Fates*, breaking off before parallel structures recur.

Compare 167-8, *ne mihte he gehealdan heardne mece,* / *wæpnes wealdan*. The first line of this "economical" passage could stand alone without the phrase *wigan to wige*, since *byldan* does not require a prepositional object and *oþer* can be used absolutely, without any associated noun. Such a line would accord perfectly with the normal use of formulas and systems in *Maldon* (cf. line 70, *Ne mihte hyra ænig oþrum derian*; 169b, *hyssas bylde*). Hence the phrase *wigan to wige* must be regarded as optional material, added to vary the pattern. The new a-verse dislodges *þa hwile ðe he wæpna* from its normal position, but the poet has no desire to discard his routine expression. Instead, he collapses the entire whole-line formula into a single b-verse. This is accomplished by deleting the main verb, which will be supplied in the line below. In addition, *móste* becomes *mæge*, for metrical reasons; the latter, with its short vowel and open syllable, can be resolved to provide the second arsis of a Sievers type B verse. The poet must still supply a new predicate. To that end, he puts *wæpen* in the accusative case, so as to accommodate what must surely be one of the most ancient Germanic formulas, *habban and healdan*.[27] Such varied diction is not pretentious or even innovative. It is a tour de force of unobtrusive skill. The poet has not forgotten the tradition; he is showing us his mastery of it, his ability to use one traditional verse in paraphrasing another, and to adapt old language to new metrical environments. It is important to note that although the parallel themes of *Maldon* contain no repeated whole-line formulas or alliterative patterns, repeated systems are everywhere, and they often express closely related concepts. Such a state of affairs cannot plausibly be ascribed to the influence of literacy, except insofar as writing may have aided the poet in perfecting work of a traditional type. It can only be explained by the operation of analogy in the mind of a poet who had mastered a formulaic diction, and who placed a high value on varied expression.

Two possibilities remain. The best Anglo-Saxon poets were either genuinely transitional or they were oral poets with skills not foreseen by Parry, Lord, and Magoun. In either case, formulaic theory is refuted, not only as it applies to Old English works, but in general. Suppose first that perfect variety of diction can only be achieved by a process of literary editing in which the poet reviews his work to eliminate offensive repetition. The existence of such poetry would invalidate the arguments by which Parry sought to show that Homer composed orally. Homer's much greater economy does not, in itself, prove that he was illiterate. If transitional poets exist, there is no reason to suppose that they all seek the kind of variety so characteristic of Old English verse. Transitional Greek poets might have an especially strong reverence for traditional language, or they might have different aesthetic priorities: even narrative advance, massive scale, and clear overall design, for example. Most scholars now agree that Homer's economy cannot be explained solely in terms of the demands of live, improvisational performance, since it is much greater than that of modern oral poetry.[28] It must therefore be explained on some other grounds. Perhaps

[27]Quoted by Fr. Klaeber as one of a number of typical Germanic formulas in *Beowulf and the Fight at Finnsburg*, 3rd ed. (Boston, 1950), p. lxvi.

[28]According to G. S. Kirk, "neither the Yugoslav poetry nor any other oral poetry of which we know has anything like the strict formular system, with its high degree of economy and scope, that is exemplified throughout the Iliad and Odyssey" (*Songs*, 88).

what Lord and Parry have portrayed as the aesthetic of the oral poet is simply the aesthetic of some poets who use formulas. Lord may be right in saying that "there are periods and styles in which originality is not at a premium" (*Singer*, p. 45). Not all such periods and styles need involve oral composition.

It is also possible that skilled oral poets could provide perfect variety in repeated minor themes. That may seem unlikely, but the human mind is no inconsiderable thing, and some have objected to *a priori* claims about the limitations of illiterate artists. R. F. Lawrence warns twentieth-century scholars against depending on their "instinctive knowledge of what is or is not appropriate to early oral poetry" ("Formulaic Theory," p. 173); and Ann Watts can conceive of oral composition with constraints against repetitive diction (*Lyre and Harp*, p. 119). It may seem plausible to argue that formulas are necessary for the production of any oral epic, and that all such epics must be improvised without deliberation or revision; but as two Homeric scholars have recently pointed out, such claims have never been supported with any evidence.[29] Formulas might be needed only by beginners or by singers of limited talent. The best oral artists might be able to exploit almost constantly, should they so desire, the much more powerful and creative process of analogy. The Yugoslavian guslars do in fact seem capable of providing varied diction in sequentially repeated themes. During his discussion of the letter-writing theme, for example, Lord quotes a series of six opening lines used to introduce six letters one after the other (pp. 84-5). The lines all occur close together, and they all convey the same idea exactly: "then he wrote another letter." No two are alike in form, however, and one looks in vain for any explanation of the variance, which cannot be due to forgetfulness. These six lines seem to me quite sufficient to refute most of the theoretical claims in Lord's previous chapter.

If there are oral singers who provide varied diction, then it is not true that all such singers seek economy under all circumstances. In accordance with this notion, Homer has been viewed as the product of a near-perfect tradition in whose spare efficiency can be seen a kind of noble or "phidian" plainness.[30] All oral poets are said to work toward this state of affairs by rejecting duplications of useful phrases. If their works lack Homer's economy, that must be because their traditions have not yet been "perfected" (Kirk, *Songs*, p. 89). Any discernible impulse away from economy in any oral poet invalidates this claim. If *Beowulf, Maldon,* and *Fates* were orally composed, their variety of phraseology might make Homer seem limited rather than "perfected." Even the smaller amount of variety in the songs of guslars must raise suspicions of this kind. One line of defense against such unflattering comparisons has been the contention that Yugoslavian and Anglo-Saxon verse forms are "looser" than Homer's, so that an economy like that of Greek epic never became necessary (Whallon, *Formula, Character and Context*, p. 158; Kirk, *Songs*, pp. 88-90). Adam Parry points out that those who hold this view have failed to specify what they mean by "loose" (*Making*, p. xl, n. 1). However that may be, the supposed differences in prosodic strictness are beside the point. Lord states

---

[29]Hainsworth, *Flexibility*, p. 16; A. Hoekstra, *Homeric Modifications of Formulaic Prototypes* (Amsterdam, 1965), p. 18.

[30]Milman Parry was committed to this aesthetic point of view from the very beginning of his graduate work. See A. Parry, *Making*, pp. xxiv-v.

that all oral poets must invent new lines by analogy in order to sing at all (*Singer*, p 43). This talent must be exercised frequently (p. 45). Homer may have faced a more difficult task in acquiring the necessary facility, but once possessed of it he had a power to alter his diction comparable to that of any other singer. One may properly ask whether he cultivated that power, or even wished to do so; that he possessed it is beyond dispute.

We can conclude that the Parry-Lord hypothesis is fundamentally wrong. Either some literate poets could use formulas in a wholly traditional way, or else some oral poets could compose with utter contempt for the utility of repeated phrases. If there are any formal criteria for isolating oral poems, they remain to be discovered. The type of necessary connection between form and manner of composition which Lord and Parry describe simply does not exist. From an aesthetic point of view, however, one thing is clear: Old English verse is not to be blamed for its lack of economy. At least three Anglo-Saxon poets valued the richness of their tradition and exploited that richness systematically in their works. Where one ancient phrase would have done, they stocked their memories with several. Where a ready-made formula would have served, they were willing to create a new line by analogy. Their diction stands out as superior because they knew more of the tradition than singing demanded, and controlled it with greater facility.

Tradition and Design in *Beowulf*

By Theodore M. Andersson

The poets responsible for the earliest versions of medieval heroic legend appear not to have invented their stories, but to have fixed already existing oral stories in written form. So much holds true for French Carolingian epic and the scattered remnants of Germanic heroic poetry. By extension, it is generally assumed that there is a traditional core in *Beowulf*. If the stories of Count Roland and Sigurd the Dragonslayer were traditional, why should the story of *Beowulf* be less so? The folktale roots have been laid bare in an effort to recover the lost tradition, but folktale is not the immediate root of other heroic stories in the Germanic area and only serves to underscore the isolation of *Beowulf* in the context of this heroic literature. Dorothy Whitelock carefully argued the traditional status of Hygelac, but Hygelac is not the hero.[1] Larry Benson espoused a fairly thoroughgoing inventionist view and conferred traditional status only on the swimming contest with Breca, but this is a peripheral episode.[2] The central adventures of Beowulf's life continue to defy tradition. If we think that the poem is inherited because we know this to be generally true of medieval heroic poetry, we must look elsewhere for the traditional elements. They cannot be found in the exploits ascribed to the hero Beowulf.

In an interesting but not widely cited essay on 'Unity and Intention in Beowulf' P. G. Buchloh attempted to clarify the structure of the poem against the background of the heroic lay.[3] Buchloh advanced the idea that the Norse lays *Hamðismál*, *Atlakviða*, and *Hlǫðskviða* share a common narrative pattern involving a 'Journey,' an 'Arrival,' a 'Drinking Feast,' a 'Quarrel with Words,' and a 'Fight with Weapons.' (He adds that this pattern does not hold true for *Vǫlundarkviða* or the *Hildebrandslied*, while the *Finnsburg Fragment* and the

---

[1] Dorothy Whitelock, *The Audience of Beowulf* (Oxford: Clarendon, 1951), pp. 39-55.

[2] Larry D. Benson, 'The Originality of *Beowulf*,' in *The Interpretation of Narrative: Theory and Practice*, Harvard English Studies, I, ed. Morton W. Bloomfield (Cambridge, Mass.: Harvard Univ. Press, 1970), pp. 1-43 (esp. 20-22).

[3] P. G. Buchloh, 'Unity and Intention in *Beowulf*,' *English Studies Today*, 4th series, ed. Ilva Cellini and Giorgio Melchiori: Lectures and papers read at the sixth conference of the International Association of University Professors of English held at Venice, August 1965 (Rome: Edizioni di storia e letteratura, 1966), pp. 99-120. In footnote 18 (p. 107) Buchloh announces the appearance of a Kiel *Habilitationsschrift* by Dietrich Jäger entitled *Erzählformen des Beowulf: Vergleichende Untersuchungen über die Gattungsmerkmale des ursprünglichen heroischen Epos* and scheduled for publication in 1967. According to Buchloh this study entails a comparison of *Beowulf* to 'other Old High German and Old Icelandic lays,' but to my knowledge it did not appear. I owe the reference to Buchloh's paper and much else to my colleague Joseph Harris.

Reprinted, by permission, from *Old English Literature in Context: Ten Essays*, ed. John D. Niles (Cambridge: D. S. Brewer, 1980), pp. 90-106 and 171-72.

Brot af Sigurðarkviðu are too incomplete to judge.) It takes very little reflection to grasp the application of this pattern to *Beowulf*. As Buchloh puts it (p. 102): 'After the introductory part (1-193) the Geats set out on their "Journey" to the Danes (194-228), and the ensuing "Arrival" has two stages, the meeting with the coast sentinel (229-319) and the "Arrival" proper (325-494). The Danes are feasting in their hall, and soon the "Quarrel" between Beowulf and Unferth arises. After the "Banquet" there follows the "Fight" with Grendel. This formal pattern, with a few variations, is repeated three times in *Beowulf*.'

The proposal is suggestive. In the absence of a known story about the adventures of Beowulf, it gives us some insight into the poet's point of departure in tradition and his elaboration of a pre-established narrative framework. The weakness lies in the incomplete correspondence of Buchloh's abstract pattern to the actual content of the extant lays. He reads the pattern from only three of these lays and even in those three the fit is imperfect. *Atlakviða*, for example, can be abstracted as follows: 1) introduction, 2) the messenger's journey, 3) arrival, 4) banquet, 5) invitation and consultation (but no 'Quarrel'), 6) departure of Gunnarr and Hǫgni, 7) journey, 8) the sighting of Atli's hall and a mention of sentinels, 9) Guðrún warns her brothers, 10) battle, 11) the slaying of Hǫgni, 12) Gunnarr's exultation, 13) the slaying of Gunnarr, 14) Guðrún's deceitful reception of Atli, 15) Atli's Thyestean banquet, 16) Guðrún's slaying of Atli, 17) the burning of the hall, 18) praise of Guðrún. It is clear that Buchloh's five-part structure does not adequately represent this narrative; there are two journeys, two arrivals, two banquets, but no quarrel, and there are important scenes for which Buchloh's pattern does not allow. The same strictures hold true for *Hamðismál* and *Hlǫðskviða*. *Hamðismál*, for example, contains an introduction, an incitation (Guðrún incites her sons Hamðir and Sǫrli to avenge their sister), a departure, the killing of Erpr by Hamðir and Sǫrli, the arrival at Jǫrmunrekkr's hall, a battle, the maiming of Jǫrmunrekkr, and the death of the brothers. Again, there is no quarrel (unless Guðrún's incitation or Jǫrmunrekkr's unanswered boasting is pressed into service) and no banquet except by implication in the mention of drinking vessels in stanzas 20 and 23.

What remains true in Buchloh's presentation is a certain similarity of characteristic scenes in the older heroic lay and *Beowulf*. I should therefore like to alter the emphasis in Buchloh's argument and stress not so much the overall structural correspondence, which seems to me partial, as the correspondence in scenic inventory. This altered perspective allows us to go beyond the three lays used by Buchloh and include the evidence provided by the other remnants of the Germanic heroic tradition. It will be seen that these sources are not less significant if we adopt looser terms and think of the typical scenes which the *Beowulf* poet may have inherited, in no particular order, from the older lay.

I begin by reviewing ten categories of scenes that account for much of the action in *Beowulf*:

1. Battle scenes in the open (Hygelac's raid, Ravenswood, the dragon).
2. Hall scenes of conviviality or celebration (mostly at Heorot).
3. Hall battles (Grendel and his mother at Heorot and Grendel's mother in her aquatic hall).

4. Journeys in quest of heroic confrontation (to Denmark and back, to the mere and back).
5. Sentinel scenes (the coastguard and Wulfgar).
6. Welcoming scenes (at Heorot or in Hygelac's hall).
7. The use of intermediaries (corresponding to the sentinel scenes in *Beowulf*, though not generally in heroic poetry).
8. The consultation of the hero with kings or queens (Beowulf with Hygelac, Hrothgar, or Wealhtheow).
9. Incitations or flytings (Unferth).
10. Leave-taking scenes (at Hygelac's court or Heorot).

If we call to mind the half dozen or so survivals of the heroic lay—the *Fight at Finnsburg*, the *Hildebrandslied*, *Atlakviða, Atlamál, Hamðismál, Hlǫðskviða*, and whatever constructs we surmise behind the Sigurd and Walter stories as well as vanished lays adumbrated in prose epitomes—we may quickly establish a very similar set of characteristic situations for this genre: (1) battle scenes (throughout), (2) hall scenes of (ominous) conviviality,[4] (3) hall battles,[5] (4) journeys in quest of heroic confrontation,[6] (5) sentinel scenes,[7] (6) welcoming scenes,[8] (7) the use of intermediaries,[9] (8) the consultation of heroes with kings or queens,[10] (9) incitations or flytings,[11] (10) leave-taking scenes.[12]

Almost every situation in *Beowulf* is in some way reminiscent of the ancestral form. Even the dynastic review at the outset of the poem can be seen as an expanded and itemized version of the invocation of antiquity traditionally used to preface the heroic lay. The similarity extends to the point of verbal echo since the 'in geardagum' of *Beowulf* has its counterpart in three Eddic lays: 'Ár var alda, þat er arar gullo,' 'Ár var, þatz Sigurðr sótti Giúca,' 'Atli sendi, ár til Gunnars' (where 'ár' may mean 'messenger' and not 'in days of

---

[4]The following Eddic references are to *Edda: Die Lieder des Codex Regius nebst verwandten Denkmälern*, ed. Gustav Neckel, revised by Hans Kuhn (Heidelberg: Carl Winter, 1962). This edition will be abbreviated NK (Neckel-Kuhn). *Hamðismál* 18-20 (NK, pp. 271-72); *Atlakviða* 1-2, 10 (NK, pp. 240-42) and 34-35 (NK, p. 246); *Atlamál* 8-9 (NK, p. 249); *Hlǫðskviða* 15 (NK, p. 306); the lost Rosimund lay in Paul the Deacon, *Pauli Historia Langobardorum*, ed. Georg Waitz (Hanover: Impensis bibliopolii Hahniani, 1878), p. 104; the *Waltharius*, ed. Karl Strecker, *Monumenta Germaniae historica: Poetae latini medii aevi*, VI, I (Weimar: Hermann Böhlaus Nachfolger, 1951), lines 310-12 (pp. 36-37).

[5]*The Fight at Finnsburg; Hamðismál* 23 (NK, p. 272); *Atlakviða* 19 (NK, p. 243).

[6]Both Atli poems and *Hamðismál; Hlǫðskviða* (NK, p. 306); the *Hildebrandslied* by implication.

[7]*Hamðismál* 18-19 (NK, pp. 271-72); *Atlakviða* 14 (NK, p. 242); *Hlǫðskv.* (NK, pp. 306-07).

[8]*Atlakviða* 10 (NK, p. 242) and 33 (NK, p. 245); *Atlamál* 8-9 (NK, p. 249); *Hlǫðskviða* 6 (NK, pp. 303); *Waltharius* (edition cited in footnote 4), lines 215-26 (p. 33).

[9]*Atlakviða* 1 (NK, p. 240); *Atlamál* 4 (NK, p. 248); *Hlǫðskviða* 3 (NK, pp. 302-03).

[10]*Hamðismál* 3-10 (NK, pp. 269-70); *Atlakviða* 6-9 (NK, p. 241); *Atlamál* 11-29 (NK, pp. 249-51); *Hlǫðskviða* (NK, p. 302).

[11]*Helgakviða Hundingsbana I*, 32-46 (NK, pp. 135-37); *Helgakviða Hjǫrvarðssonar* 12-30 (NK, pp. 143-6); *Helgakviða Hundingsbana II*, 19-24 (NK, pp. 155-56); *Hamðismál*, 3-10 (NK, pp. 269-70); the *Hildebrandslied*; the lost Ingeld poem (e.g., *Beowulf*, 2047-56 and Saxo Grammaticus, *Gesta Danorum*, ed. Alfred Holder [Strassburg: Trübner, 1886], Book 6, pp. 204-13). For a listing of Germanic flytings see Carol J. Clover, 'The Germanic Context of the Unferth Episode,' forthcoming in *Speculum*. [Appeared in Vol. 55 (1980), 444-68—R. F.]

[12]*Atlakviða* 12 (NK, p. 242); *Atlamál* 34-36 (NK, p. 252).

yore').[13] The *Hildebrandslied* too vouches for tradition with the hearsay preface 'Ik gihorta ðat seggen,' and the convention persists down to the 'Uns ist in alten mæren wunders vil geseit' of redactions A and C of the *Nibelungenlied*. As the poem progresses, Beowulf's interviews with royalty in Geatland (and later in Denmark) reenact the consultation scenes in *Atlakviða, Atlamál, Hamðismál,* and *Hlǫðskviða*. The journey abroad to meet the challenge characterizes these poems and, offstage, the *Hildebrandslied* as well. The formalities of the arrival at Heorot elaborate the use of lookouts and messengers in *Atlakviða, Atlamál, Hamðismál,* and *Hlǫðskviða,* a trend pursued with fond excess by the *Nibelungenlied* poet. The feasting and distribution of treasure in Heorot recreate the traditional milieu of heroic poetry. The exchange with Unferth is modeled on the Germanic flyting abundantly illustrated in the *Edda* and Saxo Grammaticus and surprisingly well maintained in the *Nibelungenlied*. The contest with Grendel takes place in the nocturnal hall setting familiar from the *Finnsburg Fragment,* the death of Sigurd in *Skamma,* or the attack on Ermanaric as described by Bragi.[14] The remainder of the poem only recapitulates these situations—more hall scenes, more converse at the banquet, more journeys, more battles. The point would seem to be that the *Beowulf* poet had at his disposal a certain inventory of conventional situations.

The more immediate question, and the question which has preoccupied modern criticism almost to the exclusion of studies analyzing the traditional story elements, bears on the poet's organization of the scenes he inherited. How did he form his narrative and what is the broader purpose subtending the form that he chose? The supersession of the heroic lay entailed difficult new problems of 'design,' both in the sense of episodic arrangement and in the sense of an underlying intention. The dimensions of the formal problem have been clearly reflected in the critical response. In subordinating the old to the new and achieving a richer form, the poet produced a more complicated structure which has elicited comment ranging from claims of extreme ingenuity to the expression of some disgruntlement.[15] The massive scholarly tribute to *Beowulf* has obviously been taxed by an approach to the poem through its structure.

We all know that a good narrative poem should be well made, that is, susceptible of a clear and logical dissection, or in simpler terms still, possessed of a transparent plot and easy to summarize. In this respect, *Beowulf,* an

---

[13]*Helgakviða Hundingsbana I,* 1, 1 (NK, p. 130); *Sigurðarkviða in skamma* 1, 1 (NK, p. 207); *Atlakviða* 1, 1 (NK, p. 240). *Atlamál* follows suit with 'Frétt hefir ǫld ófo, . . .' (1, 1; NK, p. 248) and *Hamðismál* expands the invocation considerably (2, 1-6; NK, p. 269):

> Vara þat nú   né í gær
> þat hefir langt   liðit síðan,
> er fát fornara,   fremr var þat hálfo . . .

[14]That Bragi assigns the attack to the night hours is argued by Walther Heinrich Vogt, 'Bragis Schild: Maler und Skalde,' *Acta Philologica Scandinavica,* 5 (1930-31), 3-7.

[15]See John Nist, 'The Structure of *Beowulf,' Papers of the Michigan Academy of Science, Arts, and Letters,* 43 (1958), 307-14 and *The Structure and Texture of Beowulf* (São Paulo, Brazil, 1959). Favorable notice is given Nist's analysis by Tilman Westphalen, *Beowulf 3150-55: Textkritik und Editionsgeschichte,* Bochumer Arbeiten zur Sprach- und Literaturwissenschaft, 2 (Munich: Fink, 1967), p. 344. Another structural analysis is offered by Eamon Carrigan, 'Structure and Thematic Development in *Beowulf,' Proceedings of the Royal Irish Academy,* 66, Sec. C (1967), 1-51. Less inclined to structural subtleties is Kenneth Sisam, *The Structure of Beowulf* (Oxford: Clarendon, 1965), pp. 21-22.

eminently good poem, disappoints us. It is strangely built. It is full of temporal dilations, but it has a gaping hiatus between Beowulf's return to Geatland and his final adventure. It combines much haranguing with considerable narrative dearth; there are questions about the past and future left unanswered. The digressions are a problem in pertinence and it is hard to remember where they are inserted or in what order. The events of Swedish history in the second part are a tangle and even more difficult to retain. These anomalies of articulation are, we feel, at some level poetic deficiencies. And yet the poem is so extraordinarily satisfying that we have the nagging feeling that we are asking the wrong structural questions. The principle of goodness in the poem is clearly not narrative simplicity. It lies elsewhere.[16]

To some extent it is obvious where it lies, in elevated sentiment, rich language, elaborate courtesy, in the dramatic unfolding of achievement and failure. But there is another quality that sets *Beowulf* apart, along with Anglo-Saxon literature in general. It has to do with a persistent cultivation of mood and emotional resonance.[17] This is a quality which emerges clearly when Anglo-Saxon literature is considered in the larger Germanic context. It is not to be found until very late in the chilly verse and prose of medieval Scandinavia, nor in the bits and pieces of Old High German, nor even in the adjacent rhythms and idioms of the Old Saxon *Heliand*.

Beowulf is more remarkable in communicating an experience, or a series of experiences, than in telling a story. What holds the reader is not an orderly or even a dramatic progression of events, but the stylization of Beowulf in a series of encounters, the accomplished young man at Hrothgar's court, the high-spirited boy in the retrospective swimming contest with Breca, the complete warrior in the combats with Grendel and his mother, Hygelac's loyal retainer, the admirable ruler of the Geats, and the veteran spirit matched against the dragon in what is at once Beowulf's final victory and his crowning defeat. The heroic and personal postures in the poem are of course not so different from what we find in the lays and sagas of Germanic tradition, though the opponents are monstrous, but critics, especially since Tolkien's analysis in elegiac terms, have never been content to classify *Beowulf* as heroic poetry. Nor is the analogy to *Grettis saga* productive beyond the episodic correspondence. In the abstract, Grettir goes through the same experience, the rambunctious boy who comes of age, mellows, quells monsters, and succumbs in pathetic straits. But the similarity is only in the summary, not in the impact on the reader. The saga is full of extraneous adventures and the mood of Grettir's fate impinges on the story only now and then. The narrative economy

---

[16]Gwyn Jones, *Kings, Beasts and Heroes* (London: Oxford Univ. Press, 1972), p. 4: 'And finally, it [*Beowulf*] is by any standards a good, even a fine poem; and there have been many to think it a great one—less for its movement and action, or fable, than because they find it a statement about human life and values by an artist who—by virtue of his technical ability, his command of words and metre, his power to present narrative, argument, reflection, mood, and feeling in verse—has given lasting significance to the thing he wrote, which is now the thing we read.'

[17]See Alan Renoir, 'A Reading of *The Wife's Lament*,' *English Studies*, 58 (1977), 4-19 and 'Germanic Quintessence: The Theme of Isolation in the *Hildebrandslied*,' in *Saints, Scholars and Heroes: Studies in Medieval Culture in Honour of Charles W. Jones*, ed. Margot H. King and Wesley M. Stevens (Collegeville, Minnesota: Hill Monastic Library of St. John's Abbey and University, 1979), II, 143-78.

of *Beowulf*, on the other hand, dispenses with distracting adventures and guides the reader more concentratedly and consistently into the recesses of the experience. The mood is always at the center of the poet's preoccupation. Indeed, the mood becomes the substance of the work and when we explore the structure of the narrative, we should focus not on the sequence of events, but on the construction of atmosphere.

Much of the attractiveness of Buchloh's essay lies in the attempt to go beyond structural observations in order to analyze the *Beowulf* poet's 'intention.' The narrative amplification implies a meaning and this meaning can be found in the tension between a traditional form and a new purpose. On the one hand, Beowulf dies the traditional hero's death in defense of his kingdom, but on the other, his death turns out to be senseless because it exposes the kingdom to destruction. This result puts heroism in a questionable light and it establishes the poet as a detached spectator of heroic events. The discrepancy between heroic theme and authorial reserve is explained, reasonably enough, by the incongruity between the poet's native literary culture and his reinterpretation of this culture in epic and Christian terms. Buchloh speculates that his immediate aim may have been to support a kingship committed to the new faith and threatened by real or potential apostasies (p. 117): 'So, the *lar* of the *Beowulf* poet is that a king has to endeavour to become strong, the people have to endeavour to live in peace under his rule, but whether they may live in *frofor* and *dream* is not dependent on human endeavours, but lies alone in the hands of God, the *Metod*. If this sententia defines the basic attitude of the *Beowulf* poet towards his poem and towards his world, the discrepancy between the epic poet, who is detached from the heroic world he describes, and the Christian propagandist, who wishes to prove the validity of his principles, disappears.'

The sharp attitudinal distinction between *Beowulf* and Germanic heroic poetry may be open to some question. It could be argued that futility is always part and parcel of heroic grandeur and that some sort of social critique is always implicit in the heroic poem.[18] On the other hand, it is certainly true that the critique is formulated more insistently and more self-consciously by the *Beowulf* poet than by any of his predecessors in the heroic genre. As Buchloh points out elsewhere in his paper, futility lies at the very center of the work (p. 110): 'But the central theme, which is varied time and again, is that of the futility of all human efforts, and the almighty power of a good God.' The poet's mission may be viewed as an effort to extract meaning from the apparent meaninglessness of the heroic life. The emptiness of heroic posture is filled with the purposefulness of Christian aspiration. Beowulf's secular existence is a sequence of flickering successes capped by ultimate failure, but it is, after all, only a prelude to the vindication of the afterlife. The pessimism of the secular life is counterbalanced by the optimism of the spiritual life. Secular struggle has spiritual meaning and this is what distinguishes *Beowulf* from the antecedent lay with its grim finality, moderated only by a sort of academic glory bequeathed by the dying hero for the vicarious edification of his survivors.

The *Beowulf* poet, located between the spiritual limitations of the heroic

---

[18]Klaus von See touches on this idea in *Germanische Heldensage: Stoffe, Probleme, Methoden* (Frankfurt am Main: Athenäum Verlag, 1971), pp. 170-72.

lay and the new doctrine of salvation, resolves the conflict by putting the heroic life in perspective against the promise of a future reward. The structural problem confronting him is how to illustrate the futility of this life as a background for the permanence of the next. The raw material available to him was a stock of characteristic 'lay' scenes without spiritual implication, scenes which he proceeded to combine to form a new genre, the heroic biography. The most plausible model for this synthesis remains Virgilian epic. But the biographical dimensions of *Beowulf* are limited. There are gaps in the hero's life and the scenic traditions taken over from the heroic lay were not well adapted to provide biographical continuity. Nor does the biographical model serve in itself to convey the message of futility, which is clearly the poet's concern. When it came to the infusion of his central theme, the *Beowulf* poet was obliged to go beyond his inherited scenic inventory and Virgil's epic form.

Buchloh reviews some of the techniques of amplification (pp. 106-07)—the descriptions of sight and sound, the emphasis on emotions, retrospection and anticipation, authorial commentary—but he understands them only in terms of the poet's new autonomy in relation to his story, an autonomy that allows him to analyze and evaluate from a greater distance. I should like to supplement this view with the observation that the epic elaborations and the arrangement of episodes serve to underline the message of futility. Descriptions, emotional portraiture, narrative digressions, commentary, and the movement backward and forward in time are designed for the most part to isolate a pattern of frustration in this life. The ordering and annotation of the traditional materials therefore contribute in and of themselves to the querying of the heroic career which Buchloh and others have commented on.

The organizing principle in operation throughout the poem is mutability. Brodeur, in his *Beowulf* book, wrote about the 'dramatic reversals' of the poem.[19] No sooner is one mood established than it is superseded by its opposite. Hope gives way to disappointment, joy to grief, and vice versa. It is not just a question of occasional tonalities; the main lines of the poem as a whole can be analyzed according to this alternation.

We are introduced to the Danish scene at the acme of accomplishment and optimism, the construction of Heorot and the expansive hall joys which it houses (lines 1-100). But this luminous tableau is darkened by Grendel's ravages (100-88). Hope mounts and the spirits of the Danes are raised by Beowulf's arrival and his confident promise of salvation (189-702), but the mood plummets once more at the sight of Hondscioh disappearing into Grendel's maw (740-45). However, the setback is only momentary and Beowulf succeeds

---

[19]Arthur G. Brodeur, *The Art of Beowulf* (Berkeley: Univ. of California Press, 1959; rpt. 1971), e.g. pp. 51, 60. The ebb and flow of mood in the poem is also suggested by Joan Blomfield, 'The Style and Structure of *Beowulf*,' *Review of English Studies*, 14 (1938), 396-403, rpt. in *The Beowulf Poet: A Collection of Critical Essays*, ed. Donald K. Fry (Englewood Cliffs, N. J.: Prentice-Hall, 1968), pp. 57-65, and Herbert G. Wright, 'Good and Evil; Light and Darkness; Joy and Sorrow in *Beowulf*,' *Review of English Studies*, N.S. 8 (1957), 1-11, rpt. in *An Anthology of Beowulf Criticism*, ed. Lewis E. Nicholson (Notre Dame, Indiana: Univ. of Notre Dame Press, 1963), pp. 257-67. See also Robert B. Burlin, 'Gnomic Indirection in *Beowulf*,' in *Anglo-Saxon Poetry: Essays in Appreciation for John C. McGalliard*, ed. Lewis E. Nicholson and Dolores Warwick Frese (Notre Dame, Indiana: Univ. of Notre Dame Press, 1975), pp. 41-49. Burlin comments on 'the alternation of human security and fear, comfort and agony, the inexorable rhythm on which the poet has chosen to organize his narrative' (p. 47).

after all in rescuing the situation by routing Grendel (702-836). The relief experienced by all at the removal of this sinister force is celebrated with elaborate delight during the return from the mere and in Heorot (837-1250). But even in the midst of this celebration there are undertones of renewed woe. The success story of Sigemund, albeit a success story tempered by the reader's knowledge that not all dragon stories in the poem have a happy conclusion, is succeeded by the somber stories of Heremod and Finnsburg, illustrating the gloomy moral that promising beginnings can have sorry ends. The message is confirmed by the appearance of the unexpected distaff monster and the seizing of Æschere (1251-1320). Once more spirits droop, but briefly, for again Beowulf retrieves the situation by dispatching the monster mother in her watery haunts (1321-1590). The joy at Heorot soars (1591-1887) and persists in Beowulf's report to Hygelac (1888-2199), but here too there are counterbalancing resonances. The story of Thryth's conversion from vice to virtue is followed by the ominous implications of the Ingeld digression, intimations of doom that are borne out soon enough by the robbing of the hoard and the ravages of the dragon (2200-2323). From this point on triumph and despair merge as Beowulf encounters the new enemy (2324-2693), prevails and succumbs (2694-2820), and is consigned to the funeral pyre (2821-3182). The larger lines of the development may be tabulated as follows:

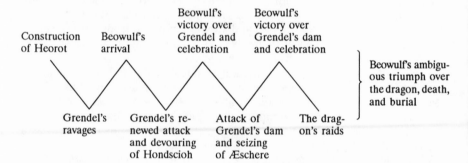

This is the larger pattern, a rising and falling of hope and fear, success and failure, joy and grief, in short, the rhythm of a mutable world. It might be argued that the pattern is implicit in the story and would exist in any narrative in which victory and defeat are interwoven. What is peculiar to *Beowulf* is the cultivation of the pattern in every segment of the poem, the smallest as well as the largest, and the explicit reminders throughout that good yields to bad or the reverse.

We observe the pattern already in the prefatory matter, the enumeration of the Danish dynasty. Scyld Scefing is 'found destitute' (7a), but by a compensation of fate becomes a great king.[20] His son, the older Beowulf or Beow, is sent by God 'as a comfort to his people' (14a) and reverses their suffering. So much is positive, but we are reminded that life ends in grief no matter how glorious the career. Scyld dies and the people mourn: 'him wæs geomor sefa / murnende mod' (49b-50a). A king is alternately a consolation

---

[20]Line references are to *Beowulf and the Fight at Finnsburg*, ed. Fr. Klaeber, 3rd ed. (Boston: D. C. Heath, 1950).

and an affliction to his people, an idea which is not far from the theme of the poem as a whole. It prepares us for the accession of Hrothgar and the mixed fortunes of his reign. His success culminates in the construction of Heorot, a scene of feasting and liberality, but hardly has this height been attained when the fall is anticipated with a mysterious reference to 'the hostile flames of hateful fire' (82b-83a). On the heels of this forecast come Grendel's depredations and the recision of hall joy. The poet specifies the ensuing grief with unremitting variation:

> Þa wæs æfter wiste   wop up ahafen,
> micel morgensweg.   Mære þeoden,
> æþeling ærgod,   unbliðe sæt,
> þolode ðryðswyð   þegnsorge dreah . . . (128-31).

(Then in the wake of feasting voices were raised in lamentation, a great clamor in the morning. The glorious ruler, the excellent prince, sat joyless, suffered and endured great sorrow for his thanes . . . .)

The perception of woe is urged repeatedly, as is the remorseless reign of terror initiated by Grendel (136b, 156a, 159b). Denmark has fallen from a peak of glory into a chasm of misery at the moment of Beowulf's appearance. The juxtaposition of Beowulf 'the mightiest of mankind' (196) to the Danish 'suffering harsh, hateful, and long-lasting' (191b-92a) sounds in itself the theme of release and the message becomes explicit when Beowulf addresses the Danish coast guard with a promise of 'relief' (280a), 'remedy' (281b), and the cooling of 'seething cares' (282). In short, his mission is the reversal of fortune. This section reduces to the following outline:

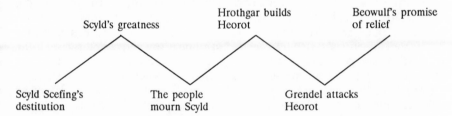

| | Hrothgar builds | Beowulf's promise |
| Scyld's greatness | Heorot | of relief |

| Scyld Scefing's | The people | Grendel attacks |
| destitution | mourn Scyld | Heorot |

Reversal is consequently the theme of the welcoming ceremonies at Heorot. Hrothgar declares that help has often appeared imminent when his warriors have vowed action over their ale cups, but the following morning the hall was again awash with the blood of murdered retainers. The period prior to Beowulf's arrival has therefore been a time of dashed hopes, a pattern which the new development promises to change. A sequence of slender and increasingly wistful hopes is replaced by a great and justified hope. This new mood is signalled by a feast during which everyone celebrates, as it were, in advance. The high spirits culminate in the flyting with Unferth, which concludes with Beowulf's rejoinder that Grendel would not have prevailed had Unferth been as fierce as he claims. Thus the debate with Unferth reemphasizes the idea that fragile remedies and false promises have yielded to a real delivery. The prospect is greeted with an outpouring of joy. The Danes rise from the nether regions of despair to a state of high expectation. The gist of the story up to this point has not been a detailed narrative of how Beowulf got to Denmark, and why, but rather an analysis of the Danish mood and how it is altered by Beowulf's presence. It is a history of sensations—grief, hopelessness, fear, joylessness and their opposites, good cheer, hope, release, confidence.

All of this changes once again with Grendel's invasion of the hall. He is a studied antithesis to the evening's celebration. He bears God's anger (711b), is deprived of joy (721a), and advances with a wrathful spirit (726a). Unlike the hall laughter of the evening's festivities, Grendel's anger is laughter distorted:

> Þa his mod ahlog;
> mynte þæt he gedælde,   ær þon dæg cwome,
> atol aglæca   anra gehwylces
> lif wið lice,   þa him alumpen wæs
> wistfylle wen   (730b-34a).

(Then his spirit laughed; the horrid monster thought to separate the life of every man from its body—he had an expectation of feasting.)

But the reader is immediately reminded that Grendel's fortunes are also labile (734b-36a): 'Fate did not decree that he should partake of more of mankind beyond that night.' The monster gulps down just one more hall-thane, then Beowulf prevails as Grendel discovers that his earlier strength is, unexpectedly, of no service to him. Beowulf's triumph appears to terminate the preceding vacillations of fortune with an air of finality and the stage is set for another celebration at Heorot.

The victory is celebrated first by an equestrian entertainment. As the troop gallops back from the mere, or perhaps at intervals in the gallop, a singer recites the tale of Sigemund's unbroken successes. But a cautionary note intrudes on this heroic elation when the singer turns to Heremod's career, which, despite great expectations—'many a wise man had trust in him as a relief from afflictions' (908b-09)—ended in crime. Case and counter-case. If the digressions are pertinent and heroes past are to be associated with heroes present, Heremod is an image of what Beowulf might become, a specious 'relief from afflictions' who ends badly.[21] The juxtaposition of the two lays is an implicit anticipation of Hrothgar's sermon; the impermanent and questionable nature of success is mixed into the careless strains of triumph.

The celebration continues in the same vein at Heorot. Hrothgar pronounces a congratulatory speech in which he greets the unexpected release from his woes, but in the midst of this expansive good feeling we are reminded that Heorot is not restored forever and that the hall-dwellers will eventually be engulfed in Hrothulf's treachery (1018b-19). The danger of strife and betrayal that always lurks in the meadhall is reinforced by the story of Finnsburg, in which Hildeburh laments 'the murderous misfortune of her kinsmen, where before she had had the greatest joy of this world' (1079-80a). The plunge from joy to sorrow in Finnsburg and the sight of slaughter in the morning look backward and forward to the carnage of Grendel and his mother in Heorot. As the respite was brief and delusive in Finnsburg, so it has been and will be in Heorot. The atmosphere of fragile hilarity and Heorot's vulnerability

---

[21]Cf. Adrien Bonjour, *The Digressions in Beowulf* (Oxford: Blackwell, 1950), p. 7.

are restated when, after a renewal of joy and convivial clamor (1160b-62a), Wealhtheow comes to Hrothulf, then to Hrethric and Hrothmund, whom he is fated to betray, and, sensing what lies ahead, appeals to Beowulf for his protection. At the conclusion of the feast, the juxtaposition of festive harmony and impending disaster is summarized one final time (1232b-34a): 'There was the best of feasts, men drank wine. They did not know their fate, the destiny determined of old. . . . Once more in outline:

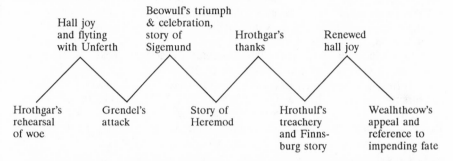

Now we turn to Grendel's aggrieved mother and destiny is fulfilled, again in the form of a sudden and unexpected reversal of fortune, a veering from respite to affliction (1280b-81a): 'The men were soon overtaken by change.' The new fiend seizes and carries off Æschere—'cearu wæs geniwod' (1303b), and Hrothgar commemorates the loss in the same words—'Sorh is geniwod' (1322b). It is as if joy can have only one natural consequence, the renewal of sorrow. But the reverse is equally true and Beowulf confronts the challenge by countermanding the word 'sorrow'—'Ne sorga,' he says (1384a) and intones the much-quoted sentiments about gaining glory before death, sentiments which have regularly been invoked to validate our notion of the fatalistic Germanic mentality, but which, in the context of the poem's mood, are another example of ambivalent enthusiasm in a gulf of underlying despondency. Beowulf promises relief, but he does so in the larger framework of rising and falling fortunes and with a consciousness that success is always tinged by the reversal that inevitably follows, in this case the ultimate reversal of death.

The ambivalence is reformulated as Beowulf arms and prepares to dive into the mere. He addresses Hrothgar on the provisions to be observed in the event of his death, so that the shadow of defeat rests on the probability of victory and confidence is mitigated by an allowance for failure. Uneasiness is characteristic of the poem throughout. Emotionally it is not single-ply, the light and dark layers blend. Whether they do so to cancel or accentuate each other is a matter of the reader's perspective.

The battle with Grendel's mother is itself described as a mounting and plunging of fortunes. Beowulf grasps Hrunting only to discover that for the first time this much-tested sword has no bite. The blade fails, but not the boldness, and he resorts to 'the power of his hand-grip' (1534a) to throw down his antagonist. She counters with what is technically known as a 'reverse' in wrestling and pins him. Only his armor saves him from the point of the knife. The climactic reversal occurs under divine auspices; God makes our hero aware of the sword among the accoutrements in the hall and he seizes it to sever the monster's head. For good measure he beheads the lifeless Grendel as well, a wanton gesture of triumph tempered by a painful flashback to Grendel's depredations in Heorot, where he devoured fifteen of Hrothgar's 'hearth-companions' (1580b).

The final extermination of monsters should be an occasion for some crowning revelry, but the poet shrinks back again. Instead of a hymn of release, we are now given a view of Beowulf's companions on the shore despairing of the outcome and fully expecting that Beowulf has succumbed. Only when Beowulf breaks the surface is the illusion of bereavement dispelled and the meters peal joy once again. The emphasis is as much on the unexpected conquest of woe as on the real achievement. In *Beowulf* victory is always extracted from defeat, a tension which makes it more valuable than foregone success. Defeat yawns under every victory and underscores the frailty of success as one of the larger themes in the poem. Even Beowulf's report at Heorot adheres to this rhythm, rehearsing how the battle would have been lost but for God's intervention.

After the slaying of Grendel's mother, the measure of success is full. Beowulf has accomplished his vow and cleansed Heorot, which stood at the beginning of the poem as the culmination of Danish hall-joy and which is once again free for the feasting. How is this splendid outcome greeted? Not by songs, merriment, drinking, or joyful converse, but by Hrothgar's somber sermon. Heremod is invoked, as after the first victory, and Beowulf is warned how pride grows and the soul succumbs:

> Nu is þines mægnes blæd
> ane hwile;   eft sona bið,
> þæt þec adl oððe ecg   eafoþes getwæfeð,
> oððe fyres feng,   oððe flodes wylm,
> oððe gripe meces,   oððe gares fliht,
> oððe atol yldo;   oððe eagena bearhtm
> forsiteð ond forsworceð;   semninga bið,
> þaet ðec, dryhtguma,   deað oferswyðeð   (1761b-68).

(Now your might flourishes for a time. Only too soon will sickness or blade deprive you of strength, or the grip of fire, or the surging of water, or the onslaught of the sword, or the flight of the spear, or relentless old age; or the brightness of eye will dim and darken; soon it will be, warrior, that death will overpower you.)

This may seem like a cold congratulatory message, but it is perfectly characteristic of the *Beowulf* poet, for whom the underside is always uppermost. Hrothgar goes on to verify the truth of what he says by reviewing the history of his own fall from glory. His words are a prudent containment of the momentary triumph and a telling anticipation of Beowulf's later career.

The same rhythm of sorrow and relief obtains on Beowulf's return to Geatland. This section is prefaced by another digression, the story of Thryth's reform from a vicious beginning to a generous end. Whatever the exact relevance of the account, it illustrates that the most startling changes are possible. Surprise is the theme of Beowulf's interview with Hygelac, who greets the returning hero with amazement and delight because he had not expected him to survive the encounter. Beowulf then launches into a report of the 'multitude of sorrows' (2003b-04) and 'persistent misery' (2005a) created at the Danish court by Grendel's ravages and the joy brought by his own victory—never had he seen 'under the vault of heaven greater mead-mirth of hall-sitters' (2015-16a). But here as always in the poem, joy is not allowed to prosper and Beowulf cannot forbear a comment on the ephemeral nature of this 'mead-mirth.' He relates the marriage plans for Freawaru and Ingeld and the hope of settling the feud between Danes and Heathobards, but the prognosis is not sanguine. The vicissitudes of the Danish court are not over and lie as much in the future as in the past. This section of the narrative yields the following synopsis:

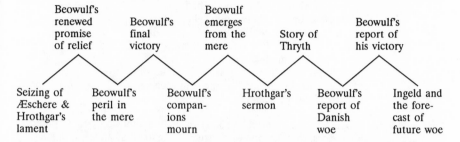

Beowulf's relation of his contests adheres to the same oscillating line: Grendel's bloody visitations followed by Beowulf's reprisals, the monster's mournful departure followed by the 'song and glee' (2105a) of the celebration, the unhappy retaliation of Grendel's mother followed by Beowulf's final triumph. The poet supplements Beowulf's version with his own summary, which is similarly structured as a series of contrasts. Beowulf is given a gift of both horses and treasure, a gesture that constitutes proper behavior toward a kinsman as contrasted to the weaving of 'nets of malice' (2167a) and the plotting of death. He in turn conducts himself bravely and with discretion, behavior contrasting to drunkenness and the slaying of 'hearth-companions' (2180a). At this point the narrator raises the mysterious matter of Beowulf's inauspicious youth and recaps his whole career with the words (2188b-89): 'The glorious man recovered from each of his afflictions.' Since the Thryth digression leads into this segment of the narrative, we may imagine that she is paradigmatic for Beowulf's career—a bad beginning and a glorious recovery.

This reading would be well and good if it covered Beowulf's total career, but the larger reversal from bad to good in the monster segment is subject to another reversal from weal to woe in the dragon segment. The dragon brooding over his treasure is an apt emblem of the latent menace that broods over the history of kings and heroes. The menace can be activated at any time by minor causes, in this case the intrusion of a thief, who removes a precious cup from the dragon's hoard. The dragon awakens from his sloth and the fiery ravages begin. But like his monstrous kin in Denmark, the dragon too is subject to reversals (2322b-23): 'He relied on his cave, his prowess, and his wall; his expectation deceived him.' Beowulf is doomed along with the dragon and the battle is prefaced by clear pronouncements of the outcome (2341b-43, 2397-2400, 2419b-20, 2423b-24). The mood is reinforced by Beowulf's recalling of Herebeald's death at the hands of his brother Hæthcyn, the Old Man's Lament, the wars of the Swedes and the Geats, and Hygelac's death. The battle itself is a sequence of bitter disappointments: the shield protects

Beowulf for a shorter time than it should, for the first time in his life he does not prevail, the sword blade fails ('swa hyt no sceolde,' 2585b), 'he who once had ruled a people suffered distress enveloped in fire' (2594b-95). But the final reversal is in Beowulf's favor. It becomes clear in his dying words:

> Ic ðas leode heold
> fiftig wintra;   næs se folccyning,
> ymbesittendra   ænig ðara,
> þe mec guðwinum   gretan dorste,
> egesan ðeon.   Ic on earde bad
> mælgesceafta,   heold min tela,
> ne sohte searoniðas,   ne me swor fela
> aða on unriht.   Ic ðæs ealles mæg
> feorhbennum seoc   gefean habban;
> forðam me witan ne ðearf   Waldend fira
> morðorbealo maga,   þonne min sceaceð
> lif of lice   (2732b-43a).

(I ruled this people for fifty winters; no king of any neighboring people dared attack me with warriors, threaten me with terror. On earth I awaited my destiny, bore myself well, sought no treacherous quarrels, nor swore unrightful oaths. Though sick with mortal wounds, I may have joy of all this. Therefore the Ruler of men need not reproach me for the murder of kinsmen when life slips from my body.)

In other words, Beowulf has lived in a way that allows him to die with satisfaction, with 'joy of all this.' He has remembered that he will die and lived accordingly so that he need not fear the judgment of the Ruler of men. His life has been mindful of death. Everything in it has been a momentary release from anguish, but the final release is secure.

The drift of the poet's thematic design should now be clear. *Beowulf* is a kind of *memento mori* dwelling insistently on the transitoriness of earthly things. It works in a way quite analogous to the verse epistle of consolation addressed by the *Beowulf* poet's contemporary Alcuin to the afflicted brethren of Lindisfarne after the viking raid of 793.[22] Alcuin uses both the life of universal history and the life of the individual to illustrate the scourge of fortune. Kingdoms fall—witness the fate of Babylon, Persia, Rome, Jerusalem, Africa, Spain, and Italy. 'This general ill,' Alcuin suggests wanly, 'relieves individual woes' (line 71). But the individual also succumbs, as Alcuin is not slow to visualize in one of those clinical descriptions of old age in which the *memento mori* excels. The only refuge in this secular wasteland is the hope of heaven.

> Your (Christ's) people await another life in the kingdom of heaven,
> Where sweet peace prevails and no battles are fought.

[22]The poem is printed in *Monumenta Germaniae historica: Poetae latini aevi carolini*, I, ed. Ernestus Duemmler (Berlin: Apud Weidmannos, 1881; rpt. 1964), 229-35. The letters written by Alcuin on the same occasion are excerpted and translated by Stephen Allott, *Alcuin of York c. A.D. 732 to 804: His Life and Letters* (York: William Session Ltd., 1974), pp. 36-41. The originals are to be found in *Monumenta Germaniae historica: Epistolae karolini aevi*, II, ed. Ernestus Duemmler (Berlin: Apud Weidmannos, 1895), 42-60 (epistolae 16-22).

As fire tempers gold, tribulation cleanses the just
So that a purer soul will rise to heaven (87-90).

And again:

Thus almighty God will test holy men with cruel
Lashes, only to bestow joyful rewards in heaven (95-96).

Alcuin's technique and message are not unlike those of the *Beowulf* poet, who is deeply preoccupied with the ephemeral nature of history and the hero. *Beowulf* is a poem essentially about mutability. The structure is not some elaborate scheme of internal correspondences, but a simple wave pattern of hope and despair redeemed only by the promise of permanent release. The traditional episodes of heroic poetry are organized according to the notion that life is unstable and is lent stability only by trust in the hereafter.

The result of this process is a larger, quasi-epic narrative illustrating the mutability of the heroic life. The poet drew his settings from the scenic repertory of the older heroic lay, but he strung these traditional scenes together with a moralizing commentary in the form of digressions, flashbacks, anticipations, authorial remarks, reflective speeches, and a persistent emphasis on unexpected reversals—all tending to underscore the peaks and valleys of human experience. In working toward an epic form, he did not transcend his tradition by creating new types of scenes, but only by introducing multiple occurrences of the old types, and of course by dilating the individual scenes. The scenery itself is traditional. What is new is the way in which the poet combines and adapts the inherited scenes. He tells us clearly enough that he knows the heroic lay because he includes references to it in his digressions. But his aim is to supersede the old form, to find a broader conception which subsumes the old one. The short lays become parenthetical exempla to serve his new purpose. He surpasses the limitations of the antecedent form, the quick succession of six or eight deeply but roughly etched scenes in which the action exhausts itself without probing the implications. His poem may be viewed as a study of the unstated implications in the anterior lay. It questions the nature of heroic success and failure by playing them off against each other in constant alternation.

Ups and downs are of course the narrative skeleton of any medieval battle sequence. The hero even in romance takes a teeth-rattling blow on the helmet, sags to one knee, and loses consciousness for a split second before he finally prevails. What distinguishes *Beowulf* is that the rise and fall of expectations is so much a part of the poetic fabric and is so consistently fixed in the reader's perception of the action by the use of explicit outbursts of joy and woe, harangues, personal discomfitures, and personal resolutions. The affiliation with heroic poetry may be justified for the poem in the revised sense that it pits the heroic temperament not against a hostile world, but against a mutable world. Traditional heroism confronts a stable spirit with stable misfortune—it is limited because it pits one mentality against one contingency. Beowulf pits a scale of emotions against a scale of conditions, good and bad. The outlook is richer and more supple.

In the final encounter with the dragon the peaks and valleys of experience tend to collapse into a uniform mournfulness over a life committed to heroism, but confined by the decrees of mortality. The power of youth is reduced to the moral stance of old age. In one sense Beowulf's record of prowess becomes meaningless. But in a larger sense, his struggle with mutability acquires a sanction unknown to pre-Christian heroic poetry because it is crowned with the certainty of divine approval. For the vivid single catastrophe of the heroic lay, into which the hero plunges without reflection or hope, the *Beowulf* poet has substituted a long life seasoned by contemplative moments and dignified by the promise of salvation. The warrior king who has borne himself well through the vagaries of fortune, so insistently illustrated by the poet's narrative rhythm, has earned the traditional hero's good name and the Christian hero's future reward.

Beowulf in Literary History

By Joseph Harris

Patristic, archetypal, new critical—these and other worthy critical trends teach a great deal about the form and meaning of Old English poetic texts, but without wishing to say anything against motherhood or apple pie, I would like to suggest that our preoccupation with interpretation since Tolkien's famous lecture—coupled perhaps with resignation over the impossibility of establishing facts—has drawn energies away from the healthy traditional approach that seeks an order of works: that is, from literary history. Recent work suggests, though, that the flight from literary history that seems characteristic of the 1950s and '60s is coming to an end. In other chronological fields there is surely a vigorous revival of literary history going on, especially in the form that interests me here: namely, how a later writer read and reacted to his source or influence. Admittedly the difficulties of constructing a *psychologically* based literary history in the manner of Harold Bloom in the anonymity of the Old English period are insurmountable, and when we enquire into the inter-textuality of Old English poetry, the terms of the question must be broader, often generic rather than specific to a textual source. But in the case of *Beowulf*, at least, there is some evidence at hand. For I mean it literally and not merely as a fashionable chiasm when I say that the reason we do not have an adequate picture of *Beowulf* in literary history is that we have ignored literary history within *Beowulf*.

Though I mean to argue that *Beowulf* has very extensive clues to its own prehistory, I do not interpret this in the sense of Berendsohn's *Vorgeschichte* or Genzmer's *skandinavische Quellen* or in the sense of the much disparaged and little read older dissectors.[1] *Beowulf* no doubt "grew" (in the organic metaphor) out of preceding stages, but I do not propose to consider its prehistory in terms of growth but of literary reception, a concept that implies perspective, attitude, and intention. In a literary history which is not mindlessly organic but composed of acts of reception, *Beowulf* seems to resemble great works like Goethe's *Faust* and Eliot's *Waste Land*, and especially Chaucer's *Canterbury Tales*—works that embodied new literary forms in their periods but which, nevertheless, were emphatically oriented toward the literature of their past. Such works are generically synthetic and punctuate or terminate a period,

---

[1]Felix Genzmer, "Die skandinavische Quellen des Beowulfs," *Arkiv för nordisk filologi*, 65 (1950), 17-62; Walter A. Berendsohn, *Zur Vorgeschichte des "Beowulf," mit einem Vorwort von Professor Otto Jespersen* (Copenhagen: Levin & Munksgaard, 1935). *Beowulf* is cited from Fr. Klaeber, ed., *Beowulf and the Fight at Finnsburg*, 3rd ed. rev. (Boston: Heath, 1950) but without macrons.

Reprinted, by permission, from *Pacific Coast Philology* 17 (1982), 16-23.

summarizing the literary past and seeming either to generate no direct progeny or to devour their own by overshadowing them in the course of subsequent literary history. For want of an established term I will call them *summae litterarum*. The *Canterbury Tales*, the clearest case of such a literary *summa*, is most obviously an anthology of medieval genres, including examples of fabliau, miracle of the Virgin, Breton lay, tail-rhyme and other types of romance, sermon, exemplum, and so on. The diversity poses the major critical problem of the *Canterbury Tales*, the problem of unity or the "idea" of the work. No one will dispute, however, that the *Canterbury Tales* can be said to present Chaucer's reading or reception of high medieval literature. In the following literary period there are spurious tales and spurious links and all manner of Chaucerian influence, but no rival work in the new form achieved high status in literary history. The *summa*, when it is a masterpiece, seems necessarily to leave behind a void.

Beowulf criticism, fixated on the unifying "idea" and determined to follow Tolkien in restoring the monsters to the center, has overlooked the poem's anthology-like characteristics and therefore its place in literary history. The *Beowulf*ian *summa* includes genealogical verse, a creation hymn, elegies, a lament, a heroic lay, a praise poem, historical poems, a flyting, heroic boasts, gnomic verse, a sermon, and perhaps less formal oral genres. In addition, a number of other genres are alluded to, just as Chaucer alludes to drama; but without paraphrases, the generic terms—for example, *spell*—are difficult to interpret.[2] As a whole, then, *Beowulf* presents a unique poet's unique reception of the oral genres of the Germanic early middle ages; like the *Canterbury Tales* it was retrospective and comprehensive, *summa*-rizing a literary period in a literary form so new and so masterful that it apparently inspired no imitators.

The constituent genres of *Beowulf* fall into two groups, those that are formally "introduced" or "marked" and those that are only "included" or "unmarked." The formally introduced genres are the heroic lay of Finnsburg, the creation hymn, the praise poem on Beowulf by the *gilphlæden guma*, the lament of the *Geatisc meowle*, the choric praise of the twelve riders, the elegy of the father for his hanged son, and several heroic vaunts. More doubtfully marked are the lament of the last survivor, the flyting, and some of the vaunts. Among the definitely unmarked, simply included genres, I will mention the genealogical introduction, the Offa-Modthryth digression, the gnomes, Beowulf's death-song, and two still more obliquely included texts: the Ingeld-Freawaru digression and Hygelac's raid on the Lower Rhine. Special problems for this approach are presented by Hrothgar's sermon, Beowulf's final salute, Wiglaf's *comitatus* speech, and the prophecy of the messenger; in fact all the constituent texts, whether they may safely be taken to represent genres or not, call for elaborate individual discussion. And by now you have realized that what I am presenting here is not the *product of*, but a *program for* research on *Beowulf* in literary history. The method I propose to follow is exemplified by two recent articles on the flyting between Beowulf and Unferth; these articles, by Carol Clover and me, attempt to establish the normal form of the flyting

---

[2]David R. Howlett, "Form and Genre in *Beowulf*," *SN*, 46 (1974), 309-25, makes an interesting, systematic attempt to interpret such terms, but the internal evidence alone is not sufficient.

as a genre by examining its occurrences outside *Beowulf* and then to characterize the *Beowulf* poet's "reading" of that genre.[3] It is a chancy and demanding method and a sprawling program, and potential objections against the philological circularity and pan-Germanic approach will already have occurred to you.

Those objections must remain unanswered here, and I have time only for a brief sample analysis of two constituent genres, the first included or unmarked, the second clearly introduced. Lines 4 through about 64 are, of course, recognized in *Beowulf* scholarship as a genealogy but have not, I think, been compared to genealogical poetry outside *Beowulf*. The lineage, you remember, is Scyld Scefing—Beowa or Beowulf I—High Healfdene—and the children of Healfdene: Heorogar, Hrothgar, Halga *til*, and a daughter. Verse genealogies, or such as were originally in verse, are to be found in relevant sources from Tacitus to Jordanes and on to *Hyndluljóð*,[4] but the best comparison is offered by the surviving group of skaldic genealogical poems from Old Norse: the *Ynglingatal* of Þjóðólfr ór Hvini from the late ninth century, perhaps just before 875; the *Háleygjatal* of Eyvindr Finnsson *skaldaspillir* from the 980s; and *Nóregs konunga tal* by an anonymous Icelander of about 1190.[5] In addition, there is the Theodoric stanza on the Swedish Rök Stone, which is drawn from a poem that resembles *Ynglingatal* so closely in meter and content that it takes the extant generic evidence back before 850.[6] The peculiarity of these Norse royal genealogical poems that especially links them with the opening of *Beowulf* is the emphasis on the death and burial of the rulers;[7] in *Ynglingatal*, for example, most of the twenty-seven surviving links

---

[3]Joseph Harris, "The *senna*: From Description to Literary Theory," *Michigan Germanic Studies*, 5 (1979), 65-74; Carol J. Clover, "The Germanic Context of the Unferþ Episode," *Speculum*, 55 (1980), 444-68; similar assumptions govern part of Lars Lönnroth's "Hjálmar's Death Song and the Delivery of Eddic Poetry," *Speculum*, 46 (1971), 1-20.

[4]Edited in *Edda: Die Lieder des Codex Regius nebst verwandten Denkmälern*, ed. G. Neckel, 4th ed. rev. Hans Kuhn (Heidelberg: Winter, 1962).

[5]These and all other skaldic poems referred to are edited in Finnur Jónsson, ed., *Den norsk-islandske Skjaldedigtning*, 4 vols. (Copenhagen, 1908-15) [AI-AII texts according to the manuscripts; BI-BII corrected texts with Danish translations]; standard discussions are in Jan de Vries, *Altnordische Literaturgeschichte*, 2nd ed. rev., 2 vols. (Berlin: de Greuyter, 1964-67). *Ynglingatal* is also in editions of *Ynglinga saga* (in Snorri's *Heimskringla*); especially handy is Elias Wessén, ed., Snorri Sturluson, *Ynglinga saga*, Nordisk filologi, A:6 (Stockholm, Copenhagen, Oslo: 1964). Good brief accounts of *Ynglingatal* may be found in Wessén, pp. xii-xviii; Hallvard Magerøy, "Ynglingatal" in *Kulturhistorisk leksikon for nordisk Middelalder fra vikingatid til reformationstid*, 20 (Copenhagen: Rosenkilde and Bagger, 1976), cols. 362-64; and de Vries, I, 131-36; full discussion in Walter Åkerlund, *Studier över Ynglingatal*, Skrifter utgivna av vetenskapssocieteten i Lund, 23 (Lund: Gleerup, 1939).

[6]Brief statements on the connection of the Rök Stone with *Ynglingatal* may be found in Magerøy, col. 364 and in de Vries, I, 132; fuller discussion in Åkerlund, especially pp. 177-89. There are no brief general accounts of the Rök Stone itself; see Elias Wessén, *Runstenen vid Röks kyrka*, Kgl. Vitterhets Historie och Antikvitets Akademiens handlingar, Filologisk-filosofiska serien, 5 (Stockholm: Almqvist and Wiksell, 1958).

[7]Snorri's "Prologus" says that in *Ynglingatal thirty* ancestors are listed and the death and place of burial of *each* is reported: "[*Ynglingatal*] . . . í því kvæði eru nefndir xxx. langfeðga hans og sagt frá dauða hvers þeira og legstað" [Wessén, *Ynglinga saga*, p. 1]. If so, the twenty-seven extant links must have been preceded by three about Odin, Njǫrðr, and Freyr, though there are some difficulties with this assumption; clearly, however, Snorri was exaggerating in

tell of the king's manner of death, e.g. stanza 19: "Brave Óttarr fell under the claws of the eagle before the weapons of the Danes; the eagle, come from afar, trod him with bloody foot." Often the grave site or the mode of burial is recorded: for example, stanza 6: "And I have often asked knowledgeable men about the corpse of the king, where [King] Dómarr was carried onto the roaring-killer-of-Hálfr [i.e. onto the funeral pyre]; now I know that the descendant of Fjǫlnir [i.e. King Dómarr], dead of disease, was cremated at Fyrir." In many of the deaths the element of Fate is emphasized; for example, stanza 32: "And Hveðrungr's maid [that is, death] invited [Hálfdanr] the third prince out of this world to a rendezvous, when [he] . . . had used up the life assigned by the norns; and the victorious men [i.e. Hálfdanr's men] buried their prince at Borre."

Clearly Þjóðólfr's difficult poem poses great problems of its own, and I am open to the charge of trying to explain the unknown by the more unknown; but I do believe the similarities with *Beowulf* are striking and that *Ynglingatal* is quite genuine and just as old as it is supposed to be.[8] Not only is it old, but it works out of an established tradition. This is supported by Jordanes, who knew that the Gothic royal family had a genealogy in which not only parentage was recorded but also the place where each member was born and where he died.[9] Irish and Welsh partial parallels are cited for the graves of *Ynglingatal*,[10] but *Beowulf* shows a more closely analogous combination of elements at an earlier date and in a literary tradition that is unquestionably closely related.

For *Beowulf* has the same conjunction of genealogy with emphasis on death and funeral; fate, too, is prominent: "Him ða Scyld gewat to gescæphwile. . ." [l. 26]. Even the element of mystery that attends Scyld's end, both his passing and his funeral, is paralleled by many of the Ynglings; we might, for example, compare Scyld's voyage, still living (*felahror*), into the unknown ("Men ne cunnon / secgan to soðe . . . hwa þæm hlæste onfeng" [ll. 50b-52]) to King Sveigðir who disappeared alive into a cliff, enticed by supernatural creatures (st. 2). Of course, *Beowulf*'s genealogy is both short and swollen with descriptive and didactic remarks; the funeral outweighs and interrupts the genealogy (but this is true of *Ynglingatal* also); and Beowa, Healfdene, and the sons of Healfdene are completely overshadowed by Scyld. Of Beowa we learn that he ruled "lange þrage," but his death is only implicit; and the same can be said of Healfdene, who ruled "þenden lifde." We clearly cannot take *Ynglingatal* as *the model* from which *Beowulf* diverged; Þjóðólfr's poem is itself almost certainly a tour-de-force that takes a free hand with an old

---

the second part of his statement since the grave sites are reported for only about nine Ynglings (cf. Magerøy).

[8]For references to the long debate over the age of *Ynglingatal* see Åkerlund. The connection between the Swedish genealogy in *Beowulf* and *Ynglingatal* is, of couse, well known in Old English scholarship, but the formal analogue is not; I hope to go into both in depth in another paper.

[9]Jordanes, *De origine actibusque Getarum*, ed. T. Mommsen, Monumenta Germaniae Historica, A. A. 5, 1 (Berlin: Weidmann, 1882), p. 76 (ch. 13): "quorum genealogia [read: genealogiam] ut paucis percurram vel quis quo parente genitus est aut unde origo coepta, ubi finem effecit, absque invidia, qui legis, vera dicentem ausculta"; cf. de Vries, I, 134.

[10]Andreas Heusler, *Die altgermanische Dichtung*, 2nd. ed. rev. (Potsdam: Athenaion, 1941), pp. 93-94; Irish models are dismissed by de Vries, I, 132; discussed at length by Åkerlund.

form.[11] But it appears that the *Beowulf* poet, from a somewhat similar starting point, has made changes not unlike those he made in the flyting: namely, condensation, elliptical suggestion of the subtext, some rearrangement, and a good deal of selective expansion. And, of course, he has integrated the genealogy into his poem as a whole, partly with the often-noted funeral-to-funeral procession. Heusler considers Norse verse of the type of *Ynglingatal* to be fundamentally praise poetry that appropriates a form from memorial or listing verse (pp. 93, 129). No doubt this is right as far as it goes, but the connections with cult were surely at least as important. In any case, the *Beowulf* poet has partly stripped away the less relevant praising function and perhaps partly converted it to direct didacticism; thus we have "þæt wæs god cyning" [l. 11b] and the like, but also "Swa sceal (geong g)uma gode gewyrcan, / fromum feohgiftum on fæder (bea)rme. . ." [ll. 20-21].

My proposals about a second example, the panegyric of the *gilphlæden guma*, should be a little less controversial. Hrothgar's thane composed a poem about *sið Beowulfes*, the exploit of fighting with Grendel [ll. 867b-915]. The content of the opening praise passage is not related, only the manner of its composition or recitation ("on sped," "soðe gebunden"), and that in very few lines; but the scop, if we may call him that, went on to tell all he knew about Sigemund, and this is paraphrased in twenty-five lines. There follows a paraphrase of about twelve lines on the negative example of Heremod and a sudden reversion to Beowulf and back to Heremod at the close of the passage. The classic question, then, is whether the generic subtext here consisted of one (imaginary) praise poem plus two narrative heroic lays or whether somehow Sigemund and Heremod were *within* the praise poem. Klaeber, Heusler, and probably most other scholars have thought there were three poems underlying the passage, the second two being, in Klaeber's words "short epic poems comparable in scale to *The Fight at Finnsburg*";[12] if this is true, the Sigemund and Heremod stories certainly burst the limits of the heroic lay— both as to form and content—as it was defined by Heusler. But I would suggest that Hoops and de Boor, who regarded the entire passage as summary of one elaborate praise poem, were right.[13] The main evidence must be the structure of the passage, beginning and ending with praise of Beowulf, and in between, two exempla, one positive, one negative; the exempla are syntactically intertwined with each other and at the end with the paraphrased praise of

[11]It also *incorporates* older genealogical verse (de Vries, I, 134-36; Wessén, p. xiv).

[12]Klaeber, p. 158; Heusler, pp. 152, 125.

[13]Johannes Hoops, *Beowulfstudien*, Anglistische Forschungen, 74 (Heidelberg: Winter, 1932), pp. 52-55, and *Kommentar zum Beowulf* (Germanische Altertumskunde, ed. Hermann Schneider (Munich: Beck, 1938), p. 410. My structural analysis is similar to that of Hoops; de Boor's idea of the type of poem at stake is not quite the same as mine or Hoops': "Er, der Kenner der 'alten Geschichten,' beginnt Beowulfs Kampf vorzutragen . . . und geht danach zu dem Liede von Sigmunds Drachenkampf über. Das weicht vom nordischen Fürstenpreise weit ab. [. . .] Die Betonung, dass der Sänger in alten Geschichten bewandert war, der unmittelbare Übergang zu einer solchen 'alten Geschichte' als Gegenbild des Grendelkampfes, machen es genugsam klar, wie sich der Beowulfdichter dieses Preislied dachte. Es war ihm Ereignisdichtung in epischer Darstellung mit fortlaufender Handlung und mit den Stil- und Darstellungsmitteln des heroischen Liedes. Lebendige Wechselrede, die Seele heroischer Handlungsführung, wird aus diesem Typus des epischen Preisliedes nicht wegzudenken sein."

Beowulf. A sense of unity is also contributed by the clear ending of the whole passage with *hwilum* [l. 916] and a return to the present scene of the cavalcade. The *hwilum*-sentence of l. 916, with its spontaneous horse race, is obviously a reprise of the *hwilum* sentence of l. 864; together they frame the *hwilum*-introduced passage on the praise poem. This technique of making a return to the present is used by the poet after the Finnsburg song, and a comparison of the "marking" of the *gleomannes gyd* of ll. 1063-1160 with that of the *spel* of the *cyninges þegn* in ll. 867b-916 reinforces, I think, the impression that a single praise poem is the imagined subtext.

But is there any external support for this view? Pindar offers similar structures, but not in a genetically related literature. The earliest surviving Norse praise poems, however, *can* be brought to bear on this problem since two of the earliest do contain narratives within a praising framework. The great difference, however, between on the one hand Bragi Boddason's *Ragnarsdrápa* and Þjóðólfr's *Haustlǫng* and on the other hand our *Beowulf* passage is that these two skaldic praise poems of the first and second half of the ninth century purport to describe scenes on painted shields. A severe objection, but two other early Norse praise poems, *Eiríksmál* and *Hákonarmál*, can be cited to support the traditional appearance of Sigemund, Fitela, and Heremod within a *Preislied*, even if their stories are not told there; and there is a similar collocation of Hermóðr and Sigmundr in *Hyndluljóð*, a late Eddic poem with Danish and perhaps English connections. A better connoisseur of skaldic verse than I might be able to produce other examples of praise poems which are also spiced with narrative exempla; Kormákr's *Sigurðardrápa* of about 960 comes to mind for its brief mythic allusions, and Snorri refers to a lost skaldic praise poem that embodied the Sigurd story.[14] All these clues together suggest that it would not be unreasonable to reconstruct the *Beowulf* poet's subtext here, whether it in some sense really existed or more probably was imaginary and modeled on a type, as a praise poem with symmetrical and traditionally sanctioned heroic exempla.[15]

Short shrift for our two sample analyses, but I must return to the view from Olympus and ask again "What kind of literary work is *Beowulf*, and does the *summa*-notion square with what little we know of other attitudes of the poet?" In my opinion the swollen lay theory may well apply to *Waldere* but does not fit the *Beowulf*ian *summa* very well. On the other hand Vergilian inspiration, not Vergilian imitation, probably did spark the *Beowulf* poet's reaction to the antecedent literature in his own tradition. In that act of reception he created a genre *sui generis*, and the agreement between his *literary* reaction and his historical, religious, and ethical reactions is striking. Charles Donahue and others and, especially elegantly, Marijane Osborn have given us a convincing picture of a poet aware of historical depth, careful to speak *to* his audience

---

[14]Þorvaldr veili was shipwrecked and saved himself on a skerry "ok hǫfðu þeir illt til klæða ok veðr kalt; þá orti hann kvæði, er kallat er: kviðan skjálfhenda eða: drápan steflausa, ok kveðit eftir Sigurðar sǫgu" (*Edda Snorra Sturlusonar*, ed. Thorleifr [sic] Jónsson [Copenhagen, 1875], pp. 211-12 [=*Háttatal*, Ch. 35 (36)], this is the only edition available to me).

[15]Heusler would not agree; on the shield poems he writes: "Auch zu dieser sehr eigentümlichen Art des Preislieds sehen wir keine südgermanischen Vorstufen," and he goes on to cite the predictable Irish influence (p. 129).

with proper epistemological assumptions but to speak *of* his characters with sympathy and cognizance of their limits.[16] Such an author could be expected to act similarly toward the texts and genres of a passing era.

But what about this notion of a genre *sui generis*, does it really exist? For all their multi-generic originality we *can* trace the inspiration for works like *Faust*, the *Waste Land*, and the *Canterbury Tales*. At the risk of further exaggerating the catalogue-like qualities of *Beowulf*, I would like to suggest a native source for the *summa*-attitude in *Beowulf*. The only major early Germanic genre that *Beowulf* does *not* contain is *Merkverse* or mnemonic verse; Hrothgar's scop does *not* regale his audience with an analogue of "Ætla weold Hunum, Eormanric Gotum / Becca Baningum, Burgendum Gifica." Could it be because the thula-impulse had been absorbed into the very frame of *Beowulf*? If so, we could see a progression of literary thulas from *Widsith* through *Deor* to *Beowulf*. In *Widsith* a fictional scop portrays his life in the most optimistic terms, listing heroes and kings, the substance of songs; he is too close to the literary tradition he sings in to see it in terms of form. *Deor* brings a sadder and wiser perspective, a sober answer to *Widsith*: heroes and kings are still listed and their stories summarized, but they stand in the service of a fragile consolation. *Beowulf* integrates its thula into narrative to a much greater degree than either *Widsith* or *Deor*, and with still more perspective the *Beowulf* poet includes the literary *forms*, the oral genres, along with the poets and heroes as aspects of the past or rapidly passing world of his forebears. Someone has said that *Beowulfes Beorh*, as Grundtvig named the poem,[17] is a barrow for heroic society; if so, we must not forget, among the hidden treasures there, the lost literature.

[16] Marijane Osborn, "The Great Feud: Scriptural History and Strife in *Beowulf*," *PMLA*, 93 (1978), 973-81; Charles Donahue, "*Beowulf*, Ireland and the Natural Good," *Traditio*, 7 (1949-51), 263-77, and "*Beowulf* and Christian Tradition: A Reconsideration from a Celtic Stance," *Traditio*, 21 (1965), 55-116.

[17] N. F. S. Grundtvig, ed., *Beowulfes Beorh eller Bjovulfs-Drapen* (Copenhagen, 1861).

Frame Narratives and Fictionalization:
Beowulf as Narrator

By Laurence N. de Looze

The author (or authors) of *Beowulf* presents all events of the epic—the digressions and the historical and heroic exempla as well as the main story of the protagonist's three great battles—as unqualifiedly true. Thus the voice of the implied author is authoritative at all times. It gives no sign of being unreliable, nor does it invent "fictional" events.[1] The narrator's method consists in selecting and emphasizing certain incidents, not in inventing them; and if modern scholars do not for a moment believe that the fights between Beowulf and his three adversaries actually took place—as opposed, say, to accepting that Hygelac indeed died on a raid in Frisia or believing that feuds between the Swedes and the Geats were not unknown in the sixth century—this discrimination is not due to any shift in the voice of the implied author but rather to the findings of modern historical scholarship and the simple fact that we no longer believe in monsters.

Even when portions of the *Beowulf*ian narrative are displaced from the authorial to one of the other narrating voices in the poem, the accounts of events are equally "reliable." In the various lays and sermons the speakers do not fantasize or invent their stories. When Hrothgar's scop, for example, takes up the tale of Finn and his followers (ll. 1067 ff.),[2] he is not fictionalizing but relating an old story well known to the *Beowulf* audience and probably accepted as true.[3] The voice of Hrothgar's scop proves as authoritative as that of the (implied) author. When one of the Danish thanes improvises a lay on the return from Grendel's mere (ll. 867 ff.), he is not "making up" a story; rather he weaves together the tales, separated in time but linked in theme, of Beowulf's and Sigemund's exploits. His is an artistic accomplishment, to be sure, but not a fictionalizing act. Hrothgar, too, draws on the past for his exemplar of the baleful king par excellence, Heremod, in his sermon to the young Beowulf, but Hrothgar by no means invents either events or exemplar. Hrothgar encourages Beowulf to use the lessons of the past to guide his course

---

[1]Throughout this paper "fictional" refers to an event so perceived by the speakers and/or audience of *Beowulf*. In this respect the term is indifferent to the ontological status modern scholars might accord to events of *Beowulf* deemed historically true or "made up." Also, I have opted, for simplicity's sake, to refer to the author(s) of the poem as "he"; in no wise, however, do I intend to imply any decision regarding who, what gender, or how many persons might have been involved in the composition of *Beowulf*.

[2]All references to line numbers and all citations refer to Fr. Klaeber, ed., *Beowulf and the Fight at Finnsburg*, 3d ed. (Lexington, Mass: D. C. Heath, 1950).

[3]In fact, Hrothgar's scop is corroborated by the independent Lay of Finn, there being "no discrepancies in subject-matter between the two versions" (Klaeber, p. 236).

Reprinted from *Texas Studies in Language and Literature* 26 (1984), 145-56, by permission of the editors and the author.

of action in the present, a method to which Beowulf will return later in life but which will prove inadequate, as we shall see. Even when an account of a particular incident is disputed, as in the flyting exchange between Beowulf and Unferth, the difference of opinion concerns not the facts of the story but their interpretation, as Carol Clover has recently shown.[4] Whether Breca and Beowulf were irresponsible and who got the better of the other are disputed questions, but not the fact that both boys leaped into the water.

In *Beowulf* there is, however, one exception to this otherwise consistent lack of fictionalizing: one instance where a character makes up and narrates a wholly fictional event. Curiously this lone fiction is told by Beowulf. Amid the flashbacks to the Swedish-Geatish wars and just prior to the final battle which Beowulf is increasingly aware will cost him his life, the protagonist narrates two tales. The first, the story of Haethcyn and Herebeald (ll. 2425-43), is historical. The second, the tale of a father forced to watch his son swing on the gallows (ll. 2444-62a), is fictional. This incident alone is not presented as drawn from the annals of Germanic history, although such incidents may well have occurred. Why should Beowulf create a fiction at this point in the text? And why should the author find it fitting that Beowulf, and only he, do so?

An analysis of the structure of the Swedish-Geatish digressions will reveal, I think, that the author carefully frames the protagonist's predicament and the narratives which Beowulf tells as a result of that dilemma. In his narratives Beowulf attempts to come to terms with his critical situation; he explores possible responses to the challenge before him, first by reviewing a historical analogue, then by creating a fantasy. This "heroic simile" is a fictional projection which allows Beowulf to distance himself from the clash of obligations facing him, to examine them more objectively, and to resolve the Hamlet-like question of whether—and how—to act or not to act.

Before proceeding to a close consideration of Beowulf's fictionalizing, let us consider the context in which it arises. The scene of the father's lament forms the structural center of a series of framing episodes, each a digression on—or, if you will, a "reflection" on and of—Beowulf's dilemma as he approaches his final battle. The backdrop to the lament scene associates two seemingly unrelated feuds: the long and murderous seesaw of wins and losses known as the Swedish-Geatish wars and the dragon's more immediate challenge. But then the two feuds are profoundly linked in that the outcome of the dragon conflict will greatly influence, perhaps even determine, the outcome of the wars. Beowulf's death in the fight with the dragon will mean a resumption of the Swedish-Geatish conflict and the near annihilation of the leaderless Geatish nation.

From a historical view Beowulf's fight with the dragon is one event—a decisive one—in the grand sweep of Swedish-Geatish relations. But in the second part of *Beowulf*, foreground and background are reversed; the *Beowulf*ian narrative brackets the Swedish-Geatish digressions within the events of the dragon's feud with Beowulf. The dragon is reawakened (l. 2287), and its attack occupies the narrative until line 2323, at which time the terror is made known to Beowulf (l. 2324) that his home and throne have been burned (ll. 2325-27).

[4]Carol Clover, "The Germanic Context of the Unferth Episode," *Speculum*, 55 (1980), 444-68.

This news causes a shift in Beowulf's plans. Although he begins preparations for revenge (ll. 2337-39), he already has an uncustomary sense of foreboding: "brēost innan wēoll / þēostrum geþoncum, swā him geþȳwe ne wæs" (ll. 2331-32). Nevertheless, because of his past successes, Beowulf has a tendency to underestimate his adversary. In contrast to the audience which has already been told unequivocally that Beowulf will not survive this fight (ll. 2341b-43a: *Sceolde lændaga / æþeling ærgōd ende gebīdan / worulde līfes*), Beowulf is of the opinion that he can still achieve victory. He does not "dread" the encounter and scorns the dragon's strength (ll. 2347b-49a: *nō hē him þā sæcce ondrēd / nē him þæs wyrmes wīg for wiht dyde, / eafoð ond ellen*).

In this shadow of Beowulf's impending battle, the Swedish-Geatish wars are evoked.[5] The first digression (ll. 2349b-96b) juxtaposes Hygelac's foolhardiness and its disastrous results with Beowulf's balance of action and thought in Frisia. Hygelac did what Beowulf might be tempted to do half a century later: to take action without considering the possible consequences or fully estimating the capabilities of the enemy. Hygelac's rashness in unnecessarily pursuing the Hetware stands in contrast to Beowulf's sobriety both in Frisia and in his deliberations before going to meet the dragon. Hygelac's fall to pride becomes a fall in battle, with the result that his kingdom is destablized. Beowulf, by contrast, has consistently acted when required, but has also restrained himself when that has seemed the better course. He avenged his lord in Frisia as was proper (ll. 2363-66) and came away with his life. But upon his return home, Beowulf became a model of restraint, *not* seizing the throne proffered him by Hygd, guarding it instead for Heardred. Indeed his restraint stabilized the realm if only for a generation. This first Swedish-Geatish digression ends by stressing Beowulf's continuing loyalty in later days (*uferan dōgrum*) to Heardred and his allies and to the principle of rightful succession through the support given to Eanmund and Eadgils (ll. 2391-96).

After this digression the poet returns briefly to the "present" of the poem. Here he shows us Beowulf's measured response to the dragon's provocation. In contrast to Hygelac, Beowulf does not act rashly. Rather he organizes a reconnaissance, staking out the dragon's barrow and gathering information on the nature and origin of the feud (ll. 2401-16). In so doing he begins to appreciate the magnitude of his adversary and the complexities of his situation. And complex it is, for it binds him to honor mutually conflicting obligations. The attack on his hall and the challenge to his authority demand that he take vengeance regardless of risks. Yet Beowulf has an equally strong responsibility to provide leadership to his people, a task which requires above all that he not sacrifice his life needlessly. These two demands are, of course, irreconcilable. Mournful, restless, and ready for death (ll. 2419b-20a), Beowulf sits down to

---

[5]In my analysis of the structure of the Swedish-Geatish digressions, I follow in some measure the divisions proposed by S. B. Greenfield in "Geatish History: Poetic Art and Epic Quality in *Beowulf*," *Neophilologus*, 47 (1963), 211. What Greenfield designates as the first Swedish-Geatish passage corresponds to my Swedish-Geatish Wars I (ll. 2349b-99a). Greenfield's second passage (ll. 2425-515) I have subdivided into its component narratives Haethcyn Episode 1, Father's Lament, Haethcyn Episode II, and Swedish-Geatish Wars II. I hesitate to call the whole of lines 2425-515 a passage on Geatish history (1) because the father's lament (ll. 2444-62a) does not portray a historical event and (2) because in line 2508b Beowulf returns to the present with an emphatic "Now shall . . ." (*Nu sceall . . .*) to utter a heroic boast (ll. 2510-15).

think aloud. And lest we forget how desperately Beowulf needs a solution to the insolvable, the authorial voice briefly reminds us, before the narrative is passed over to Beowulf for nearly a hundred lines (to l. 2514), that Beowulf's fate is very near (ll. 2423b-24: *nō þon lange wæs / feorh æþelinges flæsce bewunden*).

Beowulf takes up the narration at line 2425 with two events, one historical and one fictional, which we shall consider in detail shortly. For now let us simply observe that in both he investigates modes of response to conflicting and irresolvable demands. In lines 2425-43 he recounts the story of how Haethcyn accidently killed his brother Herebeald while hunting, an act for which vengeance was both imperative and impossible to exact since subject and object of the murder were of the same family. At line 2444 Beowulf relinquishes the Haethcyn episode, although unfinished, to embark on another narrative, the fantasy of a father forced to watch his condemned son swing on the gallows. This projection examines further the paradox of mutually irreconcilable obligations, inherent in the Haethcyn story and Beowulf's own situation, and Beowulf follows it to completion at line 2462a. At line 2462b Beowulf picks up the Haethcyn story again and completes it at 2471 with Hrethel's death. The *Beowulf*ian narrative (still in Beowulf's voice) returns now to the larger context of the Swedish-Geatish wars which preceded the introduction of the Haethcyn episode. After reviewing the Swedish-Geatish feuds and Hygelac's raid on Frisia from his own perspective,[6] Beowulf links the digression once more to his present feud with the dragon and the impending battle. At last the plot moves forward once more; Beowulf makes his heroic vows (ll. 2510-37) and goes to battle (l. 2538).

Thus a careful framing of dramatic episodes telescopes in to Beowulf's central fictional projection and then back out as follows:

1. Dragon Feud (ll. 2287-349a)
2. Swedish-Geatish Wars I (ll. 2349b-99a)
3. Haethcyn Episode I (ll. 2425-43)
4. Father's Lament (ll. 2444-62a)
3. Haethcyn Episode II (ll. 2462b-71)
2. Swedish-Geatish Wars II (ll. 2472-508a)
1. Dragon Feud (ll. 2508b ff.)

Or if we wish a less episodic division, we could describe the framing in terms of its temporal shifts. The narrative moves from present events (the dragon) to the past (the early days of the Swedish-Geatish conflicts) to a fictional time (the father's lament) and back again. Either analysis reveals the centrality of Beowulf's narrative of the grieving father. The only fantasized incident in *Beowulf* is encased in several layers of narrative shell.

When Beowulf begins his utterance (l. 2425), we have just heard of Hygelac's foolish raid on Frisia, from which national instability and a fresh round of internecine strife issued. Beowulf returns to a more distant past, to his youth—to when he was only seven years old. But far from bewailing any

---

[6]For discussions of the different points of view from which Geatish history is reviewed, see Greenfield, "Geatish History," pp. 212-16; and Arthur G. Brodeur, *The Art of Beowulf* (Berkeley: University of California Press, 1971), pp. 83-85.

loss of youthful vigor (as Hrothgar did when he recalled his youth, l. 2112), Beowulf seeks in past events an objective correlative to his present predicament. Leaping over the long series of raids and counterraids in the Swedish-Geatish wars, he returns to the time when the feud began, to how Haethcyn accidently killed Herebeald with a stray arrow. This tragic accident first destabilized the Geatish realm; it brought on Hrethel's death from grief, thus making the nation vulnerable to Swedish hostilities. Just as there is an interdependency between personal and international events that links Beowulf's fight with the dragon to the Swedish-Geatish wars—since the next "act" of the latter conflict depends on the outcome of the former—there is a similar linkage between affairs of family and affairs of state in the Haethcyn incident. Reference to Hrethel's death and the events which caused it can hardly be devoid of allusion to the wars which followed. The connection between tragic fratricide within the ruling house and internecine wars between ruling houses is both historical and psychological.

The Haethcyn-Herebeald episode invites comparison with the Swedish-Geatish wars in whose context it is inscribed. Both suggest that events are beyond human control, whether because of the freakish nature of chance or because of the snowballing of incessant violence. Both illustrate the fragility of "national security" in Germanic cultures. Hrethel's death opens his country to attack as surely as each act of vengeance in a feud will draw a counterraid. In both cases man is an unwitting partner swept along by events more powerful than he—which is also the case with Beowulf, as we shall see shortly. Yet the modes of action and response in the Haethcyn story are the very antitheses of those of the Swedish-Geatish wars. In the latter it is the recurrent cycle of vengeance that decimates the Swedish and Geatish nobility and ensures that the Swedes will be poised to attack once Beowulf is gone. But if the Swedish-Geatish wars illustrate the results of vengeance pressed with extreme vigor, the Haethcyn episode shows what happens when no vengeance is taken. In Hrethel's case it is precisely the inability to take action that causes such anguish. Since both the murdered and the murderer are Hrethel's sons, no satisfaction is possible. Forced to remain passive, he dies of grief, leaving his country vulnerable to attack. In sum, diametrically opposed responses to the call for vengeance have a common result. Consistent and vigorous vengeance or total inaction, the end is the same: death and disaster.

By evoking the Haethcyn-Herebeald episode, Beowulf evokes the two extremes of inaction (Hrethel's response) and excessive (re)action (characteristic of the wars), both of which lead to doom. The question we must ask here is why Beowulf should choose to recall the Swedish-Geatish conflict and why he should decide to narrate the Haethcyn episode at the particular moment he does. An answer to this question may reveal much not only about the psychology of the protagonist Beowulf but also about his perception of the limitations of the Germanic heroic ethos and about the function of his narratives within the poem as a whole.

I have already suggested that the Swedish-Geatish wars and the Haethcyn episode are associated not just with each other but also with the crisis facing Beowulf. More specifically, we might say that in the Haethcyn episode Beowulf seeks an object lesson for his own predicament. To guide him in the present he seeks a historical analogue which might illustrate strategies of action much as Hrothgar used Heremod as a negative exemplar. Thus in past incidents Beowulf can mentally test possible responses to the demand for vengeance. The Haethcyn-Herebeald incident is a well-chosen analogue because of the many correspondences between Hrethel's and Beowulf's respective predicaments. In both instances a man is faced with a "no win" situation in which he must decide whether to take vengeance; and in both cases to take or not to take vengeance will not alter the bleak results. For Hrethel, to take vengeance would be to wipe out his family; the logic of vengeance would oblige him to avenge one son on the other, then the second son on himself. Hrethel's only other option is to wither away in grief.[7] Beowulf's alternatives are no more promising. He can let the dragon destroy his realm, or he can enter into a battle which may claim his life and leave his realm to be ravaged by the Swedes. Furthermore, the historical analogue chosen by Beowulf literalizes the patriarchal relationship of Beowulf to his realm; the father is unable to save his charges through effective action. What is more, both episodes illustrate the same relationship between an individual leader and the larger historical sweep of events he cannot control. From Beowulf's death will follow a new series of wars, just as the first series flowed from the accidental death of Haethcyn. The freak accident is a kind of nightmarish correlative of the single combat in which one is fated to die. From Beowulf's point of view, the appearance of the dragon after a three-hundred-year sleep, and after the protagonist's peaceful reign of fifty years, must seem a freakish twist of events indeed. But then whole cycles of Germanic wars can be unleashed by the most unlikely event: the death of a single man, an arrow off course, a cup stolen.

In his choice of historical material, then, Beowulf can objectify and study his own dilemma. Far from taking rash action like Hygelac, Beowulf follows Hrothgar's example of making history instructive. Or at least he tries to. But the analogy, although well chosen, breaks down as all analogies inevitably must do. The dragon's appearance is freakish and unexpected, perhaps, but it is not accidental. The crisis facing Beowulf is not predicated upon chance as is the tragedy which undoes Hrethel. Events may be beyond Beowulf's control, but not because of pure hazard. There is a crucial element of free choice in Beowulf's situation that is lacking in the historical exemplum he reviews. Hrethel took no vengeance because none was possible. Beowulf, by contrast, is in a more delicate situation; he must choose between two courses of action, neither of which is satisfactory. Furthermore, the chance accident of the Haethcyn episode eliminates all social concerns and responsibilities save one: the ever present obligation to take revenge, which Hrethel cannot fulfill. But the anguish of Beowulf's plight is bound up with a considerably more complex web of societal institutions. To begin with, the pressures on a slave to gain favor with his master have precipitated the crisis.[8] Then there is the obligation

---

[7] Old Norse sources suggest that Óðinn created a third option when one son, Höð, shot and killed the other, Baldr. According to *Baldrs Draumar* (str. 11) and the *Völuspá* (str. 32)— and, with significant differences, Saxo Grammaticus's *Gesta Danorum*—Óðinn quickly begat on Rind a new son, Váli ("Bous" in Saxo), who took vengeance when only one day old. For Hrethel, however, this course of action is hardly feasible, since ordinary human beings cannot count on their progeny doing battle at such a tender age and, more important, because even if one son were avenged in this fashion murderer and murdered would still be within the same family.

[8] The reading *þēow* ("slave") in line 2223b is of course a restoration; in the manuscript

on Beowulf to take vengeance for the dragon's attack on his realm, an obligation which is indifferent to the effectiveness or the ultimate consequences of
such action. There is also the contrary demand on Beowulf to keep himself
alive—not to sacrifice himself needlessly, as Hygelac did. And finally there are
the demands of the heroic Germanic ethos which will go unheeded when Beowulf's retainers desert him on the field of battle, a fact Beowulf cannot yet
know but which he may in some measure sense.[9] In short, the poet depicts a
culture whose social institutions are strained almost to the breaking point. But
Beowulf has chosen an analogue from an earlier age, one more "innocent" or
at least more self-assured in its values, from which many of these cultural
tensions are absent. The analogy thus breaks down, and when it does, the
narrative of the Haethcyn episode must break off. History has been unable to
provide Beowulf with an example of a man in a "no win" paradox, bound by
certain social pressures to take revenge but constrained by others from doing
so. The wisdom of the past and Hrothgar's method of making history instructive are not adequate to the unique crisis facing Beowulf.

At this point Beowulf begins to fictionalize. Reference to past events has
failed to provide a model; so what he cannot find within known time, Beowulf
begins to search for outside of time: he fantasizes a scenario which expands
upon the conflicting demands of Hrethel's predicament in order to express
more aptly features of Beowulf's own paradoxical situation. It is perhaps
indicative of his desperation that Beowulf turns now to the fictive for answers
he cannot find in the real world. But if so, this shift also bears witness to his
sharp perception of the limitations of history as well as to the extraordinary
lengths to which he goes to determine the best course of action. Beowulf's
fictionalizing is, one might say, an excellent example of creative problem solv-
ing. Of course, there may have been well-known historical precedents for such
a scenario. But if so, it is all the more remarkable that Beowulf rejects history
and chooses instead to create through simile (*swa bið*) an analogy that is outside of time—a fictional setting into which he can project, study, and objectify
his own plight:

> Swā bið geōmorlīc   gomelum ceorle
> tō gebīdanne,   þæt his byre rīde   (2445)
> giong on galgan;   þonne hē gyd wrece
> sārigne sang,   þonne his sunu hangað
> hrefne tō hrōðre,   ond hē him helpe ne mæg
> eald ond infrōd   ænige gefremman.
> Symble bið gemyndgad   morna gehwylce   (2450)
> eaforan ellorsīð;   ōðres ne gȳmeð
> tō gebīdanne   burgum in innan
> yrfeweardas,   þonne se ān hafað
> þurh dēaðes nȳd   dæda gefondad.
> Gesyhð sorhcearig   on his suna būre   (2455)

---

only the thorn is legible. *Þegn* has also been proposed by W. W. Lawrence in "The Dragon
and His Lair in *Beowulf*", *PMLA*, 33 (1918), 551, 553-57. I follow Klaeber's reading *þ(ēow)*.

[9]Might not a certain prescience of cowardice within the ranks be inherent in Beowulf's
decision to have his men wait on the barrow, since, as he says, it is not an adventure for
them, nor fitting for any man but him alone (*Nis þæt ēower sīð / nē gemet mannes, nefn(e)
mīn ānes*; ll. 2532b-33)?

wīnsele wēstne,   windge reste
rēōte berofene,—   rīdend swefað,
hæleð in hoðman;   nis þær hearpan swēg,
gomen in geardum,   swylce ðær iū wǣron.
Gewīteð þonne on sealman,   sorhlēoð gæleð   (2460)
ān æfter ānum;   þuhte him eall tō rūm
wongas ond wīcstede.

In this poignant vision Beowulf uses a number of features which distance his narrative from any historical context and differentiate it from the earlier narrative of the Haethcyn-Herebeald episode. From the first-person voice with which he began the Haethcyn story (*Ic wæs syfanwintre*), Beowulf moves to the more impersonal, third-person voice. And from personal reminiscence in the past tense, he moves to the authenticating voice of the maximic present (*swa bið*), thus disassociating the narrative from chronological time.[10] But if the father's lament exists outside of time, it is nevertheless a more accurate evocation of Beowulf's paradoxical situation than time/history could provide. Beowulf again projects himself as a father figure, this time as an old man without progeny. Beowulf, heirless as is the old man after the death of his son, can give no thought "to gebīdanne burgum in innan / yrfeweardas" (ll. 2452-53a). The realm is the closest thing Beowulf has to an heir, and it is doomed regardless of which course of action Beowulf chooses.

More significantly, in his second narrative Beowulf replaces random chance with a conflict of obligations more like that plaguing him. Rather than being unable to take vengeance, as Hrethel was, the father of the condemned criminal finds himself subject to two strong social demands: one that he take vengeance for his son's death, the other that he take no action because his son was a condemned outlaw. The demands on Beowulf are remarkably similar: the pressure to take vengeance must be reconciled with the need to provide leadership and maintain the social administration (dependent principally on Beowulf's survival). But most important, Beowulf's fiction expresses his need to choose between unsatisfactory alternatives. The lamenting father can choose the societal obligation by which he will be bound, as does Beowulf. By replacing accidents with free choice and by substituting the obligation to fulfill two conflicting demands for the need to do the physically impossible, Beowulf creates a kind of miniature of the psychology of his own dilemma.

In his extended simile, Beowulf investigates the option of not taking action. He tries out in his projection the alternative he will discard subsequently: the old man decides to ignore the demand for vengeance. The results Beowulf sketches for such a decision are lethargy and isolation: The father takes to his bed (*Gewīteð þonne on sealman*, l. 2460) and sings sorrowful songs, one after another (*sorhlēoð gæleð / ān æfter ānum*, ll. 2460b-61a). In short, the father is headed the same way as Hrethel—to death by grief. Beowulf even makes the link between their respective emotional states explicit in the next sentence; he tells us that Hrethel felt likewise (ll. 2462b-84). Inaction, whether chosen or not, leads to disintegration and death in both of Beowulf's narratives.

It is here that Beowulf parts company with his fictional projection. Having

---

[10]For an analysis of the authenticating voice in Beowulf, see S. B. Greenfield, "The Authenticating Voice in *Beowulf*," *Anglo-Saxon England*, 5 (1976), 51-62.

explored in depth the passive alternative, he will now reject it for himself. Beowulf's own moment of inaction is a moment of reflection; it lasts no longer than the time it takes him to examine the pros and cons of his situation. He utters a couple of tales, but singing sorrowful song after sorrowful song to no effective end does not become a way of life for Beowulf. Fully cognizant of the limitations of the Germanic code, Beowulf nevertheless falls back on it as the better of two unsatisfactory alternatives. He remains faithful to the ethic he asserted many years before when, after Aeschere's death, he proclaimed to Hrothgar: "Ne sorga, snotor guma! Sēlre bi® æghwæm, / þaet hē his frēond wrece, þonne hē fela murne" (ll. 1384-85). Should we expect any different from Beowulf now? Indeed if the result of both alternatives is the death of the father figure—either by wasting away (inaction) or in the course of a feud (vengeance)—then for Beowulf to take action is nonetheless the more practical option because by fighting the dragon he at least has the hope of eliminating one of his people's prime enemies. The passive course would leave both the Swedes outside the Geatish realm and the dragon inside to be dealt with after Beowulf was gone.

Here Beowulf's fictional projection closes. He moves through the narrative frames back to the present, to his own problem. He places each episode carefully into its narrative frame. He acknowledges the psychological similarity between the fictional paradox and Hrethel's dilemma (ll. 2462b-71). Then he frames the Haethcyn episode within the "synn and sacu Swēona ond Gēata" which arose "syð®an Hrē®el swealt" (ll. 2472-508a). Finally Beowulf closes the narrative of the Swedish-Geatish wars by setting those events against the present hostilities of the dragon (ll. 2508b-09). With all this done, he at last utters his prebattle boast (ll. 2510-15), and the plot moves forward once more.

When Beowulf marches to his final battle, he does so after having carefully determined his course of action within the framework of the two polar strategies of response, active and passive. Illustrative of the active response are (1) the cycle of vengeance in the Swedish-Geatish wars and (2) the hasty action of Hygelac in his Frisian raid. The passive alternative is represented by (1) the impossibility of effective action in the Haethcyn episode and (2) the choice not to act in the fantasy of the father's lament. Through these events Beowulf is able to examine his own situation with increasing objectivity before deciding his own course of action—a middle course of considered action. In an effort to find a satisfactory solution, Beowulf reviews historical precedents, and when they fail he fictionalizes events in an attempt to resolve his own crisis, this fiction forming the structural center of a series of frame narratives. But in the end there are no solutions within the Germanic ethos, either in history or in Beowulf's imagination, and he has no recourse but to fall back on the heroic code so familiar to him: Beowulf decides to do battle. After such studied meditation he cannot be accused of having acted rashly or foolishly. Rather, in an effort to solve the insolvable, Beowulf reviews history and then creates a suitable fictional correlative to his situation before taking up arms. Seeking answers in history is the method of any man who wishes to temper *fortitudo* with *sapientia*. But the fictional projection adds something new. This uniqueness may well tell us something about the role of fiction and the fictionalizing process in Anglo-Saxon culture.

Grendel's Mother as Epic Anti-Type
of the Virgin and Queen

By Jane Chance

Throughout the epic *Beowulf*, Grendel's mother, rather oddly, is described in human and social terms, and through words like *wīf* and *ides* normally reserved for human women. She has the form of a woman (*idese onlīcnes*, 1351)[1] and is weaker than a man (1282ff) and more cowardly, for she flees in fear for her life when discovered in Heorot (1292-3). She is specifically called a *wīf unhȳre* (2120b), a "monstrous woman," and an *ides āglǣcwīf* (1259a), a "lady monster-woman." *Ides*, as we have seen in other literary works and as it is also used in *Beowulf*,[2] normally denotes "lady" and connotes either a queen or a woman of high social rank. But unlike most queens, Grendel's Mother fights her own battles, an activity that, as we have seen in *Maxims I*, 83-5, was normally practiced only by the Anglo-Saxon lord.[3]

As if to stress her inversion of the Anglo-Saxon ideal of woman, the poet labels her domain a "battle-hall" (*nīðsele*, 1513a; *gūðsele*, 2139a).[4] In addition, he occasionally uses a masculine pronoun in referring to her (*sē þe* instead of *sēo þe* in 1260a, 1497b; *hē* instead of *hēo* in 1392b, 1394b;[5] such a change in pronoun occurs elsewhere in the poem only in reference to abstract feminine nouns used as personifications and to concrete feminine nouns used as synecdoches), and he applies epithets to her that are usually applied to male figures: warrior, *sinnigne secg*, in 1379a; destroyer, *mihtig mānscaða*, in 1339a; and [male] guardian, *gryrelīcne grundhyrde*, in 2136. Indeed in the phrase *ides āglǣcwīf*, applied to Grendel's mother as a "lady monster-woman," the phrase *āglǣca* not only means "monster," as it does when directed at Grendel (159a, 425a, 433b, 556a, 592a, 646b, 732a, 739a, 816a, 989b, 1000b, 1269a) or the water monsters (1512a), but also "fierce combatant" or "strong adversary," as when directed at Sigemund in line 893 and at Beowulf and the dragon in line

---

[1]The edition used throughout is Frederick Klaeber, *Beowulf and the Fight at Finnsburg*, 3rd ed. (Boston: D. C. Heath, 1936, with supplements in 1941 and 1950).

[2]In *Beowulf*: in 620, 1168, and 1649 used of Wealhtheow, lady of the Helmings or Scyldings; in 1075 and 1117 of Hildeburh; in 1941 of Queen Thryth.

[3]*The Exeter Book*, Vol. 3 of *The Anglo-Saxon Poetic Records*, ed. George Philip Krapp and Elliot Van Kirk Dobbie (New York: Columbia University Press, 1936), p. 159 (lines 83-85).

[4]Bosworth-Toller's *Anglo-Saxon Dictionary* lists *hringsele* and *nīðsele* as compounds singular to Beowulf, underscoring the intentionality of the poet's irony.

[5]Masculine pronouns refer to the feminine personifications of Old Age (1887b) and Change or Death (2421a), and to the feminine synecdoche "hand" (1344a).

This selection reproduces Chapter Seven of the author's *Woman as Hero in Old English Literature* (Syracuse Univ. Press, 1986), pp. 95-108 and 131-5.

2592a.[6] Such a woman might be wretched or monstrous to an Anglo-Saxon audience because she blurs the sexual and social categories of roles. For example she arrogates to herself the masculine role of the warrior or lord. This inversion of the Anglo-Saxon image of woman as peacemaker is congruent with recent interpretations of the other two monsters in the epic. Grendel and the dragon have been interpreted recently as monstrous projections of flaws in Germanic civilization, portrayed by the poet as "Negative Men."[7] Grendel is introduced as a mock "hall-retainer" (*healðegn* 142a; *renweard*, 770a) who envies the men of Heorot their joy of community; he subsequently attacks the hall in a raid that is described through the parodic hall ceremonies of feasting, ale-drinking, gift-receiving, and singing.[8] The dragon is introduced as a mock "gold-king" or *hordweard* (2293b, 2302b, 2554b, 2593a), who avariciously guards his barrow or "ring-hall" (*hringsele*, 3053a),[9] and attacks Beowulf's kingdom after he discovers the loss of a single cup. The envy of the evil hall-retainer and the avarice of the evil gold-king antithesize the Germanic *comitatus* ideal first enunciated in Tacitus' *Germania* and pervading heroic and elegiac Anglo-Saxon literature; the *comitatus'* well-being depended upon the retainer's valor in battle and loyalty to his lord and the lord's protection and treasure-giving in return.[10]

Grendel's Mother differs from Grendel and the dragon in that she is used as a parodic inversion both of the Anglo-Saxon queen and mother,[11] the ideal

---

[6]*Āglæca* apparently means "fierce adversary" in *Juliana* 268b and 319a where the Devil in the garb of an angel brings tidings to the maiden; when she asks who sent him, "Hyre se aglæca ageaf ondsware," 319, in *The Exeter Book*, p. 122. Because he no longer appears to be a "wretch, monster, miscreant," the term *āglæca* must denote 'foe' in this passage. Indeed, Juliana addresses him in line 317b as "feond moncynnes," 'foe' or 'enemy of mankind.'

[7]Groundwork for this interpretation of the monsters as enemies of man was first laid by Arthur E. Du Bois, "The Unity of Beowulf," *PMLA* 49 (1934): 391 (Grendel and his mother become "the Danes' liability to punishment" for the secular sins of weakness, pride, and treachery; the dragon, "a variation upon Grendel," is "internal discord"). More recently they have been understood as adversaries of both man and God: see Richard N. Ringler, "*Him Sēo Wēn Gelēah*: The Design for Irony in Grendel's Last Visit to Heorot," *Speculum* 41 (1966): 64, in which Grendel represents *ofermōd* or *fortrūwung*, "held suspect by both Germanic instinct and Christian doctrine." See also Alvin A. Lee, *The Guest-Hall of Eden* (New Haven: Yale University Press, 1972), p. 186.

[8]For this interpretation of Grendel, see especially Edward B. Irving, Jr., "*Ealuscerwen*: Wild Party at Heorot," *Tennessee Studies in Literature* 11 (1966): 161-68, and *A Reading of Beowulf* (New Haven: Yale University Press, 1968), p. 16; also, William A. Chaney, "Grendel and the *Gifstol*: A Legal View of Monsters," *PMLA* 77 (1962): 513-20; Joseph L. Baird, "Grendel the Exile," *Neuphilologische Mitteilungen* 67 (1966): 375-81.

[9]Irving, *A Reading*, p. 209; Lee, pp. 215-16.

[10]Tacitus, *Germania*, ed. Rodney Potter Robinson, Philological Monographs No. 5 (Middletown, Ct: American Philological Association, 1935), p. 291 (cap. 14).

[11]Recently interpretations have stressed her significance in Germanic social terms, but without developing the implications of such insights: a Jungian analysis views her as symbolic of the "evil latent in woman's function, as Grendel symbolizes the destructive element hidden in Beowulf's *mægen* . . . Grendel's mother symbolizes the feud aspect of the web of peace." Further, as a destroyer she signifies "the obverse of the women we meet in the two banqueting scenes which precede Beowulf's descent into Grendel's mere," both of whom combine to form the dual mother image. See Jeffrey Helterman, "*Beowulf*: The Archetype Enters History," *ELH* 35 (1968): 13-14. To other critics she represents vengeance (Nist, Irving, Hume), false loyalty (Gardner), revenge (Leyerle). See John A. Nist, *The Structure and Texture of Beowulf* (São Paolo, Brazil: Universidad de São Paolo, Faculdade de Filosofia, ciências eletras, 1959), p. 21;

of which was embodied in the Virgin Mary. That is, the word *ides* in Latin and Old English glosses is paired with *virgo* to suggest maiden-hood, as when *on idesan* equals *in virgunculam*.[12] (It is interesting to note that Grendel's *father* never appears.) In addition, as if the poet wished to stress her maternal role, she is characterized usually as Grendel's *modor* or kinswoman (*mǣge*, 1391), the former a word almost exclusively reserved for her, although other mothers appear in the poem.[13] Her vengefulness as a mother invites implicit comparison with the love and mercy of the Virgin Mother.

These two roles, while related, are linked to her two appearances in the poem, one at Heorot, one at her mere. That is, her episode is appropriately divided into two parts, like her monstrous but human nature and her female but male behavior, which illustrate the two roles, that of the mother or kinswoman and that of the queen or lady, that she inverts. The poet constantly highlights the unnatural behavior of Grendel's dam by contrasting it with feminine ideals.

Thus the episode involving Grendel's mother is not structurally and thematically extraneous, a blot on the unity of the epic, as it so often has been termed,[14] but a vital part of the parody of social roles embodied in Grendel (1100-1200 lines, from 86 to 1250) or the dragon (1000 lines, from 2200 to

---

Irving, *A Reading of Beowulf*, p. 113, and *Introduction to Beowulf* (Englewood Cliffs, N.J: Prentice Hall, 1969), p. 57; Kathryn Hume, "The Theme and Structure of *Beowulf*," *Studies in Philology* 72 (1975): 7; John Gardner, "Fulgentius's *Expositio Vergiliana Continentia* and the Plan of *Beowulf*: Another Approach to the Poem's Style and Structure," *Papers on Language and Literature* 6 (1970): 255; and John Leyerle, "The Interlace Structure of *Beowulf*," *University of Toronto Quarterly* 37 (1967): 11-12.

Other recent interpretations have explored not only Jungian but also Scandinavian and Celtic mythic and legendary parallels, sources, or analogues of this figure: for the Scandinavian parallels, see Nora K. Chadwick, "The Monsters and Beowulf," in *The Anglo-Saxons: Studies in Some Aspects of their History and Culture Presented to Bruce Dickens*, ed. Peter Clemoes (London: Bowes and Bowes, 1959), pp. 171-203, and Larry D. Benson, "The Originality of Beowulf," in *The Interpretation of Narrative: Theory and Practice*, ed. Morton W. Bloomfield, Harvard English Studies, No. 1 (Cambridge, Mass: Harvard University Press, 1970), pp. 1-43; for the Celtic parallels, see Martin Puhvel, "The Might of Grendel's Mother," *Folklore* 80 (1969): 81-88; and for amalgamated parallels—English, German, Latin, and Scandinavian —viewing Grendel and his mother as incubus and succubus, see Nicholas K. Kiessling, "Grendel: A New Aspect," *Modern Philology* 65 (1968): 191-201.

[12]See "Kentish Glosses" (ca. 9th century) in Thomas Wright, *Anglo-Saxon and Old English Vocabularies*, 2nd ed., ed. Richard Paul Wülcker, (London, 1884) I, 88. For "on idesan" paired with "in virgunculam," see *in iuuenculam* in the gloss on Aldhelm's *De laudibus virginitatis* 29.14, in *Old English Glosses*, ed. Arthur S. Napier (Oxford: Clarendon Press, 1900), p. 57; also for *ides* as *virguncula* see the gloss on Aldhelm's *De laudibus Virginum* 191.7 and 194.14, pp. 181, 183.

[13]Used of Grendel's mother in lines 1258b, 1276b, 1282a, 1538b, 1683b, 2118b, and 2139b. In 2932a *mōdor* refers to the mother of Onela and Ohthere.

[14]If the poem is regarded as two-part in structure, balancing contrasts between the hero's youth and old age, his rise as a retainer and his fall as a king, his battles with the Grendel family and his battle with the dragon, then her episode (which includes Hrothgar's sermon and Hygelac's welcoming court celebration with its recapitulation of earlier events) lengthens the first "half" focusing on his youth to two-thirds of the poem (lines 1-2199). This view of the structure as two-part has generally prevailed since its inception in J. R. R. Tolkien's "Beowulf: The Monsters and the Critics," in *Proceedings of the British Academy* 22 (1936): 245-95, rpt. in *An Anthology of Beowulf Criticism*, ed. Lewis E. Nicholson (Notre Dame, Ind: University of Notre Dame Press, 1963), pp. 51-103.

3182),[15] her section of roughly 500 lines (from 1251 to 1784) is more than a "transition between two great crises."[16] Indeed, as we shall see, her episode should be lengthened to a thousand lines (from 1251 to 2199) so as to include Hrothgar's sermon and Hygelac's court celebration, in that the idea she represents dominates these events both literally and symbolically as do Grendel and the dragon the events in their sections. We turn first to an examination of the female ideal in Beowulf, then to a detailed analysis of the episode involving Grendel's mother and its two parts, and finally to some conclusions regarding the way in which her episode is key to the structural unity of the entire epic.

I

The role of woman in *Beowulf*, as in Anglo-Saxon society, primarily depends upon peace making, either biologically through her marital ties with foreign kings as a peace pledge or mother of sons, or socially and psychologically as a cup-passing and peace-weaving queen within a hall. The *Beowulf*-poet takes care to remind us of this role: Wealhtheow becomes a peace pledge or *friðusibb folca* (2017) to unite the Danes and Helmings; Hildeburh similarly unites the Danes and Frisians through her marriage; and Freawaru at least intends to pledge peace between the Danes and Heathobards.

In addition, woman functions domestically within the nation as a cup-passer during hall festivities of peace (*freoþo*) and joy (*drēam*) after battle or contest. The mead-sharing ritual and the cup-passer herself come to symbolize peace-weaving and peace because they strengthen the societal and familial bonds between lord and retainers. First, the literal action of the *freoðuwebbe* (peace-weaver, 1942) as she passes the cup from warrior to warrior weaves an

---

[15]This increasingly popular view of the structure as tripartite has been advanced by H. L. Rogers, "Beowulf's Three Great Fights," *RES* N.S. 6 (1955): 339-55, rpt. in Nicholson, pp. 233-56; Gardner, "Fulgentius's *Expositio Vergiliana Continentia* and the Plan of Beowulf," 227-62; and most recently, Hume, "The Theme and Structure of Beowulf," 1-27. Hume's fine analysis includes an extensive survey of the various approaches to and interpretations of structural and thematic unity in Beowulf (see pp. 2-5). She declares, p. 3, "That critics should disagree over whether the structure has two parts or three is hardly surprising. Those concentrating on the hero tend to see two, those on action usually prefer three. But neither camp has produced a structural analysis which does not, by implication, damn the poet for gross incompetence, or leave the critic with a logically awkward position." For example, William W. Ryding, *Structure in Medieval Narrative* (The Hague: Mouton, 1971), first regards the middle of Beowulf as "a point of maximum logical discontinuity," p. 40, and then, contradicting himself, as more difficult, more intense, more exciting combat than the fight with Grendel, illustrating a "varied repetition" of the same narrative motif, therefore implying logical continuity (p. 88).

[16]Adrien Bonjour, "Grendel's Dam and the Composition of *Beowulf*," *English Studies* 30 (1949): 117. Other early *Beowulf* studies similarly ignored Grendel's mother or treated her as a type of Grendel. See also Tolkien, pp. 51-104, in which he declares, "I shall confine myself mainly to the monsters—Grendel and the Dragon" in Nicholson, p. 52. Similar treatments occur in T. M. Gang, "Approaches to *Beowulf*," *RES* N.S. 3 (1952): 1-12; Bonjour, "Monsters Crouching and Critics Rampant: or the *Beowulf* Dragon Debated," *PMLA* 68 (1953): 304-12; and even more recently, in Margaret Goldsmith, *The Mode and Meaning of Beowulf* (London: Athlone, 1970), e.g., p. 144; Lee, *The Guest-Hall of Eden*, pp. 171-223; and Daniel G. Calder, "Setting and Ethos: The Pattern of Measure and Limit in *Beowulf*," *Studies in Philology* 69 (1972): 21-37. For a cogent summary of the problem, see Alexandra Hennessey Olsen, "Women in *Beowulf*," in *Approaches to Teaching Beowulf*, ed. Jess B. Bessinger, Jr., and Robert F. Yeager (New York: Modern Language Association, 1984), pp. 150-56.

invisible web of peace: the order in which each man is served, according to his social position, reveals each man's dependence upon and responsibility toward another. For example, after Wealhtheow gives the cup to Hrothgar she bids him to be joyful at drinking as well as loving to his people (615ff). Then she offers it to the *duguð* (old retainers), then to the *geoguð* (young retainers), and finally to the guest Beowulf. Second, her peace-weaving also takes a verbal form: her speeches accompanying the mead-sharing stress the peace and joy contingent upon the fulfillment of each man's duty to his nation. At the joyous celebration after Grendel's defeat Wealhtheow concludes her speeches with a tribute to the harmony of the present moment by reminding her tribe of its cause, that is, adherence to the *comitatus* ethic. Each man remains true to the other; each is loyal to the king; the nation is ready and alert; the drinking warriors attend to the ale-dispenser herself (1228-31). Yet minutes before she attempted to forestall future danger to her family and nation by preventive peace-weaving: she advised Hrothgar to leave his kingdom to his sons, and then, as if sensing the future, she reminded Hrothulf, his nephew, of his obligations to those sons (obligations he will later deny). Third, the peace-weaver herself emblematizes peace, for she appears in the poem with her mead-vessel only after a contest has been concluded. Thus, Wealhtheow enters the hall only after the contest between Unferth and Beowulf (612); she does not appear again until after Beowulf has overcome Grendel, when the more elaborate feasting invites the peace-making speeches mentioned above. After Grendel's mother is defeated, the poet preserves the integrity of the pattern of feminine cup-passing after masculine contest by describing the homecoming banquet at Hygelac's court, where Hygd conveys the mead-vessel. This structural pattern to which we shall return simultaneously weaves together the Danish part of the poem with its Geatish part.

Most of the other female characters figure as well in this middle section so that the female monster's adventures are framed by descriptions of other women for ironic contrast. The role of mother highlights the first half of the middle section with the *scop*'s mention of Hildeburh (1071ff) and the entrance of Wealhtheow, both of whom preface the first appearance of Grendel's dam (1258) in her role as avenging mother. Then the introduction of Hygd, Thryth, and Freawaru after the female monster's death (1590) stresses the role of queen as peace-weaver and cup-passer to preface Beowulf's final narration of the female monster's downfall (2143). The actual adventures of Grendel's mother cluster then at the center of the middle section of the poem.

II

In the first part of the female monster's section, the idea is stressed that a kinswoman or mother must passively accept and not actively avenge the loss of her son. The story of the mother Hildeburh is recited by the *scop* early on the evening Grendel's Mother will visit Heorot. The lay ends at line 1159; Grendel's Mother enters the poem a mere hundred lines later when she attacks the Danish hall, as the Frisian contingent attacked the hall lodging Hildeburh's Danish brother in the *Finnsburg Fragment*. The *Beowulf*-poet alters the focus of the fragment: he stresses the consequences of the surprise attack rather than the attack itself in order to reveal Hildeburh's maternal reactions to them.

Hildeburh is unjustly (*unsynnum*, 1072b) deprived of her Danish brother and Finnish son, but all she does, this sad woman (*geōmuru ides*, 1075b) is to mourn her loss with dirges and stoically place her son on the pyre. In fact, she can do nothing, caught in the very web she has woven as peace pledge: her husband's men have killed her brother, her brother's men have killed her son. Later the Danish Hengest will avenge the feud with her husband Finn, whether she approves or not, by overwhelming the Frisians and returning Hildeburh to her original tribe. The point remains: the peace pledge must accept a passive role precisely because the ties she knots bind *her*—she *is* the knot, the pledge of peace. Her fate interlaces with that of her husband and brothers through her role as a mother bearing a son: thus Hildeburh appropriately mourns the loss of her symbolic tie at the pyre, the failure of her self as peace pledge, the loss of her identity. Like Hildeburh, Grendel's dam will also lose her son and thus her identity as mother. However, she has never had an identity as peace pledge to lose since she was never a wife.

As if reminded of her own role as mother by hearing of Hildeburh's plight, Wealhtheow demonstrates her maternal concern in an address to Hrothgar immediately after the *scop* sings this lay. In it she first alludes to Hrothgar's adoption of Beowulf as a son: apparently troubled by this, she insists that Hrothgar leave his kingdom only to his actual kinsmen or descendants when he dies (1178-79). Then she urges her foster "son" Hrothulf (actually a nephew) to remember his obligations to them so that "he will repay our sons with liberality" (1184-85). Finally, she moves to the mead-bench where the adopted Beowulf sits, rather symbolically, next to her sons Hrethric and Hrothmund (1188-91). The *past* helplessness of the first mother, Hildeburh, to requite the death of her son counterpoints the anxiously maternal Wealhtheow's attempts to weave the ties of kinship and obligation, thereby forestalling *future* danger to her sons. Later that night, Grendel's Mother, intent on avenging the loss of her son in the *present*, attacks Heorot, her masculine aggression contrasting with the feminine passivity of both Hildeburh and Wealhtheow. Indeed, she resembles a grieving human mother: like Hildeburh she is guiltless and *galgmōd* ("gloomy-minded," possibly "gallows-minded," 1277a); her journey to Heorot must be sorrowful (1278) for she "remembered her misery" (1259b). But a woman's role as peace pledge was reserved for her husband, not for her son, according to the Danish history of Saxo Grammaticus.[17] Perhaps for this reason Grendel's Mother is presented as husbandless and son-obsessed to suggest to an Anglo-Saxon audience the incestuous dangers inherent in woman's function as *friðusibb*.

However, her attempts to avenge her son's death could be justified if she were human and male, for no *wergild* has been offered to her by the homicide Beowulf.[18] The role of the masculine avenger is emphasized throughout the

---

[17]See the stories of the treacherous wife but loyal mother Urse in the twelfth-century *Saxonis Grammatici Gesta Danorum*, ed. Alfred Holder (Strassburg, 1886), pp. 53-55. (*The First Nine Books of the Danish History of Saxo Grammaticus*, tr. Oliver Elton [London, 1894], pp. 64-65 [2. 53-54]).

[18]Dorothy Whitelock, *The Beginnings of English Society* (Harmondsworth: Penguin, 1952), p. 41; on duty to one's kin, see pp. 38-47; on duty to one's lord, see pp. 31ff. Duty to one's lord superseded duty to one's kin (p. 37). See also *Saxonis Grammatici Gesta Danorum*, p. 254 (7), for the retainer's duty to lord; in cases of blood revenge the son remained most deeply

passage (1255-78) in defining her motivation to attack: she performs the role of avenger (*wrecend*, 1256b) "to avenge the death of her son" (1278b). Whatever her maternal feelings, she actually fulfills the duty of the kinsman. Unlike Hildeburh, she cannot wait for a Hengest to resolve the feud in some way; unlike Freawaru, she cannot act as a peace pledge to settle the feud. Tribeless, not kinless, forced to rely on her own might, she seizes and kills Aeschere, Hrothgar's most beloved retainer, in an appropriate retribution for the loss of her own most beloved "retainer" and "lord"—her son. She thus implicitly parodies the Virgin in response to the loss of her son.

The monstrosity of her action is at first not evident. Hrothgar suspects she has carried the "feud" too far (1339-40). And from the Danish and human point of view she possesses no legal right to exact compensation for her kinsman's loss because Grendel is himself a homicide. However, Beowulf later implies that the two feuds must remain separate, as she desires her own "revenge for injury" (*gyrnwracu*, 2118a). Perhaps he is thinking of her as a retainer duty-bound to avenge the death of his lord, regardless of the acts he has committed. If so, then she behaves monstrously in only one way. It is monstrous for a mother to "avenge" her son (2121) as if she were a retainer, he were her lord, and avenging more important than peace making. An analogy conveying her effect on the men in Heorot when she first appears suggests how unusual are her actions in human terms. Her horror "is as much less as is the skill (strength) of maidens, the war-horror of a woman, in comparison to a (weaponed) man, when the bound sword shears the one standing opposite" ("Wæs se gryre læssa / efne swā micle, swā bið mægþa cræft, / wīggryre wīfes be wæpnedmen, / þonne heoru bunden . . . andweard scireð," 1282-87). In their eyes recognizably female, she threatens them physically less than her son. But because female "peacemakers" do not wage war, the analogy implies, by litotes, that her unnatural behavior seems *more* horrible. If we compare her vendetta to the Virgin's forgiveness, it becomes even more monstrous.

In the second part of her adventure, Grendel's Mother no longer behaves solely as an avenging monster, antitype of Hildeburh and Wealhtheow, who are both through marriage "visitors" to the hall like Grendel and his dam. Such hall-visitors contrast with the hall-rulers of this second part: the *merewīf* as queen or guardian (*grundhyrde*, 2136b) protects her "battle-hall," the cave-like lair, from the visiting hero like the regal dragon guarding his ring-hall, and like King Beowulf his kingdom, in the last section of the poem. Accordingly, the stress on the relationship between mother and son delineated in the first part of her adventure changes to a stress on the relationship between host and guest.

As a tribeless queen or lady (*ides āglæcwīf*) she rudely receives her "hall-guest" Beowulf (*selegyst*, 1545a, *gist*, 1522b) by "embracing" him and then "repaying him" for his valor not with treasure but with "grim grips" ("Hēo him eft hraþe andlēan forgeald / grimman grāpum," 1541-2) just as the dragon will "entertain" him in the future.[19] Indeed, the parody of the hall-ceremony

---

obligated to his father, pp. 75, 96 (3), then to his brother or sister, pp. 53, 280 (2, 8), finally to his grandfather, p. 301 (9).

[19]The poet uses similar word play in describing the "reception" of the guest Beowulf in the "hall" of the gold-lord dragon. First, Beowulf does not dare attack (or more figuratively, "approach") the gold-lord dragon in his ring-hall (*hringsele*, 2840a, 3053a): Wiglaf admits "hē

of treasure-giving is complete when a *"scop"* (Beowulf's sword, acting as bard) sings a fierce "war song" off the side of her head ("hire on hafelan hringmǣl agōl / grǣdig gūðlēoð," 1521-22a). It is interesting to note that this "hall-celebration" of the mock peace-weaver to welcome her valorous guest Beowulf following her attack on Heorot and her curiously listless "contest" with Aeschere duplicates the pattern of mead-sharing ceremonies involving peace-makers which follow masculine contests throughout the poem.

It is also interesting to note that the contest between this apparently lordless "queen" and her "guest" contrasts in its mock-sensual embracing and grasping with the other two major battles of the hero—the briefly described arm-wrestling between Grendel and Beowulf and the conventional sword-wielding of Beowulf against the fire-breathing dragon. Indeed, before Beowulf arrives at the "battle-hall," Hrothgar introduces the question of how Grendel was begotten when the king of the Danes admits that they do not know of a father (1355), or of possible additional progeny in addition to Grendel, apparently engendered incestually upon Grendel's Mother by her own son (1356-57). The mystery of his begetting and conception hints at a possible parody of the conception and birth of Christ. While Hrothgar's ostensible point is to warn Beowulf of additional monsters lurking nearby, it serves as well to remind the reader that Grendel's mother has a monstrous or sexual nature very different from that of a civilized *ides*. For, during the passage describing their battle, the poet exploits the basic resemblance between sexual intercourse and battle to emphasize the inversion of the feminine role of the queen or hall-ruler by Grendel's Mother. This is achieved in three steps: first, the emphasis upon clutching, grasping, and embracing while they fight; second, the contest for a dominant position astride the other; and third, the use of fingers, knife, or sword to penetrate clothing or the body, the latter always accompanied by the implied figurative kinship between the sword and the phallus and between decapitation and castration. The personal and physical nature of the battle symbolizes her monstrosity as mock-peace-weaver as effectively as Grendel's arm-wrestling and the dragon's sword-battle symbolizes theirs as mock-retainer and mock-lord.

She welcomes him to the *mere* with an almost fatal embrace similar to the "embrace" (*fæðm*, 2128) to which Aeschere has succumbed. She "grasped then towards him" (1501a), seizing him with "horrible grips" (1502a) envisioned earlier by the hero as a "battle grip" (1446a) and a "malicious grasp" (1447a). Second, inside the "castle" (*hof*, 1507b) where she has transported him, each grapples for a superior position over the other. After his sword fails him, for example, he "grasped her by the shoulder," hurling her to the ground. The poet, conscious of the monster's sex and Beowulf's definitely unchivalrous behavior, drily protests that in this case "the lord of the Battle-Geats did not at all lament the hostile act" (1537-38). Then, as "reward" for his valor, this lady "repaid" him with the treasure of her "grimman grāpum," forcing him to stumble and fall (1541-44), after which she climbs, rather ludicrously, on top

---

ne grǣtte goldweard þone" (3081), literally because of the danger from fire, figuratively because of the dragon's avarice. Instead, *wyrd* will dispense or distribute his "soul's hoard" for which Beowulf has paid with his life (*wyrd* will seek his "sāwle hord, sundur gedǣlan / līf wið līce," 2422a-23a; he "buys" the hoard with his life in 2799-800). After this "treasure-giving," the cup-passer—Wiglaf—pours water from the cup—Beowulf's helmet.

of her "hall-guest" (*selegyst*, 1545a), intent on stabbing him and thereby (again) avenging her only offspring (1546-47). Third, the battle culminates in very suggestive swordplay, and wordplay too. Earlier her "hostile fingers" (1505b) tried to "penetrate" ("ðurhfōn," 1504b) his locked coat-of-mail; now she tries unsuccessfully to pierce the woven breast-net with her knife. Previously Beowulf discovered his own weapon was impotent against the charm or spell of the "sword-greedy" woman (*heorogīfre*, 1498a), who collects the swords of giants. Now the "sword-grim" hero substitutes one of these swords, an appropriate tool to quell such a woman. The "sword entirely penetrated [*ðurhwōd*] the doomed-to-die body" (1567b-68a). After this final "embrace" of the "grasping" of her neck, the "sweord wæs swātig, secg weorce gefeh" ("the sword was sweaty, the warrior rejoiced in the work," 1569). The alliteration links *sweord* and *secg*, to identify the bloody sword with the rejoicing, laboring "man-sword" (*secg*); the "battle" appropriately evokes erotic undertones. The equation of the sword and warrior, with the subsequent sexual connotations, resembles the synecdoche controlling Riddle Twenty, "The Sword," in which the sword becomes a retainer who serves his lord through celibacy, foregoing the "joy-game" of marriage and the "treasure" of children, and whose only unpleasant battle occurs with a woman, because he must overcome her desire while she voices her terror, claps her hands, rebukes him with words, and cries out "ungod."[20] Similarly, in Beowulf, once the sword finally penetrates the body, its blade miraculously melts—like ice into water —either from the poison of Grendel's blood or of his mother's, the poem does not specify which (1608). And even the *mere* itself, in whose stirred-up and bloody waters sea monsters lurk and the strange battle-hall remains hidden, and the approach to which occurs only through winding passageways, slopes, and paths, symbolically projects the mystery and danger of female sexuality run rampant.

Such erotic overtones in descriptions of battles between a male and female adversary are not especially common in Anglo-Saxon literature but can be found, in sadomasochistic form, as we have seen, in various saints' lives in the *Old English Martyrology* (ca. 850) and in *Aelfric's Lives of Saints* (ca. 994-early

---

[20]*The Exeter Book*, pp. 190-91. The sword declares:

Ic wiþ bryde ne mot
hæmed habban,   ac me þæs hyhtplegan
geno wyrneð,   se mec geara on
bende legde;   forþon ic brucan sceal
on hagostealde   hæleþa gestreona.
Oft ic wirum dol   wife abelge,
wonie hyre willan;   heo me wom spreceð,
floceð hyre folmum,   firenaþ mec wordum,
ungod gæleð.   Ic ne gyme þæs compes. (27b-35)

For a discussion of the double entendre of this riddle and an alternate solution ("Phallus"), see Donald Kay, "Riddle 20: A Revaluation," *Tennessee Studies in Literature* 13 (1968), 133-139. Similarly erotic riddles include no. 21, "Plow"; no. 25, "Onion"; no. 44, "Key"; no. 45, "Dough"; no. 53, "Battering Ram"; no. 62, "Poker" or "Burning Arrow"; and no. 91, "Key" or "Keyhole." Some of these erotic riddles and the sexual implications of others have been analyzed in full by Edith Whitehurst Williams, "What's So New about the Sexual Revolution?" *Texas Quarterly* 18.2 (Summer 1975): 46-55: no. 25, "Onion", no. 45, "Dough"; no. 61, "Helmet" or "Shirt"; no. 12, "Leather"; and no. 9, "Key" or "Keyhole."

eleventh century),[21] and in another epic poem, *Judith*, contained in the same manuscript as *Beowulf*.[22] In Ms. Cotton Vitellius A.xv, this fragmentary epic portrays similar sexual overtones in Judith's "battle" with Holofernes. As in *Beowulf* a warrior battles a monster: the blessed maiden grapples with the "drunken vicious monster" (*se inwidda*, 28a) Holofernes. However, the sexual role behavior of *Beowulf* occurs in reverse in *Judith*: Holofernes parallels Grendel's dam, but whereas the *wīf* is aggressive and sword-greedy, Holofernes seems slightly effete (his bed enclosed by gold curtains, for example) and impotent from mead-drinking: "The lord fell, the powerful one so drunken, in the middle of his bed, as if he knew no reason in his mind" (67b-69a). These hypermetrical lines heighten the irony of his situation, for the warrior swoons on the very bed upon which he intended to rape the maiden. Having lost his head to drink, in a double sense he himself is penetrated by the virgin's sharp sword, "hard in the storm of battle" (79a), therefore literally losing his head. But first Judith draws the sword from its sheath in her right hand, seizes him by the hair in a mock loving gesture (98b-99a), then pulls him toward her "shamefully" ("teah hyne folmum wið hyre weard / *bysmerlice*," 99b-100a). The "b" alliteration in line 100 ("*bysmerlice*, ond þone *bealofullan*") draws attention to *bysmerlice*, which as a verb (*bysmrian*) elsewhere suggests the act of "defiling" (intercourse).[23] In this line what seems shameful is apparently her embrace of the warrior's body while she moves it to a supine position. As in *Beowulf*, the female assumes the superior position; she lays him down so that she may control (*gewealdan*, 103a) him more easily in cutting off his head. The ironic embrace and mock intercourse of this couple parallels that of Beowulf and the *ides āglǣcwīf*: the aggressive and sword-bearing "virgin" contrasts with the passive and swordless man (Holofernes, Aeschere, and even Beowulf are all momentarily or permanently swordless). The poet's point in each case is that a perversion of the sexual roles signals an equally perverse spiritual state. Holofernes' impotence is as unnatural in the male as the *wīf*'s aggression is unnatural in the female; so the battle with the heroine or hero in each case is described with erotic overtones to suggest the triumph of a right and natural sexual (and social and spiritual) order over the perverse and unnatural one. In the latter case, Grendel's dam and her son pose a heathen threat to Germanic society (the macrocosm) and to the individual (Beowulf the microcosm) as Holofernes and the Assyrians pose a heathen threat to Israelite society (the macrocosm) and to the individual (Judith the microcosm).[24]

In this second part of the adventure of Grendel's Mother, Hygd and Freawaru as queens or cup-passers contrast with the *wīf* just as Hildeburh and Wealhtheow as mothers were contrasted with Grendel's dam in the first part.

[21]See *An Old English Martyrology*, ed. George Herzfeld, EETS O.S. 116 (London, 1900). For example, see the discussion of St. Lucia, p. 218, discussed previously in Chapter 2.

[22]Although the poems were written by different poets, *Beowulf* in the late seventh or eighth century and *Judith* in the middle or late tenth century, the second *Beowulf* scribe did transcribe all of the *Judith* fragment, probably in the late tenth century. All references to *Judith* derive from Elliot Van Kirk Dobbie, ed. *Beowulf and Judith*, Vol. 4 of *The Anglo-Saxon Poetic Records* (New York; Columbia University Press, 1953).

[23]See, again, the life of St. Lucia in the *Martyrology*, p. 218.

[24]For a discussion of these planes of correspondence in *Judith*, see James F. Doubleday, "The Principle of Contrast in *Judith*," *Neuphilologische Mitteilungen* 72 (1971), 436-41.

Hygd, the first woman encountered after the defeat of Grendel's mother, truly fulfills the feminine ideal of *Maxims I*, just as Wealhtheow does. Her name, which means "thought" or "deliberation," suggests that her nature is antithetical to that of the bellicose *wīf* and possibly that of the war-like Thryth, whose actions, if not her name, suggest "Strength" (only in a physical sense; the alternate form of her name, "Mod-Thrytho" or "Mind-Force," implies in a more spiritual sense stubbornness or pride).[25] Although Hygd, like the *wīf* and Thryth, will be lordless after Hygelac's death, she does not desire to usurp the role of king for herself: doubting her son's ability to prevent tribal wars she offers the throne to Beowulf (2369ff). In addition, this gracious queen bestows treasure generously (1929b-3la), unlike the *wīf* and Thryth, the latter of whom dispense only "grim grips" and sword blows upon their "retainers."

The Thryth digression is inserted after Hygd enters to pass the cup upon Beowulf's return to Hygelac. Its structural position invites a comparison of this stubborn princess and the other two queens, Hygd and the *wīf*. She appears to combine features of both: she begins as a type of the female monster, but upon marriage to Offa changes her nature and becomes a much loved queen. According to the poet, Thryth commits a "terrible crime": she condemns to death any retainer at court caught staring at her regal beauty. That she abrogates her responsibilities as a queen and as a woman the poet makes clear: "Such a custom—that the peace-weaver after a pretended injury deprive the dear man of life—is not queenly for a woman to do, although she be beautiful ("Ne bið swylc cwēnlic þēaw / idese tō efnanne, þēah ðe hīo ænlicu sȳ, / þætte freoðuwebbe fēores onsǣce / æfter ligetorne lēofne mannan," 1940-3). The label "peace-weaver" (*freoðuwebbe*) seems ironic in this context, especially as she does not weave but instead severs the ties of kinship binding her to her people and also the bonds of life tying the accused man to this world. That is, for any man caught looking at her, "the deadly bonds, hand-woven, were in store; / after his arrest it was quickly determined / that the sword, the damascened sword, must shear, / make known death-bale" ("ac him wælbende weotode tealde / handgewriþene; hraþe seoþðan wæs / æfter mundgripe mēce geþinged, / þæt hit sceādenmǣl scȳran mōste / cwealmbealu cȳðan," 1936-40a). If she weaves at all, then she weaves only "deadly hand-woven bonds" binding him to a grisly end. The "peace-weaver" cuts these bonds—imprisoning ropes—with a sword, simultaneously shearing the bonds of life to "make known death-bale." She resembles that other ironic

---

[25]See Klaeber's discussion of Thryth's possible prototypes, 1931-62*nn*. Thryth's name resembles that of Quendrida (Queen Thryth?) and that of the Scottish queen Hermutrude, whose story is related in Saxo Grammaticus' *Danish History*, p. 124. (*Gesta Danorum*, pp. 101-102 [4]). Hermutrude, loved by Amleth, remains unmarried because of her cruelty and arrogance, similar to Thryth's. Finally, note the similarity between the following descriptions and those in *Beowulf*: Offa murdered many without distinction, including King Ethelbert, "thereby being guilty of an atrocious outrage against the suitor of his daughter," in William of Malmesbury's *Chronicle of the Kings of England: From the Earliest Period to the Reign of King Stephen*, tr. J. A. Giles (London, 1847), p. 238; in Latin "nefarium rem in procum filiae operatus," from *Willelmi Malmesbiriensis Monachi De gestis regum Anglorum libri quinque; Historiae novellae libri tres*, ed. William Stubbs, 2 vols., *Rerum Britanniarum Medii Aevi Scriptores*, No. 90 (London, 1887), p. 262 (2. 210). Compare *Beowulf*: "Mōdþrȳðo wæg, / fremu folces cwēn, *firen' ondrysne*," lines 1931b-32. Did the Beowulf poet confuse the father of Modthrytho with the daughter herself?

peace-weaver, the *wīf*, who tried to penetrate the braided breast-net of Beowulf with her knife.

Both antitypes of the peace-weaving queen behave like kings, using the sword to rid their halls of intruders or unwanted "hall-guests." Unlike Thryth, the monstrous *wīf* remains husbandless, having lost her son, wife only to the *mere* she inhabits both in life and in death. At this moment in the poem, both Thryth and Grendel's Mother belong to the past. If they represent *previous* inversions of the peace-weaver and cup-passer, and Hygd who is passing the mead-cup to Beowulf's weary men in celebration signifies a *present* cup-passer, so the poet introduces a final queen, this time a cup-passer of the *future* who will fail in her role just as Hildeburh, the first womam, failed in hers.

Freawaru, like Hildeburh, seems innocent of any crime. She is envisioned by Beowulf as a queen married to Ingeld of the Heathobards in a digression (2032-69) immediately preceding his summary of the battles with Grendel and with his mother. She will fail in her role as peace-weaver because of an underlying hostility—an old Heathobard warrior's bitterness over ancient Heathobard treasure acquired through previous wars and worn by a young Danish man accompanying the new queen. The fragility of this role is heightened even further when, in the third section involving the dragon, Beowulf inhabits a queenless kingdom and when Wiglaf must become the cup-passer, pouring water from the "cup" of Beowulf's helmet in a futile attempt to revive his wounded lord.

Indeed, three female characters appear outside this middle section to convey dialectically the idea that woman cannot ensure peace in this world. First, Wealhtheow, unlike other female figures, appears in the first (or Grendel) section of the poem to pour mead after Grendel's challenge has been answered by the hero. This first entrance symbolizes the ideal role of Germanic woman as a personification of peace, as we have seen. In antithesis, Beowulf's account of the fall of the *wīf unhȳre* appropriately ends the poem's second (Grendel's Mother) section which has centered on this role: the personification of discord, the antitype of feminine ideal, has been destroyed. But in the poem's third section a synthesis emerges. The nameless and unidentified Geat woman who appears, like the other female characters, after a battle—this one between Beowulf and the dragon—mourns at the pyre. This damaged one-line reference undercuts the role of the peace-weaver because it broadens the context in which she appears. That is, the efforts of the peacemaker, while valuable in worldly and social terms, ultimately must fail because of the nature of this world. True peace exists not in woman's but in God's "embrace" (*fæðm*, 188).

III

This idea is implied in Hrothgar's sermon (1700-84), which occupies a part of the middle section of Beowulf dominated by the female monster and which at first glance seems unrelated to it or her. In the sermon Hrothgar describes three Christian vices—envy, pride, and avarice—in distinctly Germanic terms. Impelled by envy, Heremod kills his "table-companions" (1713-14); next, the wealthy hall-ruler in his pride is attacked by the Adversary while his guardian conscience sleeps within the hall of his soul (1740-4); finally, this same hall-ruler "covets angry-minded" ("gȳtsað gromhȳdig," 1749a) the ornamented treasures God has previously given him by refusing to dispense any to his warriors. Each of these three sins is personified in the poem by the three monsters: Grendel personifies envy, like Heremod, because he killed the Danish retainers; the dragon personifies avarice, like the hall-ruler he mocks, when he stands guard over a treasure. So the monster that specifically epitomizes pride in *Beowulf*, as does Eve in *Genesis B*, is female—Grendel's Mother—thematically related to Thryth or Mod-Thrytho, whose name (if it can be said to exist in manuscript in that form) means "pride." Grendel's Mother substitutes war-making for the peace-weaving of the queen out of a kind of selfish pride—if she were capable of recognizing it as such. Although the poet portrays the monsters as antitypes of Germanic ideals, his integument conceals a Christian idea. The city of man, whether located in a Germanic or Christian society, is always threatened by sin and failure.

These three sins alienate Christian man from self, neighbor, and God; they alienate Germanic man primarily from other men. Note that although each of the three monsters in Beowulf is described as guarding or possessing a type of hall, whether Heorot, a watery cavern, or the treasure of the dragon, each remains isolated from humanity (and from each other—Grendel and his mother live together, but they never appear together in the poem until he is dead). Ideally, when the retainer, the queen, and the gold-lord cooperate they constitute a viable nucleus of Germanic society: a retainer must have a gold-lord from whom to receive gold for his loyalty in battle; the peace-weaver must have a "loom"—the band of retainers and their lord, or two nations—upon which to weave peace.

Despite the poet's realization that these roles cannot be fulfilled in this world, this Germanic ideal provides structural and thematic unity for *Beowulf*. Grendel's Mother does occupy a transitional postion in the poem: as a "retainer" attacking Heorot she resembles Grendel, but as an "attacked ruler" of her own "hall" she resembles the dragon. As a monstrous mother and queen she perverts a role more important socially and symbolically than that of Grendel, just as the queen as peace pledge or peace-weaver ultimately becomes more valuable than the retainer but less valuable than the gold-giver himself.

If it seems ironic that a Germanic ideal that cannot exist in this world can exist in art, unifying the theme and structure of the poem, then Grendel's Mother, warring antitype of harmony and peace, must seem doubly ironic. The structural position of her episode in the poem, like woman's position as cup-passer among members of the nations, or as a peace pledge between two nations, is similarly medial and transitional, but successfully so.

Beowulf 505, 'gehedde,' and
the Pretensions of Unferth

By John C. Pope

Whether or not Unferth's name is meant to suggest 'un-friδ' ('mar-peace'), there is no doubt that he enters the poem in a quarrelsome mood as he tries to discredit Beowulf with his (and Breca's) version of the swimming adventure, and that he has provoked among modern critics wide disagreement about his character, his status in Hrothgar's court, and his future participation, if any, in the supposed machinations of Hrothulf against the sons of Hrothgar. The various interpretations of his name and the disputes about his character and his position as 'þyle' were sensibly surveyed by the man we honour in this volume as recently as 1972,[1] but exploration and debate continue, not without profit, especially in attempts to relate Unferth's status and role to Germanic traditions that may have been familiar to the poet and his audience, yet would no doubt have been locally modified in ways we can only dimly surmise.[2]

---

[1]Stanley B. Greenfield *The Interpretation of Old English Poems* (London and Boston 1972) 101-7. Among the many suggested interpretations of Unferth's name mentioned by Greenfield, that which combines a negative, 'un-' with 'friδ' ('peace') rather than 'fer(h)δ' ('spirit') seems clearly preferable, both for its possible application to the character and for Old English usage, since, as a second element in proper names, West Saxon '-ferδ' regularly corresponds to Anglian '-friδ,' and 'friδ,' not 'ferhδ,' is a common Germanic name-element. But I have recently received from Professor R. D. Fulk the draft of an essay (soon to be published in *Modern Philology*) in which he advances reasons that seem to me of considerable weight for supposing that Unferth's name is a Germanic inheritance having nothing to do with etymological characterization on the part of the poet. In any case, it is clearly dangerous to use a doubtful etymology of the name as a guide to the characterization in preference to what Unferth says and does in the poem and what the poet tells us (though too meagrely) about him and about what other characters think of him.

[2]Among numerous recent articles on problems connected with Unferth, the following are particularly relevant as background to the present much more limited discussion: James L. Rosier 'Design for Treachery: The Unferth Intrigue' *PMLA* 77 (1962) 1-7 (as certain glosses suggest but do not prove, Unferth as 'þyle' may have been little more than a scurrilous jester, but one destined to conspire with Hrothulf in plotting the overthrow of Hrothgar's sons); Norman E. Eliason,'The Þyle and Scop in *Beowulf*' *Speculum* 38 (1963) 267-84 (Unferth a harmless though scurrilous and cowardly fool, possibly identical with the scop[!]); J. D. A. Ogilvy 'Unferth: Foil to Beowulf?' *PMLA* 79 (1964) 370-5 (cautionary observations on Rosier's speculations and, in a final note, on Eliason's); Ida Masters Hollowell 'Unferð the *þyle* in *Beowulf*' *SP* 73 (1976) 239-65 (Germanic tradition supports the possibility that Unferth as 'þyle' held a dignified and privileged position, one distantly associated perhaps with pagan wizards or priests); Geoffrey Hughes, 'Beowulf, Unferth and Hrunting: an Interpretation' *ES* 58 (1977) 385-95 (a defence and extension of the views of older critics: Unferth a warrior of

---

Reprinted, by permission, from *Modes of Interpretation in Old English Literature: Essays in Honour of Stanley B. Greenfield*, ed. Phyllis Rugg Brown, Georgia Ronan Crampton, and Fred C. Robinson (Univ. of Toronto Press, 1986), pp. 173-87.

Until recently, however, there has been substantial agreement about the purport of the passage, lines 499-505, with which the present essay is concerned, in spite of early uncertainties, almost forgotten, about the lexical identity and meaning of a word in line 505 that stands in the manuscript as 'gehedde.' It is the passage in which the poet first brings Unferth to our attention, introducing him with an abrupt 'Unferð maþelode' and preparing us for his carefully slanted disparagement of Beowulf by assigning a motive for it. Klaeber prints the passage as follows:

> *Un*ferð maþelode,   Ecgláfes bearn,
> þē æt fótum sæt   frēan Scyldinga,
> onband beadurūne—   wæs him Bēowulfes sīð,
> mōdges merefaran,   micel æfþunca,
> forþon þe hē ne ūþe,   þæt ænig ōðer man
> æfre mærða þon mā   middangeardes
> gehē*d*e under heofenum   þonne hē sylfa—:[3]

In line 505, Klaeber altered the spelling of ms 'gehedde' to 'gehēde,' since he accepted Holthausen's explanation of 'gehedde' as a corrupt spelling of the preterite third singular subjunctive of 'gehēgan,' which was thought to mean, in this context, 'perform, carry out, achieve.' Holthausen had printed 'gehēdde' (ie 'gehēde') in his first edition of the poem (Heidelberg 1905-6) and 'gehēgde' in later editions. Other editors (eg Dobbie, von Schaubert, Wrenn) retained the manuscript spelling on the chance that it was not an error but a late variant involving, as some thought, both a lengthening of the consonant and a shortening of the preceding vowel; but prior to 1973 all major editions since Klaeber's of 1922 had treated the ms 'gehedde' as preterite of 'gehēgan,' which appears unmistakably as an infinitive in *Beowulf* 425 and as the preterite 'gehēde' in *Andreas* 1496. Accordingly, although every translation I have consulted differs in some shade of interpretation from every other, the following version, with its parenthesized alternatives, may serve as the general sense of the passage during the greater part of the twentieth century:

Unferth spoke, son of Ecglaf, who sat at the feet of the lord of the Scyldings, unbound words of strife. The undertaking of Beowulf, the brave seafarer, was a great vexation to him, for he would not allow (or grant) that any other man on earth should (or could) ever achieve more glory (or perform more glorious deeds) under the heavens than he himself.[4]

---

some importance, not a jester; a foil to Beowulf, whose superiority he grudgingly recognizes; yet a treacherous fratricide and an ominous figure of discord); Carol J. Clover 'The Germanic Context of the Unferth Episode' *Speculum* 55 (1980) 444-68 (brings the widespread Germanic conventions of flyting to bear on the poet's treatment of the Unferth-Beowulf exchange, establishing the extent and importance of its conventional features).

[3]Fr. Klaeber ed *Beowulf and the Fight at Finnsburg* 3rd ed with First and Second Supplements (Boston 1950) lines 499-505.

[4]Johannes Hoops *Kommentar zum Beowulf* (Heidelberg 1932) 77, observed that 'þon mā' should mean 'noch mehr,' modern English 'the more' (thus being an adverbial expression modifying the verb and correlative with 'þonne' in the next line), and 'mærða' should be accusative plural, object of 'gehedde,' which he did not emend but accepted as preterite of

But this peaceable agreement among editors and translators was challenged by Fred C. Robinson, first briefly in 1970 in an article entitled 'Personal Names in Medieval Narrative and the Name of Unferth in *Beowulf*,'[5] then with fuller explanation in 1974, in 'Elements of the Marvellous in the Characterization of Beowulf.'[6] In the latter article, as part of an argument (inspired in some degree by the articles of Rosier and Eliason to which I refer in note 2) that Unferth's name can be interpreted as 'unintelligence' or 'folly' rather than 'discord' and his official title as 'þyle' can point to a position something like that of the later court jester,[7] Robinson turns to the traditional text of lines 501-5, saying,

Surely this clear statement justifies Bonjour's inference that Unferth is 'jealous of his own glory' and that only a man 'of his prominent position,' 'a distinguished and glorious thane,' would harbour such concern for his martial reputation?[8] So it would seem, but the cited passage will bear scrutiny before the point is granted. As quoted, the passage says that Unferth was unwilling to admit that 'any other man on earth should perform glorious deeds.' But this meaning is achieved only by means of an emendation of the verb 'gehedde' to 'gehede,' which is then interpreted as preterite subjunctive of 'gehegan' and assigned the meaning 'to perform (deeds).' Elsewhere in Old English the verb always occurs with 'þing,' 'seonoð,' 'spræc,' or 'mæðel' as its direct object and means 'to hold (a meeting).' Left in its original manuscript form, 'gehedde' would be preterite of 'gehedan' ('heed, care for') (see Klaeber's glossary s.v. 'hedan'). If the sentence is read this way, then Unferth emerges as a character with a most unheroic, Falstaffian attitude toward heroic deeds: he did not want to grant that other men cared for glory or for deeds of glory ('mærða') any more than he himself did. This is not an inappropriate sentiment for a man who, the poet later tells us, willingly 'forleas ellenmærðum' (1470-1). Perhaps there is more than a little of the swaggering coward in Unferth, and the speech reminding Beowulf of a past failure is motivated by a desire to scare the hero out of his commitment to face Grendel. If the speech is successful, then Unferth will have shown the Danes that he is not alone in his distaste for derring-do.[9]

I have quoted this passage in extenso, because I wish to distinguish between my willingness to accept 'gehedde' as the preterite of 'gehedan' ('heed, care for'), and my uneasiness at the interpretation Robinson has placed upon the

---

'gehēgan' ('vollbringen, vollführen'). A grammatically close translation (though modern 'the more' doesn't quite fit) would thus give the rather awkward 'should (*or* could) ever perform glorious deeds (*or* achieve glory) in greater measure than he himself.' Klaeber's glossary offers an alternative between the construction advocated by Hoops and 'mā' as substantive object of the verb, governing 'mærða,' genitive plural, a partitive construction not possible with the new interpretation of 'gehedde' discussed below.

[5] *Essays in Honor of Richebourg Gaillard McWilliams* ed Howard Creed, *Birmingham-Southern College Bulletin* 43:2 (Birmingham, Ala 1970) 43-8. On 'gehedde,' see 48n1.

[6] *Old English Studies in Honour of John C. Pope* ed Robert B. Burlin and Edward B. Irving, Jr (Toronto 1974) 119-37

[7] This conception of the character, developed in an extreme form by Eliason (above n2), was partially suggested by W. J. Sedgefield *An Anglo-Saxon Verse-Book* (Manchester 1922) 164: 'Unferth was the king's *þyle*, O.N. *þulr*, *i.e.* an orator clever at repartee, whose function was to amuse the company in the hall. He may have been the earlier stage of the king's jester of later times.'

[8] Adrien Bonjour *The Digressions in Beowulf* (Oxford 1950) 17-22. Robinson does Bonjour

clause, lines 503-5. For this interpretation, as it seems to me, is only one of two grammatically possible interpretations, and not, in the immediate context or the wider context, the likelier of the two. But first, the word itself. It has been a problem to editors from the beginning, though they have made little noise about it, and a brief survey of its various interpretations may be useful. Robinson's interpretation will, I think, emerge as the most probable, but we shall see that there are complications that have rendered that interpretation less than obvious and may still allow dissent.

Before Holthausen declared for 'gehēgan,' 'gehēdan' had been the leading candidate; but the early editors were not satisfied to attribute to it the same meaning as that which was clearly present in the unprefixed 'hēdde' of *Beowulf* 2697: 'ne hēdde hē þæs heafolan,' which Klaeber explains as 'he [Wiglaf] did not care for (i.e. aim at) the head.' Actually, the only other occurrence of 'hēdan' in the poetry is in *Exodus* 584, 'hēddon herereafes,' where it has been interpreted as meaning more than 'heeded,' namely 'took charge or possession of,' and this sense is partially supported by examples in the prose of Ælfric and the laws, though the prose also has examples of simple 'heed, care for.'[10] As for the prefixed 'gehēdan,' the only recorded instance (and that a disputed one) in Old English verse or prose, apart from 'gehedde' 505, is the present subjunctive 'gehede' in the *Meters of Boethius* 27.15. It occurs in the passage describing Death as a hunter who will not leave any trail 'ær he gehede / þæt he hwile ær // æfter spyrede' ('before he "gehede" what a little earlier he was tracking'). The general if not the exact meaning of 'gehede' ('catches, seizes, possesses, obtains'?) is evident not only from the context but by its correspondence to 'gefehð' ('seizes') in the prose version. Unfortunately, scribal error has been suspected because of the unusual meaning, and error plus dialectal substitution of Kentish 'e' for 'y' is possible, since the manuscript has traces of Kentish spellings elsewhere in the *Meters*. Emendations range from 'gehende' to 'gehyðe.'[11]

But right or wrong, this lonely 'gehede' undoubtedly had a part to play in early interpretations of 'gehedde,' certainly by Grein's time if not before.

---

the justice to refer the reader to his more temperate but still not completely derogatory view of Unferth in his *Twelve Beowulf Papers* (Neuchatel 1962) 129-33.

[9]'Elements of the Marvellous' (as above, n6) 128-9.

[10]See 'hēdan' in Bosworth-Toller, both *Dictionary* and *Supplement*; also the glossaries in the editions of *Exodus* by E. B. Irving, Jr (New Haven 1953): 'hēdan, take care of (here virtually "seize")'; and Peter J. Lucas (London 1977): 'hēdan, HEED, take charge of.'

[11]W. J. Sedgefield ed *King Alfred's Old English Version of Boethius De Consolatione Philosophiae* (Oxford 1899) 197, Met xxvii. 15 and 124, line 9, the corresponding prose. For the uncertainty of 'gehede' in such a sense and some proposed emendations, see E. A. Kock 'Interpretations and Emendations of Early English Texts. XI' *Anglia* 47 (1923) 268, no 332, and G. P. Krapp's note on *Meters* 27.15 ASPR 5 (New York 1932) 236. I agree with Sedgefield that 'gehede' in *Meters* 20.151 is probably a Kentish spelling of 'gehyded' ('hidden'), though Toller in the Bosworth-Toller *Supplement* thinks it belongs properly to 'gehēdan' with the sense 'keep, store up,' and compares 'hēddærn' ('storehouse'). A. Campbell in his *Enlarged Addenda and Corrigenda* to Toller's *Supplement* (Oxford 1972) has made confusion worse confounded by referring both 'gehede' in *Meters* 27.15 and 'gehedde' in *Beowulf* 505 to 'gehēgan,' as if 'gehede' in the *Meters* were not a present but a preterite subjunctive! (In my pronouncements here and elsewhere about recorded forms in both verse and prose I have depended on Antonette diPaolo Healey and Richard L. Venezky *A Microfiche Concordance to Old English* Toronto 1980).

Kemble, in the second volume of his enlarged second edition of *Beowulf*, though he referred 'gehedde' 505 (= 1004 in his lineation) to 'gehēdan' and defined it in his glossary as 'observare,' added a question mark, and preferred the notion of possession in this translation of the clause: 'because he granted not that any other man should ever have beneath the skies, more reputation in the world than he himself.'[12] Grein's verse translation in 1857 gave a similar interpretation of 'gehedde' and its clause:

> da er durchaus nicht gönnste, dass ein anderer Mann
> je mehr das Ruhmen in dem Mittelkreise
> besässe unterm Himmel, denn er selber hatte.[13]

Grein was clearly influenced by the 'gehede' of the *Meters*, for in the *Sprachschatz* accompanying his *Bibliothek der angelsächsischen Poesie*,[14] under 'gehêdan, gehŷdan,' he listed as the sole examples of sense 4, 'asciscere' (here evidently meaning 'to take or appropriate to oneself, take possession of'), 'gehede' of *Meters* 27.15 and 'gehedde' of *Beowulf* 505. Again, in his separate edition of *Beowulf* in 1867, Grein defined 'gehêdan' as 'sich einen Sache bemächtigen, erwerben,' quoting lines 503-5 and proposing 'Ruhm erwürbe' for 'mærða . . . gehêdde.'[15] Moritz Heyne's third edition (Paderborn 1873) gives 'erwerben' alone. Whether in part by Grein's example, or Heyne's, or entirely from *Meters* 27.15 and some of the prose uses of 'hēdan' to which I have referred above, 'gehēdan' (as infinitive of 'gehedde' 505) was defined as 'obtain' in the glossaries of A. J. Wyatt's first two editions (Cambridge 1894 and 1898) and in the first two editions of W. J. Sedgefield (Manchester 1910 and 1913). In short, then, for a considerable period in German and English editions, 'gehēdan' was assumed to be the infinitive of 'gehedde,' but was given such meanings as 'erwerben,' 'take possession of,' 'obtain,' rather than the simple 'heed, care for' or 'hüten' that was recognized by all editors for the 'hēdan' (pret 'hēdde') of *Beowulf* 2697. The potentially perfective sense of the prefix 'ge-' may have had some influence on the preference for 'obtain,' but the combined influence of *Meters* 27.15 and the context, *Beowulf* 501-5, were probably of greater importance.

Nevertheless there may always have been an uneasiness about 'gehēdan.' Grein, in the very glossary of his 1867 edition I have quoted for his definition of 'gehēdan,' adds as an alternative interpretation, 'wenn nicht etwa *gehêdde* für *gehêde* von *gehêgan* steht ("Ruhmthaten vollbrächte").' For the 'gehêgan' of line 425, where it certainly occurs, he gives the definition "vollbringen, ausführen,' more or less corresponding to 'perform, bring about.' We are already on the way to Holthausen's settling for 'gehêgan' and its subsequent

---

[12]John M. Kemble *A Translation of the Anglo-Saxon Poem of Beowulf, with a Copious Glossary Preface and Philological Notes* (London 1837) 21. This is the second volume of Kemble's second edition. The first volume was entitled *The Anglo-Saxon Poems of Beowulf, The Travellers Song and the Battle of Finnesburh* (London 1835). Kemble's first edition (London 1833) was limited to a single volume.

[13]C. W. M. Grein *Dichtungen der Angelsachsen, stabreimend übersetzt* 2 vols (Göttingen 1857-9) 1:236

[14]4 vols Göttingen 1857-8 (text); 1861-4, *Sprachschatz*

[15]C. W. M. Grein ed *Beowulf nebst den Fragmenten Finnsburg und Valdere* (Cassel and Göttingen 1867). Grein's first edition was in the *Bibliothek* vol 1 (1857).

almost universal adoption as the infinitive of 'gehedde.' The last faint protest came from R. W. Chambers, in whose revision of Wyatt's edition (Cambridge 1914) we find a footnote on 505 'gehēdde': 'This is usually interpreted "obtain" or "achieve," and is explained either as a compound of hȳdan, "to hide" (Bosworth-Toller; cf. 2235, 3059), or of hēdan, "to heed" (so Sedgefield). But it may be, as Holthausen (who reads gehēgde) and Schücking suppose, . . . from gehēgan (line 425), "to carry out," in which case mǣrða = "deeds of glory." Grein adopted all three interpretations in turn.' Chambers, mercifully, does not favour 'gehȳdan,' but his glossary offers a free choice between 'gehēdan' and 'gehēgan.' After Chambers, 'gehēgan' prevails and seems not to have been challenged until Robinson's protest against it.

The main trouble with 'gehēgan,' as we have seen, is not the spelling but the question whether it has any right to such meanings as 'perform,' 'achieve.' Looking only at Beowulf 425-6, '[ic sceal] āna gehēgan // ðing wið þyrse,' and at 'gehedde' 505, one might translate the first, 'I shall bring about, or carry out, alone a meeting with the giant,' and decide that 'bring about' and 'carry out' were not dangerously far from 'perform' or even 'achieve.'[16] But when one adds twelve occurrences of 'gehēgan' in other poems,[17] all agreeing with Beowulf 425 in governing an accusative (or, in 'mæðelhegende,' the first member of a compound) signifying a meeting or conference or a formal address, where 'hold' or 'convoke' or 'attend' or even 'bring about' might fit one of these instances or another but 'perform' or 'achieve' are hardly possible for any of them, the 'gehedde' of 505 looks very lonely as a would-be member of the 'gehēgan' family. There is, to be sure, an infinitive 'hegan' in Daniel 207 that has been associated by two editors of the poem with 'gehēgan' and defined by them as 'perform, do.'[18] But both the Grein-Köhler Sprachschatz and the Bosworth-Toller Supplement assign this word with great probability to 'hēgan,' 'exalt,' a weak verb formed on 'hēah,' cognate with Gothic 'hauhjan' and appearing in Old English also as 'hēan.' The participle 'geheged,' clearly meaning 'exalted,' appears in Early English Homilies from the Twelfth Century MS Vesp. D. XIV. ed. Rubie D. N. Warner, EETS OS 152 (London 1917) 99; line 13. Some scholars may feel that such a meaning as 'perform' for 'gehēgan' cannot be ruled out, since the basic etymological meaning of prehistoric Germanic '*haujan' has not been determined; but a definition of 'mæðelhēgende' in Bosworth-Toller ('Attending, holding, or addressing an assembly or council, consulting, conversing'), with a pertinent reference to Icelandic 'þing-heyjandi,' helps to suggest the usual range of meanings of 'gehēgan' and makes it very difficult to deduce such a meaning as 'perform (deeds)' or 'achieve (glory).'[19]

---

[16]W. J. Sedgefield in the glossary of his Anglo-Saxon Verse-Book (Manchester 1922) refers 'gehēdde' of Beowulf 505 (49; line 7 of his Selection 14) to 'gehēgan' ('venture on, risk'), an erratic definition seemingly without a past or future.

[17]Andreas 157, 262, 609, 930, 1049, 1096, 1496; Elene 279 (ms 'meðel hengende'); Phoenix 493; Vainglory 13 (ms 'mæþel hergendra'); Maxims I 18; Judgment Day I 9.

[18]F. A. Blackburn ed Exodus and Daniel (Boston and London 1907); R. T. Farrell ed Daniel and Azarias (London 1974).

[19]The Cleasby-Vigfusson Icelandic-English Dictionary (Oxford 1874) gives, as the first definition of 'heyja,' 'hold, perform,' but although this may have encouraged the assignment of 'gehedde' to 'gehēgan' in the sense 'perform,' the examples that follow in the dictionary do not seem to support 'perform' in the sense of performing deeds. On the uncertainty of our

It seems advisable, therefore, in the present state of our understanding of the two verbs, 'gehēdan' and 'gehēgan,' to refer 'gehedde' to 'gehēdan,' and since we cannot be sure of the validity of such a meaning for 'gehēdan' as 'obtain,' which might otherwise seem attractive, to rest content with the meaning 'care for,' 'be concerned about,' as Robinson has recommended. This interpretation has two advantages besides the spelling. First, the word can bear in this context (though the early editors did not seem to think so) an easily substantiated meaning, rather than an unsubstantiated modification of its normal meaning as the supposed preterite of 'gehēgan.' Secondly, though this is perhaps a very minor consideration, it clarifies the grammar of the clause, since 'hēdan' (and therefore presumably 'gehēdan') normally takes a genitive object. Thus 'mærða,' as a genitive plural governed by 'gehēdde,' is clearly separated from the adverbial 'þon mā,' whereas the translators of what has become the standard version, whether they regarded 'mā' or 'mærða' as the direct accusative object of 'gehēde,' were virtually compelled by modern usage to write 'more glory' or 'more deeds,' as if 'mā' were the object with 'mærða' a partitive genitive.

Thus I am glad to observe that Robinson's interpretation of 'gehedde' has been accepted by at least two editors. W. F. Bolton, in revising the glossary for the third, posthumous edition of Wrenn's *Beowulf,* has listed 'gehēdde' as preterite subjunctive singular of 'gehēdan,' with genitive, stating the change of identity and meaning, though without giving any authority for it or including any comment on the passage.[20] A second editor, Howell D. Chickering, Jr, has printed 'gehēdde' in his text, with the translation 'care . . . for' on the opposite page and a partially approving reference to Robinson's 1974 article in the Commentary.[21] But alas, as we have learned,

> 'Tis with our Judgments as our Watches, none
> Go just alike, yet each believes his own.

As I have already said, I am uneasy about Robinson's interpretation of the clause, 503-5, in which 'gehedde' occurs, and I should be reluctant to accept his interpretation of the word if I did not think it at least equally consonant with a different, less revolutionary interpretation of the clause. Robinson has given us a paraphrase rather than an exact translation of the clause, and his paraphrase is weighted towards a negative view of Unferth's concern for glory, partly by the disparaging comments that precede it, and partly by the run of

---

understanding of 'gehēgan,' see E. G. Stanley 'Two Old English Poetic Phrases Insufficiently Understood for Literary Criticism; *þing gehegan* and *seonoþ gehegan'* in *Old English Poetry: Essays on Style* ed Daniel G. Calder (Berkeley 1979) 67-90. This includes a fully documented account of the connection with Old Frisian use of the cognate 'heia.'

[20] C. L. Wrenn ed *Beowulf* 3rd ed revised by W. F. Bolton (London 1973). It seems likely that Bolton's attention was directed to the problem by Robinson's interpretation of 'gehedde' in the 1970 article (above, n5). Bolton refers to the article in the glossary of proper names sv 'Unferð.'

[21] Howell D. Chickering, Jr ed and trans *Beowulf: A Dual-Language Edition* (Anchor Books, Garden City, New York 1977). Two other recent editions, Gerhard Nickel's (Heidelberg 1976) and Michael Swanton's (Manchester 1978), take no notice of Robinson's interpretation of 'gehedde.'

the sentence itself: 'he did not want to grant that other men cared for glory any more than he himself did.' Our modern 'any more than,' though it does not have to be deflating, is frequently used to reduce the importance of what precedes it by comparison with something already known to be small or commonplace. This kind of effect can be achieved in Old English when the second term of the comparison is familiar and known to be slighter in some way than the first would normally be. For example, the normal value of fire is reduced to that of sunshine by the poet of *Daniel* in order to describe the miraculous protection of the three children from the blazing furnace into which they have been thrown: 'Næs him se sweg to sorge / ðon ma þe sunnan scima' ('The roaring flame was no more painful to them than sunshine').[22] Indeed, the formula 'þon ma þe' or 'þe ma þe,' though it occurs only a few times, and with varied effect, in verse, occurs frequently in prose and has much the same colloquial tone as 'any more than,' but neither the modern expression nor the Old English need be reductive.[23] It is mainly the nature of the two terms rather than the formula of comparison that matters. When the first term is more easily evaluated than the second, it is the second that is freshly defined and may be magnified. In *Genesis B*, for example, Eve beautifully expresses the bitterness of her own, previously unstated, grief at what she has done by denying that Adam's, which he has made all too plain in the course of his denunciation of her, is any greater:

> 'Þu meaht hit me witan,   wine min Adam,
> wordum þinum;   hit þe þeah wyrs ne mæg
> on þinum hyge hreowan   þonne hit me æt heortan deð.'[24]

'You may blame me for it, my friend, Adam, with your words; but it cannot grieve you worse in your mind than it does me at my heart.'

Here what precedes 'þonne' serves to increase the magnitude of what follows it. If now we look again at *Beowulf* 503-5,

> forþon þe hē ne ūþe,   þæt ænig ōðer man
> æfre mærða þon mā   middangeardes
> gehēdde under heofenum   þonne hē sylfa

for he would not grant that any other man on earth could ever, under the heavens, care more for glorious deeds than he himself did,

we shall see that the comparison differs a little from both of the examples just given, since both terms are somewhat uncertain, but resembles the second

---

[22]*Daniel* 264, ed R. T. Farrell (as above, n 18); numbered 263 in Krapp's edition ASPR 1:118

[23]For examples, see G. W. Small 'The syntax of *the* with the comparative' *MLN* 41 (1926) 300-13. The author distinguishes between 'þon (þe) ma' alone and 'þon (þe) ma þe.' He denies (questionably) that 'þon ma þe' is equivalent to 'þon ma ðonne' (of which he gives no examples) and does not even mention *Beowulf* 504-5, 'þon ma . . . ðonne,' which appears to be a unique variant. At least I can find no exact parallel to this combination in either verse or prose, and the peculiar word order, obviously dependent in part on the poet's unusual emphasis combined with the metrical requirements, helps to set the clause apart.

[24]*Genesis* 824-6 ed Krapp ASPR 1:28

example, from *Genesis B*, more than the first, from *Daniel*, in that we should suppose that Unferth knew as well as we do that there have been a number of men in the world who cared a good deal for glorious deeds, whereas nothing at all has yet been established about how much Unferth cared. The normal assumption, therefore, since Unferth is said not to grant that anyone could surpass him in caring, is that he himself cared a great deal. This assumption is strengthened, it seems to me, by the poet's hyperbole, the piling up of 'ænig,' 'æfre,' 'middangeardes,' and 'under heofenum.' Such exaggeration is mere nonsense if Unferth did not care at all. It becomes a mildly satirical anticipation of Unferth's discomfiture if it suggests that he not only cared a great deal but had deluded himself into supposing that nobody on earth could ever have cared more.

Thus, if my interpretation of the clause is correct, the acceptance of 'gehedde' as preterite third singular (probably subjunctive because hypothetical) of 'gehēdan' rather than 'gehēgan' need not alter the usual view, that Unferth was upset out of jealousy for his own reputation. The emphasis merely shifts from actual performance of glorious deeds to a concern for such performance. What most immediately troubled Unferth was Beowulf's professed daring to undertake what no one in Hrothgar's comitatus, since the unhappy demise of a few overbold thegns some time ago, had thought of attempting. If Unferth could show, as he tried to do, that Beowulf had been foolhardy in the past, that another man had beaten him, and that he was now promising more than he could reasonably expect to perform, Unferth would not lose face by his own prudent unwillingness to encounter Grendel. Nobody, in fact, could have blamed Unferth any more than the other Danes for not wanting to be killed and eaten, if only he had not tried to downgrade a rival. It is the jealousy born of his own excessive pretensions, made reckless no doubt by drink and an incautious reliance on hearsay, that exposes him to Beowulf's scornful rejoinder and to the poet's later reminders of his loss of glory.

Much as we should like to know exactly what the poet meant by 'gehedde,' it is far more important to agree on the general purport of the passage in which the word occurs, and this turns out, I believe, to have been adequately understood long ago. Stanley Greenfield, in his new translation of the poem,[25] has not made an issue of the word. His version of lines 499 to 505 runs as follows:

> Then Unferth, son of Ecglaf, who sat
> at the feet of the Scyldings' lord, spoke
> and stirred up strife; the bold seafarer
> Beowulf's venture made him envious,
> for he would not grant that anyone
> on earth could ever gain more glory
> under the heavens than he himself.

Here, although the rendering is deliberately free, the use of 'could gain' for 'gehedde' suggests the sense 'achieve' questionably attributed to 'gehegan,' certainly not 'care for,' though it is not far from the sense 'obtain' formerly attributed to 'gehedan.' There is a clear difference between gaining glory and caring

---

[25]*A Readable Beowulf: The Old English Epic Newly Translated* by Stanley B. Greenfield, with an Introduction by Alain Renoir (Carbondale, Ill 1982)

for it, but in either case Unferth's resentment is attributed to the same fundamental cause, what I have called jealousy and Greenfield envy. Critics have
differed at this point, but where self-love and vainglory are concerned, envy of
another's achievements and jealousy for one's own reputation are blood brothers.
It seems to me, therefore, that Greenfield, who is aiming at a 'readable' style
in syllabically measured verses, has successfully conveyed what is essential to
the meaning of the original, though not of course its own inimitable nuances.

There is much that we can never know for certain about Unferth, not only
because we cannot tell precisely what meaning the poet and his audience
attached to the term 'þyle,' but still more because we do not know whether or
not Unferth had any part to play in stories the poet knew, and expected his
audience to know, outside the limits of this particular poem. Was there a well-
known tale involving the fratricide with which Unferth was charged by Beowulf
and by the poet himself? Or was this charge invented for the occasion of the
flyting and, though treated by the poet as true (at line 1167), never elaborated? That the poet knew a story about Hrothulf's dealings with the sons of
Hrothgar after the latter's death, and that it probably involved what could have
been called treachery on Hrothulf's part, seems to me the most reasonable
explanation of the poet's emphasis, during his description of the banquet scene
(1017-19 and 1164-5), on the absence, for the present, of discord or treachery
between uncle and nephew, and on Wealhtheow's anxieties for her sons (1169-
87). It seems less clear but altogether possible that Unferth had a sinister part
to play in that story. Scandinavian tales partially corroborate such a story
about Hrothulf, though they say nothing of anyone corresponding to Unferth.
Readers of *Beowulf* will never cease to speculate about these matters, and a
novelist might well invent a tale that would incorporate what little the poem
actually says about either Unferth or Hrothulf into a complicated tragedy.
What is important for the poem about the poet's comments on the relations
of Hrothgar, Wealhtheow, and Hrothulf is the sense that appears elsewhere
too, that life cannot long escape tragic conflicts and betrayals, whatever
interludes there may be of joy and good fellowship. Whether or not Unferth
was included in these forebodings matters very little to our appraisal of the
poem. Within the poem he is mainly, and expertly, used as a foil to Beowulf,
helping primarily to allow Beowulf, in the flyting, to reveal his astonishing
powers in anticipation of his defeat of Grendel, and secondarily, in the lending
and failure of the sword Hrunting, to allow a tacit acknowledgment on
Unferth's part of Beowulf's superiority, and at the same time to enforce that
superiority by contrasting the best of man-made swords with the great sword
of the giants, which alone could overcome the magic spells of the monsters
and which only Beowulf could have wielded.

I agree, therefore, with those who have seen in the poet's and Beowulf's
comments on Unferth later in the poem, especially in the banquet scene
(1165-8) and in the passages dealing with the loan and return of Hrunting
(1455-72, 1488-91, 1807-12) a clear indication that Unferth was in fact a
warrior of some standing, deservedly a 'widcuð man,' as Beowulf calls him
(1489), though one at least of his exploits had been morally reprehensible and
nothing he had done could match the least of Beowulf's achievements. Nobody
has ever ventured to find Unferth a lovable character, so far as I know, but
in the matter of his being a respected fighter among the Danes as well as a

privileged spokesman, I tend to agree with Bonjour's carefully reconsidered estimate in his *Twelve Beowulf Papers*[26] and with the more recent paper of Geoffrey Hughes.[27] He is certainly no professional entertainer, and though he thinks too well of himself, not a man to be despised. Those who have deduced from Hrothgar's failure to reproach him for his discourteous attack on Beowulf that he was not only a privileged character but one whose sallies, like those of later professional fools, were not taken seriously, will find much to ponder in Carol J. Clover's study, 'The Germanic Context of the Unferth Episode.'[28] By showing how many features of this flyting are well-recognized conventions in traditional heroic fiction, she suggests that the poet's audience would have been much less shocked by Unferth's behaviour than some modern critics have been. There are several reasons besides these conventions (which do not of course render less remarkable the specific relevance and individuality of the whole episode) that can be offered for Hrothgar's failure to scold Unferth. One is that Beowulf has put his adversary so firmly in his place. Another, somehow overlooked in the excitement of debate, is that the poet has chosen to emphasize what is vastly more important for the progress of the narrative than a royal rebuke to Unferth, namely the joy that Hrothgar feels at hearing in Beowulf's reply so unexpected and so persuasive a confirmation of the hope that at last a champion has been found who can defeat Grendel.

I have allowed myself to digress a little from the limits of my narrow theme. It is my hope, however, that most of what I have said about Unferth's character and behaviour in the poem as it unfolds will appear consonant with what I believe to be the tenor of lines 499-505, with or without the new interpretation of 'gehedde.'

[26] Above, n 8
[27] 'Beowulf, Unferth, and Hrunting' above, n 2
[28] Above, n 2

Index of Lines and Passages in *Beowulf* Quoted or Discussed

Numbers before the colon refer to Klaeber's edition of the poem; numbers after the colon refer to pages above.

277

R. D. FULK is Associate Professor of English at Indiana University. His writings include studies of medieval English, Norse, and Celtic subjects, along with Germanic and Indo-European linguistics.